Blackcoats among the Delaware

David Zeisberger, 1721–1808. Portrait by John Valentine Haidt, painted in 1771. *Courtesy of the Moravian Church Archives.*

Blackcoats among the Delaware

David Zeisberger
on the Ohio Frontier

Earl P. Olmstead

THE KENT STATE UNIVERSITY PRESS
Kent, Ohio, and London, England

© 1991 by the Kent State University Press, Kent, Ohio 44242
All rights reserved
Library of Congress Catalog Card Number 90-47576
ISBN 0-87338-422-9 cloth
ISBN 0-87338-434-2 paper
Manufactured in the United States of America

Unless otherwise noted, illustrations are reproduced through the courtesy of the Moravian Church Archives, Bethlehem, Pennsylvania.

Library of Congress Cataloging-in-Publication Data

Olmstead, Earl P., 1920–
    Blackcoats among the Delaware : David Zeisberger on the Ohio
frontier / Earl P. Olmstead.
        p.   cm.
    Includes bibliographical references and index.
    ISBN 0-87338-422-9 (cloth : alk. paper) ∞ — ISBN
0-87338-434-2 (paper : alk. paper) ∞
    1. Zeisberger, David, 1721–1808.   2. Delaware Indians—Missions.
3. Delaware Indians—History—Sources.   4. Missionaries—Ohio—
Tuscarawas County—Biography.   5. Moravian Church—Missions—Ohio—
Tuscarawas County.   6. Tuscarawas County (Ohio)—History—Sources.
I. Title.
E99.D2Z456   1991
977.1'03'092—dc20   90-47576
[B]

British Library Cataloging-in-Publication data are available.

To Barbara, Jacqueline, and Hazel—
three great ladies
who made this book possible.

There are those who have little and give it all.
These are the believers in life and the bounty of life
and their coffers are never empty.
—*Kahlil Gibran*

Contents

Foreword   ix
Preface   xi
Acknowledgments   xv

Part 1 The Wilderness Years, 1772–1798
1 The Ambiguous Delaware   3
2 The Great Dispersement   34
3 From Disaster to a New Beginning   51
4 Return to the Ohio Country   64
5 Pettquotting: The New Salem   76
6 From the Detroit River to the Retrenche   87

Part 2 The Goshen Mission Years, 1798–1821
7 The Goshen Mission   107
8 Goshen Mission Life: An Overview   124
9 Without Their Beloved David   152

Part 3 Record of Burials, the Goshen Mission Cemetery
Origins of the Goshen Biographical Sketches   175
Burials 1–44, 1799–1823   177

Appendixes
A Moravian Missions in North America, 1740–1821   241
B The Goshen Mission: Annual Population Statistics   243
C Population Graph: Goshen Mission, 1798–1821   244
D Map of Interments, Goshen Mission Cemetery   245
E Statutes of Languntoutenunk and Welhik-Tuppeek   246
F Genealogies: William Henry and Ignatius Families;
   Josua, Sr., and John Papunhank Families   248
G Grave Registry, Goshen Mission Cemetery   249

Notes   255
Bibliography   267
Index   273

~~~~

Foreword

The death of the Bohemian reformer John Hus at the stake on July 6, 1415, signaled the beginning of the reformation struggles that gave birth to the Unitas Fratrum on March 1, 1457. This early pre-Reformation church pioneered in worship in the vernacular, Scripture as the rule and source of all life, congregational hymn singing, and education for both sexes. While much of its life in the first two hundred years was hidden away from the public eye because of the Counter-Reformation reactions in Bohemia and Moravia, the influence of this group was felt beyond its limited membership.

John Amos Comenius, the world-renowned educator and prophet of peace, was a bishop of the Unity who traveled extensively throughout Europe in the work of education and as a servant of his church. His educational contributions of graded curricula, illustrated textbooks, training for female students, and education as the evangelistic arm of the church earned for him the epithet of "Father of Modern Education."

Following a period of underground existence in family cells, the Unity was renewed in 1727 on the estate of Nicholas Ludwig von Zinzendorf in Saxony. This Count of the Holy Roman Empire was a Lutheran pietist whose religious interests far outweighed his professional training in law. The refugees of the Unitas Fratrum found a hospitable environment for their families and their church on his lands, where they renewed their church life. The establishment of their town, Herrnhut, with its unique organization and focus provided a base for their worldwide efforts in missions, which began in 1732 when their first two missionaries went to Saint Thomas in the West Indies to work among black slaves. Within ten years, the work was spread over four continents and the British Isles.

Growing out of the concern of Count Zinzendorf for the unevangelized peoples of the world and the understanding of the Moravians (the count's nickname for the members of the Unitas Fratrum), a base was established in Savannah, Georgia, in 1735 to provide a center for operations in the New World and to serve as a center for the envisioned mission work among the American Indian population. In spite of the fact that the community failed and a new center was established at Bethlehem, Pennsylvania, in 1741, the work among the native American people was begun by Christian Frederick Post and Christian Henry Rauch in the early 1740s.

Finding a hospitable reception among the Delaware peoples, a mission was started among them and continued for well over a century and a half. The Indian mission stations at Schoenbrunn, Gnadenhutten, Lichtenau, Salem, New Schoenbrunn, and Goshen were all part of this work, led through the later years of the eighteenth century by David Zeisberger with a deeply committed group of assistants including Johann Georg Jungmann, John Roth, John Heckewelder, Benjamin Mortimer and others who served for short periods of time.

The Goshen history which follows is a fascinating part of a nation's history that is often overlooked and yet rich in lessons for today's struggles for peace and equity for all.

Dr. Albert H. Frank
First Moravian Church, Dover, Ohio

≈≈≈≈

Preface

Tuscarawas County, the site of my childhood, is unique among the eighty-eight counties in Ohio. It was there in the last quarter of the eighteenth century that David Zeisberger, a Moravian missionary, established his first mission of Christian Indian converts in the Ohio country. There in 1772 in the Tuscarawas River valley (called the Muskingum in Zeisberger's time) he founded Schoenbrunn, the first organized settlement in Ohio. There he built Ohio's first church and schoolhouse. When he arrived with his Indians, the Ohio country was a primordial wilderness. For millennia this land had been the home of native American Indians. Roaming the timbered hills and expansive valleys were the Shawnee, Delaware, Mingos, Munsee, Wyandot, Miami, Ottawa, and Ojibwa. Along the northern branches of the Muskingum River, where Zeisberger first settled, were the homes of the native Delaware. He lived there, among the Delaware, for nine years in relative peace. Then, caught between the opposing forces of the American Revolution, he and his Indian congregations were forced to leave. After wandering in the wilderness of the Ohio country and Canada for seventeen years, he returned to his cherished valley and established Goshen, his last mission. Ten years after founding the Goshen mission he gave up his quest and passed on into eternal peace.

As the years passed, most of the evidence of Zeisberger's six missions on the Tuscarawas quickly disappeared, and this interesting period of American history was virtually forgotten. All that remained at Goshen was the mission cemetery with the graves of David Zeisberger; William Edwards, his assistant; and the forty Indian converts.

In November 1908, on the occasion of the one hundredth anniversary of Zeisberger's death, and through the cooperation of the Ohio Historical Society and the local Moravian church authorities, there was a resurgence of interest in Zeisberger's life. The following year, 1909, the graves in the Goshen cemetery were marked with appropriate gravestones by Luther Demuth and J. E. Weinland, a local Moravian minister.

Their work progressed slowly until 1921 when a group of interested local citizens, spearheaded by Reverend Weinland, founded the Tuscarawas County Historical Society. In September 1923, with the assistance of the Ohio Historical Society and the local organization, an archaeological excavation began on the Schoenbrunn site. In the meantime, two maps of Schoenbrunn were discovered in the Moravian archives at Bethlehem. (These maps were drawn in 1772 by John Ettwein, one of the leaders of the Moravian church in Bethlehem, who came on a visit to inspect the new mission.) Using the maps, the expedition located the original fireplaces in the Zeisberger home and the adjoining church. Four years later, in 1927, this information enabled archaeologists making another excavation to discover the forty-five graves in the original Indian cemetery at Schoenbrunn. At the same time reconstruction of some of the village cabins was begun.

Childhood experiences have an uncanny way of affecting later incidents in our adult lives. One such event in my life is responsible for this narrative. In 1929 my father decided his nine-year-old son should share in some of the local historical excitement caused by the current discoveries in the county. Thus on the brisk Sunday afternoon of November 17, 1929, we arrived at the small abandoned mission cemetery in the village of Goshen, several miles south of New Philadelphia. This was to be my first meeting with David Zeisberger, on the 121st anniversary of his death. As we strolled through the graveyard, my father related a brief history of Zeisberger's life. For the first time I heard the exciting Indian story. It was an unforgettable day.

Except to a small number of religious scholars, most members of the Moravian church, and a section of the general citizenry that live near the sites of his former missions, David Zeisberger is a relatively unknown historical figure. An eighteenth-century Moravian missionary, born in 1721, he lived to be eighty-seven years old, a remarkable feat in itself in that era. He spent almost sixty-three of those years conducting missionary activities among the North American Indians, a record unequaled by any other Protestant Indian missionary.

While certainly not a principal participant in the major historical events of the eighteenth century, his activities often intruded into or were affected by each. Any study of Zeisberger clearly shows how the history of America shaped his life and preserved for us today a capsulized version of the eighteenth-century wilderness. The thousands of extant pages of his diaries provide the modern scholar with a detailed record of this period.

These written accounts may be Zeisberger's greatest contribution to American history.

Three major historical events came to their climax during his lifetime; all irrevocably shaped the history of North America. The first was the French and Indian War (1754–63). During the previous one hundred years, France and England had contended for control of the continent east of the Mississippi. With the Treaty of Paris in 1763, and after six years of bloody fighting, the question was resolved. The English finally possessed all of the territory formerly held by the French.

Within a short twelve years came the second major upheaval. Colonial Americans became dissatisfied with their English landlords, threw off the "yoke of tyranny," and proclaimed their freedom. Eight years later, shorn of the shackles of British rule, the negotiators again sat down in Paris in 1783. To the astonishment of the American delegation, England ceded to the colonial rebels all of their territory from the Atlantic coast to the Mississippi River, with the exception of Canada, Spanish Florida, and several other small areas. From that vast territory these same colonials formed a new nation—the United States of America.

Finally, the most important event affecting Zeisberger's work involved the struggle of Europeans to wrest the vast continent from its native inhabitants. Long before the twenty-two-year-old Zeisberger entered the missionary field, that contest had begun. One of the first European exploratory efforts was made as early as 1524, when the Italian Giovanni da Verrazano (working for the French) anchored in New York Bay. He spent two weeks conversing with the Mahican chiefs in the area. Eighty-three years later, on May 14, 1607, John Smith and his 105 English settlers ("Gentlemen" and "men of the common sorte") debarked from their small ships and founded the first permanent settlement at Jamestown. By the time David Zeisberger died in 1808, the Indian question was effectively resolved. All that remained was a "wipe up" operation to be completed in the nineteenth century. The final solution would come as close to genocide as ever was witnessed on the North American continent. (It is not this author's objective to make observations or judgments as to the wisdom or the methods used by our forefathers. There is enough blame to be shared by all antagonists regarding the fate of the Indians on this land.)

This small volume is designed to give the reader a glimpse of the last thirty-two years of David Zeisberger's exciting life, and to provide a brief insight into the problems that the Indians encountered during their daily lives as members of a Protestant Christian mission. Part 1 of the narrative covers the years of Zeisberger's life from the close of the

Schoenbrunn mission in 1777, until the "Great Dispersement" in 1781. It then follows eleven years of wandering deep within the North American wilderness, until his small band of Christian converts arrived in Canada and built the Fairfield mission (1792). He lived at Fairfield for six years. In 1798, responding to the call of the church leaders, the seventy-seven-year-old Zeisberger returned to the Muskingum River valley and founded his last mission, at Goshen.

Part 2 is the history of the Goshen mission. Unlike most Protestant missionaries in North America, Zeisberger quickly learned that success with the peace-loving Delaware required delicate skill to combine the two radically different cultures. But like most religious zealots, he believed in the singular correctness of his own religious beliefs. Pluralism was not part of his religious philosophy. The rules governing village life were strict, but there was some room for compromise, and forgiveness to transgressors was granted in most instances. Part 2 deals with Zeisberger's efforts at Goshen to find a common ground for Indians and whites to live in peace and harmony.

Part 3 is a chronological record of the deaths at the Goshen mission and a biographical sketch of each interment. During the period between 1798 and 1823, forty Indian converts died at Goshen and were buried in the quiet tree-lined cemetery on the banks of the Muskingum River. This is unique. Rarely do we find Indian cemeteries in America. When they are discovered, never do we know the intimate details of the Indians' personal lives. Thanks to the missionaries who served this small congregation, we have a daily record of the events that occurred at the village. These diaries are now preserved at the Moravian Church Archives in Bethlehem, Pennsylvania. They clearly show the intense struggle the native Americans encountered as they attempted to adapt to European civilization.

Most human events begin and end with a story. These anecdotes are the essence of history. There is a remarkable consistency about the drama of human life, regardless of the time in which we live. The humdrum monotony of the daily routine, the sanguine days, the tragedies, all seem to be similar, regardless of the generation. The reader of this narrative will be reminded of the similarities. Except for a few amenities, the struggle remains the same. This, then, is a story of Americans not unlike you and me; only time separates us.

~~~~~

Acknowledgments

The sportswriter Red Smith once wrote: "There is nothing to writing, all you do is sit down at the typewriter and just open a vein." I presume that a Victor 9000 word processor could be substituted for the typewriter. While I found the process bloodless, writing is still a lonely and self-revealing business.

The valley of the Tuscarawas, where my wife and I have lived and raised four children, is steeped in the history of Zeisberger. Unfortunately, with the exception of several small monographs, there has never been a definitive account of Zeisberger's life since Edmund De Schweinitz wrote his full-length biography in 1870. For many years I have believed there was a need for a twentieth-century version of this great man, written from a secular rather than a religious point of view as is De Schweinitz's. In the spring of 1981 I began the project.

In the course of doing my research, I have followed Zeisberger's trail on twenty-three trips to date. He has taken me to many remote places in Pennsylvania, New York, Connecticut, Ohio, Indiana, and Canada as I traced his movements from mission to mission. Early in the spring of 1987 I discovered the microfilm copies of Benjamin Mortimer's Goshen diaries; Mortimer was Zeisberger's assistant at Goshen. With few exceptions, virtually nothing has been published on the Goshen mission. Here within the eight hundred pages of Mortimer's daily record was a microcosm of the four hundred years' struggle between the white European and the native American Indian. Mortimer's perceptive insight and deep understanding of this problem convinced me to interrupt the Zeisberger biography and spend the next year recording the events that occurred at this final mission of David Zeisberger. Goshen represents the last valiant effort of the Leni Lenape (Delaware) to live in harmony on the Muskingum River with the white man.

Without the experience, knowledge, and patience of many persons this book could not have been written. I am therefore grateful to many people. The principal source of Zeisberger material is found in the thousands of pages of original documents at the Moravian Church Archives in Bethlehem, Pennsylvania. I am deeply indebted to all of those many fine and helpful folks—especially to Rev. Vernon Nelson, the chief archivist, for his patient understanding; to Lother Madeheim, the assistant archivist; and to Margaret Groman and Margaret Wilde. Also to Bob Brown, who on so many occasions provided a bed for a weary traveler and gave access to his marvelous collection of Moravian memorabilia. I wish also to extend my special thanks to Dean David Schattscheidner of the Moravian Theological Seminary for his words of encouragement; to Henry L. Williams, the immediate past head librarian of the Reeves Library, and to his successor, Thomas Minor, both of whom have been most helpful; and finally to Rev. Arthur Nehring, the president of the Moravian Historical Society, and to his lovely wife Rose, who both patiently read the Zeisberger manuscript.

Fortunately for the Zeisberger researcher, in 1970 most of the Moravian archives were microfilmed by Research Publication, Inc., of New Haven, Connecticut. There are forty reels of Moravian material. Thirteen cover the Zeisberger years. With my microfilm reader and a printer furnished by Michael Kobulnicky of the Tuscarawas branch of Kent State University at New Philadelphia, I was able to read and study the original records from the comfort of my home. Research Publication also published the Fliegel *Index* (four volumes) in 1970. An explanation of this publication and its value to the Zeisberger story is contained in the narrative. I am therefore grateful to Mindy Greenleas and Laurie Fusco of Research Publication for assisting me in securing the appropriate microfilms, a copy of the microfilm index, and the Fliegel publication.

Substantial translations of the original Zeisberger German manuscripts have been located in strange places. Derek McKown and Chase Putnam of the Warren County, Pennsylvania Historical Society provided copies of the manuscript translations in the Merle Deardorf collection covering the Zeisberger years between 1767 and 1772. These were the years immediately prior to his removal to the Ohio country. Gary Arnold, chief librarian of the Ohio Historical Society, introduced me to the August Mahr translations of the Zeisberger years from 1772 through 1781. The Bethlehem archives contain the William Schwarze translations for the same period. All Zeisberger researchers are indebted to Eugene Bliss, who one hundred years ago—in 1888—published a translation of the Zeisberger diaries from 1781 through 1798, following Zeisberger's removal from the Muskingum valley. Within the Moravian Church Archives we find the marvelous English diaries by Benjamin Mortimer from May 1798 until November 1812, which represent the principal years covered by this narrative.

Many libraries and historical societies have played a major role in my research. I am especially grateful to Theresa Snyder, research assistant at the Historical Society of Pennsylvania, who kept all things regarding Philadelphia in the eighteenth century in their proper perspective, and for the informative maps she furnished of Philadelphia and its environs in 1776 and 1777. Thanks to Helen Wilson, the head reference librarian at the Western Pennsylvania Historical Society at Pittsburgh, who on short notice mailed copies of many pertinent Pennsylvania Colonial Records, and frequently played the gracious hostess on numerous trips to Pittsburgh. I am especially grateful for the friendship of Jack Hetrick, president of the Northumberland Historical Society at Sunbury, Pennsylvania, who led the archaeological excavation and discovered the blacksmith shop at the Moravian mission at Shamokin in Sunbury— Zeisberger's first mission assignment.

Special mention must be given to the late distinguished scholar Dr. Donald Kent, the former head archivist at the Pennsylvania Historical and Museum Commission at Harrisburg, Pennsylvania, who spent two hours in May 1983 with an absolute stranger, outlining a list of books that were required reading for a novice eighteenth-century researcher. I wish to acknowledge the assistance of Jonathan Sayer and Linda Ries, also at the Harrisburg museum, who provided over twenty maps and many land deeds from their fine eighteenth-century collection. I extend my appreciation to Beth Pearce and Bishop Edwin Sawyer of the Moravian Historical Society at Nazareth, who provided many back issues of their publication *Transactions,* shedding further information on the early activities of the Moravian mission program, and to Bishop Sawyer for his guided tours of the sites where Zeisberger lived for short periods in the Bethlehem area.

Throughout my many research trips I have visited libraries located near the sites of Zeisberger's former missions, especially in New York, Pennsylvania, and Ohio. To all of these local librarians may I offer my grateful thanks. Special recognition among this group must go to Ann Sindler of the Western Reserve Historical Society Archives, who led me through the microfilms of the Draper Manuscripts discovering the original correspondence written by Zeisberger and Heckewelder during those critical years of 1777 to 1781. These letters gave a totally new dimension to the Zeisberger saga. But especially am I indebted to the Dover Public Library in Dover, Ohio, and to Dan Cooley and his head reference librarian, Jacqueline Metzger. With patience, they steadfastly ferreted out well over 150 rare and out-of-print books that deal with the life and times of David Zeisberger.

I owe a debt of gratitude to Dr. Amos Loveday, chief curator of the Ohio Historical Society in Columbus, a resolute friend who recognizes the importance of the Zeisberger story, and who has been supportive of the author's work with many kind words of encouragement. And to Dr. George Knepper, Distinguished Professor of History at Akron University, who also read the manuscript. Their close review and critical suggestions have strengthened and improved the narrative.

I am also indebted to my many friends among our own Tuscarawas County Historical Society who have permitted me to sit in the chair of that great Zeisberger scholar, Rev. Joseph Weinland, who in 1921 with his other colleagues helped to found our society. Today the reconstructed Schoenbrunn mission village, begun by Rev. Weinland in 1927, still flourishes under the capable management of Susan Goehring, curator, and Linda Flynn, assistant curator—employees of the Ohio Historical Society. They and their capable staff entertain thousands of visitors annually, thus keeping the Zeisberger story alive.

Four special people are directly responsible for this narrative. Without their assistance it would have never been written. First, I wish to express my gratitude to my good friend Dr. Albert Frank, pastor of the First Moravian Church at Dover, Ohio. Having taught at the Moravian Theological Seminary, Dr. Frank is a well-recognized and acknowledged Zeisberger scholar who cheerfully read the manuscript and kept all things Moravian historically accurate. He is also the president of the Board of Trustees, Ohio Outdoor Drama Association, which produces "Trumpet in the Land," the historical drama of Zeisberger's Schoenbrunn years. It plays annually at New Philadelphia to over twenty-five thousand visitors. I am deeply indebted to and delighted to extend my special thanks to my editor, Barbara Entress, former reader representative of the *Christian Science Monitor* newspaper, Boston. Relentlessly she rearranged the hard-to-come-by words of the author (disregarding the fact they were her father's) to make sense to the general reader. Next is my dear friend and gracious octogenarian Hazel Lightel, who taught many years in the New Philadelphia public school system. Unflinchingly she rooted out the various misspelled words and misplaced commas of the author. Fortunately Hazel is from the old school, which believes such things are akin to mortal sin. And finally, I am grateful to Jacqueline, my friend and wife of forty-nine years, for her patience and forbearance while this narrative inched forward toward completion. She always lightened my literary burden with cheerful words of encouragement and gave me the space required for writing.

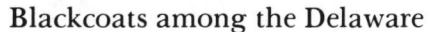

Blackcoats among the Delaware

≋

Part 1
The Wilderness Years
1772–1798

~~~~~~

ONE

The Ambiguous Delaware

A warm fall sun cast bright shadows across the river. Oak, sycamore, and hickory leaves—victims of an early frost—floated on the water like miniature boats. The children played at catching them as the canoes skimmed by. It was October 4, just fifteen months before the close of the turbulent and bloody eighteenth century. Thirty brown, weatherworn Indians silently and rapidly propelled downstream a flotilla of seven canoes laden with supplies. An old man with an expectant look on his face knelt behind William Henry, the helmsman in the lead canoe. As they rounded a slight bend in the river, the old man quietly tapped Henry on the shoulder and said, "There it is, Billy, there it is." David Zeisberger had finally come home.

One by one the canoes rounded the bend and pulled to shore. As the lead canoe struck the bank, Billy Henry, now sixty-one, agilely jumped from the canoe like a young man and pulled it safely onto the shore, then turned and said, "Let me help you, Brother David." For the past seventeen years, David Zeisberger and his small band of Christian converts had been wandering in the pristine wilderness of North America, seeking a haven of peace and tranquility. Six times they fled from hostile native Indian tribes or British and American military armies. Two years before the close of the century, in 1798, they planned to try again to return to the lush, green forest-covered valley of the Muskingum.[1] This narrative is a story of those seventeen years and the subsequent years of Zeisberger's life at the last mission he would found, at Goshen. He had desperately longed to return to this valley, the site of his greatest achievements. It was as close as he ever came to having a permanent home.

Despite his seventy-seven years he remained agile and alert and continued to perform the strenuous missionary schedule, only conceding the daily writing of the mission diary to his assistant, Benjamin Mortimer. Mortimer had been specifically dispatched to him at a suggestion of the elders back in Bethlehem, and Zeisberger reluctantly agreed. For fifty-three years he had lived among his cherished Indian Brethren, but it had been a hard life, one filled with hope and sorrow, success and failure. Here on the banks of the Muskingum he had achieved his greatest success. Perhaps his blessed Savior would again show him the way.

Early on, as a young man of nineteen, he had chosen the direction of his life. While roaming the green forest-covered hills of eastern Pennsylvania, he made his first contact with the Delaware Indians, frequently visiting old Chief Tatamy's village just north of Bethlehem, where he lived as a young man. Intrigued by their gregarious nature, he returned time and again until he could carry on rudimentary conversations in their native tongue. He loved the wilderness and he loved these people.

Even as a young man he displayed those tendencies that would mark him later in life. Slightly over five feet tall, Zeisberger was a quiet, reticent, and reserved young man who despite his stature and retiring personality could inspire trust and confidence in all who surrounded him. Intensely brave, he never flinched despite the danger to his own life, never once losing faith that his beloved Savior would guide him over the paths and through the precarious trials of his long life. But unlike some of his contemporaries, he always minimized dangers and seldom discussed the details of the many life-threatening events he faced.

Zeisberger was born on Good Friday morning, April 11, 1721, in the small village of Zachtenthal, in the Moravian province of the Catholic Kingdom of Bohemia (now Czechoslovakia). He was the oldest child of a moderately successful freeholder; his father, David, and his mother, Rosina, were clandestine members of the Unity of Brethren Church, a Protestant group forbidden by the pope and the Catholic monarch of Bohemia.

In his sixth year, 1726, David's family, including his infant sister Anna, fled across the tortuous Carpathian Mountains into Protestant Saxony and joined the other Unity Brethren at the village of Herrnhut. Founded in June 1722, the new village became the center for their renewed church. His father and mother remained at Herrnhut until 1736, when they left him in the care of fellow church members at Herrendyk, Holland, to complete his education. His parents were among the first group of the Brethren to emigrate to America and establish a mission at the new Georgia colony in Savannah. Two years later David joined his parents in Georgia.

By 1740, with the failure of the Georgia mission caused by the outbreak of war between England and Spain, the few Brethren remaining in Georgia moved to Pennsylvania. Nineteen-year-old David became one of the fifteen people to found the new village of Bethlehem, Pennsylvania.

The little settlement quickly grew and became the headquarters of the Moravian Church in America and the focal point of the far-flung Moravian Indian missions throughout the North American continent. Here they began to train the many missionaries—called "Blackcoats" by the Indians—required to service the missions. Theirs was a unique missionary approach. Previous Protestant efforts traditionally measured their success by the number of converts. The Moravian philosophy, as developed by their benefactor and mentor, Count Nicholas Zinzendorf, departed from this objective and became a simple three-point program:

> First, silently observe to see if any of the heathen were prepared, by the grace of God, to receive and believe the word of life. Second, if even ONE were found, preach the gospel to HIM because God must give the heathens ears and heart to receive the gospel, otherwise all of his labors would be in vain. Third, preach chiefly to such heathens, who never heard the gospel. We were not to build on a foundation laid by others nor to disturb their work, but to seek the outcast and forsaken.[2]

This became Zeisberger's creed, a one-on-one approach used on countless occasions during his life.

Three years after the founding of Bethlehem, the Brethren began their first Indian language school. Zeisberger became its star pupil. Early in January 1745 he was chosen for his first assignment, accompanying Christian Frederick Post. The pair left Bethlehem in the middle of January, headed for the Mohawk village of Chief Hendricks (on the Mohawk River in present New York State). Here they were to live and learn the language of the Mohawk. Shortly after arriving they were arrested and taken to New York, accused of being spies for the French; the English and the French were involved at that time in King George's War (1740–48). Despite their innocence, they were jailed for fifty-one days, where Zeisberger spent his twenty-fourth birthday suffering, he wrote, "For the Saviour's sake."

Less than a month after returning from New York Zeisberger headed back into the wilderness, accompanying Augustus Spangenberg, the leader of the Bethlehem Brethren, on their first trip into Iroquois country. Their destination was the Onondaga village of the same name near present Syracuse, New York. The purpose of the trip was to secure the Onondaga's permission to let several Brethren live among them and learn their language, a prerequisite to founding a mission among the Iroquois. While receiving a favorable response, the events of King George's War in America delayed the implementation of the program for another five years. Zeisberger then led the Moravian missionary vanguard among the Iroquois.

In the meantime, during the spring of 1746, Zeisberger and the missionary Martin Mack founded a new mission at Gnadenhutten, on the Mahoning Creek, twenty-five miles north of Bethlehem (see appendix A, number 5). Although it was only a temporary assignment, Gnadenhutten was the beginning of the Zeisberger ministry. Within two years, by 1748, he was permanently assigned as Martin Mack's assistant at the new Shamokin mission (now Sunbury, Pennsylvania). The following year he was ordained a deacon and could now serve as a full-fledged missionary. He remained at Shamokin as head missionary until May of 1750, when he was chosen to begin the first of four visits among the Six Nations Iroquois confederacy.

Over the next five years Zeisberger conducted a turbulent and frustrating experiment among the Iroquois. After he had traveled over fifteen hundred miles and was on the threshold of success, the program was interrupted by the outbreak of the French and Indian War. All of his long and tedious effort came to nothing. After the war the Brethren abandoned their work among the Iroquois. Unfortunately, the reason behind this decision has been lost in the unwritten pages of Moravian history.

The French and Indian War in 1755 and the Pontiac Uprising in 1763 brought devastation to the Moravian missionary movement. In 1755 it wiped out the prospering mission of Gnadenhutten on the Mahoning Creek, and almost cost Zeisberger his life. Just moments before he arrived on a trip to the village, French Indians assaulted the mission and killed ten white mission workers. Because of its exposed position, the Shamokin mission was also abandoned during the same year.

Gathering together the remnant of converts from Gnadenhutten and Shamokin, the Moravians founded new missions at Nain and Wechquanach, near Bethlehem. These two missions were subsequently destroyed in 1763 during the Pontiac Uprising, and the 125 converts were taken by Zeisberger to Philadelphia and placed under the protective custody of the Pennsylvania colonial government.

With the resumption of peace in 1765, the Moravian church leaders clearly recognized that they could never again conduct missionary efforts near white settlements. Thus began the movement to remove the missions far afield from white civilization. Zeisberger now became the point man for the Moravian missionary effort and served as such until his death in 1808.

In the spring of 1765 he led ninety converts to the banks of the Susquehanna River and the Indian village of Wyalusing (now Wyalusing, Bradford County, Pennsylvania). Here they founded the mission of Friedenshutten on the Susquehanna. It flowered and became one of the most successful of all the Moravian missions.

Two years after founding Friedenshutten, Zeisberger—again attempting to expand the mission effort—became the first white man to cross the Forbidden Path, a Seneca Indian trail prohibited to all whites. Traveling west, he came to the headwaters of the Allegheny River, near present Tionesta, Pennsylvania. The following year, in 1768, he founded there the mission of Goschgoschunk (Go-sch-go-schunk). He remained on the Allegheny for two years, until April of 1770, when he moved again further westward to the Beaver River and established the mission of Friedensstadt (south of present New Castle, Lawrence County, Pennsylvania). These missions are shown in appendix A, numbers 12 through 16.

During this period, Zeisberger encountered a new problem. In the past, his work had been impaired by the hostile attitude of on-rushing white immigration. Now, on the Beaver River, he confronted similar interference from the native Indian leaders. (Zeisberger frequently differentiated between the two groups of Indian by referring to the native or unchristian Indians as "natives" or "Wild Indians." The converts were called "Christian Indians" or "converts." Other whites or native Indians occasionally called them "praying Indians.") Even though the population of most of these mission villages never exceeded one hundred persons, some converts were coming from previously untapped native Indian tribes. The Moravian missionary effort may not have been deliberately designed to weaken tribal government, but the native leaders looked upon the mission work as a threat to their culture. The missionary program did unwittingly weaken those tribes, by drawing off members. But Zeisberger, the true believer, had his own mission—spreading the work of the Lord. He struggled on despite the difficulties.

By early spring of 1772 Zeisberger became convinced that he should consolidate the two missions of Friedensstadt and Friedenshutten. Few converts had been gained at the Friedensstadt mission on the Beaver River. To the east, Friedenshutten was threatened by encroaching white settlers. Fortunately Zeisberger had been invited by Netawatwes (Net-tuh-waht-wes), the head chief of the Delaware, to make a trip to the Muskingum valley the previous year. Five years earlier, Netawatwes had visited Friedenshutten and was favorably impressed with the mission work. Since that time, the chief had also heard good reports about the missions in western Pennsylvania. During the spring visit in 1771, Zeisberger had received an invitation to bring the "praying Indians" to the Muskingum valley. Impressed with Netawatwes's sincerity, he firmly believed that the Lord had solved his problems.

Thus on May 3, 1772, Zeisberger arrived at the new location on the banks of the Muskingum with eleven converts, several native Indian helpers, and a handful of children. The village of Schoenbrunn began to

The Power of the Gospel was painted by Charles Schussele in 1862—a fanciful depiction of Zeisberger preaching at Goschgoschunk in the spring of 1767. The painting measures more than six feet high by nine feet long, and hangs in the Moravian Church Archives Building in Bethlehem, Pennsylvania.

take shape. Before the year ended, the converts had arrived from Friedens-hutten and an additional mission was founded at Gnadenhutten.[3] David Zeisberger, the experienced missionary, supervised both villages. At Schoenbrunn he was assisted by Johann and Anna Margaretha Jungmann. John Heckewelder, a new missionary, was the school-teacher. Johann and Johanna Schmick, the former head missionaries at Friedenshutten, occupied the same position at Gnadenhutten.

During the first four years, they lived in relative peace. The missions thrived, and life was comfortable. Both villages contained sturdy log homes, large fenced fields, and gardens surrounded by fruit trees. As 1775 came to a close (the last year in which the Schoenbrunn census was re-corded), the mission diarists listed 263 inhabitants at Schoenbrunn and 136 at Gnadenhutten—almost 400 Indian converts. It was the apex of the Moravian missionary effort.

The deed for the sale of the Friedenshutten Mission, executed on June 22, 1772, granted the mission land and improvements to Job Chillaway, a Christian convert who remained behind following the congregation's move to the Muskingum valley. It is signed by John Papunhank; Josua, the Mahican; and former chief John Martin, trustees of the Christian Indians departing for the new mission. It is noteworthy for the totemic signs representing their marks on the bottom right of the deed.

Back in the eastern settlements, sixteen years of seething colonial resentment against the British landlords finally exploded into violence. The minutemen from Lexington and Concord, standing in the village green, fired "the shot heard around the world." That shot sparked the American Revolution. It also destroyed the Moravian missions in the Muskingum valley. This is the story.

The success of the Muskingum valley Christian missions can be attributed to Chief Netawatwes and two of his principal advisors, Gelelemend (Kuh-lay-luh-mund) and White Eyes (Ko-que-tha-gach-ton). In 1772, at the time of the converts' arrival, the Delaware lived at their capital village of Gekelemukpechunk (Kuh-lay-luh-muk-pe-chunk) near present Newcomerstown, Ohio.

Nearing ninety, Netawatwes for two decades had been among the three principal chiefs of the Leni Lenape tribe, known as the Delaware. A member of the Unami (Turtle) clan, he was revered and profoundly respected among his people as indicated by his name, which meant "One who is a skilled advisor." Zeisberger's relationship with the chief dated back almost ten years when Netawatwes, called "Chief Newcomer" by the whites, lived on the Allegheny near present Tionesta, Pennsylvania. Their first contact came in July 1766 when the Moravian converts were living at Friedenshutten mission on the Susquehanna. The occasion was a peace message sent to Friedenshutten, which was to be passed on to the Iroquois at Onondaga. Their next contact came three years later, in the spring of 1769. By then the chief had moved his village to Gekelemukpechunk on the Muskingum, and Zeisberger was ministering to his Christian flock at Lawunakhannek on the Allegheny River. Netawatwes was now the head chief of the Delaware. His immediate predecessor, Tamaqua or Beaver, had died early in the year. In the following three years (1769–71), Netawatwes repeatedly appealed to Zeisberger with invitations suggesting he move the converts to the Muskingum valley near the old chief's village.

Netawatwes's grandson was Gelelemend, the designated heir to his head chieftainship. In 1771, at the time of Zeisberger's visit, he was thirty-four and one of Netawatwes's principal advisors. John Killbuck, his father and Netawatwes's son, was another active member of the Delaware Council. Then known as the Killbucks among the whites, both father and son played major roles in the Delaware history of this period. The father, sometimes called Bemineo (Be-min-eo), was a renowned warrior and highly respected. He had been active during the French and Indian War, fighting with the French, and participated in raids against the eastern colonial settlements. In 1758, following the war, he became

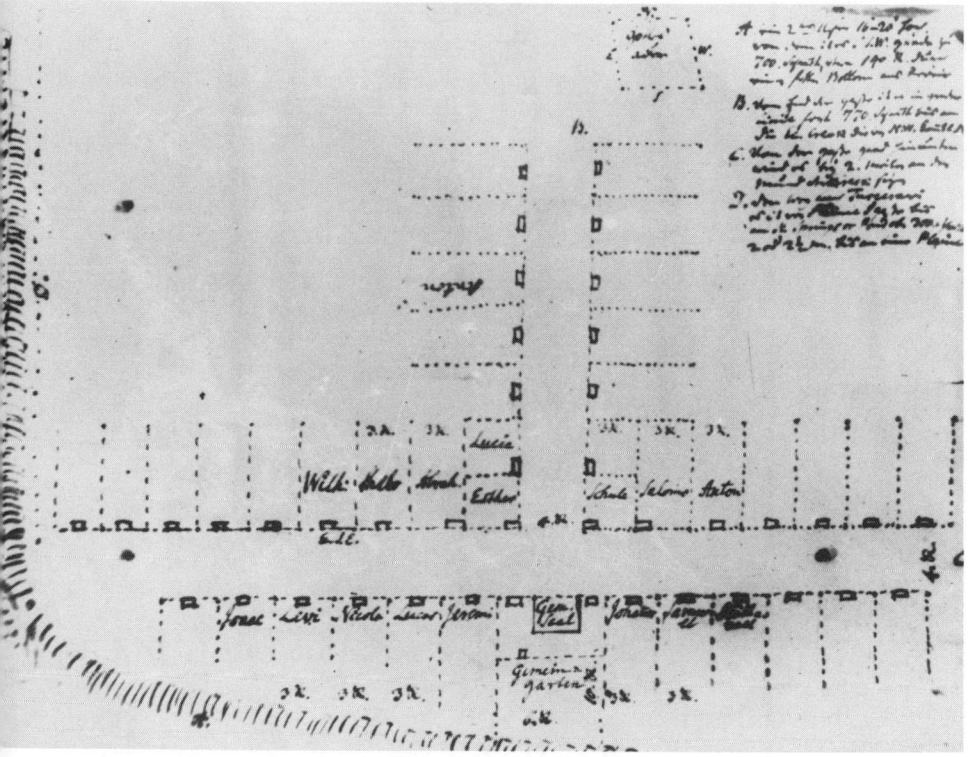

This original map of Schoenbrunn was drawn by John Ettwein in August 1772.

Netawatwes's counselor of the Wolf clan (as White Eyes was for the Turkey lineage). He later moved to the Muskingum and was one of the Delaware deputies sent to make peace with Sir William Johnson in 1765 following the Pontiac Uprising. Three years later he was a delegate at the important Treaty of Fort Stanwix. He took a pro-American stance during the Revolution. However, unlike his son he was never fond of the Moravians and was generally antagonistic toward missionary activities.

Gelelemend, like his mother of the Turtle lineage, was born near the Lehigh River in 1737. (The Delaware were matrilineal and took their clan affiliations from the mother rather than from the father. Only those men from the Unami [Turtle] clan could assume the head chieftainship.) From the very beginning of his contact with the Moravians Gelelemend became enamored with their Christian philosophy. As a young boy, he

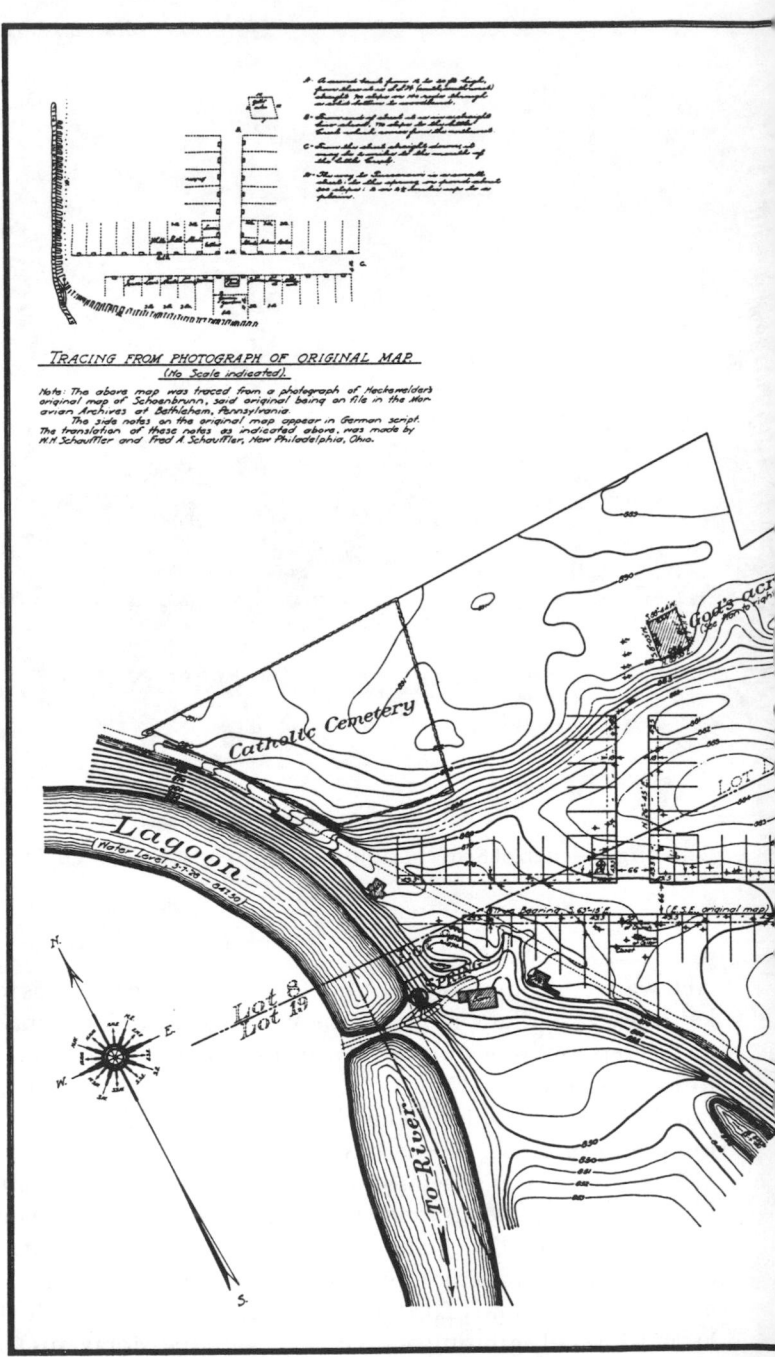

TRACING FROM PHOTOGRAPH OF ORIGINAL MAP
(No Scale indicated).

Topographic map of Schoenbrunn, drawn in 1929 by Waldo Hartline and Al
Rosch, New Philadelphia, Ohio. Once the hearthstone of the original chu
was discovered in 1923, it was possible to place the village in its exact locati
Hartline and Rosch superimposed Ettwein's map (shown in the upper left-h
corner) on their topographic drawing. Subsequent excavations located the ce
tery in 1927 (shown in the upper center of the map) and the fences, lots,

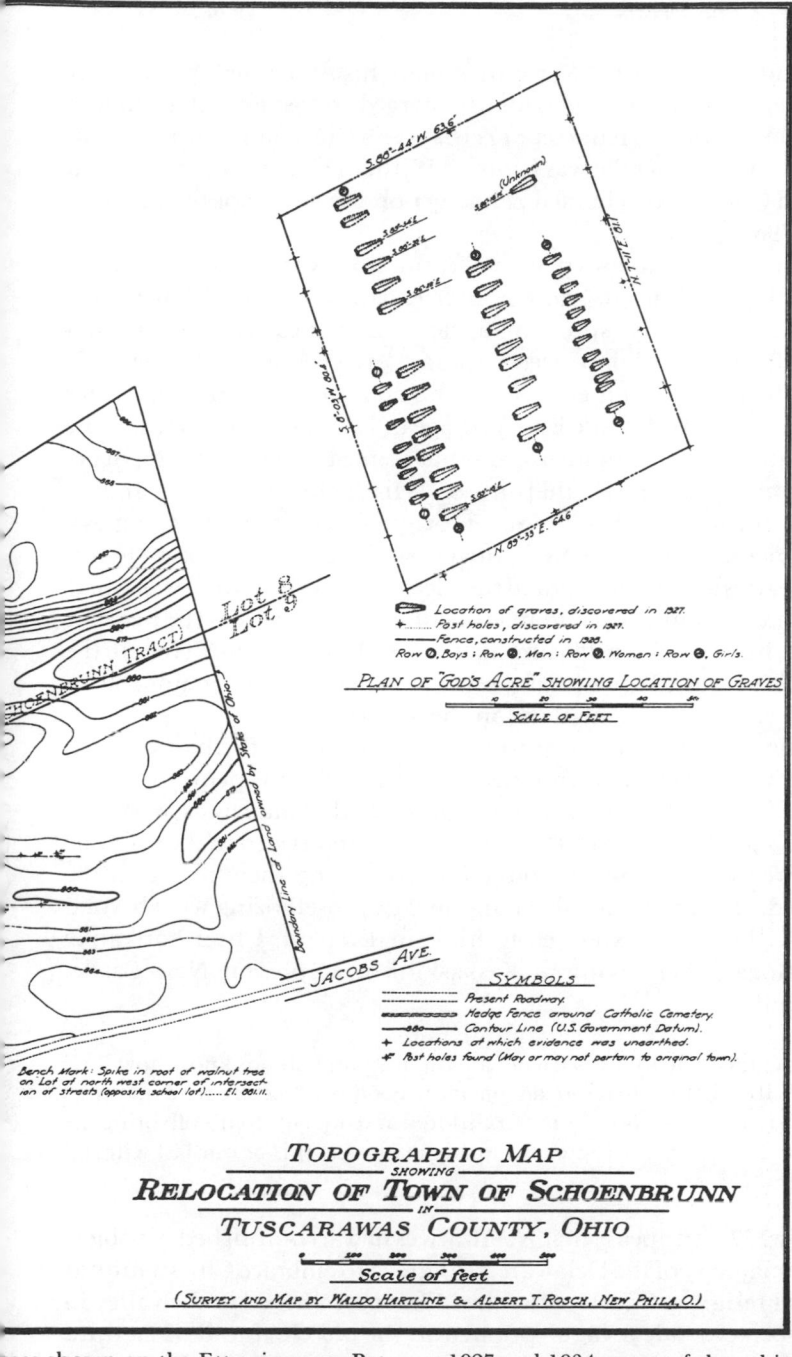

Location of graves, discovered in 1927.
.... Post holes, discovered in 1927.
——— Fence, constructed in 1935.
Row ⊙, Boys ; Row ⊙, Men ; Row ⊙, Women ; Row ⊙, Girls.

PLAN OF "GOD'S ACRE" SHOWING LOCATION OF GRAVES

SCALE OF FEET

SYMBOLS

.... Present Roadway.
▬▬▬▬ Hedge Fence around Catholic Cemetery.
——880—— Contour Line (U.S. Government Datum).
+ Locations at which evidence was unearthed.
✦ Post holes found (May or may not pertain to original town).

Bench Mark : Spike in root of walnut tree
on Lot at north west corner of intersect-
ion of streets (opposite school lot).... El. 881.11.

TOPOGRAPHIC MAP
——— SHOWING ———
RELOCATION OF TOWN OF SCHOENBRUNN
—— IN ——
TUSCARAWAS COUNTY, OHIO

Scale of feet

(SURVEY AND MAP BY WALDO HARTLINE & ALBERT T. ROSCH, NEW PHILA, O.)

...ses shown on the Ettwein map. Between 1927 and 1934 many of the cabins
...e reconstructed, including the church, schoolhouse, and the Zeisberger
...l Jungmann houses. The spring, the mission's main source of water, is
...wn near the base of the hill next to the lagoon which provided access to the
...r by canoe.

was shy and introspective. As a grown man, his nonviolent personality was anathema to the sometimes highly charged atmosphere of his Indian village. The pacifistic character of Zeisberger's Christianity was irresistible to him. Much later, he was baptized William Henry—the helmsman in the lead canoe that relanded Zeisberger on the shores of the Muskingum in 1798.

Another of Netawatwes's principal counselors was White Eyes. Flamboyant and gregarious, he was a stout friend of the colonial Americans. As the Delaware tribal spokesman, he was once called by Christian Frederick Post "One of the cleverest Indians" he ever met.[4] The key to his fame can be found in an entry from the diary of the Baptist minister David Jones. Visiting White Eyes's village in 1773, he wrote, "He was the only Indian I met with in my travels that seemed to have a design of accomplishing something [in the] future."[5] His dream of a separate Indian state never became a reality, despite its original acceptance by Congress. As the principal advisor to Netawatwes, White Eyes was a party to numerous treaties and embassies and traveled extensively in the eastern part of the country. Ambitious and intelligent, he passed across the pages of American history like a blazing meteor, only to be murdered at the height of his career. However, for seven years he played a major role in the life of the Christian missions on the Muskingum.

Like his grandson, Netawatwes was captivated with the Christian philosophy of peace and tranquility. He longed for his people to reject their warlike ways and embrace the brotherhood of man as expressed in Zeisberger's teachings. From the time the converts arrived in the valley he worked tirelessly among his council, encouraging them to accept the Christian doctrine as their tribal religion. His proselytizing went beyond his own village and extended to his tribal friend, Chief Pankanke (or Custaloga), then living at Kaskaskink near present New Castle, Pennsylvania.

> Both you and I, he told his friend, are old men and do not know how long we shall live. Let us therefore do one more good work before we depart this temporal life and let us leave to our children and our children's offspring the message that we have accepted the word of God. Let this be our last will and testament.[6]

By early 1775 it appears that Netawatwes had accomplished his objective and a majority of the Delaware had agreed to embrace Christianity as their tribal religion. Shortly after the Moravians arrived in the valley in 1772, Zeisberger made a vague promise to the old chief to build a third village near the Delaware capital. On September 29, 1775, on their way to the treaty at Fort Pitt, the entire council stopped at the village to deliver a formal request from Netawatwes, who was ill and unable to make the trip. Zeisberger recorded their message in his diary.

The 29th.

Brethren and Friends: It is now three years since you have come to this region, at which I and we all rejoice and for which we are thankful. You informed us, immediately upon your arrival, that you were minded to found two or three towns for the believing Indians in this region. Now there are two and we see that they are fully occupied. Since now after much and long consideration we [the Delaware Council] have unanimously decided to accept the Word of God, we think that now the time has come to found the third town, so that as many people as would become believers may see that they have a place. We, therefore, urge you that you will take action as soon as possible. You are to make the beginning, to lay the foundation, to plant the Word of God there and try to introduce the arrangement you best understand right from the start. . . . He [Netawatwes] wishes that the matter be taken up as soon as possible that he might see a beginning made before he dies, for he cannot live long.[7]

Despite the urgency of the request, Zeisberger delayed his decision until the following year. In the meantime, Netawatwes had moved his village to Goschachgunk (Go-sch-ach-gunk) at the forks of the Muskingum, approximately twenty miles west of his old village, at present Coshocton, Ohio. Because of their dependency on corn, they always found it necessary to begin a new village early in the spring with sufficient time to clear the fields and plant the spring crop. On February 4, 1776, Zeisberger received another more urgent request from the old chief. Five days later he, Schebosh, and five Indian Brethren left Schoenbrunn for Goschachgunk, the Delaware capital. Arriving on February 10, they spent the next two days searching for an acceptable site. Three miles below the Delaware village they found "an extraordinarily fine piece of land." Zeisberger remarked: "We were so pleased and our hearts filled with such joy that we could hardly conceal our satisfaction."

Before leaving Goschachgunk he confided to his diary the love he felt for Netawatwes.

He is a dear venerable old man, who is concerned about the well-being of his people and has great confidence and trust in the Brethren that they will make the Indians a happy people. . . . During this visit we have noticed a different atmosphere; a different spirit rules among the Indians. We have seen many who in times past, were our bitter enemies and would neither hear nor know anything of God's Word and now show themselves very obliging and confiding toward us, cultivating our companionship as long as we were with them. There have been great changes within a year.[8]

The Zeisberger party arrived back in Schoenbrunn on the evening of February 13, 1776, completely oblivious of the storm that was building back in the eastern settlements. Within a year he would be fighting for the very existence of the mission program.

LICHTENAU, "THE PASTURE OF LIGHT"

Meanwhile, the next two months were spent in preparation for the move to Lichtenau, the new village. By April 9 eight families had been chosen to provide the seed congregation. The diary for the next few days describes the departure of those who were to establish the new settlement.

April 9, 1776.
   The 9th. The Brethren and Sisters that are to move to the new settlement prepared for their departure, and the canoes were loaded. Finally we decided between ourselves, in the presence of our dear Lord that the new town to be laid out should be called Lichtenau, that was announced to all the Brethren and Sisters.

April 10, 1776.
   The 10th of April. During the morning service, Br. David Zeisberger baptized the baby girl, born last night to Brn. and Sr. Leonard and Rachel, to the name of Hanna . . . and then he left with Br. Heckewelder and 7 families of Brethren and Sisters from here to Lichtenau.[9]

The party, some traveling by land driving the cattle and the others in canoes carrying the baggage, spent the evening of April 10 at Gnadenhutten, where several additional families joined the group. There were now thirty-five converts in the contingent. The following day they passed White Eyes's town, which was six miles below present Newcomerstown, Ohio. On the evening of April 12 they arrived at their destination. The next day they began to stake out the town. Nine days later the new mission village was solemnly inaugurated in the presence of Chief Netawatwes and a great number of his people. The old chief was ecstatic. His people could now conveniently visit the village and hear the Word of God preached daily.

Unfortunately, the ninety-year-old Netawatwes did not live out the year, dying in Pittsburgh on the last day of October 1776. His death shortly changed the hegemony of the Delaware Indian nation—a crucial element in the survival of the mission program. Thus almost from the beginning the future of the Lichtenau mission was placed in jeopardy, since the success of the new village required a receptive and friendly Delaware native council.

Netawatwes's successor and grandson, the thirty-nine-year-old Gelelemend, while personally competent, never enjoyed the prestige of his grandfather. He was a quiet, self-reflecting man and much preferred the life of the mission villages to the politically contentious aura of the native Delaware capital. It was a precarious chieftainship. White Eyes, his principal advisor, would live only one more year. Memocanund (Memo-ca-nund), White Eyes's cousin, and six other subchiefs warmly supported Gelelemend and the missions; Tete-pach-kschus, the speaker of the council, Big Cat, Delaware George, and several other important chiefs secretly opposed the Gelelemend faction. Captain Pipe, the head chief of the Munsee Delaware, had abandoned the council and was now living in the northern part of Ohio firmly allied with the British and the Wyandot. But despite these defections, Gelelemend in the fall of 1776 adroitly handled his council and kept the Delaware neutral.

In December Zeisberger welcomed William Edwards, a new man to the mission field, to Lichtenau. Over the next twenty-six years the two men became close associates and personal friends.[10]

At the beginning of 1777 the British stepped up their activity in the western theater. Their strategy was to create disturbances in the area, compelling Gen. George Washington and the provincial Congress at Philadelphia to divert troops from the eastern campaigns to quell any disorders that might develop in the western Ohio and Pennsylvania theater. Henry Hamilton, the new British lieutenant governor at Detroit, began to circulate the war belt—a tomahawk wrapped in a red-and-white beaded cloth. His plan was to augment his meager British forces with Indian allies. The belt was immediately accepted by the Shawnee, Wyandot, Mingos, and Captain Pipe's Munsee Delaware. Only Gelelemend, White Eyes, and their Unami Delaware at Goschachgunk demurred, maintaining their neutrality.

By 1777 the Revolution had reached the western frontier and a state of war now existed between the British and American forces. The Muskingum Christian missions were located in the middle of the battle zone. Hostile British Indian war parties passed weekly through the Moravian villages bound for attacks against the western colonial settlements. Zeisberger's instructions to mission personnel were to treat all visitors hospitably, regardless of whether friend or foe. During their frequent visits to the area, the British-led Indians began to exert pressure on the Delaware Council to abandon its neutrality and to convince the Indian mission converts to join their war parties.

During the nine months following the founding of Lichtenau, the British and colonial political manipulations continued to escalate among the various Ohio Indian tribes. The first evidence of this pressure had now reached the Christian congregation with the defection of convert Augustinus, the former Delaware chief Newellike. On February 13, 1777, Heckewelder, now the temporary resident missionary at Schoenbrunn, recorded this entry:

> On the 13th, Augustinus (otherwise called Newellike) moved away from here with his family to his property which he had already established in the previous fall. Although such incidents always affect us deeply, and although it is painful for us to see people turn away from the light and chose darkness again, yet in the case of this man, we could not help but thank the Saviour for having rid us of such bad influences as Augustinus had been.[11]

Newellike and his family were Munsee, cousins of the Delaware, and had thrown in their lot with that of Captain Pipe, the leader of the Munsee at the Delaware Council. Pipe was now firmly allied with the British. Heckewelder's relief at the departure of Newellike was genuine. Since the chief's first contact with the missions in 1765 he had been a vacillating and unstable influence among the converts.[12]

Eleven days later Heckewelder received a letter from Zeisberger advising that the Shawnee tribes, with few exceptions, were actively waging war against the Virginians. The confusion among the missions continued to accelerate. On the evening of February 27, Josua (German for the English Joshua) came from Gnadenhutten with a string of wampum from the councilors at Goschachgunk. Heckewelder recorded the following entry: "In this letter it was stated that now the war seemed to be spreading over the entire country, and the enemies of the Delawares threatened to kill all white people whoever they may be, who may be found in the Indian country and that in case this or that Indian should undertake to take white people under his protection such an Indian would forsake his head."[13] The chiefs further suggested that a representative from Schoenbrunn and Gnadenhutten be sent immediately to Goschachgunk to discuss the situation. Nathanael and Cornelius were dispatched the next day.

With the coming of March winds, rumors continued to blow across the valley. Nicolaus, the son of Thomas the Munsee, visiting Schoenbrunn to purchase corn, told of a party of Mingos plotting to "snatch Bro. and Sr. Schmick and the Jungmanns out of town during the sugar-boiling season because at that time it would be rather empty." According to the report, they were either to be killed or sent to Detroit for ransom. Also, from the Cuyahoga they received news that all British traders had been recalled to Detroit for their protection. The colonials at Fort Pitt were threatening all British traders caught on the frontier.

Nathanael and Cornelius returned from the Goschachgunk council on March 14 with uncertain news. White Eyes promised during the series of meetings that he would do all in his power "to take care of, and stand up for, the safety of the Brethren.'' But additional rumors circulated of a general dissatisfaction with White Eyes's speech.

Nine days later Zeisberger arrived at the Schoenbrunn village. Heckewelder explains the reason for the sudden visit.

> On the 23rd. [March] in the morning, there was a sermon. After the sermon our dear Bro. David accompanied by the two brethren Isaac and Abraham, arrived from Lichtenau, entirely unexpectedly. He at once informed us about the purpose of his visit, namely, that the chiefs, in view of the present warlike times, and dangerous circumstances, and for the sake of greater safety for us, were positively demanding that we, here at Schoenbrunn, as well as our brethren and sisters at Gnadenhutten should move to Lichtenau.[14]

Zeisberger agreed with the council's assessment of the situation and informed the Schoenbrunn converts that he planned to move both villages to Lichtenau. Almost immediately Zeisberger's plan to abandon Schoenbrunn and Gnadenhutten caused a heated controversy. Most of the converts agreed, but the remaining Munsee faction refused to move. At a meeting with Zeisberger the next day they loudly professed their disapproval and announced, ''We are through believing.'' Some of the missionaries also disagreed. In fact, Johann Schmick, the head missionary at Gnadenhutten, not only objected to the plan, but categorically refused to comply.

While Zeisberger appreciated the ''dangerous circumstances'' expressed by the native chief at Goschachgunk, he was also well aware of the contentious atmosphere at the Delaware capital and must have surmised that it was simply a matter of time until the Delaware would join the British. Because Lichtenau was less than three miles from the Delaware capital, there was easy communication between the Lichtenau mission and the native village; any evidence of hostility on the part of the Delaware Council could be quickly perceived. With all of the converts gathered together in one area they could be moved rapidly to a safe location.

The Zeisberger party returned to Lichtenau on March 26, and Heckewelder and the Jungmanns vowed to continue on at Schoenbrunn until they could make an orderly move. The next day Heckewelder recorded in the diary ''Fifty-two communicants partook for the last time in this place of the Lord's Supper.''[15] At the break of day on March 30, they gathered in the church to celebrate Easter and the resurrection of their beloved Savior.

On the morning of April 1, Schebosh and his family departed from Schoenbrunn for Gnadenhutten with most of their possessions in three canoes.[16] Near evening, Sem, a friendly native Indian, paid one of his frequent visits to Schoenbrunn. He brought alarming news, which was

The reconstructed Schoenbrunn evokes frontier life at the mission. Photograph taken by Carl C. Kempf in 1987.

confirmed by the converts Jacob and Nicolaus, who arrived several hours later. Heckewelder recorded the message: "Eighteen warriors were at the forks of the Tuscarawas [twelve miles north of the village] and it was their intention to kill us white Brethren and Sisters both here and at Gnadenhutten."[17] Without delay and in the dead of the night, the Jungmanns and the Conners boarded canoes manned by Jacob and Nicolaus and left Schoenbrunn for Lichtenau. En route they stopped at Gnadenhutten early the next morning. After a brief rest, they continued downstream to Lichtenau. Heckewelder, who left Schoenbrunn at the same time, traveled by land and arrived at Gnadenhutten at midnight.

The following day they received news that the Mingos' party had continued toward Fort Pitt, abandoning its original plan to attack the missions. During the day an advance party from Lichtenau arrived at Gnadenhutten to facilitate the removal of the Schoenbrunn contingent. They picked up Heckewelder and continued on to Schoenbrunn. While

the immediate crisis was resolved, the Brethren and sisters were happy to
see some of the missionaries return and observed "that all sorts of good-
for-nothing rabble filled the town in the last several days."[18] The proposed abandonment of the village quickly spread among the native
riffraff that frequently roamed the countryside looking for a free lodging
soon to be available.

Zeisberger arrived with another Lichtenau party on April 12. Seven
days later, their possessions were loaded into the canoes and the moving
plans completed. Heckewelder made his final entry:

> On the 19th Br. David conducted the early meeting, the last time in this
> church. In conclusion, the congregation went down on their knees, and Br.
> David offered a further prayer. He thanked the Saviour for everything that He
> had done in this place for our hearts, and asked Him for His continued sover-
> eignty and gracious guidance of this people. . . . Immediately after the
> meeting, the roof was torn down from the meeting house and all kinds of
> other things were done to it in order to ruin it for further use.[19]

The following morning they left Schoenbrunn for the last time. It was a
sorrowful procession that drifted down the Muskingum toward Lichtenau. Thus came to an end one of Zeisberger's most successful missions.

For more than two hundred years controversy has swirled around
Zeisberger's decision to abandon Schoenbrunn. A recently discovered letter written by Johann Schmick on May 24, 1777, six weeks after the converts departed from the village, explains Schmick's objection to the
move. This important and revealing letter was written to his good friend
Matthaeus Hehl at Lititz. While it should not serve as a definitive answer
to the dispute, it does explain Schmick's position. It further describes the
importance of "the lot" and the frequency with which the Moravian missionaries resorted to its use.

The Moravians were fond of using this procedure when confronted
with major decisions. The use of the lot was a powerful influence in the
early history of the Moravian church. Prior to 1769, its use was haphaz-
ardly observed, but at the general synod held at Marienborn in Germany
in 1769, it became a recognized important principle of the church's
decision-making process. At this synod the Brethren leaders determined
that all elections, appointments, and other important decisions, including the settlement of church policy, should be ratified by the lot. The
method was to place three pieces of paper in a box and then appoint
someone to draw one from the three. "If the paper was positive, the resolution was carried; if the paper was negative, the resolution was lost; if
the paper was blank, the resolution was laid on the table. The weightiest
matters were settled in this way." The whole process was treated with

Moravian Mission Sites on the Tuscarawas River

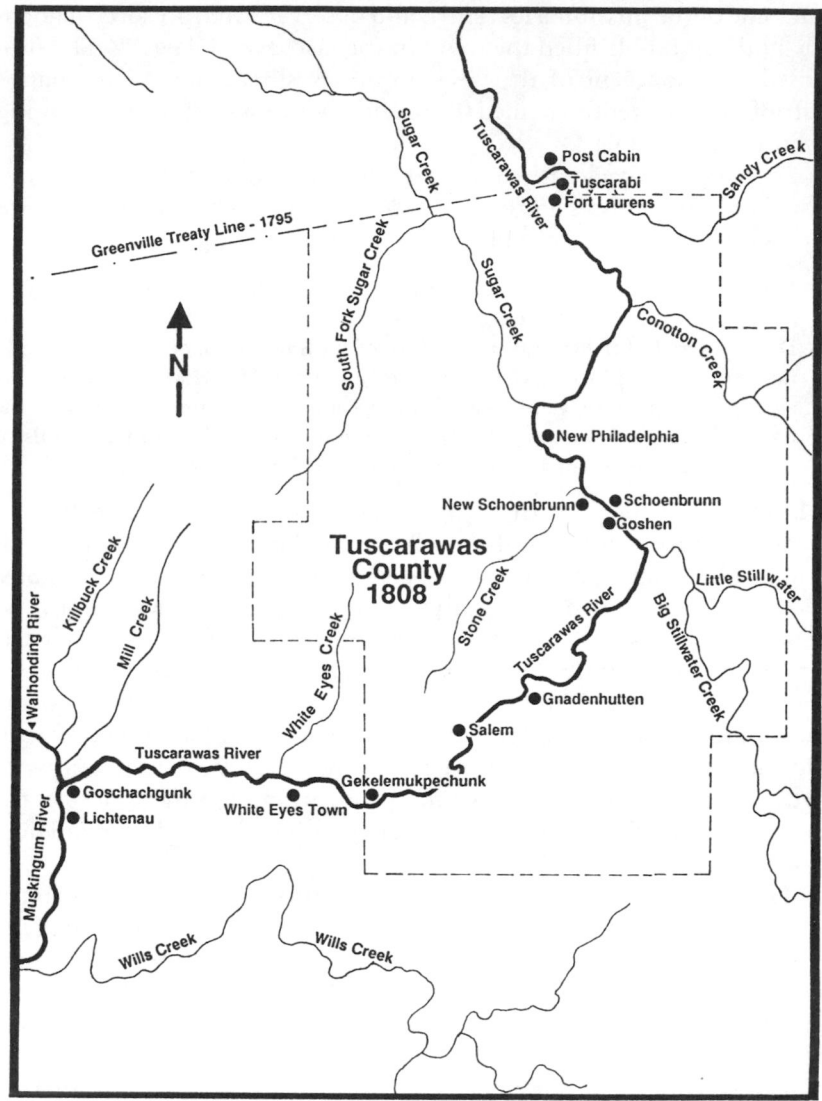

Map by Christy Reed - *Carrousel Graphics*

great solemnity, prayer, and deliberating before the Savior. To some crit-
ics the practice appeared to be a symptom of lunacy. But the Moravians
quickly pointed out the example of the eleven Apostles as recorded in
Acts I, verse 26, "And they gave forth their lots; and the lot fell upon
Matthias." They also cited Christ's promise, "Whatsoever ye shall ask in

my name, I will do it." However, by the middle of the nineteenth century, the practice fell into disfavor and was finally abolished.[20] Perhaps the greatest effect of the lot was the power and legitimacy it conferred on the decision. Regardless of the results, the resolution of the question was now validated by the voice of God. Zeisberger frequently resorted to this method to decide all of the significant mission questions including convert baptism, proposals of marriage, mission policies, and election of village leadership. Interestingly, most of those affected by the decisions willingly accepted the results.

Schmick's letter indicates that Zeisberger did not use this procedure in arriving at his decision to abandon Schoenbrunn. He further describes some of the activities that took place immediately prior to the move and subtly suggests the influence Zeisberger was under from the Delaware Council at Goschachgunk. The letter is also most remarkable for its candor. Seldom do we find any diary references to disagreements among the missionaries. Since the diaries were written for general consumption and usually read to the congregation at Bethlehem, then sent to Herrnhut, the church headquarters in Germany, all contentious matters were omitted.

Because of its importance, the Schmick letter is quoted in its entirety:

Gnadenhutten, May 24, 1777.

My dearest Brother Matthaeus.

Your last letter, of March 14 of this year, I did receive May 8. It was forewarded from Lichtenau, where it had lain, until there was an opportunity to send it and the list for the Daily Texts for May and June to us. It made us very happy that you, dear Brethren, have so much sympathy with our more or less difficult and often life-threatening circumstances, and that you remember us before the Saviour. This remembrance and the prayers of the congregation and [all] the Brethren has surely helped us a lot. We thank the Saviour from the bottom of our hearts for it and we pray that he may bless them for the future.

I hope that you received my last letter, of Febr. 28, of this year; it was addressed to you and dear Br. Nathanael [Seidel] and contained also the diary for 2 months Nov. and Dec. and the memorabilia of the last year. The good advice and proposal to exchange positions with the Jungmanns last autumn was not followed, since there was no asking the "lot," and at the present it is totally out of the question, because Schoenbrunn was left by all the Brn., and that on request of the Chiefs at Goschachkueng [Goschackgunk] with the consent of the brn. Zeisberger and Jungmann, without thinking and deliberation before the Saviour [i.e., asking the lot in this matter]. The Jungmanns fled immediately at night on account of the rumors which were only lies, namely that the Mingoes wanted to kill them and us. They went in a hurry to Lichtenau, in order to keep this station, as agreed upon with Br. David even before one even could think of being so suddenly called away. Now one can see clearly and exactly, why they were not willing last autumn to change places with us. However, it is said that the congregation of Schoenbrunn got away [i.e., was abandoned] in such a cunning way through the machination of the evil enemy, that the Brethren got dispersed and lost their houses and plantations. They could have as well quietly stayed there, as we did at Gnadenhutten, even though our people had also been requested by the Chiefs to move away. If they had only acted as we did and given the same answer to the chiefs as our Brethren, namely: Friends, we listened well to your words and have thought about it, but it is difficult for us to get up. We want first to wait for the answer of the Delemattonses [i.e., Pomoacan and his Wyandot] and hear what they have to say about the speeches of you and Colonel Morgan. If they had done that, they would still be in Schoenbrunn. However they were not allowed to think and to answer that way, because they were told by Br. David: There is nothing to deliberate about, you just have to get away; there is nothing else to do; you have to move down; it will be war. The chiefs request it and take you from here and leave you near Lichtenau, in order to be close to Goeschach-kuenk [Goschachgunk], to be strong with them when the war will break out. These latter words mean as much as if they had said: If it will be war, you fight together with us. However, Brethren shall not do that because they love peace and want to live with others in peace. Eight of the families moved to us, namely Schebosch. Nathanael Davis, Leonhard, David, A. Johanna, Anton, Joseph and Wilhelmina with three children, also the widow Noah left behind. And Schoenbrunn is now a place where run-aways and partly hermits are living, who took possession of the houses and plantations of the Brethren.

Br. Heckewelder came also to us to live with us; but he is now going for a visit to Bethlehem and can report to you more and even better than I can write it. Br. Heckewelder is in a hurry. Therefore I will finish for this time and send regards to you and your wife, Br. Grube, and the respected Brethren of the Conference. I and my wife greet you very cordially. We recommend us into your prayers. Be respectfully greeted by your humble Br., J. J. Schmick.[21]

In retrospect, little can be accomplished by speculating on the wisdom of the Schoenbrunn removal. If Schmick's contention is to be believed, Zeisberger relied too strongly on the decision of the Delaware Council, and why he abandoned his longtime practice of consulting the lot we will never know.

Despite Zeisberger's efforts to placate the Delaware Council, their relationship continued to deteriorate throughout the spring and summer of 1777. By August 6 contentions had become so critical that Johann and Anna Margaretha Jungmann, Zeisberger's former assistants at Schoenbrunn, considering their family's safety, accepted his suggestion to leave Lichtenau and return to Bethlehem. (Heckewelder had also been sent back on May 27.) Four days later Johann and Johanna Schmick left Gnadenhutten and returned to Lititz, a Moravian community in Lancaster County, Pennsylvania. It must have been a heartrending experience for the Schmicks. For twenty-six years they had been actively connected with the Indian missions and since 1763 were associated closely with Zeisberger. As noted above, the Schmicks had violently opposed the Schoenbrunn move. Now, with the safety of their family threatened and embroiled in the confrontation with Zeisberger, they decided to leave. Within six months after their departure Johann Schmick died in his sixty-fourth year, on January 23, 1778. A brilliant career had come to an end. Living under the shadow of the great Zeisberger, he has unfortunately never been given the recognition he deserves. Zeisberger and Edwards were now alone at Lichtenau, and Gnadenhutten was unattended. The hostility among the members of the native Delaware Council at Goschachgunk had reached the turning point. In typical stoic Zeisberger style, he told Edwards, "If we perish, we perish."

At the beginning of August 1777, two days after the Jungmanns left Lichtenau, Pomoacan (Po-Mo-a-can), the proud and arrogant Half-King chief of the Wyandot, and two hundred of his colorfully dressed warriors arrived at the Goschachgunk village. Zeisberger was waiting for him. He had been warned of the approaching contingent and carefully laid his plans for their reception. Sending a large quantity of their choicest provisions, the converts met the Wyandot north of the village. From his old mentor, Augustus Spangenberg, Zeisberger had learned "Never talk to an Indian on an empty stomach." The Moravian delegation was headed by Isaac, the famous former captain of the Delaware Wolf clan called Glikhikan (Glik-hi-kan). As Isaac met with the Wyandot at the council house at Goschachgunk, the other converts remained at Lichtenau, ready to depart hastily. At the door of the council stood a messenger on watch, who was to mount his horse at the first sign of hostility from the Wyandot. Glikhikan delivered his speech and presented several strings of wampum. Surprisingly, both were favorably received. After a brief consulation with his captains, Pomoacan rose to speak: "I rejoice to hear that the believing Indians have accepted the Word of God, and have two white teachers among them to proclaim it. Let them continue to hold their daily councils, undisturbed by passing warriors. Their teachers I herewith acknowledge as my father; the Wyandots are their children. I will make this known among the nations, and tell it to the Governor of Detroit."[22]

The following day the Indian war party visited the Lichtenau mission. Without exception, each of Pomoacan's warriors pledged his hand to Zeisberger and Edwards in an unusual display of friendship. Cautiously

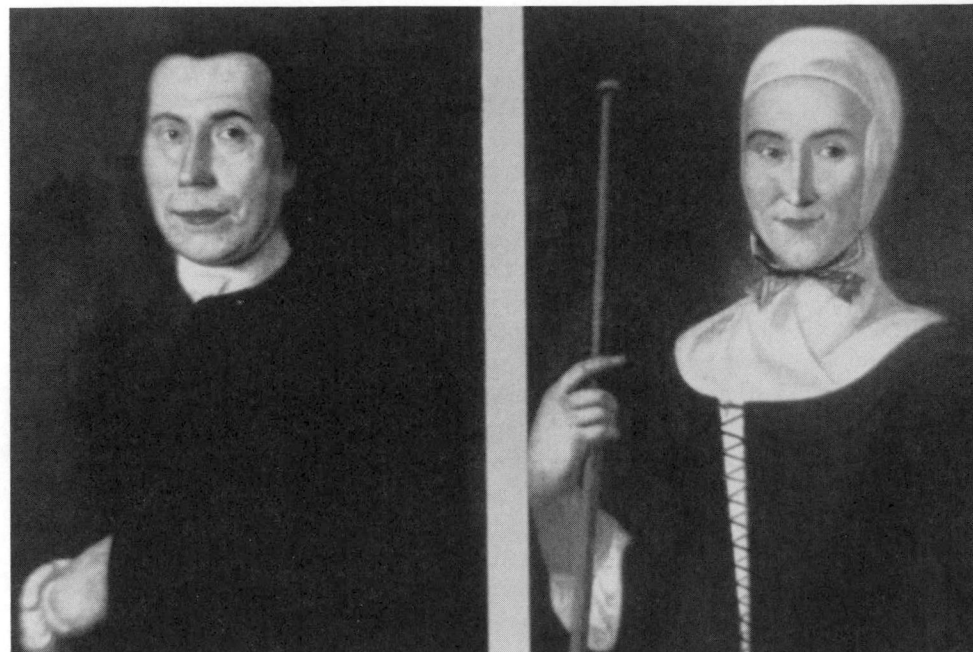

Moravian missionary Johann Schmick (1714–78) and his wife Johanna Heid Schmick (1721–95).

the missionaries responded to their friendly greetings, knowing full well they must remain wary of this haughty chief and his Wyandot warriors. Notwithstanding, everyone at Lichtenau breathed a sigh of relief.

Pomoacan, however, had additional items on his agenda. His forces left Lichtenau on August 10, en route to attack Fort Henry (Wheeling) on the Ohio River. Unexpectedly they met a small force of armed backwoods borderers (unauthorized by Gen. Edward Hand, the commander at Fort Pitt) who were marching west—advancing toward the Delaware capital. After defeating them, Pomoacan turned his fury on Fort Henry. On September 1, 1777, they attacked the fort with great resolution; however, the assault failed. Suffering numerous casualties, the Indians broke off the engagement and subsequently returned to their village on the Upper Sandusky.

Although the repulse of the Wyandot at Fort Henry was a minor incident, it marked the first occasion of circulated British reports that

Zeisberger alerted the fort of their approach.[23] It also may be the reason the Moravians later gained the Half-King's everlasting hatred.

Buffeted on both sides by the British and the colonial forces, Zeisberger's position in 1777 continued to deteriorate until 1781, when it became intolerable. For the next five years he conducted a veritable barrage of correspondence with the commander at Fort Pitt. Hidden within the Draper Manuscripts at Madison, Wisconsin, are forty-three letters written either by him or by John Heckewelder to Fort Pitt and letters from Fort Pitt to both men. This figure does not include many additional letters written between the chiefs at Goschachgunk and Fort Pitt. Since the chiefs were illiterate, most of the letters originating from the Indian village were either written by Zeisberger or Heckewelder for the chiefs. There also could have been additional correspondence that has been lost.

While General Hand, the commander at Fort Pitt, must have been advised by Zeisberger of the coming attack against Fort Henry, no letter is extant. However, seventeen days after the attack Hand did advise the Goschachgunk chiefs to refrain temporarily from sending any additional messages to the fort. He feared reprisal by the angry whites in the area against the Indian messengers in particular and against all Indians in general following the attack on Fort Henry. Shortly after Hand's message to the chiefs on September 17, Zeisberger responded on September 22. It was a long, detailed, and informative letter explaining his apprehension concerning the attitude of the white frontier population. In part it read:

> Capt. White Eyes & the councellors Are very sorry that the Communication and Correspondence with you is stopped & they shall hear Nothing now from you not knowing in what Condition they are and what they have to expect, because we hear that the white People would come & attack Goschachgunk & the delaware Towns which has set all the Indians in Consternation & fear, expecting every day that they will be upon them. A late report we had that the white People were already on their March hither *caused our Indians at Gnadenhutten to fly & left their town and we are now altogether here nigh Goschachgunk.* Therefore, pray Sir, let us know if we the Christian Indians, or the Delawares are in any Danger, & if we have any Thing to fear of the white People. I cannot leave my People the Christian Indians for I see it before hand that they all will be scattered if I leave them & the Brethren's Labor which so many Years and with so much Difficulty have continued with success would be entirely lost. . . . I hope you will remember us, & as much as lies in your Power to assist us that we may be able to keep our Ground & remain in Possession of our Towns. Capt. White Eyes and the Delaware Chiefs are yet determined to stand fast and not meddle with the War, they want to live in friendship with white People if they only knew that the white People has no

bad design against them. As long as they remain quiet and peaceable I wish my People shall keep with them or nigh them, but should we see that they drop friendship, then we should be obliged to separate ourselves from them. . . . The Wiondots & Mingoes are all gone home again. According to their Knowledge they killed 14 People at Weelunk (Wheeling, or Fort Henry), had one Wiondat killed & 6 of 7 Wounded one of the last died since.[24] [Emphasis added]

This letter clearly reveals that Zeisberger concluded that his best interest lay with the colonials. If the missions were to be saved, he had to put his trust in the American rebels. He had little choice. His help and assistance to operate the missions came from the east at Bethlehem. His and his church's connections were with the colonies, not with England.

The evening that Zeisberger wrote the above letter, he received another from General Hand. The next morning, before dispatching the first, he wrote a second letter detailing the position of the Miami Indians on the Wabash. They had just rejected the tomahawk belt sent to them by Governor Hamilton at Detroit, and decided to remain neutral and "follow the example of their Grandfathers the Delawares." Near the end of the letter he again furnished intelligence useful to the commander at Fort Pitt, who at the time was considering an expedition against Detroit.

By information of a white Man from Detroit who came here two days ago but doth not choose to have his name mentioned I can give you the following Account. That there are six Companies of Militia amounting to about 300 Men in the whole. . . . About 70 men in the garrison only. An Entrenchment is round the fort on the Land Side & about 50 Pieces of Cannon in the fort & 7 Pieces of Cannon on the Wharff. If an Army should come against the fort every Man is to march out to meet it & they are to be reinforced from Niagara. Great Stores of Provision is at Detroit & the inhabitants full of Cattle. At the Sandusky there in 100 head of cattle & the People to whom they belong will have nothing against it if they fall in the Hands of the Army. [There are] Six vessles on the Lake the largest two of 16 Guns. If an Army should march there late then there will be large Cargo of Goods at Sandusky.[25]

Following Pomoacan and the Wyandot's departure from Lichtenau on August 20, Zeisberger assigned William Edwards to head the unattended mission at Gnadenhutten. Edwards arrived during the third week in August 1777 to find the congregation in an uproar. All the villagers insisted they move to the west, away from the activities of the roaming bands of Wyandot and the threat of an invasion of white militia from the east.

Despite his assurances of Pomoacan's friendly intention, Edwards was forced to relent. They left Gnadenhutten on September 15 and moved west beyond Goschachgunk to a camp on the Walhonding River—his people preferring to stay by themselves rather than live at Lichtenau. Here they were placed well beyond any mischief that might result from Pomoacan's activity or an attack from Fort Pitt. The congregation spent three weeks on the Walhonding, then returned to Gnadenhutten during the first week of October. The crisis for both Gnadenhutten and Lichtenau was temporarily over.

Edwards remained at Gnadenhutten until the spring of 1778. It had been more than six months since the Bethlehem officials had heard from those on the Muskingum. Concerned for their safety, the church leaders dispatched John Heckewelder and Joseph Schebosh on a hasty trip to the villages. They arrived at Gnadenhutten on April 6, 1778, just as the congregation was about to undertake another move. The day before they arrived, Edwards, at Gnadenhutten, had received instructions from Zeisberger to move his converts to Lichtenau. With Heckewelder's and Schebosh's help, Edwards organized the village for the move. Three weeks later, the Gnadenhutten congregation arrived at Lichtenau. Zeisberger now had well over three hundred converts gathered at the forks of the Muskingum less than two miles from the native Delaware capital.

The Gnadenhutten move was prompted by rumors, rife among the Delaware, that the Americans had suffered a crushing military defeat and the remnants of the army were heading west to destroy the Indians. The source of most of the gossip came from Alexander McKee, Matthew Elliot, and Simon Girty, who had just escaped on March 28, 1778, from protective custody at Pittsburgh. All were charged with aiding and abetting the British. In the weeks after their escape from Fort Pitt they had been circulating among the Shawnee spreading the word. When Heckewelder and Schebosh (after their famous ride from Pittsburgh to Gnadenhutten) arrived on April 6 with dispatches from General Hand, the rumors were dispelled.[26] Actually, the American forces had defeated and captured the entire British army of General Burgoyne.

In October 1778 Zeisberger received devastating news. White Eyes had been shot and killed by an American colonial militiaman. The official word from Fort Pitt contended that he died of smallpox.[27] Had the truth been known the Delaware would have destroyed every colonial white person they found. White Eyes was accompanying an expedition to capture Detroit led by Gen. Lachlan McIntosh, Edward Hand's replacement at Fort Pitt. The army had advanced as far as the Great Crossing Place on the Muskingum, and because of the lateness of the season, McIntosh stopped there and built Fort Laurens.

With the loss of their great chief, Gelelemend began to lose his allies at the Delaware Council. Slowly they began to drift toward the British,

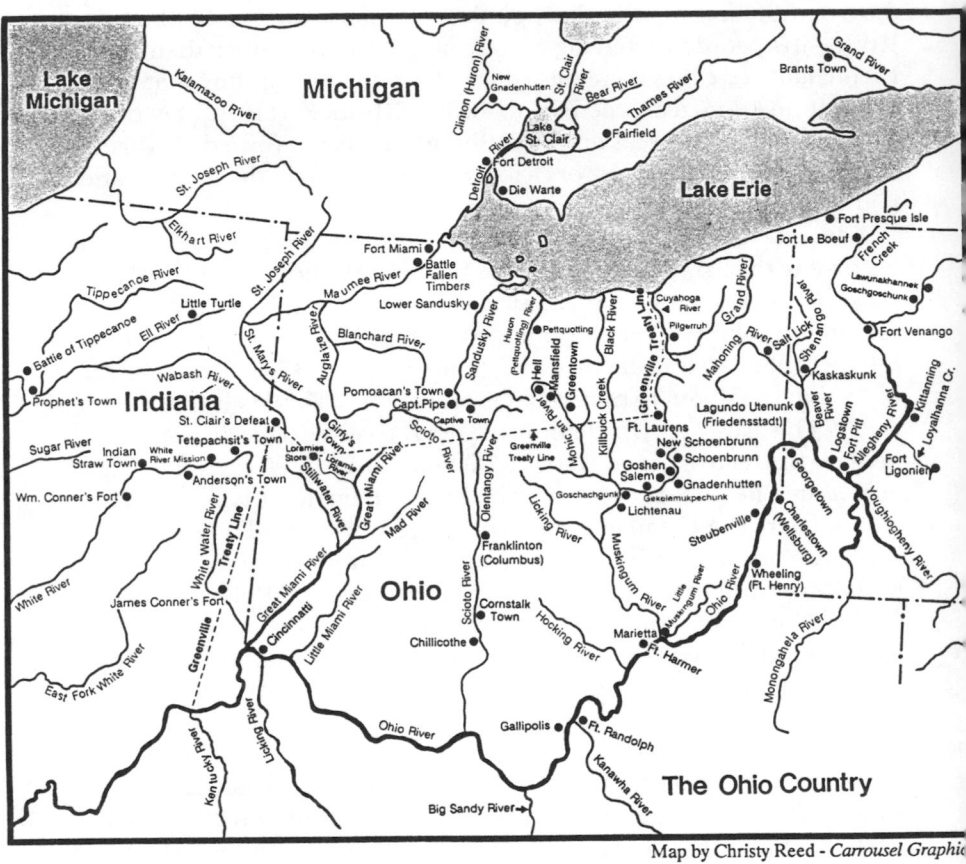

Map by Christy Reed - *Carrousel Graphic*

abandoning their neutral position. Only the successful campaign of George Rogers Clark in the Illinois country postponed further action on the Ohio frontier, delayed the Delaware decision for another two years, and gave Zeisberger time to reevaluate his own position.

For courage, daring, and bravery, Clark's attacks against the British settlements in Illinois have very few equals in the American annals. He left Redstone (Brownstown, Pennsylvania) in late May 1778, picked up stores in Pittsburgh and Wheeling, and sailed down the Ohio. By July 5 he had secured Kaskaskia, and by July 8 had captured Cahokia, both on the Mississippi River. Several weeks later he sent Captain Helms to capture the British stronghold of Vincennes, which surrendered after mild resistance. In the meantime, Clark wooed and won over the local Indians with sweet talk and treaties. In Detroit the British governor Hamilton reacted quickly. He mounted an expedition and retook Vincennes in December. Feeling secure, Hamilton settled down for the winter at Vincennes, but his peace and tranquility were rudely interrupted on the morning of February 24, 1779. Leaving Kaskaskia on February 5, Clark's troops had marched through forests and waded up to their necks in ice-choked rivers and marshes to arrive on the doorstep at Vincennes, completely undetected by Hamilton. Several hours after Clark's forces had surrounded and laid siege to the fort, Hamilton asked for a three-day truce. Clark's demand was "Immediate, unconditional surrender." On the next day, February 25, Hamilton surrendered himself and the entire garrison. The governor was taken to Williamsburg, where he was ordered confined in chains and fed on bread and water. Only General Washington's intercession secured humane treatment for him as a prisoner of war.[28]

Hamilton's capture and Clark's victories temporarily destroyed British aggressiveness, and the Delaware Council returned to its neutral position. With this new development, Zeisberger revised his strategy. Because of White Eye's death and the recent erratic nature of the Delaware Council, he no longer felt safe at Lichtenau. It was only a matter of time until the Delaware would drop their neutrality. If this occurred, it would be a disadvantage to reside close to their village. With this in mind, he began to decentralize the missions and move the converts away from the forks of the Muskingum.

On April 5, 1779, he directed Edwards to reoccupy the Gnadenhutten mission. Five days later, twenty of the former Mahican families moved back into the deserted village. While Edwards supervised the reorganization of Gnadenhutten, Heckewelder was given his first assignment as head missionary and placed in charge of the Delaware congregation remaining at Lichtenau.

NEW SCHOENBRUNN

Several days later Zeisberger proceeded north with many of the Lichtenau converts to find a new location near old Schoenbrunn, some thirty-five miles from Goschachgunk. The proposed village site overlooked the Muskingum River, approximately 1.75 miles west, across the river from the old village.[29] On April 10 they arrived in the area. Five days later they began to clear the land and build fences. The village would be called New Schoenbrunn. Meanwhile, the workers lived near the "beautiful spring," at the site of old Schoenbrunn. Unlike most mission construction, work went slowly. By April 15, most of the land was cleared and the fences erected, but it was not until July 12 that they staked out the town, and September 4 before they cleared the main street. On December 6, 1779, they occupied their new homes.

SALEM

With Zeisberger and some of the Lichtenau congregation at New Schoenbrunn and Edwards and his Mahicans at Gnadenhutten, Lichtenau was abandoned. On March 28, 1780, Heckewelder began to move the remaining Delaware converts twenty-five miles east of Goschachgunk to a new village site called Salem. The new mission lay in a beautiful alluvial plain on the west side of the Muskingum, just across the river and a few miles from Gnadenhutten.[30] By the third week in April, the move to Salem was completed and Lichtenau was deserted. The church at the new village was completed on May 22, just in time for a gala wedding celebration for Sarah Ohneberg and Johann Gottlieb Ernest Heckewelder. The little chapel overflowed with the happiness and exuberance of the celebrants.

At the end of the year Zeisberger reported 143 residents at New Schoenbrunn; Edwards had 135 at Gnadenhutten; Heckewelder 102 at Salem—a total of 380. This meant a population loss of only nineteen residents since 1775 and a remarkable achievement for the three men, considering the five years of confusion and uncertainty they had just experienced.

By the beginning of 1781 the British had successfully recovered from the loss of the Illinois country and replaced Hamilton with Major Arent Schuyler De Peyster at Detroit. On instructions from General Washington, the colonial commander of Fort Pitt, Gen. Lachlan McIntosh, abandoned his campaign to capture Detroit, withdrew from Fort Laurens, and was replaced by Gen. Daniel Brodhead. Both De Peyster and Brodhead were about to begin aggressive military actions.

Brodhead moved first with an expedition against the Delaware Indian capital at Goschachgunk at the forks of the Muskingum because he suspected that the Delaware had joined the British. His troops left Fort Henry early in April. By forced march, the three-hundred-man militia arrived at Goschachgunk on the evening of April 19, 1781, completely surprising the Delaware village. Owing to the high water, the villagers on the west side of the river escaped, but all on the east bank were captured without firing a shot. Sixteen of the warriors were taken below the town and killed by the direction of a council of war held in Brodhead's camp. The next morning, Red Eagle, the successor to White Eyes, called from the opposite side of the river for the "Big Captain" (as they called Brodhead), saying he wanted to make peace. Receiving assurance he would not be harmed, the chief came across the river. When he arrived and approached the Brodhead party, legend has it, the notorious Indian fighter Lewis Wetzel stepped from behind the general and tomahawked and killed the chief. Some authorities believe the deed was done by Wetzel's brother Martin. Before leaving the area, the expedition burned the abandoned Lichtenau mission, then occupied by some straggling bands of Delaware. Only the previous friendly relationship with the Moravian missionaries prevented Brodhead's men from destroying the Indian missions at Salem and Gnadenhutten. The army began its return march with twenty prisoners. Within a few miles of the village, the volunteer guard in charge of the prisoners massacred all except a few women and children.[31]

On the afternoon of April 20, the abandoned Lichtenau village lay in smoldering ruins. A lazy column of smoke also rose over Goschachgunk, the pride of the Delaware's old chief Netawatwes. Their head chief, Gelelemend, roamed the hills in exile east of Gnadenhutten with his wife and family—including his newborn son, Benjamin. No longer did the great Gelelemend sit among his counselors and direct the fortunes of the Delaware. With the destruction of their village and the massacre of their warriors, there was no longer any question—the Delaware were now firmly under British control, led by their war chief, Captain Pipe. Because of his friendliness with the colonials, Gelelemend was now considered a renegade. The destruction of Goschachgunk marked a turning point in Delaware Indian history. Zeisberger would never again sit among friendly faces at a Delaware council.

De Peyster's plans for the new year were unknown to Zeisberger, as the missionary organized one final trip back to Bethlehem to attend a synod called by Johann Reichel, a visiting bishop from Germany. (Zeisberger lived for another twenty-seven years, but he never returned again to Bethlehem.) The party left New Schoenbrunn on March 23, 1781, just nineteen days before Zeisberger's sixtieth birthday. He arrived back on the Muskingum four months later, on July 15, with a wife, thirty-seven-year-old Susan Lecrone. The marriage, conducted at Lititz, was a spontaneous decision, as he had long ago given up any thoughts of matrimony. Convinced by his friends in Bethlehem, who urged him to take a "help-meet" who would be "warm comfort in the storm and strife" of his old age, he relented of his earlier resolve and proposed to Susan. To Zeisberger's surprise, and the gratification of his friends, she accepted and remained at his side until his death in 1808.

~~~~~

TWO

The Great Dispersement

Christianity, from its inception, has been an evangelical and proselytizing religion. Jesus Christ preached the spiritual conquest of the world, and both the Old and New Testaments relate the epic story ending in the Last Day of Judgment.[1] Conversion is essential to its very nature and missionaries are the life's blood of its survival. The earliest history of the Europeans on the North American continent includes the sixteenth-century diaries and journals of the French and Spanish Catholic missionaries who were aboard the ships of the first explorers. Protestant Christians, especially the English, were late in their arrival on the scene. But they quickly made up for the lost time.

Cotton Mather, that stalwart Englishman and promoter of Christian missions, called the proselytizing of the Indians "the wars of the Lord." Mather himself gives us a glimpse of what motivated him and his friends to evangelize the Indians. In the opening words of his "Address of Christianized Indians," he said:

> Behold, ye Indians, what care, what cost, has been used by the English here for the salvation of your precious and immortal souls. It is not because we have expected any temporal advantage, that we have been thus concerned for your good; no, it is God that has caused us to desire his glory in your salvation; and our hearts have bled with pity over you, when we have seen how horribly the Devil oppressed you in this, and destroyed you in another world. It is much that has been done for you; we have put you into a way to be happy both on earth while you live, and in Heaven when you die.[2]

"The glory of God" was thus the prime factor that motivated Mather and his friends to attempt Indian conversion. In fact, the whole planting of New England was directed toward this "glory." A sense of guilt and indebtedness never occurred to those New Englanders who robbed the Indians of their land and eventually destroyed the Indian culture. Any display of indebtedness was supposed to be shown by the Indians. They may have lost their land, but they had received God's glory and English salvation.

While the Puritans clearly abhorred the Indian life-style, to their credit they never doubted that the Indian was truly human. It was for these souls that Christ had died. It was therefore the responsibility of the missionary to save them from the Devil's grasp. It was God's will working through Divine Grace that called for their salvation.[3]

Recently, James Axtel, in his *The Invasion Within*, discussed this dilemma confronting the prospective Indian convert. He notes that Christian Scriptures speak of the "born-again man," the shucking of the old and putting on the new person, created in righteousness and true holiness. Unlike the converted European, for the Indian the transition amounted to cultural suicide. The Indian was required to peel off his or her "savagery" in order to prepare for the whitewashing in the "blood of the Lamb," and compelled to adopt the Calvinistic philosophy of "severe discipline, sharpe laws, a hard life and much labor." The Indian was given "Civilitie for their bodies" as well as "Christianitie for their souls," which inevitably stripped them of their own culture.[4]

After Cotton Mather, a host of English Protestant missionaries followed in his wake: David Brainerd, Jonathan Edwards, Samuel Hopkins, John Sergeant, Sr. and Jr., and Eleazer Wheelock, to name a few.

The arrival of the Moravians in 1735 introduced a different breed of Protestant missionary. Unlike the English, who had generally lived in North America since their birth, the Moravians were newly arrived from Europe. They were dispatched from Germany, dedicated exclusively for missionary work and chosen by the use of the lot. After an aborted stop in Georgia, the Moravians moved north in 1740 to the Lehigh valley in Pennsylvania. Here they founded the settlements of Bethlehem, Nazareth, and later Lititz, in Lancaster County. At first, English and Dutch settlers, and especially their clergy, were hostile to these new arrivals. It was not until after the Revolution that the Moravians became heroes and leaders in the missionary work in America.

Cotton Mather and his early contemporaries whose efforts were piecemeal and sporadic were unlike the Moravians who came with determination specifically to serve the Indians. The Moravians brought an entirely different philosophy to the American Indian mission field. Although their mission settlements were not closed communities, they were governed by a strict set of rules to which all residents had to comply, otherwise leave the settlement. Those who remained in the Moravian villages were organized to serve the workers in the field. The entire machinery of the church was dedicated to the missionary program.

Industry and prayer were required of all. David Zeisberger soon became the vanguard of their missionary effort.

Unlike the English, who served for the glory of God, the Moravians served for the love of God in Christ, a distinctly different approach from Puritan philosophy. This love of God and his redemption in the Christ called for simple preaching of his story of salvation everywhere. Compassion for the despised and oppressed filled Moravian hearts. Interestingly, the Moravians did not primarily seek conversion of the Indian. God in his own way and his own time would settle that question. Despite repeated failures and defeat, they pushed on with their message confidently, believing that they could change the hearts of all people through the telling of the story of the Lamb of God.[5]

The singularity of the Moravian approach can be found in the diary of Rev. David McClure. McClure visited the Moravian mission of Friedensstadt on June 19, 1772.[6] A would-be missionary, the new minister had just graduated from Yale College. He spent several days at the mission conversing with Zeisberger and John Ettwein, a visiting elder from Bethlehem and assistant to Nathanael Seidel, the leader of the Moravian Church in Bethlehem. From these two men he received detailed information on the Moravian missionary activities among the Indians.

> The Moravians appear to have adopted the best mode of Christianizing the Indians. They go among them without noise or parade, & by their friendly behaviour conciliate their good will. They join them in the chace, & freely distribute to the helpless & gradually instil into the minds of individuals, the principles of religions. They then invite those who are disposed to harken to them, to retire to some convenient place, at a distance from the wild Indians, & assist them to build a village, & teach them to plant & sow, & to carry on some coarse manufactures.[7]

The uniqueness of the Zeisberger approach to Indian conversion left him without peer among his Protestant contemporaries. Fully aware of the cultural shock required when the Indian left his or her tribe and joined the mission, he "without noise and parade" tried to find a halfway station that borrowed some elements from both cultures. Left undisturbed from external white interference, the success of the Muskingum valley missions was proof that the plan could succeed.

When Zeisberger and his new bride returned to the Muskingum valley on July 15, 1781, there were six missionaries on the Muskingum: Zeisberger and Johann Jungmann at New Schoenbrunn; Gottlob Senseman and William Edwards at Gnadenhutten; John Heckewelder and young Michael Jung at Salem. The missions continued to prosper.

But was it all a mirage? Major De Peyster, the British commander at Detroit, was about to bring an unwelcome change to the Muskingum valley Christians.

De Peyster was certainly the architect of the coming scheme, but those late escapees from Fort Pitt—Alexander McKee, Matthew Elliot, and Simon Girty—were the executioners. Girty had already been active just thirteen miles north of the New Schoenbrunn mission. With a force of 200 Wyandot he had besieged the Fort Laurens garrison throughout most of its nine-month existence. In early summer of 1779 General Washington gave up the campaign to capture Detroit, and in August he ordered General McIntosh to withdraw the garrison. Zeisberger had been correct when he warned all of the missionaries in July not to place too much confidence in the security the fort might provide to the Christian villages.[8]

McKee, Elliot, and Girty, like thousands of their fellow colonists, made the decision not to defect from the British cause. All three men, for most of their adult years, had been in the service of their king and were loyal subjects of England. Their lives and fortunes depended on the outcome. Like all combatants, they believed in their cause and fought to defend what they thought to be just, remaining loyal to the Crown.

After De Peyster assumed command at Detroit, his Indian allies regularly besieged him with complaints against the Moravian missionaries, accusing them of furnishing intelligence to the commander at Fort Pitt. The most strident accusations came from the Wyandot Half-King and the Delaware Captain Pipe. After the stinging Brodhead attack on the Delaware at Goschachgunk, the Indians abandoned their neutrality, left the Muskingham valley, and moved to the northwestern Ohio country along the banks of the Sandusky near Pipe's village. In the summer of 1781 De Peyster gave orders to his Indian allies to remove the Christian Indians and their teachers from the valley. McKee, the British Indian agent, was to develop the details. The Wyandot and Pipe's Delaware were to carry out the mission. Elliot was appointed the captain of the expedition.

Caught between the two hostile forces, Zeisberger and his fellow missionaries attempted to continue in peace by providing hospitality without preference to both the English and the colonials. However, Zeisberger's frequent correspondence with the commanders at Fort Pitt leaves little doubt as to the side on which his sympathy lay. We must further remember that his financial support, missionary instruction, and other assistance came from the church headquarters at Bethlehem. In fact, one of General Washington's hospitals was located at Bethlehem. Zeisberger did not view this correspondence with Fort Pitt as a treasonable act but rather as an effort to keep on friendly relations with those officials. Despite the failure of Fort Laurens, he hoped that the colonials would continue to assist in the promotion of his missions and assure some protection for the Christian congregations. For over two hundred years controversy has clouded his action during this period; however, there is no question that during the Brodhead expedition in 1780 he had regularly contacted Fort Pitt. Had he not continued on friendly relations with Brodhead, undoubtedly the general would have destroyed the missions during his expedition. Many of Brodhead's men insisted they do just that. Notwithstanding, the British and the Wyandot suspected him of "duplicity."[9] Thus De Peyster concluded that it would be prudent to remove those who might be working against the British.

During the hot August days of 1781, Zeisberger learned from a friendly native Delaware "that a strong party of warriors was on the March for our towns."[10] Shortly after he received the first message, a runner arrived from the Wyandot party bearing a dispatch from Pomoacan. The believing Indians were all to assemble at Gnadenhutten. By the morning of August 20, over three hundred Wyandot and Delaware warriors had taken up their quarters in huts built at Gnadenhutten and the Salem missions. Zeisberger noted: "Their chief men were: first an English captain [Matthew Elliot], with several others, among whom were also Frenchmen; the Wyandot Half-King, from Sandusky, with his warriors; Pipe, and his Delawares [now the implacable foe of the Moravians]; some Shawnee, Chippewas, and Tawas."[11]

On the afternoon of August 20, Pomoacan outlined his plans to the missionaries. They were to follow him in a peaceful manner to his village on the Sandusky, where, he assured Zeisberger, all would be safe under his protection. Zeisberger's response was a diplomatic but unqualified *no*. Thus began the protracted negotiations. Initially, Pomoacan seemed satisfied with a suggestion made by Zeisberger. If they were to move, it would be more convenient to do so in the spring, giving the converts time to gather the fall harvest, organize the congregation, and make an orderly departure at that time. But Matthew Elliot had his orders from Detroit. If the Wyandot wanted British food and supplies in the coming winter for their hard-pressed people, he demanded that Pomoacan promptly remove the Christians. The negotiations then turned ugly. Zeisberger noted, "We felt the power of darkness, as if the air was filled with evil spirits."[12]

The converts were called together at Gnadenhutten on September 3, when Pomoacan made one last appeal. Getting a negative response from the missionaries, the veil of kindness immediately dropped. In the next several days all the missionaries were seized, stripped to the waist, threatened with their lives, and held as prisoners. The villages were sacked and the converts harassed. By September 8 Zeisberger capitulated, realizing that he no longer had control of the situation. He then did his best to bring order out of the chaos and prepared to move. The New Schoenbrunn converts were ordered to Gnadenhutten. In the afternoon, with but meager possessions, they began the arduous journey later referred to as the Great Dispersement. That evening the missionaries, who traveled by water, reached Salem, where they waited two days for the remaining Brethren, who were traveling on foot, to arrive. On the morning of September 11 they broke camp and "as if in a dream so as to hardly know our senses" they left their beloved valley, most of their possessions, and all of the crops. The three beautiful and orderly little villages lay in scattered ruins, with dead animals rotting in the streets, and many of the crops and fences trampled and destroyed. For nine years they had been struggling to build these model Indian communities—never again would they be duplicated on such a scale. It was the end of the most stable period of Zeisberger's work.

From Salem, the refugees traveled a long trail down the Muskingum to the old site of Goschachgunk (Coshocton), then up the Walhonding River northwest to the Kokosing headwaters, where they walked overland to the Sandusky River. They reached the Wyandot country on October 1, after twenty arduous days on the trail. It was a journey of unspeakable hardship and travail. Some of the converts left the congregation and faded back into the wilderness, but the nucleus prevailed.

CAPTIVE TOWN

Zeisberger and his Christian band spent the next fifteen and one-half months on the Sandusky.[13] While the exact location of their village is not precisely known, it was probably five miles south of the present city of Upper Sandusky on the south bank of the Sandusky River.[14] They lived temporarily in the abandoned huts of an old Wyandot village, spending the first few days searching for a probable permanent site to settle. The location finally chosen was "a mile up the creek, where there was good timber." They began to cut the logs required for their hew houses. By October 12 they had their "small and slightly built" homes under roof.

Several days later, they received word from De Peyster at Detroit. The information came in a roundabout fashion to the Delaware chief

Wingenund [Win-gay-noon'd], one of the current captains of the Wolf clan, and delivered by the chief, accompanied by the brother of Captain Pipe. The message had been sent to the Wyandot and Delaware, with instruction to be carried to the believing Indians. It is a classic example of the diplomatic language used in dealing with the Indians and records the clever metaphors and distinct similes of the native dialects. Contained in the message are the reasons for De Peyster's actions: "The hindrances are out of the way . . . the birds will no longer sing." Zeisberger recorded De Peyster's dispatch:

> My children, your father over the lake has been much pleased at the news which you have brought of the believing Indians and their teachers, so that now all nations may be one and that the hindrances are out of the way; that the birds will no longer sing in the woods and tell many lies. And now the Virginians will be in darkness and light will shine for them no more. . . . In a few days a boat is expected for you from Detroit at the Miami (Maumee) river with goods. You must all go there to receive them. [This was the Indians' payment for the accomplished mission.]
>
> Your father over the lake requests also that Capt. Pipe and Wingenund should bring to him the ministers with some of the principal believing Indians, for he would like to see them, and he says: "I know better how to talk with them than you do, for I know them; I can also better take care of them, and entertain them than you can, since I have the means therefore."[15]

Zeisberger expected a summons from De Peyster. However, had it not arrived he would have gone to Detroit without a subpoena for an explanation of De Peyster's action. Desperate as they were for food and supplies, the converts' Helpers' Conference resolved not to accept any of the gifts sent via the boat mentioned in the dispatch, gifts which were to be distributed to the local tribes as payment for moving the Moravians out of the Muskingum valley.[16]

Following receipt of the message, the missionaries spent the next several days preparing for the journey. Securing the necessary food to supply the villagers had been a constant problem for the missionaries ever since their arrival on the Sandusky. Some help came from the local tribes, but Zeisberger complained that the price of corn was exorbitant. Concern also mounted for the Indian wives and children and the missionary families who were to be left behind. Fortunately, when the official Indian delegation arrived to announce De Peyster's summons, Zeisberger extracted a concession from the chiefs permitting the missionary families to remain on the Sandusky under the protection of Brothers Johann Jungmann and Michael Jung.

THE TREASON TRIAL AT DETROIT

The missionaries left Captive Town on October 25. The party consisted of Zeisberger, Edwards, Heckewelder, and Senseman, accompanied by the Indian converts William, Tobias, Isaac Eschicanahund, and Josua, all members of the Helpers' Conference. The first stop was ten miles downstream at the Wyandot village where they were to pick up their escorts, Captain Pipe and Chief Wingenund. Pipe was not present, and Wingenund was in no condition to travel, having spent the previous night celebrating. The Zeisberger party proceeded downstream toward Lake Erie. Two days later, they arrived on the Maumee River, where they met Pipe. He advised them to remain overnight and meet Captain Elliot the next day. They spent the next two days on the Maumee talking with Elliot, who instructed them about what to do after arriving at Detroit. Gathering their horses on October 31, they plunged back into the wilderness. Three days later they arrived at Detroit and, after a short delay, were escorted into De Peyster's quarters. The first formal interrogation was brief. Zeisberger recorded the conversation:

Question: Are you the Moravian Ministers from the Muskingum?
Answer: Yes.

Q: Did all of the Ministers come with you?
A: We left two of our number behind us in Sandusky with our wives and children, for we could not leave them alone since they needed help and could not rightly be left with the [native] Indians.

Q: Why have you not brought your wives and children as I plainly ordered?
A: We had expressly inquired of the chiefs whether our women also were summoned, and they said to us, no.

Q: Do you know why I have removed you from the Muskingum? It is because you corresponded with the rebels to harm the government here, for many complaints came against you.
A: We did not doubt at all that much must have come to your ears about us. This we could infer from the treatment we had to endure, but you must have been wrongly and ill-informed about us. We are accused of things which, when investigated, should prove us innocent.

Q: Who came with you? Where are the balance of your Indians? How many are they, how many men, and do you propose to return to their village?

A: Four of our Indians came with us, and the balance of the con-
       gregation are now on the Sandusky. Altogether there are three
       to four hundred converts. We plan to return to the village as
       soon as we are set free. We can not look upon our separation as
       a trifling matter for to be apart from our mission, which has
       been entrusted to us, it would of itself go to destruction, and
       all of our labor for the last forty years would have been in vain.

Q: Think you so? But if your Indians were harmful to the
       government?

A: They would not be harmful but useful, that you will learn, if
       you be better acquainted with us, for they are industrious,
       laborious people.

Q: Have your Indians ever gone to war?

A: No.

De Peyster: That is all, you are dismissed.[17]

Although this first interview was brief, Zeisberger was most favorably impressed with his humane treatment from De Peyster. To be accused of treason, despite his own belief of innocence, had caused him great concern. A conviction would surely mean being banished and separated from the converts with little hope of return. Arrangements were made by the commander to house the party with a local Frenchman named Tybout and his wife. The entire contingent, including the Indians, were most hospitably entertained. Clothing and food were provided. They spent the next six days awaiting the arrival of Captain Pipe, their accuser, and entertaining visitors who inquired about their welfare.

Several attempts were made to talk to De Peyster, but all were refused. When Zeisberger learned Captain Pipe was near the village, he arranged for a meeting. Surprisingly, the Christian delegation received a cordial reception from the captain. It was an encouraging sign.

On the morning of November 9, they were called again before De Peyster to face their enemy. Pipe appeared, surrounded by his counselors and dressed in his best finery—an imposing presence. De Peyster sat in front with several of his captains. The Zeisberger delegation was placed to one side of the room. The missionaries were certainly apprehensive.

Pipe and his counselors opened the trial with a presentation to the court of several scalps and prisoners taken on recent raids against the white settlements. With this usual procedure completed, the commander called on the chief to repeat his charges against the Moravians. He arose and addressed the court: "Thou hast ordered us to bring the believing Indians with their teachers from the Muskingum. We have done so, and it has been as thou hast ordered. . . . They are now here before thine eyes, thou canst now thyself speak good words to them, and I say to thee, speak kindly to them, for they are our friends, and I hold them dear and should not like to see harm befall them." Pipe repeated the last comment several times.[18]

An astonished look passed over Zeisberger's face and his Indian delegation silently gazed at one another in amazement. This man was their bitter enemy; for years he had opposed the Christian missions. What was he saying, "speak good words," "our friends . . . I hold . . . dear," no harm should befall them? This was not the Captain Pipe they knew.

This speech obviously did not please De Peyster. He proceeded to relate the charges, brought not only by Pipe but by other chiefs. For years he had listened to their harping complaints, that Zeisberger and his "praying Indians" had corresponded with the rebels and given them prior news of warrior attacks against the settlements. If these charges were true, they had committed treasonous acts most harmful to his government. He demanded that Pipe tell the truth. "Did they correspond with the rebels?" Pipe, rising slowly from his blanket, admitted to De Peyster that "there might be some truth about the thing, for he could not say that it was all lies, but it would now not happen again since they were away from there." That answer was simply not good enough for the commander. With his anger mounting, he again spoke to Pipe: "So they have then corresponded with the rebels and sent letters to Fort Pitt; for from thine answer I must conclude that it is true."

Both the chief and the major were now becoming agitated. Pipe jumped to his feet and in an excited voice responded indignantly: "I have told thee that there is something in the matter, and now I tell thee straight out: they, who are ministers, are innocent; they have not done it of themselves; they had to do it. (He then struck himself on the breast, and shouted) I am guilty, and the chiefs who were with me in Goschachgunk; we compelled them to it and forced them; thou must hold us responsible for this, but, since they are here it will not happen again, as I have already told thee."

Zeisberger and his party were overwhelmed! Pipe was now assuming responsibility for the whole affair. De Peyster, the proper English gentleman, lowered his voice and now addressed the chief—calmly proceeding to the next question: "You have probably, at home, not only thought about the ministers, but also conferred with one another what was best to be done with them. Would you like to see them go back with their Indians or would you rather they not go back?"

At this point in the trial the Indian interpreter did not correctly translate the question. Zeisberger and his Indians immediately recognized the

error, but remained silent. After a brief delay the question was again repeated and Pipe understood the translation. He responded pleadingly:
"Father, we promised the believing Indians, when they were themselves
brought away, that their teachers should remain with them as hitherto,
and that they should have their religious services unhindered; it was not
thought that they should be robbed of their teachers; it would be pleasing
to me if they were again suffered to return to them, for they looked upon
the ministers as their friends, their flesh and blood."

De Peyster gazed at Pipe for a long silent moment as if contemplating
his remarks. Seemingly satisfied with the chief's testimony, he turned to
Zeisberger and in a quiet modulated voice began asking him a series of
questions.

Question: Were all of the white ministers at the mission ordained?
  Answer: Yes.

  Q: How long have you been with the Indians?
  A: More than thirteen years ago I came to the Ohio, the others here
     came shortly after.

  Q: Did you come among the Indians of your own accord or were
     you sent?
  A: We were sent to the Indians to preach to them the gospel.

  Q: By whom?
  A: By our church, which is an old Episcopal Church.

  Q: Where are your bishops?
  A: Here in this country and in Europe.

  Q: Where have the bishops come from, who are in this country?
  A: From Europe.

  Q: Are you ordained by those bishops, and sent to preach to
     the Indians?
  A: Yes.

  Q: Have you not got your instructions from Congress when you
     went to the Indians?
  A: No; but from the bishops.

  Q: Did Congress know about this, or did you have permission
     from the same to go?
  A: We have not been with our Indians, without the knowledge
     and permission of Congress; it has put nothing in the way of
     our labor among the Indians, but also it has prescribed to us no
     rules and given us no instructions in what way we should con-
     duct ourselves.[19]

De Peyster seemed satisfied with Zeisberger's answers. He complimented the missionary on his effort to bring the gospel to the Indians,

highly applauding his work. He also said he did not intend to interfere with the Moravian work as long as they did not engage in activity in conflict with his administration of Indian affairs. He apologized for interfering with their work, absolved them of any complicity to commit treason against his government, and said, "In God's name go back to your families and to your Indians as soon as you please."

He asked one last question: Would they take the Oath? Zeisberger responded: "No, it had never been required of us." With the wave of his hand, he said: "So, I will not burden you with it," then struck the gavel on the desk, signifying the end of the proceedings. It was over.

The commandant and his court descended from the podium and shook hands with Pipe and his counselors, then repeated the same procedure with all of the Zeisberger party. With a discreet movement of his eyes, De Peyster called Zeisberger to the corner of the room and whispered, "Please come and see me, at your convenience, and before you depart."

Promptly the next day, Zeisberger and his party returned to the fort and were ushered into the commander's private apartment, asked to sit down and make themselves comfortable. A marked difference in his attitude from the previous day was quickly obvious, and he was "in every way quite friendly." Later Zeisberger wrote:

> He said to us now, since it was found we were innocent, he wished in some way to make good the losses we had suffered. Since now we knew that a trader in the city had bought from the Indians four of our watches, we told him so, and he promised to get the same for us at once. He summoned the trader, demanded the watches, and promised to pay him again what he had given for them, and gave them all back to us. Then he gave us an order upon the commissary of the King's store, who gave us blankets, some clothing and house-utensils, for us and our sisters at home; wherefore we were joyful and thankful. . . . [Later] we went again to the Governor and asked him for a pass, which he gave us. . . . We had permission to now go back to our Indians and remain with them in order to instruct them in Christianity; that no one should put any thing in our way or injure us. . . . He made us many excuses, saying to us that we must not be too vexed with him.[20]

Almost obsequiously he assured Zeisberger, "Not only did he agree with our program but wished us success." Because of the many complaints by the Indian chiefs, he was "duty bound" and could "not act otherwise" than to remove us from the Muskingum. However, he specifically instructed Captain Pipe "not to plunder or misuse us." He now believed all of the accusations "were false and groundless," and he desperately wished "peace might soon be restored."[21]

Well aware of native Indian diplomacy, Zeisberger knew the issue between the missionaries and the natives was not closed, and he left the commander with one final message: "Since now we were going back to Sandusky, if any future complaints against us came to him, not to believe everything, but to be so good as to send us a few words, and thus we would inform him at all times about the affair, how it was in regard to truth, for among the Indians we had many enemies, who opposed the preaching of the Gospel, and on this account made up all sorts of lies about us and spread them abroad."[22]

THE RETURN TO CAPTIVE TOWN AND THE GREAT SWAMP

The stay in Detroit lasted twelve days. The Moravian party left the city on November 14 and returned to Captive Town nine days later. The return route took them down the west bank of the Detroit River, around the western end of Lake Erie, and across the Maumee River at the site of present Toledo, Ohio. The group then traveled south through the Great Swamp till they came near the present site of Fostoria, Ohio. Continuing south, they struck the Sandusky River at present Upper Sandusky, Ohio, only a few miles from Captive Town. Zeisberger succinctly describes the terrain as they traveled through the Great Swamp. It was a trip frequently taken by the Moravians in the next ten years:

> The whole country is so flat and level that no hill at all is in sight, for it has great plains, many miles in length and breadth, on which nothing grows except long grass. These, for the most part, are so flooded with water—since it is so flat and level—it cannot run off. Even when it does not rain for a long time, it is still full of water and our horses had to wade through the water up to the saddles and at times swim. . . . These plains are full of crawfish, which have their holes in the ground; therefore the game, raccoons, foxes, etc., which are here in abundance, live on the crawfish and wax fat. No practicable road can be kept there, for it would soon become a deep marsh . . . but nearly everyone makes a new track through the long grass, so that at last it becomes a broad road. . . . The land is especially clayey, which is one reason why the water remains standing and does not sink away. The bush is either beech-swamp or ash, linden, elm and other trees such as grow in wet places, yet it has many oak groves, and all around Detroit it has white-cedar swamps. Here also are to be found white and black walnut trees.[23]

His entry for November 22 modestly records: "We came then on the 22d November, happy and in good condition, to our brethren in Sandusky, who, as well as we, heartily rejoice together, and could not thank the Saviour enough."

In the short time of their absence, two children were born but five had died along with the convert Sister Johanetta. The young children were now the most vulnerable to their intolerable living conditions. Unless additional food could be secured quickly, they all faced starvation. Zeisberger quickly turned his attention to this problem. Two traders at Lower Sandusky, Alexander McCormick and a Mr. Dawson, were instrumental in obtaining some corn and other staples.

Zeisberger knew he must keep the Indians working to improve their living conditions. He also encouraged the building of a chapel. Since arriving, all of the daily religious services had been conducted in the open. On November 29 they blocked out the chapel building. By December 4 the roof was completed, and four days later they conducted the first services inside. The structure was a series of upright stakes sunk in the ground with horizontal poles between the stakes. The crevices were filled with moss, and the roof covered with shingles.

Some of the converts returned to the Muskingum and retrieved a small portion of the unharvested corn. The Shawnee provided an additional quantity, remembering that the Moravians had helped them in a time of need thirty years earlier when they were living in the Wyoming valley. They continued to purchase small quantities from McCormick, the trader at Lower Sandusky, and from the local native tribes. A bushel of corn sold for eight dollars, an enormous sum at that time. Despite all of these efforts the food situation continued to dwindle. Susan Zeisberger, David's wife, in a short autobiography gives a brief glimpse of the suffering in that unusually harsh winter: "Many times the Indians shared their last morsel with me, for many times I spent eight days in succession without food of my own."[24] The Zeisbergers rarely complained of their life, but in his journal entry of December 28, David recorded: "Many of our brethren suffer hunger, and as no corn can be had, they must subsist upon wild potatoes, which they dig up laboriously and bring from a distance."[25]

Four days later, on January 1, 1782, the strain of the situation began to show. Two converts, Josy and Abraham, who had been denied permission to go to Fort Pitt to visit relatives, left secretly.[26] Learning of their departure, the Half-King again accused them of sending messages to the colonials. Zeisberger vented his frustration in the pages of his journal: "Satan rages, and it is as if we were given over to devils to plague us utterly, to torment us and make trials of fortune with us while we are here, not only from without, but also from within. . . . [Before the entry closed he demonstrated his determination and tenacity:] We are not, however, cast down nor disheartened, but oppose with might and with all our strength, to destroy and cast out of the Church the work of Satan."[27]

The weather turned bitterly cold, adding to the suffering. "Some people in this neighborhood," the diarist noted, "say that for ten years no

winter has been so cold. Our cattle fare worse every day, for we have ourselves hardly any thing to eat, and they really nothing." The hunger became so great that most of the converts were eating the dead cows and
horses. "Never in our lives," Zeisberger wrote, "have we felt such want;
we pity these people, but we cannot, we know not, how to help them."
Then, as if crying out to God as his beloved Christ did on the cross, he
wrote, "Why then does the Saviour let all this come upon us?"[28]

On February 2 young Joseph Schebosh, his father's namesake, arrived
at the village. He had gone to Fort Pitt to search for his father who, along
with a number of the converts, had been taken as a prisoner to Pittsburgh. Zeisberger noted in the diary that Schebosh, Jr., was now the last
of the converts to return from this group, except his father who had gone
to Bethlehem to bring the first news of the removal of the Muskingum
delegation to the Sandusky. Schebosh, Jr., also brought the first communication that they had received from Bethlehem since they had been
taken into captivity.[29]

By the middle of January and throughout February over one hundred
fifty of the converts began looking for places at which they could find
food. Some traveled to Lower Sandusky to visit the white traders, others
went to the Shawnee. On February 7 a large party of over one hundred
departed for the Muskingum. Zeisberger wrote, "We were now quite
alone at the village."

During this period, frequent rumors were overheard from the Delaware, Munsee, and Wyandot villages. Purportedly, Detroit planned to
remove the missionaries from the area. But had not De Peyster given his
solemn pledge not to molest them? Zeisberger considered the rumor
preposterous and therefore discounted it out-of-hand. But the rumor
persisted. On March 1 a messenger arrived from the Half-King with a
summons for Zeisberger to come to Pomoacan's village the next day. He
had "something to tell us."

The next morning Zeisberger, Heckewelder, and two Indian Brethren
arrived at the Wyandot village, where they met Pomoacan assembled
with his council. Standing in the background, partially hidden behind
the Half-King and his council, was Simon Girty—well known to the
Moravians, especially Zeisberger. On at least one occasion Girty had tried
to kill the missionary.[30] At that time only the fortuitous arrival of a Delaware delegation saved his life. Girty, since his escape from Fort Pitt in
1778, had gained notoriety for courage, cunning, and brutality. Since
that time he had been under the direct command of the Detroit commandant. Perhaps no character in American history has gained such a
reputation for infamous behavior, much of it unwarranted.[31] A letter
from the commander in Detroit had come to Pomoacan. It was not writ-

ten to Pomoacan, but to Girty. The chief handed it to Zeisberger. To Zeisberger's great astonishment it contained the following statement, written in English: "You will please present the strings I send you to the Half-King and tell him I have listened to his demand. I therefore hope he will give you such assistance as you may think necessary to enable you to bring the teachers and their families to this place. [The Indian converts were to remain behind on the Sandusky.] I will by no means allow you to suffer them to be plundered or in any way ill-treated."[32]

Zeisberger was stunned! After all the elaborate promises and positive assurances he had been given just a few months before, now this. Why? His arms fell limp to his sides, and a great bubble of emotion began to swell within his chest. He slowly raised his eyes and pleadingly looked around the room until he saw Simon Girty. He hesitated a moment before he spoke, and then in a choked voice he said to Girty, "We will obey your command. In fifteen days we will be at the Lower Sandusky, however, we must be brought over the lake by boat as our sisters and little children cannot make the toilsome journey by land."[33]

The next day, on March 3, messengers were dispatched to the dispersed converts who were still foraging for food at the Shawnee villages and the sugar camps nearby, and to the Muskingum. The Brethren were told to return to the village at once. Slowly the converts among the Shawnee tribes began to return, and by March 7 they had received a runner from the Muskingum contingent. Within a few days they would begin their return trip.

On March 14, the day before the missionaries and their families were to depart for Detroit, they received a disturbing message from the Muskingum. A native Indian, Delaware George, passed through the village with "frightful news that all our brethren who went to Schoenbrunn, Gnadenhutten, and Salem had been captured and taken to Pittsburgh."[34] The messenger also related other disturbing details. Some converts were killed, and others bound and led down the trail to the fort. Zeisberger took heart. Surely the colonials would not harm the converts once they came under their protection.

THE RECALL TO DETROIT

Friday, March 15, was the day appointed for the departure of the missionaries and their families. The Half-King was on hand to assure their compliance with Girty's orders. It was a shattering experience for David Zeisberger. In thirty-eight years he had never been compelled to abandon his post and leave his beloved Indians. Despite the heartbreak, his faith never wavered. He fell on his knees and prayed. "We thanked the Saviour for all the goodness and comfort we had enjoyed from him in all our unhappiness and burdens, in all our needs and danger from without." Now, since he was forced to leave the mission, he "commended the Indian Church to the Saviour's care and oversight to guard and protect it." Faithful to the end, and just before departure, they baptized the "well-grown youngest daughter of Rachel, unto Jesus' death, she would be called Maria."[35]

In the missionary party was Zeisberger and his wife, Susan; John Heckewelder and his wife, Sara, and their one-year-old daughter, Johanna Maria (Polly); Johann Georg Jungmann and his wife, Anna Margaretha; Gottlob Senseman, his wife, Anna Maria, and their seven-month-old child, Christian David; Michael Jung, who had been Heckewelder's assistant at Salem; and the ever-faithful William Edwards —twelve in all. They were accompanied by several of the Indian converts and their French guide, Francis Levallie. Four days later they arrived at the small Wyandot village and trading post at Lower Sandusky (present Fremont, Ohio). Awaiting the ships to be sent from Detroit, they remained at the trading post until April 14, 1782.

≈≈≈≈≈

THREE

From Disaster to a New Beginning

The small Wyandot village and white trading post were almost deserted; most of the Indian warriors were raiding against the Americans, and the white men were in their sugar camps. A handful of French and English traders wandered around the village discussing the present and contemplating their future.

When the Zeisberger party arrived, they met the Conner family, which had moved to Lower Sandusky the previous autumn, following their removal with the other converts from the Muskingum valley. Richard Conner, his wife Margaret, and their four sons, were an interesting anomaly among the Moravian converts at the Muskingum missions. They were one of only two white couples to receive Zeisberger's permission to live at the Muskingum mission villages.[1] Richard, probably born in 1718 of Irish parents, spent his childhood in Pennsylvania near the Lehigh Water Gap.[2] About 1763 he was ranging the Ohio country trading with the Indians, particularly the Shawnee. Here he met Margaret Boyer, a young white girl who in her childhood had been captured and raised by the Indians. He fell in love with "Polly" and requested permission from the local chief to marry her. The request was granted, but with a stipulation: if the couple decided to leave the village and return to a white settlement, they must leave their firstborn son with the Indians.

Zeisberger's first contact with the Conners was in 1773 on a disappointing proselytizing trip he made among the Shawnee. During the visit he met the Conners, who then lived in Connerstown, a small Shawnee village near present Lancaster, Ohio. Never passing up an opportunity to save souls, David talked with Richard and Polly late into the night, while James, the Conners' two-year-old firstborn son, quietly slept in the corner of the small cabin. David's conversation about the Schoenbrunn mission intrigued Richard, and he discussed the possibility of moving to the village. Zeisberger discouraged the move, as the mission was designed exclusively for Indians. There were additional problems. If they left the Shawnee, they were bound by their pledge to leave their son at the Indian village.

One year later conditions had changed. The treaty signed at Camp Charlotte in 1774, following Lord Dunmore's War, mandated that the Indians give up all white prisoners. Polly was now free to leave the village, but their son, James, was forced to remain behind. The Conners left the Shawnee village and, after spending the winter at Pittsburgh, arrived at Schoenbrunn on February 24, 1775. Two months after their arrival, they applied for permission to live at the mission. Following several days of negotiations with the Native Helpers and a consultation with Chief White Eyes, who knew Richard Conner, they were accepted on May 8, but placed on probation for one year.[3] During that year Richard made two trips among the Shawnee villages trying to locate his firstborn son, James. He was successful on the second trip, ransoming the lad for forty dollars, and returning with him to Schoenbrunn on March 18, 1776. Four-year-old James came home to meet his new brother, John, who had been born the previous summer.

Settling at Schoenbrunn, the Conners built a unique but functional log cabin, which could claim the distinction of being the first duplex in the Ohio Valley. Actually, it was two rectangular cabins joined by a connecting walkway.[4] The Conners had three additional children: William in 1777, born at Lichtenau; Henry in 1780, born at New Schoenbrunn; and Susanna in 1783, born at New Gnadenhutten on the Clinton River, Michigan.[5] The family was involved in the Great Dispersement in 1781 and remained with Zeisberger and the missions until 1786. The children were later prominent in the founding of the state of Indiana, especially in the area around Indianapolis.

For eleven years, Richard Conner was a close confident of Zeisberger. He was consulted frequently on mission problems, and during the turmoil in January 1780 he carried the missionary's dispatches to Colonel Brodhead at Fort Pitt. Following the Great Dispersement in 1781, he interceded among the white authorities on numerous occasions to solve the weighty problems confronting the Indian congregation. A skilled negotiator and interpreter, he was well liked among the British officials and native Indians.

In Lower Sandusky, Zeisberger began to unravel the political intrigue involved in their removal from the area. Isolated as he was at Captive Town, he knew little of the gossip that rumbled across the Indian and white grapevine that stretched from the Ohio country to Detroit. Now at Lower Sandusky, the truth began to emerge. "We learned now what had really been the occasion of our again being called to Detroit. We had, in the first place, looked upon it as done by the commandant for our safety, and indeed it was."[6]

Since the trial at Detroit and the reactions of Captain Pipe, Zeisberger absolved the chief of any complicity in the removal decision and concluded that Pomoacan and his Wyandot were at the heart of the actions taken by De Peyster. Caught as he was between the warring English and colonial antagonists, it is little wonder that Zeisberger could not comprehend the position of the Wyandot chief. Naturally, neither man trusted the other. Zeisberger believed that all of his actions were done in the best interest of the mission Indians. Pomoacan was convinced that his military adventure against his white enemies along the Ohio River had been compromised by Zeisberger's information to the Fort Pitt commandant. It was an impasse without solution and afforded no escape for either party. Something had to give. Certainly, Zeisberger believed Pomoacan was cunning, crafty, and full of guile, but the feeling was mutual. Zeisberger may have cried to God: "Why then does the Saviour let all this come upon us? Why is there nowhere a place to be found to which we can retire and be secure?" But Pomoacan probably made the same cry. For two hundred years the chief and his forebears had fought a defensive action against the white people's encroachment. No matter how hard they fought, they lost ground.

The chief had proof that the mission Indians had recently visited Pittsburgh. He believed these visitations were a repetition of the actions taken while the missionaries were on the Muskingum. Zeisberger described Pomoacan's position, as explained to him by a local trader:

> At the instigation of some white people, the Half-King had complained to the commandant that so long as we were in Sandusky we corresponded with the Pittsburghers, and would certainly yet bring them [the Americans] here to blot them out [the Wyandot], on which account they besought the commandant to take us away. . . . The Half-King said: "His affairs would not be well so long as we [the Moravians] were there, and he feared still another misfortune to fall upon him [the Half-King]." Yes, beside this, we heard that if he [De Peyster] had not quickly summoned us, they [the Wyandot] would have put us to death.[7]

The astute Pomoacan was precisely on the mark. He correctly predicted the dramatic events of the next several months and, without stretching the credulity of the prophecy, may have saved the lives of the Zeisberger party.

On March 23, two days after the missionaries arrived at Lower Sandusky, they received the first trustworthy account of the horrible massacre of ninety Christian converts on the Muskingum. The cold-blooded murder of the converts at Gnadenhutten on March 8, 1782, ranks among the most treacherous acts perpetrated by whites against the Indians and rivals the indiscriminate killing of 350 Indians at Wounded Knee in December 1890.

The news devastated David Zeisberger. His journals, however, calmly relate the details of the event and begin by referring the reader to several prophetic scriptural verses from Isaiah included in the Daily Text. These verses applied to the Moravian Daily Text for the days of March 7 and 8, 1782: "For though thy people of Israel be as the sand of the sea, yet a remnant of them shall return. . . . And I will set a sign among them, and I will send those that escape of them unto the nations, and they shall declare my glory among the Gentiles."[8]

Zeisberger carefully checked the mission's records and could account for only eighty-six converts missing. According to the messengers Jacob and Joshua, the exact count of those killed was unknown. Zeisberger prayed, "Perhaps some were taken captive or escaped," then lamented:

> We advised them at Christmas and on New Year's Day to go there, for as long as the snow remained there was the least danger, but they did not go until the snow melted and then it was too late and dangerous; when they were there they used not the least forethought, for they believed themselves quite secure. Instead of hastening to get away again, they stayed several weeks in the towns and fields, having then enough to eat. The most wonderful thing is that while hitherto our Indians had always been careful and distrustful and fearful, and if they thought themselves at all insecure, had fled into the bush, and at least would not pass the night in the towns, now when they really saw the danger and white people before their eyes, they were not at all suspicious and went straight into danger.[9]

Bordering on the Ohio River in the western part of Pennsylvania, the white settlers in Washington County were the most vulnerable and likely victims of Indian incursions. Throughout the revolutionary period many of the Washington County settlers had been killed and their homes and farm buildings destroyed. A local pastor, Rev. Joseph Doddridge, later published an account of this period. He wrote: "It should seem that the long continuance of the Indian war had debased a considerable portion of our population to the savage state of our nature. Having lost so many of their relatives by the Indians, and witnessed their horrid murders and other depredations upon so extensive a scale, they become subjects of that indiscriminating thirst for revenge which is such a prominent feature in savage character."[10]

Reacting to these raids, the farmers of Washington County organized a local militia commanded by a well-respected member of the community, Col. David Williamson. Late in the fall of the previous year, 1781, Capt. John Biggs had led an expedition to the Muskingum, where they found a few converts gathering corn and took them to Pittsburgh as prisoners. They were later freed by John Gibson, the temporary fort commander.[11]

In February 1782 the family of Robert Wallace on Raccoon Creek, Washington County, was brutally attacked during his absence. The cabin was burned, his cattle and hogs were killed, and his wife and three children—two boys and an infant—were carried off by the Indians. This and several other incidents again sparked the muster of the militia in the Mingo Bottoms. The militia departed from Mingo Bottoms at the beginning of March, arriving on the Muskingum during the early evening of March 6.[12]

Zeisberger described the events of the next two days:

A mile from town they met young Schebosh in the bush, whom they at once killed and scalped, and near by the houses, two friendly Indians, not belonging to us, but who had gone there with our people from Sandusky, among whom there were several other friends who perished likewise. Our Indians were mostly on the plantations and saw the militia come, but no one thought of fleeing, for they suspected no ill. The militia came to them and bade them come into the town, telling them no harm should befall them. They trusted and went, but were all bound, the men being put into one house, the women into another. . . . Then they began to sing hymns and spoke words of encouragement and consolation one to another until they were all slain, and Abraham was the first to be led out, but the others were killed in the house. The sisters also afterwards met the same fate, who also sang hymns together. . . . Two well-grown boys, who saw the whole thing and escaped, gave this information. One of these lay under the heaps of slain and was scalped, but finally came to himself and found opportunity to escape. The same did Jacob, Rachel's son, who was wonderfully rescued. For they came close upon him suddenly outside the town, so that he thought they must have seen him, but he crept into a thicket and escaped their hands. . . . The boy who was scalped and got away, said the blood flowed in streams in the house, which was set on fire.[13]

Zeisberger seems to be describing the events as taking place on March 7. Actually the massacre was conducted on March 8, after the militia had gathered the converts from Salem and brought them all together at Gnadenhutten. This account was written by Zeisberger on March 23, 1782, just fifteen days after the massacre, and is remarkably accurate concerning events as they apparently occurred. It appears from this entry that he had talked to both survivors of the massacre.[14]

There were also converts at New Schoenbrunn. Fortunately, on March 7 they received Zeisberger's message to return immediately to Captive Town because the missionaries were being recalled to Detroit. The Sandusky messenger proceeded toward Gnadenhutten, but as he passed the scalped body of Schebosh just north of the village and discovered the evidence that "many white people had gone toward the village," he reversed his course and hurriedly returned to New Schoenbrunn. Those converts left the village promptly and hastened back to Upper Sandusky. Thus they were saved from death. Zeisberger closed the entry of March 23 with these words: "This news sank deep in our hearts, so that these our brethren, who as martyrs, had all at once gone to the Saviour, were always day and night before our eyes and in our thoughts and we could not forget them, but this in some measure comforted us that they passed to the Saviour's arms and bosom in such resigned disposition of heart where they will forever rest, protected from the sins and all the wants of the world."[15]

Zeisberger never forgot the gruesome incident of March 8, 1782. Some twenty years later, in his hoary old age, and again on the banks of the Muskingum at Goshen, he frequently lamented to the missionary Benjamin Mortimer about the tragic events of that day. Nor did the Indians forget that horrible day in 1782. The natives were enraged and swore revenge. For over twenty-five years it was the subject of Indian complaints against the whites and was repeatedly mentioned in treaty discussions with the United States' Indian ambassadors.

The tragic Williamson expedition against the Moravians did little to reduce the number of Indian excursions against the settlers in western Pennsylvania. Most of the attacks were made by Wyandot, Delaware, and Shawnee then living on the Upper Sandusky and the Scioto, and continued unabated. Settlers, alarmed and dismayed in every quarter, were frequently forced to retire to various small "forts" that dotted the landscape in every direction. The procedure was called "forting-up." These forts consisted of small cabins, blockhouses, and stockades. In some places, where exposure to attack was not great, a single blockhouse with an outside cabin constituted the entire fort. The space around the fort was usually cleared away so that an enemy could not conceal its approach.[16] Close by, pioneer settlers worked in their fields while sentinels stood guard; all settlers carried their weapons. It is not surprising that the white settlers were deeply resentful. The horrid scenes of their neighbors' slaughter constantly reminded them to be ever on the alert for skulking Indians.

The Gnadenhutten murders solved none of the pressing problems confronting the white settlers who committed the massacre. In fact, many of those same men lost their lives as a direct result of their participation.

THE CRAWFORD EXPEDITION

By the first week in March 1782, while Williamson's men were marching toward the Muskingum, Gen. William Irvine, Washington's Fort Pitt replacement for General Brodhead, was at Carlisle, Pennsylvania, on his way to command his new post. He arrived at the fort on March 25 only to find a persistent demand from the western settlers to mount an expedition against the perfidious Wyandot, who had stepped up their raids against the settlements. The objective was to search out the Wyandot, Delaware, and Munsee villages and destroy their capacity to continue raids against the American settlements. Thus began the aborted Crawford expedition which proposed to strike terror into the hearts of the Indians at their home villages on the Upper Sandusky.

From the beginning, Irvine gently advised both civil and military authorities from Westmoreland and Washington counties that he would be unable to furnish his regular American colonial troops to accompany any expedition. As early as seventeen days before he first arrived at Fort Pitt, he received a communication from General Washington cautioning him not to conduct "offensive operations, except on a small scale, [as they] cannot just now be brought into contemplation."[17] Irvine was reluctant to divulge this intelligence to the local militia commanders. This decision, therefore, forced the locals to rely entirely on their own militia.

Not to be dissuaded, the local county militiamen elected the fifty-five-year-old Col. William Crawford to command the army of approximately 480 frontiersmen and backwoods farmers. Crawford was an experienced Indian fighter and close personal friend of General Washington. David Williamson, who had led the notorious Gnadenhutten expedition, was second in command; he lost the election to be the commander by five votes.

Crawford's small army left the rendezvous point in the Mingo Bottoms on Saturday, May 25, 1782, and headed northwest for the Sandusky.[18] Despite the absence of federal troops, the expedition was fully supported and authorized by General Irvine, who provided Crawford with one of his most able officers, John Rose. Rose was a brilliant young physician who, "by his exemplary conduct and pleasing carriage, soon won the esteem of the army." John Slover and Jonathan Zane, two competent men familiar with the territory, acted as guides. The principal officers were experienced, well-respected militia commanders and prominent citizens of the two counties. Not one word in Irvine's instructions to Crawford mentioned the Christian converts, and later testimony by the survivors hotly disputed the claim that they were primarily concerned with these hapless Indians.[19]

By forced march Crawford reached the Upper Sandusky on June 3. The next day they met the enemy Wyandot. While the first few hours of the attack were successful, later reinforcement by a British contingent of Butler's Rangers turned the battle against Crawford. The men became confused in the strange countryside and detached from their units. The retreat on June 5 quickly became a general rout. Crawford was separated from his troops, captured, and later burned at the stake by the Indians. Only by the skill of John Rose and David Williamson, who adroitly led the retreat, was the balance of the army saved. The remaining detachments arrived back at the Mingo Bottoms on June 13. Seventy men never returned, and were either killed in the various engagements or later murdered by the Indians.[20] The defeat was a bitter blow to pioneer morale.

ZEISBERGER AT DETROIT

Six weeks before Crawford arrived at Upper Sandusky, the Zeisberger party safely reached Detroit. A few hours after they arrived on April 20, they were summoned to Commander De Peyster's quarters. Zeisberger recorded their conversation:

> He said he had not expected to see us so soon again when he sent us away in the autumn, but so many complaints had come in against us, to which he gave no credence and which he believed false that he was compelled to call us away from Sandusky, and to have us come here; he had done it against his will, but must need do it for the sake of our own safety, for he could assure us that our lives were in the greatest danger if we remained longer in Sandusky. Now that we were here, he wished to leave it to us to remain here or go home."[21]

De Peyster further assured Zeisberger that as long as they remained in the jurisdiction of his command, he would provide for all of their necessities, including food, clothing, and housing. He also suggested that a site for a new mission might be found in the Detroit area.

Initially the missionaries and their families were housed in one of the soldiers' barracks within the fort. But by June 17 the party moved to a more convenient location outside the village. After consulting with his fellow missionaries, they unanimously agreed to remain in the area. Perhaps, with De Peyster's assistance, another location could be found where they could live in relative peace. But any renewal of the mission depended on the response they received from the scattered flock. Messages were dispatched by De Peyster and Zeisberger to the Shawnee along the headwaters of the Miami and the Delaware at Upper Sandusky. Since the missionaries had arrived at Detroit, frequent communiqués received by Zeisberger indicated that most of the former converts were living in those areas.

By June 10 word of Crawford's defeat reached Detroit. Four days later a ship from Lower Sandusky brought the Conner family to the fort. From Richard they learned that both the De Peyster and Zeisberger messages had been received by the converts. Rumors reported that most former members of the congregation were living among the Shawnee.

As the days and weeks passed, the missionaries became more apprehensive, until July 8, when Samuel Nanticoke and Adam arrived with their families. They had been "forty days on the journey, had suffered great hunger, so that a sister once nearly wasted away." They left behind on the trail the families of Abraham, Zachary, and Thomas, who were on their way to Detroit. Both Samuel and Adam came from the Shawnees. They did not bring encouraging news, telling Zeisberger that they had just left the Brethren nine days ago and "most of them were rather listless and in doubt about ever seeing us again." Rumors that all the missionaries had been sent to Montreal were rampant. One Indian told Samuel that "he had seen with his own eyes" Zeisberger board the ship.[22] Several families, on the receipt of this information, gave up any thought of moving to Detroit, believing the missionaries and their families had voluntarily—or by force—returned to the colonies.

Three days after the Samuel and Adam families arrived, Zeisberger received reassuring news: "By ships in from Fort Erie the cheerful news comes that an armistice has been concluded and that there is hope of a speedy peace, wherein we had more interest and joy than the inhabitants here showed."[23] The next day, two more convert families arrived, making a total now of fourteen persons.

During this interim, De Peyster arranged with the Chippewa to provide land north of Detroit for a possible new mission site. On Monday, July 15, during an early morning visit, Zeisberger advised the commander that they would accept the Chippewa's generous offer. Three days later he returned to the De Peyster quarters to make final arrangements. The diarist recorded the commander's reaction:

> He gave us at once a written order to draw from the King's store tools, provisions and whatever we needed, and our Indians were not forgotten either; on their account he gave a separate written order for all that Br. David told him to be necessary for them. All which they took, and provisions besides. When Br. David told him at the same time that two more families were come, and that we expected others soon, this was pleasant both for him and for his lady to hear. She provided us also with seeds of all sorts for planting, and the major

was so good as to lend us his own boat, with sails to go away in, and gave us besides a large canoe to keep for our own use.[24]

On Saturday July 20, 1782, the missionaries—Zeisberger, Jungmann, their wives, and the two unmarried men, Michael Jung and William Edwards—boarded the commander's ship and sailed north, up the Detroit River into Lake St. Clair. Nineteen converts accompanied the missionaries: Abraham and Anna, Samuel and Sara Nanticoke, Adam and Sabina, Zachary and Anna Elizabeth, and eleven children—among them two teenage girls. Heckewelder, Senseman, and their wives remained behind to stay with the missionaries' children and to help forward any further converts who might arrive at the fort.

Abraham and Anna had arrived at the site five days before the group departed from Detroit. Zeisberger was overjoyed. "We had always wished this; if only he would come before our departure we should be comforted, and now praise be to God, we begin our mission anew, with four families of Indian brethren, a plain and simple beginning."[25] For seventeen years, since the Lawunakhannek mission on the Allegheny River in western Pennsylvania, the faithful Abraham had marched by Zeisberger's side as a Native Helper. They would pick up the pieces from the disasters encountered since leaving the Muskingum and share the burdens of a new beginning.

NEW GNADENHUTTEN

Sailing along the shores of Lake St. Clair, they entered the wide mouth of the Huron River twenty miles above Detroit, now the Clinton River. Passing down the Huron some ten miles, they selected a site on the south side of the river "on a height, not inferior to that at Schoenbrunn, and with the same slope, according to the compass, and the course of the river which Schoenbrunn had." Zeisberger described the location:

> The land on the site of the town is sandy, which is a token that it is not wet and marshy, as is nearly all the land in this country. The bottoms or lowlands are very rich, but very thickly overgrown with heavy timber. The common kinds of trees are oak, poplar, linden, walnut, ash, hickory, elm, beech, and a great number of sugar trees and wild cherry trees, which have a fine red wood, of which in Detroit the most beautiful cabinetwork is made, and which is much finer than walnut. There are asps and sassafras of such thickness as we had nowhere seen before, so that boards two feet wide could be cut. . . . Hills there are none, but everywhere the land is flat. . . . The hunting is good, and our Indians shot their first deer today. Thus we chose this place before all

others for our town site, as the only one in this neighborhood, and we went there today, pitched our tents, for the heavily-laden boats, too, can go even to the fork, a half mile higher up than we are, and canoes much further.[26]

The first four days were spent planting turnips, lettuce, beans, and the other garden plants they had brought from Detroit and building a bark hut for the supplies. On July 27 they laid out the town. In keeping with previous villages, the streets were four full rods (66 feet) wide and each lot was three rods (49.5 feet) wide. Five days later they blocked out the first house.

It had been ten months since Zeisberger and his large band of Indian converts arrived at the banks of the Sandusky. Stripped of most of their possessions they came close to starvation. Virtually no assistance had come from the native Wyandot and Delaware who had assured Zeisberger's Indian flock they would be cared for and safe from colonial attack. During that period Zeisberger watched helplessly as the ranks of converts dwindled to a precious few; now, with only a handful, he began again. But he carried within his heart a burning resentment, especially against the Wyandot. On August 10, 1782, this normally placid man erupted with a violence rarely found in any of his diaries.

Five days earlier, on August 5, Samuel and Adam came from the fort bringing letters for the missionaries and rumors reporting that a force of Kentucky militia was organizing to attack the Shawnee later in the fall. This would be George Rogers Clark's final expedition against the Shawnee tribe in November 1782. It worried Zeisberger that many of the former converts were living in the area and he "wished they were with us out of this danger." On August 10 another of their Indians came from Detroit reporting new attacks against the Shawnee town. "Afterwards," he recorded, "we heard the Shawnees had fled into the bush and none of them had been injured." But the incident was on his mind and his patience was near exhaustion: "Though we live here so remote from all rumors of the world, yet Satan can not rest and be content with us, but set ill-minded Indian people to say to our people, since they put themselves under English people they will all perish, and had they put themselves under their protection they would have been safe and free from all danger."[27]

This talk was not new, he had heard it before, but he now exploded and scrawled across the diary pages a vehement attack against his enemies:

What a satanic and barefaced lie and what wickedness is this! Have they not driven us away? They have not rested until they had us here. Have they not ruined us and our Indians, houses and barns, property and land, and placed us in the greatest misery, so that we must have starved and miserably perished unless also the dear heavenly Father had again mercifully upheld us and helped us through? One would think they would be content to have wreaked their vengeance so far on us, but no, for since they now see that they cannot accomplish their aim of putting us out of the way and of killing the name of the Saviour in the Indian land, but that we shall yet again settle down and assemble and moreover outside their bounds too, and since they foresee already that our Indians will follow us, they bring them wicked rumors, threats, and lies, to make our Indians fearful and to frighten them from coming here, though they are the cause of our being here, and believe that here there would be an end of us; therefore, they are now scornful and angry that their eyes begin to open and they see and they know that their nation will therefore yet come to nothing. O, what great scorn has Satan! Perhaps, however, he knows he has little time.[28]

At the height of his anger, a familiar thought must have flashed through his mind. Could all of this antagonism be the result of old Hagastaes's Seneca belt passed around among the Indian tribes so many years before? It had traveled as far west as the Mississippi and throughout the Ohio country before returning to the Allegheny. Despite the fourteen years since the incident, Zeisberger remembered it clearly. How could he forget! The importance of the symbolism was crystal clear. The belt was a great bunch of wampum, "as many strings as one could hold in one's hand," and the message was: "Cousins, who dwell in Goschgoschunk and along the Ohio and you Shawnee Indians. I have arisen and looked about me, to find out what is going on in the land. I have seen that *somebody in a black coat has arrived, beware of the black coat. Believe not what he tells you, for he will pervert and alienate your hearts*" (emphasis added).[29]

Zeisberger was concerned at the time and wrote in his diary that evening, "We alone could do nothing; it was necessary that the Indians [here at Goschgoschunk] should declare their intention, otherwise our word would signify nothing." It was a devastating blow, and he correctly assessed the possible damage. He closed the entry, "In his message the chief [Hagastaes] would stir up all the Indians along the Ohio, and even the Shawanose [Shawnee] who dwell two hundred miles below Pittsburgh, against us. May the Lord help us! for we are here at His call and command."[30]

No positive proof can be found linking Pomoacan and the Wyandot action with the Seneca black belt message. However, frequent references are found in Zeisberger's diaries and correspondence for many years following the event. It was must have been always on his mind.

Despite all of the plots and intrigue against them, the converts continued to trickle into New Gnadenhutten. By the end of the year there were fifty-three people living at the village. On one of his frequent trips to Detroit, Zeisberger met Sir John Johnson, the general superintendent of Indian affairs for the British government in Canada. Johnson brought letters from Christian Ignatius Latrobe, the British mission secretary of the Moravian church, and also a draft for £100 from the agent for the Society for the Propagation of the Gospel among the Heathen. This was like "manna from heaven." They had, however, not heard from their own board in Bethlehem for more than a year. Johnson assured the missionaries that "the mission was to be protected in every way, and the Moravian ministers to be treated with all respect and distinction."[31]

With the gentle breezes of spring and the blooming of the willow buds by the river bank, William Edwards, returning from a routine trip to Detroit, brought the first news of the general peace between the English and the colonies. The plenipotentiaries from England and America, meeting on November 30, 1782, in Paris, proclaimed a tentative peace agreement. Their plan called for a cessation of hostilities on April 30, 1783. Another seven months passed, however, before the final agreement was signed. Perhaps then peace would again return to the frontier.

~~~~~

FOUR

Return to the Ohio Country

Peace did return to America in 1783. To the Indians, the Treaty of Paris was a strange and anomalous agreement. How could the American colonials be considered the victors? Had not the previous year been the Indians' most successful since the beginning of the war? Had they not defeated Crawford on the Sandusky, and had not Girty's Indian forces successfully destroyed the garrison at Blue Lick in Kentucky? "The Indians," wrote the Canadian governor Haldimand from Quebec, "are thunder Struck at the appearance of an accommodation So far short of their expectation from the Language that has been held out to them, & Dread the Idea of being forsaken by us, & becoming a Sacrifice to a Vengeance which had already in many instances been raked [wreaked] upon them."[1] As the terms of the preliminary peace treaty slowly began to filter into the vast wilderness of the Ohio country, the Indian tribes were appalled. Article six of the treaty called for the English king to renounce and yield "to the United States all pretensions and claims whatever of all the country south and west of the great Northern Rivers and Lakes, as far as the Mississippi." Since 1777 the British had solemnly pledged to the Six Nations and the other Ohio tribes to protect their territorial lands. Relying on these promises, tribe after tribe had deserted the Americans to fight with the British. Now, not one reservation or exception in the treaty was agreed upon in favor of the tribes that lived in this vast area. They were simply left to make their own terms.[2]

With the colonials now relieved of the restraint of the war years, 1783 marked the revival of American aggression against the Indian nations. The new United States government could take revenge, and reparations for the bloody attacks against the frontiersmen over the previous six years could be demanded in the form of land cessions. Floundering and fumbling in its procedures, the American Congress began negotiating a series of treaties. Four major documents were signed between 1783 and 1790: at Fort Stanwix, New York, in October 1784; at Fort McIntosh, on the Beaver River in Pennsylvania, in January 1785; at Fort Finney, at the mouth of the Great Miami near North Bend, Ohio, in January 1786; and, finally, at Fort Harmar, at the mouth of the Muskingum, in January 1789. At Fort Stanwix, the Six Nations were forced to give up forever their claims to all territory beyond the states of Pennsylvania and New York, and they soon lost their remaining territory in those states. At Fort McIntosh, the Wyandot, Delaware, and Chippewa relinquished their titles to most of the Ohio land with the exception of some in the northwest portion of the state. At Fort Finney, the Shawnee were deprived of all their land north of the Ohio to the Great Miami River. And at Fort Harmar, the Indians were hopelessly disunited, weakening their ability to negotiate, while the Americans spoke with one voice.

Gen. Arthur St. Clair dictated the Fort Harmar treaty, and the terms simply confirmed the McIntosh and Stanwix treaties. There would be no compromise, no arguments. The Indians had fought with the British and lost. However, all of these treaties were subsequently disavowed by the tribes, and the hostile and condescending manner of the American negotiators did little to contribute to lasting peace. It is not surprising that this seven-year period, filled with turmoil and confusion, enraged the Indians and provoked the bloody Indian Wars of the 1790s.[3]

In the middle of all this turbulence was David Zeisberger and his Indian converts. The spring of 1783 brought renewed activity to the mission village of New Gnadenhutten on the Clinton River. Richard Conner left his precarious haven on the Lower Sandusky and began, on March 25, to build a home in the new village. One month later he returned to the Lower Sandusky and brought his family to New Gnadenhutten.

On Wednesday, May 7, Matthew and Renatus came with an announcement that forty Indians were on the trail to the village. Seven days later they began to arrive. Renatus was no stranger to the Moravians. Twenty years earlier, as a teenage member of the Nain mission near Bethlehem (see appendix A, number 8), he had been arrested and falsely accused of participating in the massacre of a white family near Bethlehem. He was defended by an attorney furnished by the Moravians, and, much to everyone's surprise, the white male jury acquitted him of the murder. Now, at forty-six, he was a "lost sheep" returning with his family to spend the balance of his life among the converts.

Thomas, the former Indian captain Gutkigamen, a grandson of Chief Netawatwes, arrived at the village on June 18. He had been baptized at Schoenbrunn in 1774 and became a valuable addition to the congregation. Formerly well-known and respected among the native Indians, he again became an admired assistant to Zeisberger.

On July 5 Detroit commander De Peyster (now elevated to the rank of colonel) sent an express messenger to the village requesting Zeisberger's immediate presence at the fort. The following day Zeisberger arrived and met the elder Schebosh and John Weigand (a messenger from the mission board). Schebosh had been captured in November 1781 by a militia expedition and taken to Pittsburgh, along with a number of Indian converts.[4] When they were freed by Colonel Gibson, rather than return to the mission field, Schebosh traveled to Bethlehem to carry the latest news to church officials. Two years after his release, he was reunited with his family, now living at the mission village.

It had been two long, weary years since Zeisberger had heard from Bethlehem. The messengers from the east brought the sad news of Bishop Seidel's death. For over twenty years their beloved Nathanael had led his Moravian flock and shepherded the far-flung Indian missions. The unexpected catastrophe and massacre at Gnadenhutten in March 1782 grieved Seidel to his final days. He had been replaced by Zeisberger's old friend, Bishop John Ettwein.

The Moravian missionaries remained at New Gnadenhutten for the next three years. Even with patience and understanding, the rebuilding program was a slow and plodding process. Former members, now living among the native tribes, became increasingly dissatisfied and longed for the peace and contentment of the mission village. Slowly they began to drift back. The diaries during this period reflect the confusion and uncertainty that spread among the five principal Indian tribes—Chippewa, Wyandot, Delaware, Shawnee, and Ottawas (Zeisberger called the latter, the "Tawa"). The treaties of Fort McIntosh and Fort Finney only added to their discomfort and heightened their mistrust of the Americans. Although they had been forced to sign these treaties, they certainly did not plan to comply with the terms without some resistance, even if it meant another war. To comply meant abandoning their historic homeland in the Ohio country.

While the total membership at New Gnadenhutten was far below the numbers of the Schoenbrunn and Gnadenhutten years, the missionaries did make progress. With rare exception, every missionary—especially Zeisberger—meticulously recorded the year-end census of each mission village. Interestingly, he did not record the total census for 1783 and 1784, only the births and deaths; at the end of 1785 he listed a population total of 117.[5]

As time passed, their landlords—the Chippewa—became increasingly dissatisfied with the mission village. It was well understood at Detroit that the original Chippewa agreement with Major De Peyster permitted the Moravian Indians to occupy their land only for the duration of the late war. Several mission entries explain their complaint. On

June 10, 1784, Zeisberger recorded that "The Chippewas did not like to have us on their land on account of the hunting and fishing—they did not like to see others hunting and fishing on their territory." Again, a similar entry on the following November 9 stated, "The Chippewas had expressed their discontent at our Indians dwelling here, saying that we did them great harm and damage in their hunting, and this went so far that they would not go away until they had killed a couple of us, which would be the occasion for getting us out of their land."[6]

It now became increasingly evident that Zeisberger would be forced to seek another location. He longed to return to the Muskingum valley under the jurisdiction of the new American government. Only the unsettled conditions of Indian and American diplomacy prevented the move. In the meantime, Jung, the Senseman family, and the Jungmanns returned to Bethlehem; Jung left the village on August 30, 1783, and the Sensemans and the Jungmanns left on May 17, 1785. Young Polly Heckewelder accompanied the latter, planning to begin her education at Bethlehem. With no immediate prospect for an expansion of the mission work, Zeisberger decided that these missionaries should return to the safety of the settlements. The Zeisbergers, Heckewelders, and William Edwards were now alone at New Gnadenhutten.

In an attempt to assess the condition back in the States, Zeisberger sent Edwards, the assistant missionary, and three of his most trusted converts—Samuel, Peter, and Jacob—to Fort Pitt on June 17, 1785. They returned to the village six weeks later with important news. Their visit followed, by five months, the signing of the Fort McIntosh treaty. The prevailing opinion in Pittsburgh presumed that the native Ohio Indians would comply with the terms of the treaty, which mandated that they abandon their lands in eastern and southern Ohio. Zeisberger's diary entry on July 30, 1785, reflected this opinion:

> In the first place this is the main thing; we now know certainly that there is no more Indian land across the Lake, and that the States own all the land, and take possession of it; that they will not altogether drive away the Indians, but yet will not permit them to live in their neighborhood, that is on the Muskingum and in that quarter, but must remain at a distance. In Pittsburgh, also, he [Edwards] read in a newspaper that the Christian Indians have their towns on the Muskingum, namely Gnadenhutten, Schoenbrunn, and Salem, confirmed to them by Congress, with so much land as the geographer, the surveyor general, shall hold fit; this also we knew, in part by letters from Br. John Ettwein, of May last, although it had not then been confirmed. . . . We see plainly enough that we shall not have to look about for another place to settle, than in the country on the Muskingum.[7]

The information Edwards gleaned from the Pittsburgh newspaper appears to be the first confirmed indication Zeisberger had received of the proposed congressional grants of land to the Moravian Indians. The Moravian lobby had been busy at the capital in New York. The proposed grant had been included in the last page of the land ordinance passed by Congress on May 20, 1785: "And be it further ordained, That the towns of Gnadenhutten, Schoenbrunn, and Salem, on the Muskingum, and so much of the lands adjoining to the said towns, with the buildings and improvements thereon, shall be reserved for the sole use of the Christian Indians who formerly settled there, or the remains of that society, as may, in the judgment of the geographer, be sufficient for them to cultivate."[8]

The Ohio Moravian grants had their inception early in 1783 when the Moravian church petitioned Congress for a grant of land on the Muskingum as reparation for the loss of the missions at the hands of the hostile Wyandot and Delaware in 1781. The Ordinance of 1785 was only the beginning of a long and detailed process. It took three years for Congress officially to change this resolution (on September 3, 1788) to include three grants of 4,000 acres at the old sites of Schoenbrunn, Gnadenhutten, and Salem, and another eleven years for the land finally to be surveyed (in 1797).[9]

Edwards's message from Pittsburgh was exciting news, and by August 30 Zeisberger had made his decision. That fall they would relocate at either the Tuscarabi, the old village site of King Beaver near present Bolivar, Ohio, or the former location of Schoenbrunn on the Muskingum. They set about to make the necessary canoes, calculating it would take seventeen to make the move. Messages of their decision were sent to all the former converts at the native villages.

But Zeisberger misjudged the tenor of the times. Within days a storm of objections began to arrive at the villages warning against the move. On September 18 a friendly Nanticoke messenger came from Detroit to call away his own people, warning that "the Indian nations over the lake had all declared war against the Americans which would last over thirty years." At the same time a message arrived from their friends among the Miami and Shawnee. After receiving the announcement of the planned move, they sent word to Zeisberger and the mission to remain there and wait, "for there was now no peace, and it was not advisable for us to go there, and if yet we did so, they [the Wyandot] were determined to get us all together, to hold us fast, and to bring us to the head of the Miami; for the present we should stay here and remain until perfect peace should be made." Even the disgruntled Chippewa cautioned against leaving at this time and warned, "We should do best to stay a day [year] longer." Alexander McKee, the Indian agent at Detroit, also warned against the move. Zeisberger finally yielded and delayed the plan until the next spring.[10] He wrote the governor in Detroit to advise the Chippewa accordingly.

Colonel De Peyster had been replaced the previous year by Lord George Gray, who died unexpectedly before the year closed. In early 1786, Major Ancrum was named his successor. By the time of Zeisberger's first visit to the new commander on February 8, the results of the January treaty with the Shawnee at Fort Finney were well known by the British at Detroit. Accordingly, Major Ancrum said "he saw no difficulty, and no cause for anxiety why they should not proceed with their plans to move in the spring." He also assured the missionaries that he would "send on our [the missionaries'] behalf a message to the Indians that they should not molest us." McKee, the Indian agent, also gave his assurances. Armed with these pledges, Zeisberger proceeded with his moving plans.

Major Ancrum and the Detroit trader John Askins paid a visit to the mission on March 8. Askins had agreed to purchase all of the mission holdings for a generous £400—one-half to go to the Indian Brethren and the balance to the missionaries. Zeisberger noted the visit in his diary:

> The major came with a couple of officers and Mr. Askins, in their sleighs. We had prepared for them a separate house and room, and furnished them as well as we could. They looked about our town today, visited in the Indian houses and took notice of every thing; examined a part of our fields, and especially the country, which was the main objective of their visit. Our town and its situation and the whole neighborhood pleased them exceedingly well. . . . The major will in the spring, as soon as the lake is open, take us all over to Cuyahoga in the king's ships. He and all with him were exceedingly friendly to us and showed us their good will. The next morning they went back again, very well satisfied.[11]

The morning of April 20 dawned bright and clear. After a short service in the chapel, the missionaries and their families boarded the twenty-two canoes tied to the banks of the Clinton below the village. The day marked the fourth anniversary of the Moravians' arrival in Detroit. Zeisberger noted, "None of us remained behind, save Conner's family, who himelf knew not whither to go, not what to do." The sixty-eight-year-old Richard Conner had reached the end of his pilgrimage with the Moravians and remained at New Gnadenhutten until his death on April 22, 1807. The four thousand acres of land, which included the mission site, eventually became his property and is now the site of Mount Clemens, Macomb County, Michigan. His family remained on the tract until the War of 1812. As he closed the diary entry for the day, Zeisberger mused: "How strong we are! How many have died, how many have been born!"[12]

The twenty-two-canoe flotilla cleared the mouth of the Clinton and entered Lake St. Clair on the morning of the next day, but high winds necessitated an evening camp along the shores of the lake. By noon on

April 23 they had arrived at Detroit. One month later, just prior to leaving that city, Zeisberger noted the reluctance of the Detroit residents to see them depart. "All people in Detroit showed us their sorrow, not only that we, but also that our Indians were leaving them. These left a good reputation behind them, for all merchants in the city report that they have been paid all their debts to the last penny, saying it could well enough be seen that they were honorable people and better than all the inhabitants around Detroit who do not like to pay their debts."[13]

True to his promise, Major Ancrum arranged their passage on two ships, the sloop *Beaver* and the *Mackinaw,* furnished by their friend John Askin, a partner in the firm of the Northwest Company at Michilimakinac. The ships sailed from Detroit at noon on April 28, 1786. Ancrum, in the presence of Zeisberger, gave written instructions to Captain Anderson of the *Mackinaw* to treat them well and deliver them safe at the Cuyahoga.

The first two days were uneventful. On the evening of April 29, however, they sailed into the harbor at Put-in-Bay on South Bass Island. That same evening a series of easterly gales of unprecedented severity began to blow across the lake. The high winds continued frequently for almost a month, isolating the convert delegation on the islands while the two ships remained sheltered in the harbor.

One month after their arrival, a call was received by Captain Godfrey to return the *Beaver* to Michilimakinac. Complying with this request, the *Beaver's* passengers were disembarked on the nearest land. Zeisberger, Heckewelder, and most of the converts were transported to Scott's Point, Catawba Township, Ottawa County, Ohio. This party was divided into two groups. Heckewelder and the canoes sailed along the southern shore of the lake carrying some of the baggage, and Zeisberger, with backpacks, traveled on foot. Aboard the *Mackinaw,* Edwards sailed for the Cuyahoga with the aged, the infirm, and the household goods.

By midday on May 30, the Zeisberger party landed at Scott's Point. The next day, packs were assembled, and with Samuel Nanticoke in the lead, they passed down the Catawba peninsula and arrived at Sandusky Bay. Here they borrowed canoes from the Ottawas, crossed the mile-long bay, and landed on the southern shore of the lake near present Sandusky, Ohio. Now traveling due east, they took the next eight days to arrive at the mouth of the Cuyahoga, where they met Edwards and the *Mackinaw* on the southern shore of the lake at present Cleveland, Ohio. With their supplies nearly exhausted, Schebosh was instructed to proceed to Pittsburgh to buy provisions while Zeisberger explored the river for a prospective village site.

PILGERRUH

On June 9 they bid Captain Anderson and his crew bon voyage and helped the *Mackinaw* cross the shallow Cuyahoga sandbar back into the deep waters of the lake. The long delay experienced during the lake trip caused a reevaluation of their goal to reach the Muskingum in time for spring planting. On the same day Zeisberger explained their position: "We resolved for the first thing to make canoes, most of them of bark, and as soon as possible to get away from here and to go up the creek to find out how far we could go, and if we should come upon old fields, to consider whether we should plant something."[14]

He noted further, on Monday, June 12, "Hunger begins to fall sharply upon us! May the Saviour soon help us out of our need." This was the same day Schebosh left for Pittsburgh to gather supplies from Duncan and Wilson, their friendly suppliers. Six days later, moving south up the Cuyahoga, they arrived at the site of an old Ottawa village. They had been on the road forty-one days since leaving Detroit. Already June 18 and past the best planting season, Zeisberger made his decision: "We resolved, therefore, to stay here this summer when our matters would become clearer, for at present we are confused and know not rightly how things are with us. We laid out our camp upon the east side of the creek upon a height and the day after, Monday 19, we sowed the land on the west side where we wished to plant, and found good and in part quite clear land for this purpose, only it was very wild, the weeds standing as high as a man, which we had to cut down, thus having much trouble and labor."[15] Thus began the mission village of Pilgerruh (Pilgrim's Rest), their "Night's Lodge," an Indian term for one year of residency.[16]

On July 3 the immediate threat of famine was alleviated with the return of Edwards and Andrew from Pittsburgh. The Zeisberger party used the £200 credit received from John Askin for the sale of the land at New Gnadenhutten, and Duncan and Wilson granted a bill of exchange so they could purchase from the traders' Cuyahoga warehouse all supplies required for the village. The traders, located at Pittsburgh, used packhorses to transport the goods from Pittsburgh to the mouth of the Cuyahoga. (Their log huts were the first buildings built on the present site of Cleveland.) From there, the supplies were reshipped by boat to Detroit. It was a thriving business, and most of the pack trains traveled up the Cuyahoga valley, passing the Pilgerruh village.

Edwards's arrival helped the villagers recover from a sad incident that occurred on June 30. Zeisberger's journal entry for that date described the event:

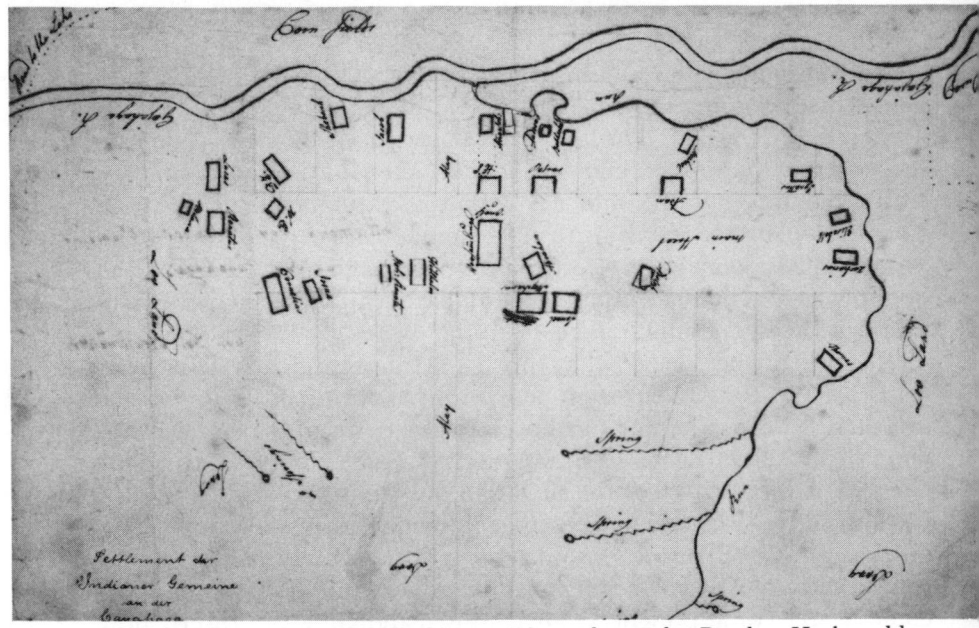

Map of Pilgerruh on the Cuyahoga River, drawn by Brother Heckewelder. Knowing they would remain there for only one year, the missionaries did not lay out the village in their usual symmetrical pattern.

We learned a sad circumstance, Thomas, who had been scalped at Gnadenhutten [on March 8, 1782], went down the creek fishing, day before yesterday, and when he remained out over night, it was supposed he had gone down to the lake. This morning, Jacob went down the creek, where he shot a deer and found his [Thomas's] canoe, which had floated down, but not him. But when search was made, he was found dead in the water. Since he was scalped, he often had fits, and this was doubtless the cause of his death, for he was one of the best swimmers. He came to us on the Huron River (New Gnadenhutten), loved the brothers, and wished not to remain among the savages; this he often said to Br. David, that he would like to be with us. He was buried here the next day.[17]

Zeisberger spent the summer and fall of 1786 attempting once again to rally the support of the apostate converts now living among the Shawnee and Delaware on the Miami and Sandusky rivers. In September Samuel and Thomas traveled among these villages talking with former members of the missions. It proved to be a fruitless quest. They did, however, gain some support from a brief visit with Captain Pipe and returned with a message for Zeisberger:

I take you by the hand and set you in the neighborhood of the Pettquotting, which is intended for you; there seek ye out a place that pleases you and is suitable for you; there ye can keep your cattle. No one shall disturb you or put aught in your way, there shall ye dwell in quiet and hold your worship of God since ye go not to war. Accept this proposal for we mean well by you. I know well that your towns on the Muskingum are given to you, it may sometime happen that ye go there, but for the time being it is not advisable, not good for you.[18]

On October 7, 1786, less than a month after Samuel and Thomas returned from their embassy, Colonel Benjamin Logan and a large force of Kentucky militiamen suddenly descended upon the Shawnee towns along the Great Miami. The expedition was in response to a supposed incursion by the Shawnee against the Kentucky settlements. (Actually the raids were conducted by the Mingos and Cherokee.) The militiamen burned seven Shawnee villages, killed ten chiefs, and did much damage to the crops and cattle. They also killed one of the Shawnee's beloved chiefs who was a warm friend of the Americans. Melanthy, approaching Logan's forces under a flag of truce, displaying the thirteen stripes, and waving the Miami treaty, was shot down in cold blood. From that time forward, the Shawnee became implacable foes and bitter enemies of the Americans. The Indian confederacy had no more loyal supporters than the Shawnee nation. Their hatred eventually culminated in the War of 1812 with Tecumseh and his brother, Tenskwatawa, the Prophet, and had galling reverberations for the Moravian Christians on the Muskingum.[19]

Two days after Samuel and Thomas returned from the Sandusky, John Heckewelder, concerned for his wife's health, left Pilgerruh with his family and returned to Bethlehem on October 9, 1786. He never again had a permanent assignment to a mission village. Before Heckewelder departed, he drew up a crude map of the village (which can be found among the Pilgerruh papers at the Moravian Church Archives). Because of the temporary nature of the mission, the layout did not follow the precise plans normally found in the Moravian villages. With the departure of the Heckewelder party, Susan and David, with the ever-faithful William Edwards, were now alone with the converts at the mission.

During October the converts constructed a new chapel and the first services were held in the building on November 10. Zeisberger's continuing correspondence with General Butler, the American commander at Fort Pitt, concerning the conditions on the frontier was not encouraging. Butler strongly recommended that the missionaries give up any attempt to return to the Muskingum at this time. The year ended with a total census of ninety-five Indians living at the mission.

With the coming of spring in 1787, Zeisberger, yielding to Butler's advice, abandoned the projected Muskingum valley move. Samuel and several of the Brethren were sent west along the lake to seek a prospective site for a new village. Leaving Pilgerruh on April 10, they returned three days later. An excellent site was discovered six to eight miles south of the lake on the Black River in Lorain County, Ohio.

One week following Samuel's return, the congregation departed from Pilgerruh and again moved westward toward the native Indian villages on the Sandusky. The second day of the journey marked the first anniversary of their arrival at the Cuyahoga. They stopped briefly at the location discovered by Samuel on the Black River; but in the meantime they had received information from Captain Pipe to push on to Sandusky, as he and Pomoacan had chosen a location eight miles from the nearest native village. Reluctantly, they continued their westward journey until they reached the Pettquotting River on May 7.[20] Since they had little stomach for living near the native villages, Zeisberger decided to remain, for the moment, at Pettquotting to determine the facts of Pipe's communication and to make a final decision. On May 12 Thomas and William made a quick trip to the Sandusky. Although they did not talk to Pipe, who had gone west to the Wabash River, they did inspect the proposed village site and found it to be only two miles from the nearest native village—a totally unsatisfactory arrangement. They then appealed to the Wyandot chief at Lower Sandusky, explaining that if they were forced to come to Sandusky, the spring planting season would be over. In one of the rare incidences of understanding, Pomoacan gave them permission to remain at the Pettquotting.

Three days later Thomas and William rejoined the Zeisberger party. After hearing their report, they unanimously decided to remain on the Pettquotting. In the meantime they had found an acceptable site "some miles up the river." Here they began to build their bark huts and clear the fields for the spring planting. Zeisberger closed the diary entry on May 15 with this remark: "There is such confusion among the Indians that it is impossible to describe it. They flee, and know not before what, and run straight into death."

During this period, Michael Jung and John Weigand rejoined the missionary staff. Weigand, however, remained for only six weeks and was then sent back to Bethlehem. This was a strange and unprecedented move. Weigand, with Schebosh, had delivered to New Gnadenhutten the first information they received from Bethlehem since their removal from the Muskingum in 1781, and his assignment was assuredly authorized by the mission board. Never in Zeisberger's long experience with fellow missionaries was a man so precipitately returned to Bethlehem. We have no explanation for this abrupt move other than this short entry on May 30: "The *Saviour favored the plan* that Br. John Weigand should go back to the Church." This indicates that Zeisberger had consulted the lot. Weigand left the congregation on June 16, "accompanied," wrote Zeisberger, "by our heartfelt blessings." If there was any misconduct or dissatisfaction with his work, Zeisberger gave us no clue.

~~~~~

FIVE

Pettquotting
The New Salem

Zeisberger and his Christian con-
verts remained on the Pettquotting for the next four years, from 1787 to
1791.[1] After Schoenbrunn and Gnadenhutten on the Muskingum, it was
his greatest achievement. Now, in the heart of the Indian country, he
could take advantage of the discontentment and alienation prevalent
within the native Indian tribes. Disgruntled and frightened with native
life, the Indians were well aware of the rising clouds of war, and they
flocked to the mission to hear the Word of God and seek the safety of the
village. The year-end statistics give some indication of Zeisberger's success. There were ninety-five converts at Pilgerruh on December 31, 1786.
During the next four years the mission population at Pettquotting increased 123 percent and they closed the last full year of residency on the
Pettquotting (1790) with 212 converts. More significant was the similar
increase in the number of communicants, which represented approximately 36 percent of the population. These were the tirelessly dedicated
converts who controlled the destiny of village life and provided the Native Helpers needed to operate the daily functions of the congregation.

A steady stream of apostates began to return to the village; most remained for the balance of their lives. Many of these men and women were
the more competent members of the native population and had demonstrated an intense loyalty to the mission program.

On June 30, 1789, Gelelemend, the once proud head chief of the Delaware nation, his wife Rachel, and their three sons, John, Charles, and the
youngest, Christian Gottlieb, returned to the village. For three years they
had been on the road fleeing from the militia at Pittsburgh. The family
camped near the village and became regular attenders of the evening services, but Zeisberger remained cautious, preferring to delay Gelelemend's
baptism. Twice the chief had been rejected from the mission during the
Muskingum valley years, and Zeisberger continued to demur wanting
additional time to evaluate his performance. Two months later, on Sep-

tember 1, Gelelemend came again for a conference. " 'I am,' he said, 'one of the greatest sinners and must be eternally lost if the Saviour does not pity me and with his blood cleanse me from my sins. In him alone I put my trust, for I believe he has died for sinners and has shed his blood for me also, therefore I await with longing to be a sharer in grace.' "[2] Zeisberger was pleased with what he heard and remarked in his journal: "Ah, how has this man, the great chief of Goschachgunk changed! How now is he become so meek that he comes like any other sinner, weeps and begs for grace at the Saviour's feet! If we are glad and have compassion, how must his [the Savior's] loving heart be disposed toward such a poor sinner!"[3]

But Zeisberger still hesitated. He waited over nine months until, on April 12, 1789, he yielded and finally baptized Gelelemend, one of his most celebrated converts. Gelelemend, so the legend goes, took his Christian name, William Henry, from a young Lancaster major who saved the eighteen-year-old warrior's life during the French and Indian War.[4] Zeisberger's confidence in this quiet and introspective man was not misplaced. He eventually became one of his most trusted and valuable lieutenants, never wavering from his baptismal vows. Gelelemend's two oldest sons, John and Charles, were baptized on May 31, and his wife Rachel on July 5. Young Christian Gottlieb, the youngest member of the family, was baptized on April 4, 1790.

The William Henry family was only the beginning of the flood of converts returning to the new mission. There was Lucas (Luke), who so long ago had come to the Moravians at Lawunakhannek on the Beaver River in 1769 and served faithfully until the New Gnadenhutten years, when he became dissatisfied and left the mission to join Captain Titawachkam's Munsee at Upper Sandusky. Togther the two spun a plot and attempted to incite the native chiefs against the Moravians, Lucas thus hoping to become a captain. However, his apostasy lasted less than a year, and by June 19, 1787, he returned to the village full of remorse, begging for Zeisberger's forgiveness. He eventually became a Native Helper and valuable leader until his death at Fairfield in 1808.

Then there was the patriarch Abraham's son, the thirty-three-year-old Gegaschamind. He visited the missions regularly during this period and Zeisberger viewed him as "a great prize." "If this man should be converted he would be useful, for he understood five Indian tongues and can speak to many the words of life." With Abraham's help, Zeisberger carefully convinced Gegaschamind to join the mission. He was baptized as Boaz on Christmas Day in 1787. As Zeisberger predicted, he played a pivotal role in opening the mission with the Chippewa in 1802.

Even venerable old men and women wandered into the mission,

seeking a final haven of rest. John Cook, a French-baptized Seneca, and his wife, Mary, one of the long line of Montours, joined the congregation on March 8, 1788. With only a few years left in his long life, he spent the next lazy years spinning long-ago tales of his witch-doctor father to the fascinated, wide-eyed children of the village.

Another interesting family came back to the missions on July 20, 1787. John and Elizabeth Lieth (Zeisberger spelled it *Leeth*), both white, had been baptized on August 1, 1780, at old Salem on the Muskingum. John, born in Lieth, Scotland, emigrated as a boy with his family and settled on the Pe Dee River in South Carolina. His father died soon after and young John journeyed to Little York, Pennsylvania. At the age of fifteen, he went to Fort Pitt where he hired himself to an Indian trader and, with the latter, started for the wilderness beyond the Ohio River. He became enchanted with Indian life and was adopted into the Wyandot tribe. There he met and married Elizabeth (Sally) Lowery, who had been captured by the Indians as a young girl. When they arrived at Salem, they had a family of two children. During the Great Dispersement they became separated from the converts, but they later received Zeisberger's permission to rejoin the congregation. They remained on the Pettquotting until 1790, when the rising specter of the Indian wars forced the family back to Pittsburgh. Following the war, they returned to the Ohio country and became farmers. Lieth died about the year 1832; Elizabeth preceded her husband in death.[5]

But there were also less sanguine days during the Pettquotting years. On September 4, 1788, Zeisberger suffered the greatest loss of his missionary career when his beloved Schebosh died. Schebosh—his Indian name meant Running Water—was a white man born John Joseph Bull of Quaker parents on May 27, 1721, at Skippack, Pennsylvania. He joined the Moravian church in 1742 and shortly thereafter was taken into the missionary service. In 1745 he and Zeisberger, both twenty-four years old, accompanied Augustus Spangenberg on the first visit into the Iroquois country. From that point on he remained at Zeisberger's side, intricately involved with all of the great missionary's activities. He married Christina, a Sopus Indian, on January 12, 1747, and that decision unalterably shaped the balance of his life. During the Zeisberger years, two Moravian missionaries married Indian women—Christian Frederick Post and John Joseph (Bull) Schebosh. Both made monumental contributions to the Moravian missionary experience, but neither was ever ordained into the Moravian ministry.[6] It is difficult not to believe they were victims of racial prejudice, although there could be perfectly logical explanations for both instances buried in the pages of Moravian history. Without Schebosh's invaluable assistance and knowledge of Indian affairs, Zeisberger's work would have been seriously inhibited. Schebosh's wife, Christina, whom he dearly loved, died on September 7, 1787, a year before his own death. Zeisberger wrote at the end of Schebosh's long obituary, "We shall long miss him among us. His stay here below will remain to us and to the Indian brethren in blessed remembrances. He is now at home in peace, and all is forever well with him."

Another death that occurred in 1788 with some historical significance was that of Joseph, the son of chief Teedyuscung, who died at the village on August 1. His father was a prominent participant in the peace efforts during the French and Indian War. Joseph had joined the Moravian Indians at old Gnadenhutten in 1774, but had a transitory mission life. Immediately after the Great Dispersement in 1781 he disappeared from the mission records until the next year. On November 20, 1782, he returned to New Gnadenhutten and begged to live again in the village. Zeisberger knew of his unsavory history during his absence and denied him permission to stay. On September 19, 1887, just prior to his death, Joseph returned to Pettquotting. The diary noted that "he was inflicted with a contagious disease," probably syphilis. But that was not the problem, Zeisberger explains: "We had indeed great doubts about receiving him, for he was one of those who tortured Col. Crawford to death in Sandusky, and he had himself scalped him while he was still yet alive."[7] Fearful of white retaliation, Zeisberger hesitated, but since Joseph was near death, he granted his request. A few months later the diary noted, "Thus he died, a repentant sinner, and so we were not sorry for the pains and trouble we had with him."

Despite Zeisberger's sadness at Schebosh's death, life continued at this oasis in the wilderness, this village halfway between the white and native culture. Slowly they began to rebuild their cattle herds and continued to expand the plantations of cultivated fields growing corn, beans, squash, and pumpkins. They fenced and planted orchards and each family in the village had its own private vegetable garden. They expanded the chapel, built a schoolhouse, and began regular school hours. While their village prospered, back in the United States other remarkable changes were occurring that would, in a few years, vitally affect Pettquotting.

Seven months prior to the Christian converts' removal from the Muskingum in March 1781, and eight months before Cornwallis's surrender at Yorktown, the Continental Congress met in Philadelphia and adopted a feeble arrangement called the Articles of Confederation. It was the first attempt to frame an instrument of unification for the new national government. To those living on the western frontier, the new government had two major problems in the trying years following the Revolution. One was the continued presence of British troops and officials at Detroit,

Michilimackinac, and other border posts on American soil. The second was the unceasing movement of the settlers and land speculators into the region claimed by the northwest tribes. The Congress could neither get rid of the first nor prevent the second.[8] Even a stronger central government would have found the problem difficult, but to the Confederation it was impossible.

We have seen in chapter 4 the frail attempts to solve this second problem with Indian treaties between 1784 and 1789; yet the Indian incursions against the wave of settlement across the Ohio continued unabated. In 1786 two filibustering expeditions from Kentucky, by George Rogers Clark and Benjamin Logan (unauthorized by the Congress), only exacerbated the situation, especially with the Shawnee.

Despite the weakness of the Articles of Confederation, which lasted from 1781 to 1789, Congress passed several important pieces of legislation that vitally affected the future of the Ohio region and the mission life of David Zeisberger. The Ordinance of 1784, which provided the first attempt to organize the region, never became operational. It was superseded by the Ordinance of 1787, which became the framework for the settlement of an immense area—later carved into five states of the new union. During May of the same year, delegates of the thirteen states gathered in Philadelphia "to form a more perfect Union." By September their document was completed, and two years later, in 1789, it was adopted as the Constitution of the United States of America. The framework for the permanent government was now in place, but the Indian problem on the frontier was still to be resolved.

Immigrants continued to pour down the Ohio River. Rufus Putnam, the father of the Ohio Company, arrived with a contingent of settlers on April 7, 1788, and founded Marietta on the east bank of the Muskingum, opposite Fort Harmar. In November, the Benjamin Sites party settled a short distance below the mouth of the Little Miami and founded Losantiville (later to become Cincinnati). As the old year passed, the first houses were erected, and during the following fall, a stockade was built by the troops from Fort Harmar and was called Fort Washington.[9] General St. Clair, the new governor of the Northwest Territory, moved his headquarters to this location and designated it as the capital of the territory, renaming it Cincinnati after the famous revolutionary society.

In January of that same year, St. Clair tried to improve the situation with the Indians. He met with them at Fort Harmar to confirm the earlier agreements, but he only embittered and aggravated the situation with his haughty demeanor.

There was nothing new with this treaty-making in the 1780s. It had been a continuing struggle since the early part of the seventeenth century. Between 1613 and 1789, well over three hundred treaties were signed by the Indians and their white antagonists.[10] Practically all involved the question of land. The insatiable demand for more land fired the western pioneer movement from the beginning of the white occupation of the North American continent. Many failed attempts were made by the British and colonial governments to prohibit or at least partially delay the westward thrust of the pioneers. In the 1750s, the Pennsylvania colonial government burned the cabins of settlers on the west side of the Susquehanna in an attempt to keep white settlements east of the river. In 1763 George III's proclamation drew a western line across the plateau of the Allegheny Mountains as far south as the Carolinas, only to have it broken five years later by the Treaty of Fort Stanwix which set the Indian territorial line at the Ohio River. The whole thrust of the treaties of the 1780s was to break this line and secure a substantial portion of the Ohio country for white settlement. But the Ohio tribes refused, and they were ready to wage war to protect their lands.

The frontier was now near an explosion point. Immigrants traveling down the Ohio were attacked frequently by Indian war parties. Many were killed and more were taken into captivity. Political pressure on the new Congress continued to build until the legislature finally authorized the president to call the militias of Virginia, Kentucky, and western Pennsylvania to assemble at Fort Washington to prepare for movement against the offending Indian tribes. What followed, sometimes called George Washington's Indian War (1790–95), had a devastating effect on David Zeisberger and his Indian converts on the Pettquotting.

Gen. Josiah Harmar, a native of Philadelphia and an accomplished Indian fighter, was ordered to lead the expedition against the Ohio tribes.[11] Harmar's first detachment of 1,133, led by Col. John Hardin, departed from Fort Washington on September 26, 1790. On October 3 Harmar and 353 federal troops caught up with the militia and spent the balance of the day organizing the troops. The following day some 1,460 men pushed north into the wilderness. The consolidated army penetrated through the headwaters of the Miami 170 miles to the forks of the Maumee and the site of Little Turtle's village at Gigeyunk (now Fort Wayne, Indiana). The untrained and disorderly militia was no match for the wily Miami Indian leader. A number of Indian villages were destroyed, but beyond that nothing was gained. Little Turtle badly bloodied Harmar in two small engagements that cost the American commander twelve officers and 171 noncommissioned officers and privates—a total of 183 men, with thirty-one men wounded. Federal troops placed the Indian losses at 120, which was probably an overestimation. Thousands of dollars worth of valuable equipment was left on the field in the army's hasty retreat to Fort Washington, placing a further strain on the young country's weak economy. Following his return, General Harmar demanded a court-martial for himself, which subsequently vindicated him. To the Indians, the Harmar affair was a great victory; their damaged villages and corn supplies could be easily replaced. They now bristled with self-confidence and resumed their incursions against the Ohio settlers.

Again, pressure on President Washington began to mount. He quickly ordered Gen. Arthur St. Clair, his most prestigious officer on the scene, to organize another expedition against the Indians. The marching and dying were not over.

The expedition was plagued from the very beginning with major supply and recruiting problems. St. Clair did not begin his northward march until September 1791—well advanced in the fall season for such a major campaign. Of the 4,128 troops authorized by the Congress, St. Clair left Fort Washington on September 6 with only 2,418. As he moved north, he stopped briefly to build Fort Hamilton on the Great Miami and Fort Jefferson near present Greenville, Ohio. Pushing north he arrived at the Wabash (Mercer County, Ohio) on November 3. His force, principally through desertion and the garrisoning of the forts he had constructed, had dwindled to 1,400 men. Throughout the night of November 3, an Indian army of over one thousand warriors led by Little Turtle of the Miami, Blue Jacket of the Shawnee, and Buckongahelas of the Delaware silently surrounded the sleeping army. At dawn the next morning, they slammed into the slowly awakening army. From the first shot, it had the marks of a catastrophe. For two hours, the Federal troops attempted to fight off their enemy in hand-to-hand combat. By nine o'clock it became a panic. With three mounts having been shot out from under him and eight bullets having pierced his clothing, St. Clair led a retreat and successfully evaded the rampaging Indians. The Americans were forced to leave on the field 637 dead officers and enlisted men, but they managed to carry the 263 wounded along with them. Of the 1,400-man army only 500 escaped, half of which were wounded. This remains the greatest loss in proportion to the numbers engaged ever suffered by an American army.[12] Although St. Clair was later exonerated of blame, the defeat of the Americans spelled the doom of David Zeisberger's mission on the Pettquotting. Three years later, in 1795, Gen. "Mad Anthony" Wayne, at the Battle of Fallen Timbers, redressed the St. Clair defeat and forced the Indians to sign the Treaty of Greenville.

But, the Harmar and St. Clair debacles were still in the future as the converts closed out the year 1787 on the Pettquotting. It had been a successful beginning. Zeisberger acknowledged the mission's accomplishments and "thanked our dear Lord for the quiet and peace he has let us enjoy." Then he philosophically closed the entry with, "If we wished to have much care and to vex ourselves it would help us not. . . . God give us peace in this land."[13]

The year 1787 also fathered positive results from the petitions to Congress initiated by the church in 1783. Now, assured of the three grants of land on the former site of the Muskingum missions, a warrant was granted by Congress in September 1787 to begin the survey of the three tracts.[14] On September 21 the Society of the United Brethren for the Propagating of the Gospel Among the Heathen (SPG), was organized at Bethlehem. The association, incorporated by an act of the legislature of Pennsylvania on February 28, 1788, held the land granted by Congress in trust for the Christian Indians. The organization of the SPG gave the Bethlehem officials another opportunity to assign John Heckewelder to the mission field. Shortly after the incorporation of the Society, he was appointed the resident agent, a post that he held for the next twenty-two years.

Essential to the development of the three tracts was the survey of the three plots. On September 10, 1788, Heckewelder left Bethlehem accompanied by Matthias Blickensderfer and traveled west to Fort Pitt to arrange the survey. Here he met Thomas Hutchins, the government surveyor, and continued traveling down the Ohio River to Fort Harmar. Heckewelder remained at the fort until St. Clair completed negotiating the Treaty of Fort Harmar. But when the treaty failed to pacify the Indians, he returned to Bethlehem without beginning the survey. Again, in May of the following year, 1789, Heckewelder and Abraham Steiner made a quick trip to the Pettquotting mission to consult Zeisberger regarding the propriety of the survey, but they found that the tribes would not consent to a surveyor trespassing on their land. Frustrated a second time, he returned to Bethlehem. It would be another eight years before the survey was finally completed.[15]

Back in Pettquotting, the popularity of the mission continued, as more of the former converts returned and new members joined the burgeoning population. The schools were expanded until Zeisberger was operating three different teaching sessions, which included many of the adult members of the mission. An entry in the diary of January 11, 1789, succinctly explained his attitude toward Indian education:

> They have a peculiar spirit in learning. They spend day and night over their books. Married brothers and sisters with three and four children go to school, and we cannot refuse them. The need is at hand we have long foreseen and feared, that if school should once begin suitable books would be lacking useful for them to read. We have been thinking about this and make preparation to prepare something for printing, yes, we wish we had something already, for it is much to be feared they will have to wait for them. Those who attended

school on the Muskingum and are married and have children have not forgotten what they learned, they can read, and those who lately began with their a b c's have in a few weeks learned to read. Thus among the Indians no trouble and labor, however little, is in vain; it aids them, is good for their future well-being, and to the Saviour brings honor and joy.[16]

In the same context, under the diary entry of November 19, 1788, Zeisberger related an interesting anecdote concerning one of John Cook's stepsons. He described him as "an unbaptized large boy"—meaning a teenager—who came to him in tears begging for his assistance. Asking what ailed him, he replied:

His step-brother, a savage, had burnt his a-b-c board, and said that if he gave himself up to this he would be a good-for-nothing-man, a worthless fellow, and had scolded him. He had complained about this among the Brethren, and yesterday cried the whole evening about it. . . . Br. David consoled him and promised to give him a book in lieu of the a-b-c board, for he had perfectly learned his alphabet in three or four days, and was already beginning to spell, for if Indian children desire anything they apply themselves to it day and night, and become not weary.[17]

Incidentally, by the following July 6, 1789, the offending brother had changed his mind about the village and become a baptized convert.

Fortunately, the three harvests gathered during their stay on the Pettquotting were bumper crops. But in the surrounding areas, especially among the native tribes on the Miami and the Maumee and even in Detroit, the Indians experienced extensive famine. Many people simply starved to death.

With the rapidly increasing mission population, Zeisberger, on May 12, 1790, gave serious thoughts to establishing another village. At the same time he requested additional assistance from Bethlehem. After a long delay, Gottlob and Anna Maria Senseman arrived on November 9, 1790. But by the end of the year the results of the Harmar invasion and the destruction of the Miami villages were well known throughout the Indian country. It now became evident that there would be an Indian war, and the rising cry for retaliation against the Harmar army destroyed any hope of extending the mission work. The bitter irony for Zeisberger was the 1790 year-end statistic. Now at the height of the mission's success, there were 212 Indians living at Pettquotting—eighty were communicants, almost eclipsing the success of the old Schoenbrunn years.

Shortly after the end of the year, rumors of war accelerated. On January 4 Zeisberger recorded, "We heard very bad and dangerous news on the part of the ill-disposed Indians, of their wicked designs against us." Following a Mission Helpers' Conference, the mission decided to send a delegation to Captain Pipe to check the validity of the rumors and to try to determine the truth of the situation. Samuel, Stephen, and Josua were dispatched to the chief on January 8. Four days later the delegation returned with disturbing news. Pipe advised them to begin to plan to leave Pettquotting in the spring. In fact, he himself planned to move further west from the Sandusky.

Later in the month Matthew Elliot paid a friendly and timely visit to the village. Zeisberger discussed the problem, and the captain assured the missionaries he would provide transportation if they were forced to move. He further assured Zeisberger they could count on assistance from his friend Alexander McKee, the British Indian agent. Ironically, these were the same men who engineered the Great Dispersement in 1781.

Rumors of war continued throughout January 1791. On February 15 a messenger arrived from the combined Indian council being held at Gigeyunk, at the forks of the Maumee. Zeisberger called it "the assembly of hell." He recorded:

> My friends, we hereby make you aware and certain that ye can no longer abide in Pettquotting. Make yourselves ready for departure and in two months time something will be told you; then ye will hear exactly, but if you refuse to arise ye will see and suffer the same as upon the Muskingum, whereupon a string was given. (A string of wampum.) We answered with our own string: My friends, we have received your word that we should prepare and make ready for departure. We are busy at this all the time and already at the work which goes well. We are also not in doubt but know what we do and are in a good way. We have made over our affairs to the chiefs [Pipe, the Delaware, and Ekuschune, the Tawa], who consider our welfare and consult us, from whom we are every day expecting a resolution. We thank you meantime for your admonition and encouragement. Whereupon, we gave him back his string.[18]

Upon the receipt of the message from Gigeyunk, Zeisberger knew his habitat on the Pettquotting was near the end. They must move as quickly as possible. He dispatched William Edwards to Detroit to discuss their plight with McKee and Elliot. Would they help? Edwards left the village on March 12 and returned March 25. Both men promised support, but they must first consult the governor in Quebec, which could take some time. In the interim, they advised Zeisberger to plant again in the spring and move in the fall. However, McKee continued, if the missionaries were forced to move this spring, perhaps a temporary location could be found on his and Elliot's adjoining farms at the mouth of the Detroit River.

Zeisberger could not wait. After Edwards's departure, the situation had further deteriorated. Runners passing through the village bound for Gigeyunk carried a message that six Indians had been killed by American militia on the Beaver River, and a hunting party of several Indian families had disappeared, either captured or killed, on the Muskingum. The same day that Edwards returned from Detroit, on March 25, Zeisberger consulted the lot for the Savior's answer. He noted the results: "Since now we had joyfulness in consulting the Saviour, being now bound to nothing and unhindered, we did so and got from him the answer: 'In God's name break from here. The Lord is with you.' This was to us a real comfort, for which we thanked him."[19]

On March 28 Zeisberger again dispatched Edwards back to Detroit to advise McKee and Elliot that they would accept their offer of the land at the mouth of the Detroit River, and to inquire whether they could furnish a ship for moving the supplies. If not, Edwards was to hire a boat from their friend Mr. Askin. Three days later they began the move. It was to be an excruciating experience. They had twice the number of converts and three times the quantity of supplies and food compared to the New Gnadenhutten move in 1786. During February the canoe builders had been planning for the move and had a fleet of over fifty canoes ready for departure. It took thirty-five days to move the entire village from Pettquotting to the Detroit River. Five days after they began, Zeisberger cried out, "O Lord, help! for one's head could hardly bear everything."

The route to Elliot's farm on the Detroit River led them down the Pettquotting (now the Huron River) to Lake Erie, then turning west, they skirted the southern shore of the lake to Sandusky Bay, where they met Mr. Askin's ship *Sagina*. Here all of the heavy supplies and most of the corn and other food were loaded onto the ship. Senseman and his wife, Anna Maria, and Michael Jung traveled on board the *Sagina*. The rest of the party continued around Scott's Point, passed present Port Clinton, then crossed Maumee Bay to the western end of the lake. There they rounded the end of the lake and headed directly north until they came to the mouth of the Detroit River. The proposed mission site was on the eastern bank of the river, near present Amherstburg, Ontario.

The Zeisberger party was the last to leave Pettquotting on April 14. They arrived at Sandusky Bay four days later, in time to watch the loading of the *Sagina* and meet both Matthew Elliot and Captain La Mot who were checking on the party's progress. Zeisberger remained at Sandusky to see the ship off as it sailed from the bay on April 21. He continued with his party on April 27 and arrived at the Detroit River mission site on May 4, 1791. It had been a safe trip, not one accident or injury. He thanked the Savior for their blessings.

≈≈≈≈

SIX

From the Detroit River
to the Retrenche

Zeisberger's decision to move to the Detroit River was farsighted and keenly perceptive. He and his Christian Indian congregation remained there nearly one year. He referred to the location once as a "Night's Lodge," and on another occasion as a "Night's Watch"—both Indian references to a stay of one year. Not until sixteen months later, at Fairfield, did he use the term "die Warte," or "The Watch Tower," when referring to the Detroit River mission.[1] During the wilderness years (1781–92), Zeisberger seldom called mission villages by name, preferring to use the river where they were located as a designation.

Just before he left the Pettquotting, Zeisberger received a copy of Loskiel's *History of the Indian Missions*. While he generally enjoyed the book that portrayed him as the hero, he did complain bitterly about the Indian orthography, calling it a disgrace to the book. He also suggested that all galling criticism of such former enemies as McKee, Elliot, and Captain Pipe be removed before the English version was published. These men were now his best friends.[2]

The Detroit River mission was located just west of the present village of Malden Centre, Ontario, and had a picturesque view of both the mouth of the river and Lake Erie. The many ships that traveled to and from Detroit could clearly be seen from the village. The McKee and Elliot plantations adjoined each other. Michael Jung and the Zeisbergers lived in the McKee home, and the Sensemans, with Edwards, were housed in the vacant Elliot property. On May 6, two days after their arrival, Captain Elliot, on his way to join McKee on the Miami, made a short stopover to check their progress. It was a warm and friendly visit.

Directly across the river from the mission was the local Wyandot village. All land traffic from Detroit came down the west side of the river and passed near this village. Josua and William Henry arrived here with the cattle on May 13. Most beasts could swim across relatively narrow

rivers, but here the river was six miles wide and the cattle had to be transported by boat—a laborious and difficult task. On May 17 they finished
the final load and all the animals were now contentedly grazing in the
newly fenced fields next to the mission village.

The providential gift of land from Elliot and McKee, and the subsequent relocation into British territory, made possible one of Zeisberger's
more sagacious moves. They were now beyond the jurisdiction of the
new American government and beyond most of their Indian enemies,
who were locked in a bitter war of survival. Elliot, on one of his frequent
visits, assured the missionaries, "You now are living in a secure and safe
place, as well protected as any you have lived in the past twenty years."
The requested meeting with Elliot concerned a message Zeisberger had
just received from the Wyandot and Delaware at Gigeyunk, demanding
that the Christian converts join the war parties now gathering on the Miami. Elliot advised Zeisberger that the British "government would not
merely look on, but would interfere," if any harm came to the converts
from that quarter.[3]

The mission was not, however, protected from the frequent war parties that passed through the village. Zeisberger was surprised and genuinely concerned with the effort now abroad among the tribes to mold a
working confederacy. Joseph Brant, the famous Mohawk chief from the
Grand River area, was the prime leader behind the formation of the
union. On June 14 Zeisberger recorded this entry: "It has never happened
in former years that the nations have been so united as at present, and for
this very reason it is a hard time for our Indian church, such has never
been before. Had we remained in Pettquotting we could well have expected something of the sort that our Indians would be summoned to the
war, but here, and particularly on English ground and soil, we had yet
hoped to be spared this."[4] On the same day he sadly relates, "So today ten
young people went away there [to Gigeyunk] without asking us and
without orders, among them some who never had a gun, and most of
them went from curiosity to see and hear something new." The Native
Helpers William and Thomas followed along after the party to keep
them out of trouble.

Indian intelligence was always aware of any major military movement that encroached into their vast territory. Even Zeisberger at the Detroit mission was privileged and benefited from the Indian grapevine.
On May 27, 1791, he recorded the following entry: "We got news that the
traders are all fleeing from the Miami, from the Americans' advance, and
it is said they were on the Hockhocking [Hocking River, at Hocking-
port, Ohio]."[5]

These were St. Clair's troops traveling to Fort Washington for their
coming campaign in September. Between the defeat of General Harmar's

forces at Gigeyunk on October 21, 1790, and the St. Clair disaster on November 4, 1791, there were two small punitive expeditions against the Indians. Both originated in Kentucky and were authorized by President Washington. But in 1791, before President Washington cleared the road for General St. Clair, he made one more effort to bring the western tribes to the peace council. He commissioned Col. Thomas Proctor to meet with Cornplanter, the principal chief of the Seneca. They hoped to use the Iroquois, especially the Seneca, to intercede with the western tribes and convince them to accept the Ohio River boundary. If the latter refused, it was hoped that the Seneca would take up arms against the Wabash tribes. The peace effort had good intentions, but the mechanics of the plan were ill conceived and poorly executed. In the end, it served only to alienate the Indians further. While Proctor, during his meeting with Cornplanter, was making some progress, the chief received a message from St. Clair urging the Iroquois to take up the hatchet against the Wabash tribes. This action completely discredited the peace mission, and although Cornplanter was not disposed to go to the aid of the Wabash Indians, they had nothing but contempt for those who suggested they attack their own race. On receipt of St. Clair's message, Cornplanter flatly refused to have anything more to do with Proctor.[6]

When word of the collapse of the peace mission arrived at Fort Washington, St. Clair proceeded with the military phase of Washington's plan. If St. Clair was not ready to advance by May, Brig. Gen. Charles Scott was to lead a contingent of Kentucky militia to the Wea village along the Wabash. This might prevent further incursions along the Ohio from that village. A second expedition from Kentucky, to be led by Lt. Col. James Wilkinson, was planned if St. Clair had not moved by August. Since St. Clair did not leave Fort Washington until September, both expeditions began to move. Scott led seven hundred Kentuckians to the Upper Wabash, where he destroyed five Wea villages, killed thirty-two warriors, and brought back fifty-eight prisoners. Wilkinson led five hundred militia to the same region with minor success.[7]

Scott crossed the Ohio River south of Fort Washington on May 23. He completed his destruction at the Wea villages (just south of Loganport, Indiana), and by June 6 left the area and returned to Kentucky. Zeisberger, at the Detroit mission 171 miles from Scott's attack, had the news twelve days later. By June 19, he noted in his journal:

> We had already yesterday heard through Mingoes and today Chippewas who came from Miami, got certain news that the army had come as far as the head of the Miami, had destroyed a couple of Twightwee towns whereby fifty Indians are said to have perished, and was back again, so that they have not come into that place on the Miami, where the Indians had assembled and were waiting for them. . . . This was interesting news for us, for from this we shall

breathe again and be free from our trouble and anxiety and our Indians will no more be summoned to war. But although the army is back again, *the Indians do not cease on this account, but go out strongly for murdering.*[8] [Emphasis added]

The native Indians were fighting for their very existence. A few villages destroyed and a few of their men killed was not enough to deter them. They continued to carry the war to the enemy in the only way they knew how—by attacking and killing those white settlers who attempted to invade their country.

Nevertheless, these raids did not deter the Wilkinson expedition. He left Fort Washington on August 1 and headed north to the Eel Indian villages on the Wabash. The troops arrived at their destination just five miles above the mouth of the Eel River on August 6. Finding no Indians or villages, they turned south, found a small Eel village, and destroyed it—killing six warriors, two women, and one child. The party continued down the Wabash until they arrived at a Tippecanoe village the following day. Since the inhabitants had fled, they destroyed the village and proceeded down Scott's trace to the Ohio River with a handful of Indian prisoners.

Within a few days, Zeisberger, at the Detroit mission, received news of the Wilkinson excursion. While the account he received was wildly exaggerated, it did contain a grain of truth. He recorded this entry: "From the Miami came back David and Jacob, who went there with Elliot several days ago bringing news that an army had advanced to the forks of the Miami and had surrounded an Indian town; that another army advanced upon Gigeyunk, and a third fell upon the Wabash, and the Indians were everywhere in flight."[9]

Three months later Zeisberger received a detailed account of St. Clair's disastrous attack on the Wabash. The battle took place on the morning of November 4, 1791. Within eleven days they received the first report at the mission village. The information continued to flow into the mission for the next four days, and the diary reflects the euphoric Indian interpretation of the battle. Although wildly exaggerated concerning the numbers killed, the reports do explain the extent of the disaster and the amount of materials captured.

Tuesday, [November] 15.

By ship which came to anchor here in which Capt. Elliot, Assistant of Indian Affairs, came, we heard the affecting news that the army of the States had again been beaten in Gigeyunk, that twelve hundred men were killed [almost double the actual number killed], and that they had lost two-thirds of their cannon, namely six, that two generals had fallen, but how many Indians is not reported. May God in his mercy look upon us and help us through these evil times, may he wish to do it, the trustworthy and true, amen, and not bring to shame our hope in him.

Wednesday, [November] 16.

Michael held early service. We heard more accurate news about the battle of Gigeyunk. We had hoped that not the whole army was beaten, but only a part thereof, but it becomes plain that the whole army, with cannon, cattle, horses, tents, provisions, and ammunition, in short, all had been lost. Gen'l Butler with twelve hundred men killed, and the rest pursued, so that but few of them will get home.

Saturday, [November] 19.

From the Miami came a party of Munsee warriors back, who had been present in the battle all of whom confirmed what has already been told about it, and they said further that they had made great booty, and that a strong party of Indians was following the fleeing, that women with children were taken also, who in part, fell into the hands of the Indians.[10]

Not since Braddock's defeat on the Monongahela in 1755 had an Indian force so decimated a white army. Little Turtle had struck a telling blow for Indian unity. There would be no compromise, no retreat from the Ohio River boundary. The Americans must surrender all of their claims and return the land to its rightful owners. But it was not to be. Three years later, on August 20, 1794, on the banks of the Maumee, Indian pride, Indian hegemony, Indian influence in the Ohio country ended. Assured of British support, an Indian army led by the Shawnee Blue Jacket was decisively defeated at Fallen Timbers by Gen. Anthony Wayne, as the British stood by and watched.

But Fallen Timbers was three years in the future. Comfortably sheltered in front of a warm fire, on December 31 David Zeisberger scrawled out four pages of finely written script in his diary, summarizing the events of the year 1791. All things considered, he was grateful. There were 158 Christian Indians living at die Warte, just fifty-four less than the previous year at Pettquotting. Near the end of the entry he crystallized his thoughts in one paragraph:

If now we look only at the trouble and the unpleasantness we have had to experience here, we cannot but thank the Saviour, who has thereby redeemed us and freed us from yet greater need, danger, and hardship. We cannot without horror and amazement, think of what we should have had to suffer on Pettquotting; had there been a possibility of staying there we should have been, as it were, in hell, should have at once been given over to the Satanic warrior-folks, who would have not spared us, while here we have remained protected from all and have heard little of war-stories. And, although at present we are still living always in uncertainty, and have no abode, yet we hold to the name of the Lord, trust in him, look to him, who led us here and will further lead us, so that we shall praise him therefore. We have held our daily meetings, have let the word of Christ live plentifully among us, have had baptisms and communions, and the most comforting and blessed things, for which we heartily thank the Saviour.[11]

In short, it had been a good year. Zeisberger may have complained about having "no abode," but shortly that situation would be resolved. However, time was taking its toll among the old stalwarts who remained with the mission. During the year they had lost two of their venerable members. In September, William died. He was the former Billy Chelloway, a Delaware baptized by Schmick in Friedenshutten on the Susquehanna in 1771. During the intervening twenty years, he was a faithful convert, a Native Helper, and a confidant of Zeisberger's. Then, in November, they lost Abraham. He had been baptized by Zeisberger on Christmas day 1765, in the first months of the Friedenshutten mission. Once a famous captain of the Munsee tribe of the Delaware—he was called Sekima in those days—he had accompanied Zeisberger on journeys to the Iroquois during the formative years at Friedenshutten. He continued to follow the Christian congregation for the next twenty-six years as a valuable Native Helper and as Zeisberger's intimate counselor on Indian affairs. Several members of Abraham's family also became prominent converts. (Some evidence of Abraham's influence is indicated by the 219 entries referring to him in the Moravian mission diaries recorded in the Fliegel Index.[12])

Throughout the winter months of 1791–1792, the converts made baskets and brooms, taking them to Detroit for sale, and Zeisberger continued his Detroit correspondence with McKee and Elliot, planning for the move to a more permanent location in the spring. On February 25 McKee visited the village, and Zeisberger and Senseman "went to him and spoke about their moving away from here. . . . He advised us to seek out a place on the Retrenche River [now the Thames], pleasing to us, and give him notice of this, then he would take measures with the Chippewas about it, and make matters right. He said they [the Chippewa] would all go away from there any way farther westward."[13] Three days following this conversation, Samuel and five other converts were dispatched to make an inspection of the Retrenche location.

Events now began to move rapidly. On March 16 Senseman went to Detroit to make the final arrangement for the move, and on March 18 the converts were advised of the new plan. Elliot visited the village on March 23 and promised a transport.

With a lovefeast, on April 11 the mission celebrated the seventy-second birthday of their beloved leader, David Zeisberger. The following day they held the last services in their little chapel at the mouth of the Detroit. Upon completion of the ceremony, the canoes were loaded, and at noon they bade farewell to die Warte—leaving the village, bound for Detroit. Unknowingly, they were now going to their "permanent abode."

FAIRFIELD, ON THE RETRENCHE

They planned to travel up the Detroit River to the fort, where they would debark and board the ship furnished by Alexander McKee. From there, they would continue up the Detroit into Lake St. Clair. Bearing right after entering the lake, they would shortly arrive at the mouth of the Retrenche River. From there they planned to sail up the Retrenche to its head, debark, and travel by foot to a site yet to be selected. The cattle, driven by Michael Jung and a party of the Brethren, would pass along the eastern bank of the Detroit and the southern bank of the Retrenche to the selected location. Most of the Brethren would travel the entire distance by canoe.

But the trip was not without problems. Because of contrary winds, they were unable to reach Detroit and spent the first night on Fighting Island a few miles south of the city. The next day they arrived at the fort and boarded the ship furnished by McKee. Two days later they left Detroit and entered Lake St. Clair, encountering stiff winds blowing hard across their bow. Before adjustments could be made, the mast broke and fell overboard—sails and all. Jury-rigging a temporary sail delayed them for several hours, but finally they arrived at the mouth of the Retrenche well after dark. Unfamiliar with the channel, the sailors grounded the ship on a sandbar. Waves broke over the vessel all night long, and both crew and passengers were soaked to the skin. On the morning of April 16 they borrowed canoes from the local Chippewa and partially unloaded the ship until it broke loose from the sandbar. Reloading, they sailed up the Retrenche until they arrived at the small village of Sally Hand, a community of English, German, and French settlers. The Zeisbergers remained there, residing with Mr. Row, who had been the steersman on the boat that brought them from Sandusky, while Senseman and Edwards pushed on upstream to look for a suitable location. On April 19 Josua arrived with his family, and two days later Jung arrived with the cattle. On April 23 most of the converts and their families arrived. Two days later they all began the trip upstream to find Senseman and Edwards.

A site was chosen and the layout of the village began on May 1. But seven days later a far more acceptable site was found three miles downstream, and all work at the first site was discontinued. The new location

provided a flat area on the north side of the river and permitted plantations on both the north and south sides of the river. By May 8 the new
village was staked out, and when the Zeisbergers arrived the next day,
they found a comfortable temporary hut ready for their occupancy.

Unknown to this great and tireless leader, David Zeisberger and his
Christian Indians had arrived at their "permanent abode." He had spent
his seventy-second birthday at die Warte preparing for this move to Fairfield. Forty-seven years earlier, to the day, he had languished in a New
York jail, arrested because he believed the message of his Savior should
be taken to his beloved "brown brethren." In all of those intervening
years he had never wavered from that belief—a singlemindedness of
purpose seldom found in any human soul.

Away from the Indian war that now raged in the United States, the
Fairfield mission prospered. However, at no time did it eclipse the earlier
successes at old Schoenbrunn and Gnadenhutten. While the next six
years spent at Fairfield were relatively pleasant and tranquil, Zeisberger
longed to return to his cherished Muskingum valley, the site of his greatest achievement.

FROM FAIRFIELD TO THE MUSKINGUM

Fairfield, on the Thames River, became David Zeisberger's greatest leg-
acy. It remained an Indian mission under the control of the Moravian
church missionary program from May 8, 1792 until April 1, 1903, just a
few weeks short of 111 years. Today, almost two hundred years since its
founding in 1792, Chief Richard Snake and 400 of his tribesmen, calling
themselves The Moravian on the Thames Band, still reside peacefully on
the site. Famous family names like "White Eyes" still remain among the
residents. That must please the soul of David Zeisberger.

In 1792, isolated as he was at Fairfield under British protection, he
lived the next six years in relative safety as the fragile Indian confederacy
along the Maumee, Great Miami, and Wabash destroyed itself. During
those six years, the historic events taking place back in the States had a
profound effect on the remaining years of his life. Anthony Wayne's victory at Fallen Timbers in August 1794, and the subsequent Treaty of
Greenville one year later, forced the Indian confederacy to concede large
portions of the Ohio country to the United States.

The Greenville treaty line ran from Lake Erie south, down the Cuyahoga to the headwaters of the Tuscarawas River, at that time a branch of
the Muskingum River. It then continued down the Tuscarawas to pres-

ent Bolivar, Ohio. Turning west-southwest, the line ran near present Fort Loramie, Ohio (Loramie's Store), then northwest to Fort Recovery. There it turned south in a direct line to the mouth of the Kentucky River on the Ohio. All land south of this line was ceded to the United States, and all territory north of the line, with the exception of sixteen small separate tracts including lands and forts, remained with the Indians.[14] The Ohio country was now opened to the insatiable demands of the frontier pioneers. The Greenville treaty also made the Goshen mission possible.

Earlier we noted the difficulty that Heckewelder had in surveying the grants given to the Moravians by an act of Congress in 1788.[15] The Greenville treaty now freed the territory from the western Indians and cleared the way for surveyors. In the meantime, the Society of the United Brethren for the Propagating of the Gospel among the Heathen took measures to secure the original grants. On June 1, 1796, Congress renewed the 1788 statute and Pres. John Adams signed the deeds shortly thereafter. In the following spring, Heckewelder and a party of Pennsylvanians, including Judge William Henry, Gelelemend's namesake, came to the site of old Gnadenhutten. Heckewelder went on to Marietta to notify Gen. Rufus Putnam, the surveyor general. Putnam, his son William, and Heckewelder returned to Gnadenhutten to complete the surveys in the spring of 1797. There were three tracts of land, each containing 4,000 acres, located on the former sites of Schoenbrunn, Gnadenhutten, and Salem. The Goshen mission was located near the southeastern border of the Schoenbrunn tract.[16] The stage was set for Zeisberger's return to the Muskingum valley. Now, with the congressional grants, they would have title to their own land and be free from the fear of losing possession to the onrushing tide of land-hungry white settlers. Zeisberger had no way of knowing that within five years he would again confront the same problem—he would be surrounded by white neighbors, some quite hostile to his missionary endeavors.

In the spring of 1798 the mission board at Bethlehem chose Heckewelder and an enthusiastic young missionary, Benjamin Mortimer, to carry the news of the completed survey to Zeisberger at Fairfield. The mission board at Bethlehem had chosen the thirty-one-year-old Mortimer to be Zeisberger's new assistant. He proved to be an excellent choice.

The two men set out on the long and tedious journey from Bethlehem on the morning of April 30.[17] The route Heckewelder chose to take was entirely by land, via the old road to the former Friedenshutten mission on the Susquehanna. From there they traveled north to Tioga Point (now Athens, Pennsylvania), crossed into present New York State, proceeded west to Niagara Falls, and crossed into Upper Canada. Skirting

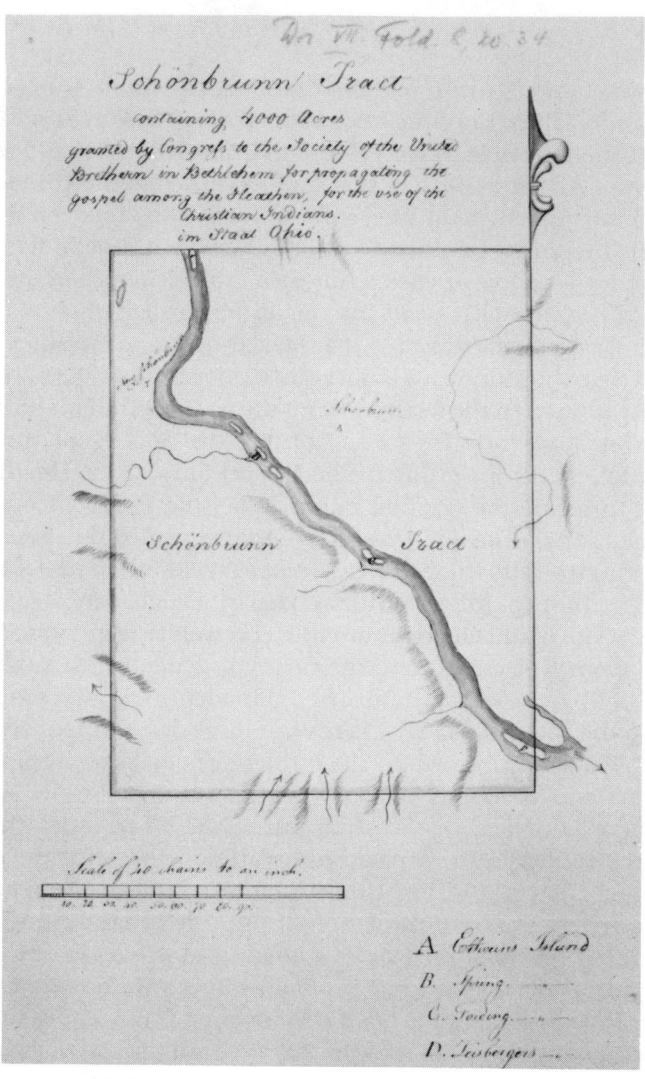

This sketch and survey of the Schoenbrunn tract was made in 1797 by William Rufus Putnam, the son of Rufus Putnam, Surveyor General of the United States. The Schoenbrunn plot is one of three tracts of land granted by Congress—originally in 1787 and confirmed on June 1, 1796—to The Society for the Propagating of the Gospel Among the Heathen. By these grants, Congress gave recognition to the services of the missionaries in the 1770s and made some restitution for their loss of property at that time. Each of the three plots—Schoenbrunn, Gnadenhutten, and Salem—consisted of four thousand acres and can still be found on current Tuscarawas County maps. The Goshen mission was founded the year following the survey, and was located on the west side of the river at the bottom right section of the tract opposite Zeisberger Island.

the northern shores of Lake Ontario, they continued west toward their destination, arriving at Fairfield on May 22, just twenty-three days after their departure—remarkably good time in which to cover 530 miles.

Their arrival prompted Zeisberger to record the following journal entry:

Tuesday May 22th.

We had the very special joy of seeing come to us our dear brothers, John Heckewelder and Benjamin Mortimer, from Bethlehem by way of Niagara, through the bush. They came so unexpectedly, for we had not thought of their coming before June or July, that we rejoiced the more, like children, on both sides, they too, for they had come a very long and hard way until they reached our bounds. In the evening service Br. Zeisberger made announcement of this with many hearty greetings from the Church, at the time also Br. Benjamin Mortimer was come not alone for a visit, but to remain with us, which gave us much pleasure.[18]

Heckewelder stayed at Fairfield nine days, resting and enjoying the balmy spring weather, while he observed the busy activities of the mission village. By May 31 Zeisberger had formulated his plans to relocate. Heckewelder, William Edwards, and a small party of the converts were to return to the valley to choose an appropriate location for the new village. In the meantime Mortimer began his duties as Zeisberger's new assistant. Throughout his long career, Zeisberger had always insisted on keeping the mission diary. On May 31, the day of the Heckewelder party departure, Mortimer assumed this responsibility. Well-educated and with a keen insight into human nature, Mortimer kept the mission diaries well beyond the aging missionary's death in 1808. He recorded his first entry:

May 31st.

This morning all the Indian brethren and sisters came to Brother Edwards to bid him farewell. The many tears they shed evidenced their affection for him, as their faithful servant in the gospel, who has for their sake, endured many hardships as a good soldier of Jesus Christ and is at length grown gray and infirm in their service. . . . He and Br. Heckewelder, and the whole company who go now to the Muskingum had been recommended by Br. Zeisberger to the prayers of the brethren and sisters. . . . The Indian brethren who go are Nicholas, Leonard, Renatus, Bartholomew, and Christian Gottlieb and the boy, Samuel, who are to assist Br. Heckewelder in laying out and opening roads, and in preparing for the formation of the intended settlements at Schoenbrunn, Gnadenhutten, and Salem. Br. Heckewelder, with some of the Indian brethren went from here by land; the rest followed with Edwards in a canoe. They will all go by the way of Detroit, and thence proceed partly by land and partly by water, to the place of their destination.[19]

The plan called for Zeisberger and a few of the converts to leave Fairfield near the middle of August. This was a departure from the previous moves when all converts participated in the exodus. For six years the Indian congregation had lived in peace at Fairfield and had closed the previous year with 172 converts registered as living at the mission. It was a prosperous village and many of the residents had extensive holdings, including cultivated land and valuable buildings. Returning to the States, despite the peaceful nature of the times, involved some risk. The mission board at Bethlehem, interested in expanding their work, decided to try a small experimental contingent to test the waters. The stipulations connected with the Muskingum valley grants stated they were to be held in trust for "propogating of the Gospel Among the Indians." To meet this condition, some Indian must live on the land; otherwise it could possibly revert to the government.

Zeisberger took the next two and a half months to make final arrangements for the journey. He was anxious to return to his beloved Muskingum valley. By the end of July, those who were to be included in the Goshen party had been notified. Unfortunately, the Fairfield diaries are silent on the specific list of names. We can, however, identify a few of the participants from several entries. Of the six Indians who accompanied Heckewelder on May 31, the diary notes that four returned to Fairfield before the Zeisberger party departed. Of the four, only Christian Gottlieb Henry returned with the Muskingum expedition. The remaining two Indians in the Heckewelder party, Renatus and Nicholas, met the Zeisberger party on the road and accompanied them back to the Muskingum. Christian Gottlieb's father, William Henry, was the "Vorsteher," or leader, of the Indian converts and was accompanied by his wife, Rachel, and their sixteen-year-old son Benjamin. Eight other converts can be identified positively as members of the Muskingum expedition: Johannes Thomas and his wife Catharina, with their daughters, Juliana and Gertraud; James and his wife Sophia, with their son Francis; and Brother John Adams.

Another meeting of the prospective Goshen group was held on August 6. Mortimer's entry explained the various activities of preparation for the converts' departure.

August 6th.
   The brethren who are to go to the Muskingum were called together and informed that we proposed setting off on the 15th. They said they would all be ready by that time. Sundry arrangements were made respecting the journey which will be performed chiefly by water. Many of them are now busily engaged in the wheat harvest, that they may have some provisions to take along

with them. [The Indians at Fairfield were among the first to plant and harvest wheat.] Most of the wild Indians can live on animal food alone, but ours are so accustomed to grain of different kinds, and to soups and vegetables, that they do not like to be without them for any length of time. According to the accounts that we have received, there will be excellent hunting on the other side of the lake.[20]

Final arrangements for the trip were now made, and the departing Indians began to dispose of their Fairfield property. Mortimer's diary is instructive and describes some of the transactions. He estimated that the value of their total improvements was between £200 and £300. One of the Brothers had just finished "a commodious two story house covered with shingles." His entry of July 31 notes the method of disposing of several other properties: "One brother presented his house to a friend, who in return gave him a cow; another exchanged his dwelling for a horse; a third sold his barn and threshing floor for eight dollars; and a fourth made his house, barn, wheat, and cornfields to another brother, on the condition that he would pay all his debts for him."[21]

Well before sunup on August 15, the little village began to stir. The August day promised to be typically warm and sultry. The Fairfield Indians who remained behind were again being separated from their beloved Brother David. Mortimer had preached a eulogy to Zeisberger's departure the previous evening and included one of the rare references to Susan Zeisberger.[22] He closed the entry with this note:

> He [Zeisberger] loved them all most tenderly and longed for nothing so much as that they might all know & love their Saviour. This, their venerable, faithful & much esteemed teacher & faithful father was now going to leave them, and the greater part of them would probably never see his face no more in this world. Their dear Sis. Susan had been for years their kind and affectionate mother. For our Saviour's sake she willingly came to live among them, out of love to them had suffered much, & with her husband had always taken a near & tender share in their welfare.[23]

The canoes were loaded. Promptly at noon they pushed away from the banks of the Thames at Fairfield. There were thirty-three converts, in seven canoes, plus the Zeisbergers and Mortimer. Several of the converts drove the horses along the banks of the river. The seventy-seven-year-old Zeisberger was making his last journey on behalf of the faithful.

Space does not permit a detailed description of the trip. Mortimer used forty-four pages of minute script to give a fascinating account of the events. They sailed down the Thames to Lake St. Clair, then down the Detroit River to the fort, arriving there on August 19, having covered 103 miles by water. The normal route over land and water was only sixty-two miles. They remained in Detroit until August 21, then moved nine miles down the Detroit River, camped overnight, and continued on the next morning. By August 26 they had entered Lake Erie and were camped near the River Rasin, now Monroe, Michigan. Mortimer gives us an interesting description of canoes and lake travel:

> By return of fair or rather still weather, we had nothing like a storm but a light breeze, such as at this season of the year would be very acceptable to every one on the land, [but it] so ruffles the surface of the lake that it cannot be navigated by canoes. This will be quite conceivable to any one that has seen the waves of the sea, (whose waters are heavier by being salt), and knows that a canoe is merely a hollowed tree, cut as to rest equally on & proceed swiftly through the water. (We have been informed that in some parts of Germany, canoes are called "Seelen Verkaufer" or "Sellers of the Soul"; a name which sufficiently implies the idea of danger in the use of them. They are only used on the rivers.)[24]

By September 1 the party had rounded the western end of Lake Erie and arrived at Sandusky Bay. Three days later they reached the mouth of the Pettquotting. The previous day, Nathaniel, the little infant son of Johannes and Catharina, died, a victim of the harsh wilderness travel. On September 3 they traveled the five miles down the Pettquotting and buried the tiny bundle in the cemetery of the old Pettquotting mission. Not one building was left in the village; all had been destroyed by the native Indians. Here they met Renatus coming back from the Muskingum and he joined the party.

On the morning of September 5, the mission party left the mouth of the river and continued along the southern shore of the lake, arriving at the Cuyahoga on the morning of September 11. Mortimer calculated that they had traveled 220 miles in nineteen days. At the Cuyahoga they found two families from Connecticut who had, a year earlier, settled on the present site of Cleveland. After an appropriate visit with the new settlers, they began the trip up the Cuyahoga, safe now from the vagaries of the lake. Mortimer explained the routine of a normal day (paraphrased here):

1. Arise at daybreak awakened by the Vorsteher, William Henry, our leader.
2. Early morning prayer service.
3. Young men go on the hunt till nine or ten o'clock, and women prepare the breakfast.
4. Eat breakfast.
5. Reenter the canoes and travel until five to six o'clock.

6. Prepare supper and the night's lodging. Within twenty or thirty minutes all families had a cooking fire and began preparing the supper meal.
7. Evening services and the congregational meeting to plan the next day.[25]

Mortimer closed the entry acknowledging that "Indians are everywhere at home in the woods."

On September 16 they proceeded up the Cuyahoga to within ten miles of the Cuyahoga "Carrying Place." That evening they were surprised to greet Nicholas, who was traveling north to meet them. He carried a dispatch from Heckewelder, on the Muskingum, who stated, "All is in order for your arrival." Nicholas came at a propitious moment. None of the party had ever been up the Cuyahoga, and while the passage had not been as horrendous as originally described by the native Indians, it had taken its toll on morale. The shallow water, large rocks, and fallen trees required considerable effort even to these native woodsmen. Nicholas provided that additional spark necessary to encourage them to continue the trek.

By September 20 they had arrived at the Carrying Place, now called the Portage Path and currently found on the Akron, Ohio, city maps. Here the Cuyahoga turns east, then north. They crossed eight miles of the portage and dropped down into the headwaters of the Muskingum. This section of the river (from here south to the Great Crossing Place) was known as the Tuscarawas or the "Tuscarabi," an old Wyandot word meaning "Open mouth of a stream." The large mouth of Sandy Creek joins the Tuscarawas at this location, thus the name.[26]

To both Indians and the white missionaries, the Great Crossing Place was a strategic location, a junction where several important Indian paths diverged and where numerous historic events occurred. It lay on the Great Trail from Fort Pitt to Detroit. The Salt Trail from the Mahoning River met the Muskingum Trail, which continued on to the Ohio River at present Marietta, Ohio. It was also the western terminus of the Beaver Trail from Fort McIntosh. Forty-eight years earlier, in 1750, Christopher Gist had passed the location on his exploration for the Ohio Company. Here had been the capital of the Delaware nation in 1758 and the home of their head chief, Shingas, and his brother, King Beaver. In 1761 Christian Frederick Post, a Moravian missionary, had built a cabin on the banks of the Tuscarawas near the Delaware village. The following year he returned with nineteen-year-old John Heckewelder to form a Christian mission, but it was aborted before the end of the year with both men fleeing for their lives. The disgruntled Delaware were preparing to join Pontiac and the other western Indians and drive the white settlers into the sea. It was the beginning of the Pontiac Uprising. In 1764 Colonel Bouquet, during his expedition against the Delaware and the

Shawnee, erected a storehouse near Post's old cabin site. During the Revolution in 1778, Fort Laurens was built at the same location and, finally, in 1795, became the northern line of the Greenville treaty.

South of the Great Crossing Place, as late as 1808, the river was still called the Muskingum.[27] Later, the full length became the Tuscarawas until its junction with White Woman's Creek (now the Walhonding) at Netawatwes's old village of Goschachgunk (Coshocton). From there, the two rivers form the present-day Muskingum.

Before beginning the last leg of the journey, Christian Gottlieb was dispatched with a letter to Heckewelder informing him of their arrival on the Tuscarawas. But there were new complications. The canoes were intentionally not brought across the Cuyahoga portage, but Mortimer failed to record the reason for this decision. On the headwaters of the Tuscarawas they could only find small trees that were not adaptable for building large canoes. Two small craft were made and strapped together to form a raft that was adequate to carry the large baggage. The rest of the party departed on September 26 on foot with backpacks, carrying some of the provisions and the small children. Nicodemus had brought a canoe for the missionaries.

The following day they lost another infant. According to the diary, he was called George. The names of the parents were not recorded, but Mortimer did note that "the grave was well-protected with logs and timbers to prevent its being opened by wolves."

They had now passed into country dense with heavy timber. At the evening camp on September 29, the Indians began to construct larger canoes, and with the first rays of daylight on the next day, they continued their work. They were back on the river by eleven o'clock. Mortimer described the last three days of the journey:

Oct. 1st.
   The banks of the river exhibited every token of fertility, in the appearance of the timber, the height and rankness of the weeds, and the abundance of grape-vine loaded with fruit, which as it were, offered us their ripened clusters to regale and refresh us. Those who went by land often found an abundance of honey in the trees. At times the bed of the river presented us with the diverting spectacles of thousands of fish of various kinds, while numerous flocks of geese, ducks & turkeys seemed to tell us that they had a particular attachment to the Muskingum. It ought to be noticed however, that this was the most plentiful season of the year for game.
   The 3rd. We passed the Tuscarabi, properly so called, and not far from thence the place where Fort Lawrence (Laurens) formerly stood. [Unknowingly they had also just passed the site of the Christian Post and John Heckewelder mission cabin in 1762.]

The 4th. was the last day of our journey. It rained hard in the morning, but the sun shone bright when we reached Schoenbrunn at 1 o'clock in the afternoon. We felt glad and thankful that our Saviour had brought us safely to the place of our destination.

Thus after a period of about 17 years, since the Indian congregation was obliged to leave the Muskingum, a small part of the remainder of them is going to form a new settlement there again. . . .

Upon the whole, we are of the opinion, that no combination of circumstances more favorable than the present, can with propriety be looked for; to induce the making of vigorous attempts to spread the ever blessed gospel of our Redeemer far and wide among the Indian nations. Throughout the continent of North America this is a time of profound peace.[28]

~~~~~

Part 2
The Goshen Mission Years
1798–1821

〜〜〜

SEVEN

The Goshen Mission

After fifty-one days of toilsome struggle and considerable risk, the small flotilla of canoes carrying thirty-one Indian converts arrived at their destination. They came ashore at the site of the old Schoenbrunn village, camping there for several days as Mortimer traveled to Gnadenhutten to discuss the available food supply with Heckewelder. "Brother Heckewelder," Mortimer wrote, "offered us all the present relief in his power."

On October 7, 1798, following the usual morning service, the entire contingent traveled the short distance to the proposed site of the new mission. Mortimer describes the day's activity.

> All the brn. went to the place which had been designated as most suitable for a town to be built on. The situation was approved by all present. It will, we believe, prove healthy & pleasant, and as convenient as could be chosen. It lies on a level highground on the W. side of the river, about 1-3/4 miles S.E. of the place where formerly New Schoenbrunn stood, & half a mile distant from our S. & W. lines. Nearly opposite to the intended town is Zeisberger island, so named by the surveyor who laid off the tract last year, according to the act of Congress [see page 96]. The main street will be made parallel with the River at a distance of 25 yards.[1]

The following day they moved the baggage to the new location and began to lay out the town. Mortimer recounts the procedure. "The 9th the town was laid out, & divided into lots 3 rods [49.5 feet] in front. The street is 5 rods [82.5 feet] wide. The Indian brn. went immediately to work to cut down the high timber and thick underwood with which the place is covered. Our land here, and the adjacent country, has acquired such a wild appearance since we left in the year 1781, that we can hardly know it again."[2]

Early on the morning of October 10, the Indian Brethren built a temporary dwelling for the Zeisbergers. These huts were crude, hastily built structures, but Mortimer notes in his diary, "Such a temporary habitation is very acceptable after a long peregrination in the wilderness; it, however, is but a poor defense against the winter's cold."[3] Thanks to John Heckewelder, David and Susan Zeisberger would not spend the winter, like most of the converts would, in their temporary shelter.

As we have seen, Heckewelder left the mission field twelve years before Zeisberger returned to Goshen. In 1786, during the converts' sojourn at Pilgerruh, he and his family returned to Bethlehem. Heckewelder was never again assigned to serve as a permanent missionary. During the intervening years, he visited Zeisberger three times—once at New Salem on the Pettquotting in 1789 and then at Fairfield in 1793. The last meeting, again at Fairfield, in 1798, was just prior to their move to the Muskingum. Heckewelder was now living at the site of old Gnadenhutten mission and working as a land agent for Godfrey Haga, a prominent and wealthy Philadelphia Moravian. He also served as the agent for the Society of the United Brethren for the Propagating of the Gospel Among the Heathen."[4]

Heckewelder became the first resident and founder of the new white settlement. Gnadenhutten was the key to an ingenious scheme hatched back in Bethlehem. Located on a broad alluvial plain on the high bank above the Muskingum River, the new site was within a block of the former Gnadenhutten mission. Populated by friendly white Moravians from the eastern settlements, the new settlement was to be the trading outlet for the Indian goods manufactured at the new Goshen mission. Here the Indians would trade their furs, meats, baskets, and other goods for the eastern products so essential to their survival. Goshen, would then become the training ground for white missionaries and Indian Native Helpers, thus providing seed congregations for additional missions to the west in the heart of the Indian country. Zeisberger at Goshen and Heckewelder at Gnadenhutten would direct operations in each settlement.

After returning to the Muskingum in 1798 with William Edwards and the party of six converts, Heckewelder remained at Gnadenhutten awaiting the new congregation's arrival. He planned well for the Goshen move and now would become a valuable adjunct to the critical needs of the thirty-one Christian converts. At Gnadenhutten he accumulated a small quantity of corn, pumpkins, and turnips. He also arranged to build a permanent and secure log cabin for the Zeisbergers, requisitioning Johann Schmick and the Colver brothers, Nathaniel and John, from Nazareth, Pennsylvania, to erect the cabin. The crew began work ten days after the converts arrived, and by October 19 they raised the new house. The roof was added and the building was completed by November 3.

JOHN ADAMS, *President of the United States of America,*

To all to whom these presents shall come, Greeting:

Know ye, *That in pursuance of the act of Congress passed on the first day of June 1796, entitled "An Act "regulating the grants of Land appropriated for Military services, and for the society of the United Brethren for "propagating the gospel among the Heathen;" and of the several acts supplementary thereto passed on the second day of March 1799, and on the eleventh day of February and first of March 1800, there is granted unto John Heckewelder*

a certain tract of land estimated to contain Three Thousand eight Hundred nineteen and six tenths acres being the second quarter of the eighth Township in the second Range of the tract appropriated for satisfying Warrants for Military services;

surveyed and located in pursuance of the acts above recited — To have and to hold the said described tract of land, with the appurtenances thereof unto the said John Heckewelder, and to his heirs and assigns forever, subject to the conditions, restrictions and provisions contained in the said recited acts.

In Witness *whereof, the said* **John Adams,** *President of the United States of America, hath caused the Seal of the said United States to be hereunto affixed, and signed the same with his hand, at the City of Philadelphia the eighth day of March in the year of our Lord 1800 ; and of the Independence of the United States of America the twenty fourth.*

John Adams

By the President,

Timothy Pickering Secretary of State.

This original land patent signed by President John Adams, March 28, 1800, was for one of the numerous plots of land owned by the Moravian merchant Godfrey Haga, a wealthy Philadelphia land speculator. John Heckewelder acted as Haga's on-site real estate agent and held his power of attorney, so the patent was in Heckewelder's name. This plot lay immediately west of New Philadelphia, and included a portion on both sides of the Tuscarawas River.

Upon the outset of the Goshen mission, the Ohio country was a virgin wilderness inhabited by small and scattered bands of native Indians. The only exceptions were an occasional English and French trader and a ten-mile-wide strip of white-occupied land along the western shores of the Ohio River. The nearest white settlement to the new mission was at Buffalo Creek in Pennsylvania. Mortimer, writing at Goshen in October 1798, described the neighborhood.

The 17th.

In these days some of the Indian brethren were employed in opening anew the old path thither [to Gnadenhutten] which was in many places hardly discernible. Three brn. set off today for Charleston on Buffalo Creek to get guns repaired & see if provisions could be procured from there. Charleston, the nearest town to us, is about 65 miles distance from here [now Wellsburg, West Virginia]. The settlements of the white people extend ten miles from thence westward—so that our nearest neighbors (the brethren at Gnadenhutten excepted) are about 55 miles distant.[5]

However, within six months Georgetown, another white settlement along the Ohio River, was also discovered as an additional supply center. There they had successfully secured a blacksmith for gun repairs.[6] These two communities represented the limits of white penetration and served for a number of years as supply bases for Goshen.

As the Christian converts began their new settlement on the Muskingum, the Brethren in Bethlehem were dreaming up plans for Goshen. Both Zeisberger and the Provincial Helpers' Conference believed that they were on the threshold of a great expansion of the missionary movement. Using Goshen and Fairfield as seedbeds and field bases of operations, they hoped to establish additional Christian missions farther west, near the heart of the Indian population.

Just before the close of the century, most of the more receptive tribes, particularly the Ottawas (Zeisberger's friendly Tawa), were located along the mouth of the Sandusky. Along the Miami (now the Maumee) were several villages of Ojibwa (Zeisberger's Chippewa), who also occupied their old homeland on the Clinton River north of Detroit. Although a village of Munsee Delaware lived near the former site of New Salem on the Pettquotting, most of their Delaware cousins lived on the White River in Indiana (near the site of present Anderson, Indiana). They called their village Woapikamikunk. The majority of the more hostile Indian population lived at the old site of Gigeyunk (now Fort Wayne, Indiana). These were the Miami, Shawnee, and a few small bands of Delaware. A tentative peace returned to the Ohio country following the Treaty of Greenville, but among the native tribes there was much confusion, indecision, and bitter resentment against the harsh terms they were forced to accept at Greenville.

While future expansion of the Indian missionary movement lay in those widely dispersed Indian tribes many miles to the west, the real threat to the Goshen mission lay just a few miles to the east. With thousands of acres of prime Ohio land now open for settlement, large groups of settlers began to pour across the river into this new territory. The small Indian mission at Goshen lay in the path of this invasion.

Through Heckewelder's urging, white Moravians living at Lititz, Nazareth, Bethlehem, and other Moravian communities were encouraged to emigrate westward to the Ohio country. The expansive mind of John Heckewelder was dreaming of a new Bethlehem on the Muskingum. These Pennsylvania immigrants settled on the Moravian tract at the site of old Gnadenhutten. The new village about to emerge on the Muskingum plains was only a microcosm of the white invasion. However, it does provide evidence of the speed and volume of white westward immigration to Ohio. At the end of 1799 there were twenty-five whites living at Gnadenhutten, while fifty Indian converts lived at Goshen. Five years later, in 1804, the Gnadenhutten population had grown to 159 residents, and immediately across the river was the rapidly growing little Moravian settlement of Beersheba. At the same time thirty-seven Christian Indians were living at Goshen.

The settlers at Gnadenhutten and Beersheba were all Moravians and were friendly, well-known faces to the missionaries at Goshen. Furthermore, they understood and were supportive of the missionary program. But there were soon to be other settlers, strangers to Zeisberger and Mortimer. How would they react to an Indian mission at their doorstep? Mortimer provides us with three entries in 1803 and another in 1804 in which he expressed his concern.

August 27th.
Mr. Kneisley [John Knisely], the owner of a large tract of land adjoining ours to the northward, and ten other persons, gave us a friendly call on their way up the river & expressed their desire to attend our divine service when they came to settle in our neighborhood—to which we made them heartily welcome. We sincerely hope that we may find these people as well-disposed to our settlement as our worthy neighbors to the southward [Gnadenhutten].[7]

October 27th.
Mr. Kneisley [Knisely] passed through here with about thirty persons who designed to settle on the section of land which borders on ours to the north. By permission they cut a wagon road through our premises to enter into that which goes from here to Gnadenhutten.[8]

November 26th.
Mr. Wells from Somerset [Pennsylvania] passed through here on his way up-river in order to lay out a town on Mr. Kneisley's land about 3 miles from here. *We shall have much reason to be thankful if the projected improvements there do not become a source of trouble to us.*[9] [Emphasis added]

Sunday June 10th [1804].
The public preaching by Br. Mortimer from Luke 14:16 etc. was attended by more white people than Indians. About fifty persons are come this spring to settle in & near the town of New Philadelphia, which is only three miles from here.[10]

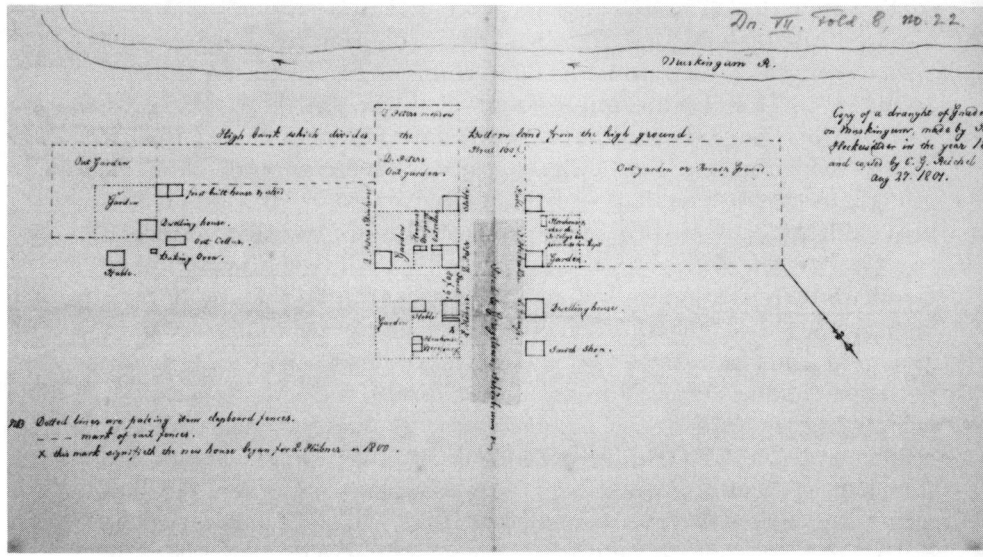

This map of Gnadenhutten was drawn by John Heckewelder in 1800, two years after its founding. At that time there were fifty people living at the village. The street in the center of the print is now called Main Street; perpendicular to it is Cherry Street. Ignatius, the Christian convert and master builder, constructed the first combination church and parsonage in the village in 1800, which is labeled as the Huebner dwelling on the left side of Main Street in the center of the map. Rev. Louis Huebner was the first pastor at Gnadenhutten.

Mortimer had a genuine reason to be concerned. These settlers at New Philadelphia would eventually prove to be a serious threat to the missionary program.

Meanwhile, the year 1798 rapidly came to a close, and David and Susan Zeisberger were comfortably installed in their new quarters. With the essential organization now in place and the daily routine of the Goshen mission established, Mortimer returned with Heckewelder to Bethlehem for the winter. He left the village on November 1, picked up Heckewelder at Gnadenhutten, and on November 4 headed down the Charleston trail for Pittsburgh, then on to Bethlehem. Mortimer spent the winter at the Moravian headquarters searching for a "helpmeet." He married Bethiah Warner, and on April 24 they began the return journey to Goshen with the missionaries Oppelt and Jungmann and their wives. After an interesting but fatiguing trip of 410 miles, recorded on forty diary pages, they arrived back in Goshen on June 14, 1799. On this return trip, they hired a group of men to cut a wagon road to Goshen from Georgetown, then considered the major source of supply for the mission.[11]

For the next thirteen years, Benjamin Mortimer was the guiding light, the stalwart soldier, the literate diarist, and the sympathetic listener for the Indian congregation at Goshen. Zeisberger had just celebrated his seventy-eighth birthday. By early nineteenth-century standards, he was an ancient man. However, despite his age, he continued, until several months before his death in 1808, to maintain an active schedule—always intimately involved in the mission's activity. Because of his advanced age, Zeisberger needed an active and capable assistant. The appointment of Benjamin Mortimer the previous May was the wise and perceptive choice of the Bethlehem fathers. Unfortunately, Mortimer is seldom recognized among Moravian scholars, always overshadowed by the towering presence of his mentor. It was Mortimer who held the Goshen mission together following Zeisberger's death, even making considerable progress among the mission converts.

Mortimer's diaries are among the most interesting, insightful, and introspective of all those of the Moravian missionaries. The diaries, kept for thirteen years, if printed would be equivalent to several large volumes. They described the activities of the mission, covering many subjects: religious activities; the growing, hunting and harvesting of food; building construction; conducting schools; developing crafts; health care and providing for the sick; relations with their white and native neighbors; the seemingly never-ending problems with liquor; and finally such interesting subjects as meteorites, earthquakes, snakes, and problems with the village dogs.

It is not possible in this short narrative to relate in great detail the regular daily events over the twenty-three-year life of the Goshen mission. However, those years may be divided into a number of rather neat categories. The reader can compare these different periods to the annual population statistics shown in appendixes B and C. Using this population profile we can trace the ebb and flow of the internal and external forces affecting mission life. We can also account for the annual fluctuation in the number of converts and generally follow the historical pattern of the mission.

There were four major events that changed the population at Goshen. Two were part of the overall plan for expanding the mission program, and one was the result of the failure of these plans. The fourth event was the result of a wrenching internal decision.

Following the signing of the Greenville treaty in 1795, most of the native Delaware settled on the White River in the Indiana Territory. Many of those natives were apostates and former members of a Zeisberger mission. They became, in the minds of the church leaders at Bethlehem, a fertile field for redemption. In an entry on September 3, 1799, Mortimer (with Zeisberger's assistance) calculated that there were 232 former converts living among the natives in the wilderness—most of these at the White River villages.[12] The following year, on April 14, the converts received a large wampum belt at Goshen, sent by the Delaware head chief Tedpachxit, with an invitation suggesting that the Christian Indians at Goshen permanently move their village to the White River.[13]

It was a warm, friendly greeting and while Zeisberger had no intention of moving to the White River area, he knew their response must be skillfully couched in typical Indian diplomatic language. He also was aware that the invitation could play into Bethlehem's overall plans for the expansion of the mission program. Both Tedpachxit's invitation and the Goshen Christian Indians' response are classic examples of the poetic nature of Indian diplomacy. Mortimer records the messages along with his own comments.

"My Friend!*

We have received your message [this was the second request of a similar nature sent to Goshen], and our chief and great captain, our warriors and young men, our women and children, were all rejoiced thereat. The reason why we did no sooner send you another was, because my people were not at home. As soon as they returned, I made it known to them, and they were all glad to hear it.

My Friend!

We have a large district of country that belongs to us; therefore I take Gelelemend (my brother William Henry),+ and your friends softly by the hand, and lift you up, and place you here near to me on the Woapikamikunk."

*The Delaware word signifies *relation* as well as *friend*.

+The speeches of the Indians are often addressed to one person in particular when all the inhabitants of the town in which he lives are meant to be included. Our brother Willm. Henry was very properly named in this occasion, as he was formerly a Delaware chief. He resigned his office merely in order to live with the Indian believing congn., & has since refused to resume it again agreeable to the request of the tribe to which he belongs.[14]

Mortimer also noted that the message was accompanied "according to custom, with a long and beautiful string of wampum."

There was almost unanimous agreement among the Goshen converts to give an immediate favorable response to the request, despite their general satisfaction with the situation at Goshen. Mortimer noted one of the Native Helpers' comments, "How can our friends on the Woapikamikunk believe, or learn to understand the gospel unless it is preached to them? To this end, no message sent to them or anything else will suffice, but

teachers go to live among them and preach to them from day to day."
Zeisberger, in order to gain time, proposed to defer the answer until he
could communicate with the elders at Bethlehem. In the meantime they
drafted the following response, which was returned by the messenger
two days after he arrived at the village.

> My Friend!
> When I saw my friend arrive in this place where I live, & beheld his face, I
> was rejoiced, and felt hope from him in my heart. Then I thought also on
> what our late chief Netawatwes had said to us formerly, when we lived on the
> Susquehanna. And as I heard, my friend, that you take me softly by the hand,
> lift me up, and place me near to you on the Woapikamikunk, I was glad.
> My Friend!
> I let you know that I live here on my own land. But yet I accept your words.
> I cannot however, my friend, immediately rise up. I must first make your
> words known to my brother over the lake, who lives far off from me. When I
> receive his answer I will let you know in what manner I have made myself
> ready. How long it will be before I can send you word again, I cannot say.
> Perhaps it will be next spring.
> My Friend!
> From this day forward, I will always think of you with pleasure, as you do
> of me.[15]

THE WHITE RIVER MISSION, 1801–1806

Tedpachxit's invitation to Goshen gave the elders at Bethlehem precisely the opening they needed to expand their missionary program on
the White River. They promptly responded to the call. As early as
September 19, 1800, Zeisberger received word at Goshen of the appointment of John Peter Kluge and Abraham Luckenbach as new missionaries to serve the proposed mission. They both arrived at Goshen on
November 18 with plans to stay through the winter, studying for their
new missionary work with Zeisberger. The thirty-three-year-old Kluge
had served for six years in Surinam, Dutch Guiana, among the Arawak
Indians. The twenty-three-year-old Luckenbach was a novice. Neither
spoke a word of Delaware nor had any knowledge of the American Indians. It was a combination designed for disaster. On March 24 of the
following year, they and thirteen of Zeisberger's most valued converts departed in five large canoes.

The population chart (appendix B) shows a reduction of seventeen
communicants during the year 1801. Thirteen of these were the departing members of the White River contingent, and four left Goshen for

White River by the end of the year. The communicants were to be the heart of any Christian mission. They were the tenacious and tough Christians who provided the leadership, strength, and respect that the missionaries needed to keep the wayward and undecided on the beaten path. Among those communicants accompanying the missionaries to the White River were: Johannes Thomas and his wife, Catharina; Jacob Pemahealend (Zeisberger's first baptism at Goshen) and his wife, Mary; and the widow Abigail. But finally, and by far the most important loss, was Josua, Jr., who was to serve as the new mission's interpreter.[16]

Kluge and Luckenbach stayed at White River for five years and four months. They spent most of that time living in mortal fear for their lives. They were threatened almost daily with death. For sixty years, and with more than thirty separate missions, the Moravians had lived with the Indians of North America. Except for ten white mission helpers who were massacred at Gnadenhutten on the Mahoning in 1755, none of the white missionaries was ever molested or harmed. The Kluges and Abraham Luckenbach came as close as any. During most of their time on the White River, they suffered indescribable hardship and witnessed unspeakable and terrifying events. By the end of 1805 there remained only nine converts at the White River mission—most of them old women, widows, and children. Josua was the last man in the congregation. During the following year, 1806, the Kluges and Luckenbach witnessed the death of their old friend, Chief Tedpachxit, who had initially invited them to the area. He was brought to their little village, tomahawked by his own son, and thrown half-alive on "a pillar of fire" built in the center of the town. Their beloved Josua was then seized and several days later suffered the same fate, as did Anna Caritas, a faithful old convert who had lived among the congregation almost all of her life.[17]

Unfortunately, the missionaries had arrived just when the Delaware were under the spell of Tenskwatawa, "The Prophet," brother of Tecumseh. These were events that sprung from his new vision of the Shawnee God, "The Master of Life," given to him while in a drunken trance. They eventually contributed to the War of 1812 on the western frontier. The black sun and witchcraft killings would continue for several years. It was no time for white men to be living among the native Indians.[18] Following the death of Josua in March 1806, Kluge appealed to Bethlehem to abandon the mission. On receipt of their approval, the missionaries left the White River, returning the following September to Bethlehem. The loyal converts who had left Goshen with high expectations on that brisk March day in 1801 had now become apostates, fading into the native population, lost forever to the missionary program.

THE PETTQUOTTING SECOND EXPERIENCE, 1804–1809

While Kluge and Luckenbach were struggling to hold the White River mission together, a similar mission project was being planned for the Pettquotting River. The Bethlehem elders had authorized the Fairfield mission to attempt another settlement near the site of Zeisberger's old mission at New Salem.[19] Most of the seed converts for this new mission were to come from Fairfield, and a few from Goshen. However, Zeisberger and Mortimer had been entrusted to train one of the new missionaries. On May 15, 1802, Johann Benjamin Haven arrived at Goshen to begin his training. At the same time, Gottfried Oppelt, now on his way to Fairfield, was appointed to be the head missionary at Pettquotting.

During the almost two years he spent at Goshen, Haven taught the mission school and gained some proficiency in the Delaware language. Among other chores, he placed a tombstone on William Edwards's grave, a rare event for an Indian mission cemetery. Haven left Goshen for his new assignment at Pettquotting on May 2, 1804, arriving a few days later. Awaiting the arrival of new congregation, Haven spent some time with the local French trader who insisted on selling liquor to the local natives. The new missionary, however, quickly became disgusted with the confusion and combative atmosphere of the local Munsee village, whose residents were frequently under the influence of the French trader's liquor. He crossed the river, traveled several miles downstream, and built himself a small bark hut in which to await Oppelt's arrival.

The official Bethlehem plan called for the new congregation to leave Fairfield early in the spring. But Oppelt encountered some resistance among his converts, who preferred to remain at Fairfield. They did not depart from the village until April 28, with thirty-six Indians, eight canoes, nineteen cows, and eight horses. It was an excruciatingly slow seventy-day journey, vividly described by Oppelt, the new head missionary and one of the few Moravian missionaries on the North American continent to write his diaries in the first person. It is a lively journal full of interesting items, frequent complaints, and surprisingly frank personal comments. The new congregation arrived at the proposed site on June 9, 1804, where they met Haven, who had been patiently waiting for over a month.

The founding of the Pettquotting mission again diminished the population at Goshen. Mortimer's diary entry of August 14, 1804, noted that ten converts had left to reside at the new mission. His year-end summary entry for 1804 recorded a total of fourteen residents moving to Pettquotting during the year (see appendix B, note b).

But just thirteen months after Oppelt and his Indian congregation arrived at the mission site, Mortimer, at Goshen, recorded another seemingly innocuous entry into the Goshen diary. "23rd. [July 1805] By Mr. Flemming [a trader], who arrived here yesterday from Pettquotting we had an opportunity of sending [letters] to our brn. there. As Mr. Flemming was present at the late Indian treaty on the Miami [Maumee River] he could give us some account of the transaction there."[20]

What Mr. Flemming told the Goshen missionaries is not recorded, but apparently it was very little. What occurred on the Miami, however, was an earth-shattering decision, at least to the missionary program on the Pettquotting. The treaty, signed at Fort Industry on the west bank of the Maumee (present Toledo, Ohio), provided for the sale of almost three million acres of land to the government of the United States.[21] This was the first major Indian concession after Greenville in 1795. At the meeting on July 4, 1805, the Ottawas (Tawa), Wyandot, Delaware, Chippewa, Shawnee, and the Pottawatami agreed to sell to the American commissioners a massive chunk of land running west from the Tuscarawas branch of the Muskingum to the mouth of the Maumee near Sandusky, including what was known as the Fire Lands (now the counties of Erie and Huron). Within the Fire Lands was the site of the Pettquotting mission. Unlike Goshen, no government grants protected the Pettquotting mission from purchases by white settlers. It took four years before the sale of the land around the mission became known to the missionaries; nevertheless, the Fort Industry treaty marked the beginning of the end for Pettquotting.

While the Kluges and young Abraham Luckenbach were fending off the machinations of Tecumseh's brother, The Prophet, and the Oppelts and Johann Haven were beginning their Pettquotting experience, an event occurred in Goshen that literally tore the mission apart, striking at the very roots of Zeisberger's and Mortimer's Christian philosophy. On the evening of March 30, 1805, Henry, the rebellious and unmanageable young son of Ignatius and Christina, committed suicide by drinking poison.[22] This was an uncommon method of suicide. It is evident through Indian literature that poisoning was not unusual among Indians and was frequently used to destroy an enemy, but it was seldom self-inflicted.

With possibly the exception of William Henry, Ignatius and Christina were the most respected and loyal converts among the congregation at Goshen. Ignatius had been baptized by Zeisberger at Schoenbrunn on January 6, 1773, and Christina had been baptized at Gnadenhutten by Schmick on the same day one year later. For thirty-two years, both Indians had remained loyal to Zeisberger and the mission program. During that time they had moved ten times. Never once had they left Zeisberger's side. Ignatius and Christina lived a life that represented everything Zeisberger preached, everything he envisioned for the converted native— they were industrious, hard working, moral, sober, and fully committed to the Savior. Skilled in log construction, Ignatius was more than a good carpenter; he was a master builder and an expert husbandman. His wife, Christina, was a loving and caring mother. Both were communicants and for many years members of the Helpers' Conference. But when Henry died, Zeisberger became intractable and unforgiving and refused to permit the young man to be buried in the mission cemetery. Henry had, in Zeisberger's mind, committed an unforgivable sin. The day following the suicide, his grieving and heartbroken parents buried the body of their son in the hills behind the village, without a Christian burial and without their beloved David in attendance.[23]

The memories of those days with young Henry must have flooded back. It was twenty-one years since Zeisberger stood by the side of his assistant, William Edwards, and watched him baptize this infant son of Ignatius and Christina. Who could forget that cold, blustery February evening on the banks of the Clinton River at New Gnadenhutten? During those years, as they moved from mission to mission, he had watched the growing child become a young adult, observing the many perplexing problems experienced by the distraught father as he tried to cope with this exasperating teenager, his firstborn son. Zeisberger had seen Ignatius return from a three-week search for the wayward boy, who at seventeen was roaming the forest with his native Indian friends. Even the exasperated Mortimer had followed Henry's three marriages, only to see him return to the village each time without his new wife. On the night of March 30, 1805, he returned for the last time. As Mortimer described it, he killed himself "in a fit of refractory disobedience." Mortimer further noted, "Nothing like this has ever before occurred in an Indian congregation." In the next six months, the Goshen mission began to disintegrate.

Up to the time of Henry's death, the mission had been singularly free from problems with liquor and drunkenness. Constantly on the alert and frequently admonishing the congregation concerning the prohibition against drinking, the missionary's efforts had been effective. Only minor incidents involving traders and native Indians were recorded as violations against their strict rules. On May 31, 1801, Mortimer wrote "it had been almost a year since they had experienced any drunkenness." Only one episode occurred in 1803, another in 1804. Both of these involved Indians but none of the Goshen congregation.

It may have been sheer coincidence, but beginning on April 12, just thirteen days following Henry's death, two men began to appear frequently in the Goshen mission diaries. They were merchants—a David Pfautz and a Mr. Shane—living near New Philadelphia. They sold liquor (among other products) and became, in the next year, villainous characters in the eyes of Benjamin Mortimer and many of the white citizens of the community.

The series of events began on April 8, 1805, just prior to the Easter weekend, four days before Zeisberger's eighty-fourth birthday and nine days after Henry's death. Ignatius and his family served notice; they planned to leave Goshen in the near future. Three days later, on Maundy Thursday, the missionaries held the regular communion and lovefeast. Mortimer ominously noted: "Four of our brethren and sisters, the near relations of the late Henry, were not present with us." The next day, April 12, Good Friday, began as usual. Mortimer described the activities: "Good-Friday 12th. Yesterday and today, in six meetings, we read together the history of our Saviour's passion. Late at night the full half of the adult inhabitants here got intoxicated with whiskey, which they had procured from our new neighbors, the Misters Pfautz & Shane of New Philadelphia. This drinking was continued throughout the greater part of the next day so that we could have no lovefeast."[24]

The following day was Easter morning. They held their usual sunrise services "partly in the church and partly in the cemetery." Less than one-half of the normal congregation was present. The previous night, the other members had fled to their nearby sugar camps and continued their drinking. By noon on Easter morning, they returned to the village—all roaring drunk. One person was brandishing a tomahawk and threatening to kill Kaschates before sundown. Mortimer wrote, "Fortunately, the latter was sober and prudently retired with his family down the river."[25]

Two days following the Easter brouhaha, Zeisberger had a long and intimate conversation with Ignatius who, with his family and friends, was responsible for the disturbance. The family commanded such influence in the village that only five of the communicants had not participated in the debacle. Ignatius freely admitted his culpability and attributed his actions to the death of his son, but he felt no sense of remorse. Added to this already melancholy scene was the death of Abel, a brilliant but controversial convert, on April 22.[26]

On May 2 the broken-hearted Ignatius and his family left Goshen to live at the new Pettquotting mission. Mortimer could not bring himself to admit that Ignatius was responsible for the late indiscretions. He wrote this entry the day of his departure. "2nd. [May] Ignatius also set off for Pettquotting. He appeared much cast down, & took to himself all the blame of the late disturbances here. We believe, however, that they are principally to be attributed to his wife and one of his daughters. Br. Zeisberger endeavored to revive his drooping spirits by assuring him that there was still help for him if he sought it in the right way of our Saviour."[27]

Between the date of his departure and July 25, 1805, Ignatius returned twice to Goshen, each time with the mail from Pettquotting. Both were short visits, and there appears to have been no reconciliation. There would be another short visit on July 11, 1806, then another one week before he came home to Goshen to die.[28] The incident is perhaps the most tragic event in the history of the Goshen mission and presents a classic example of the sometimes futile attempts to acculturate native Americans. The chasm between Zeisberger and Ignatius was just too wide to bridge. Mortimer indicated in his obituary of Ignatius on September 12, 1806, that a rapprochement did occur, but one wonders if this was not written for the folks back in Bethlehem.

The departure of Ignatius and his family on May 2, 1805, did not, however, end the incidents of drunkenness at the village and the embitterment over the burial of Henry. The situation deteriorated even further. The second Sunday subsequent to the family's departure Mortimer recorded the following entry.

Sunday, [May] 19th.
    Br. Zeisberger spoke in these days privately with some of our people concerning their late highly unbecoming behaviour, but we have to lament that they discover as yet no tokens of penitence. In the afternoon some of them went to Pfautz and Shane's and got drunk. A scene followed in the evening the like of which had perhaps never before been known in an Indian congn., but of which we forebear [*sic*] giving any particular description. During the whole night we could hardly obtain any sleep. Our hearts were filled with grief, we could only sigh to our Saviour, and implore his aid and the guardianship of his holy angels.[29]

An exhausted Zeisberger was approaching the end of his patience. He gave the Brethren an ultimatum. Mortimer explained:

[May] 20th.
    Early, Wm. Henry (the only man here who had remained sober) came to Br. Zeisberger quite disheartened. He said it would be better that they all went away from here, than that they should continue to grieve us any longer with their wicked life. . . .
    At noon, the majority of the upgrown inhabitants here, assembled by appointment in the house of Wm. Henry. Br. Zeisberger told them that their behaviour for some time past, had been the worst that he had ever seen among the Indians. That they were unworthy that ministers should any longer live among them.[30]

The strain of the last few months began to affect the old man's health. Desperately sad and disillusioned, Zeisberger took to his bed for days at a time. By June 23 he was sufficiently recovered to conduct the Sunday morning service. Mortimer gives us a graphic picture of the situation.

> *[June] 23rd.*
> Our dear Br. Zeisberger was so far recovered from his late severe indisposition, as to be able to keep the meeting of the congn. which he did with a heavy heart. He remarked afterwards, that he felt no more disposed to weep over, than to speak to them. To Br. Zeisberger, who had witnessed for a long succession of years, very blessed times among the Indians, it must be peculiarly distressing, that the gospel at present meets with so poor a reception everywhere among them & that even here, nearly half of our small congn. has lately deserted us. The number of Ind. communicants is now only five.[31]

Time, of course, moderated disagreements, and as the days and months passed, the incidents of drunkenness became less frequent. But mission life never returned to the sanguine days before Henry's death.

PETTQUOTTING ABANDONED, 1806-1809

Back on the Pettquotting, Oppelt and Haven were having modest success. They closed 1806 with a total of sixty-nine villagers—sixty-two were baptized, including eighteen communicants, and seven unbaptized natives. Oppelt was a unique character. From his departure at Fairfield to his final leave-taking at Pettquotting, his diaries and letters back to Bethlehem were filled with a steady stream of childlike complaints, criticisms, and denunciations. No one was spared. The Indian Brethren were shiftless and lazy and refused to help either him or his wife. He despised his miserable life-style and complained of overwork. There was a constant series of critical comments against Haven, while at the same time Haven's letters to Loskiel, back in Bethlehem, were filled with great tenderness and respect for the Oppelts. When the Mortimers tried to give Oppelt advice, he complained of the easy life they led at Goshen and suggested Mortimer replace him at Pettquotting. In a November 6, 1806, letter to Loskiel, he caustically observed that "he could manage as well as Zeisberger" if he had as little work to do as they did at Goshen. In the same letter Susan Zeisberger's "easy" life at Goshen also became the subject of his envy: "Concerning Sis. Zeisberger, she had nothing else to do than to take care of her small household, where on the other hand, my wife with her big household as she surely had to cook 4 to 5 times as much, bake, wash, & mind her 3 children to tend & now expects the 4th."[32]

Bethlehem finally recalled him, but not before he engaged in another heated dispute with his replacement, Christian Frederick Denke, assistant to Johannes Schnell at Fairfield. The Oppelts left Pettquotting on June 1, 1807, and returned to the Bethlehem settlement. Within three years, however, he would be back on the Muskingum in a most unusual capacity.

Denke was well known at Goshen. He had visited the mission for three months in 1800 before leaving for service in Fairfield. During this interim, he had spent five unsuccessful and frustrating years among the Chippewa, baptizing not even one convert. At the time of his new appointment to Pettquotting, he had reluctantly given up the mission among the Chippewa and was back at Fairfield assisting Schnell. But Denke's hard-luck experience among the Chippewa followed him to the Pettquotting. On April 25, 1809, just one month short of two years, he was forced to abandon the mission. Like the Chippewa years, the conditions were beyond his control. The results of the Fort Industry treaty in 1805 were beginning to take effect and the white settlers were buying land near the mission. By the beginning of 1809, the mission land proper had been sold. The first settlers arrived on April 18. Eight days later Denke abandoned the village and returned to Fairfield with most of the Pettquotting congregation.

Haven, his assistant, had been instructed to return to Goshen. On May 12, he arrived back on the Muskingum accompanied by Joachim and his interesting and provocative wife, Anna Maria. Within twenty-four days, Anna Maria died.[33] Some of the remaining converts from Pettquotting straggled into Goshen over the next several months. Mortimer's Goshen diary entry on July 30, 1809, included this comment: "30th. In the afternoon Boaz, Nicodemus, David & others, lately belonging to the Pettquotting congn. and also a number of heathen Indians, arrived here. We sighed to our Lord that he would cause the stay of these people here to be a blessing to them."[34]

Unfortunately, the Brethren coming from Pettquotting had little effect on the Goshen population or on the internal operations of the mission. None of these returning members of the Pettquotting congregation was a Native Helper. Both Boaz and David, with their families, left the mission before the close of 1809 (see appendix B, note d). By then, more than a year had passed since Zeisberger's death. Mortimer had made the transition and was now fully in charge as the head missionary, with Johann Haven as his assistant.

EIGHT

Goshen Mission Life
An Overview

During his thirteen years at the Goshen mission, Benjamin Mortimer wrote over eight hundred pages of diary manuscripts. Beyond the broad major historical events occurring at the small villages, the record is filled with the routine of daily mission life. A careful study reveals the uniqueness of the experience and gives the reader a flavor of what it meant to live in a Moravian Christian mission.

When David Zeisberger arrived in the Muskingum valley on October 4, 1798, he was celebrating his fiftieth year in the mission service. With minor exceptions, from the Shamokin mission in 1748 where he served as an assistant to Martin Mack to his last mission at Goshen on the banks of the Muskingum, he lived those fifty years among the Christian Indians and, like all of his fellow Moravian missionaries, served without any personal compensation.[1] During that period, he developed a style of operation which, over the years, he altered and perfected to meet the changing conditions. Unlike most of the early Protestant Christian missionaries, he quickly recognized and appreciated the vast chasm that lay between the native Indian and Euroamerican culture. To bridge that gap, he developed a program that delicately balanced the native village life with his Christian mission settlements.

Early on he formulated a set of rules to govern the villages. At first they were loosely written, but after a mission conference in August 1772, and beginning with the Schoenbrunn mission, they were formalized and recorded (see appendix E). Each January, or at other appropriate times, the rules were read and discussed at a congregational meeting, at which time every convert pledged to abide by all statutes. There were nineteen specific regulations, which are more meaningful if broken down into four separate categories. In the following list, the number assigned to each rule represents its respective position in the original list.[2]

1. Statutes pertaining to the religious activities of the village.

    1. All converts must worship one God, but the one and only true God, who made us and all creatures, and came into this world in order to save sinners; to him alone we pray.

    2. We will rest from work on the Lord's day, and attend public service.

    3. We will honor father and mother, and when they grow old and needy we will do for them what we can.

  12. A man shall have but one wife, he shall love and provide for her; and a woman shall have but one husband, be obedient to him, care for his children, and cleanly in all things.

  16. Young persons shall not marry without the consent of their parents and the missionaries.

2. Conditions for village residency.

    4. All residents must have prior approval from both the Native Helpers and the missionaries before they can live in the village.

    5. All residents must refuse to have any association with thieves, murderers, whoremongers, adulterers, and drunkards.

    9. There must be prompt obedience to the missionaries and the Native Helpers who are appointed to preserve order in the village.

  14. Prior consent must be received from Native Helpers before contracting any debt or selling any goods from traders.

  15. Permission must be received from the Native Helpers before going hunting.

  17. All members of the village must willingly assist in community projects, such as building fences, repairing public building, etc.

  18. Hospitality must be shown to all strangers. All residents must contribute corn from their private stores whenever needed, or sugar for lovefeast.

  19. No villagers will go to war or buy anything from warriors taken in war. [This statute was adopted during the revolutionary war.]

3. Prohibition against native practices.

    6. All dancing, sacrifices, heathen festivals, and games are prohibited.

    7. Witchcraft will not be permitted during hunting.

    8. All villagers must renounce and abhor tricks, lies, and deceits of Satan.

  13. All villagers must renounce the use of rum, and traders are prohibited from bringing liquor into the village.

4. Personal relationships with fellow villagers.

  10. We will not be idle, nor scold, nor beat one another, nor tell lies.

  11. Whoever injures the property of his neighbors shall make restitution.

To us in the twentieth century, village life under these rules must seem quite restrictive. Not so to these late eighteenth-century native Indians. Many were intrigued by the Christian promise of eternal life, and the communion and association with what Zeisberger proclaimed as the "one and only true God." Others admired the peace and orderliness of the villages and the security from hunger, a constant threat in native villages. Some truly believed they could accommodate and adopt the white people's life-style and live peacefully as their neighbors. Possibly these white teachers, whom they loved and admired, could make this a reality.

Despite the number of restrictive rules, in practice Zeisberger held a loose rein. Little attempt was made to restrict the wanderlust nature of the native life-style. There was never any interference with the spring and winter hunts or the spring sugarmaking. Visitations by native friends and relatives from other Indian villages were never discouraged and, likewise, requests to visit their native friends were seldom denied. During any week, the mission village entertained numerous native and white visitors. Many of these, both Indian and white, were only curious strangers; however, they intrigued and excited the inquisitive nature of the Indians.

Zeisberger's mission villages were not communal settlements. Each of the converts built and owned his own home, fenced and planted his own "plantation" (or his own plot of ground), and was responsible for the care and feeding of his own family. Tending the orchards, however, was a community project. The harvest was divided among the residents and a portion sold to their white neighbors to help cover village expenses. The Brethren also sold some of their shares to their neighbors for cash or trade.

Life at the Goshen mission in 1798 differed greatly from the missions at old Schoenbrunn and Gnadenhutten twenty-six years earlier. Two distinct factors contributed to the differences. First, the Goshen converts were a totally new group of second-generation converts. While many were baptized as infants at the old missions, most had lived for only short periods in mission villages. With scattered minor exceptions, gone were those Indian families who had spent most of their lives in Christian mission villages. Those great men and women of the Schoenbrunn and Gnadenhutten years—Abraham, Esther, Isaac, Sophia, Johannes, Anton, Lucia, Josua, and many others—were long in their graves. Zeisberger, with his fifty-plus years among the natives, had lived through two generations of Indians. Second, at Goshen Zeisberger was almost immediately confronted with a growing white population. When Schoenbrunn was founded in 1772, most of the frontier still lay well to the east of the Allegheny Mountains, several hundred miles from the mission villages. The restrictive village statutes were easily enforced at Schoenbrunn, where Zeisberger encountered little or no white interference. At Goshen it was a different situation. Within four years of the founding of the village, Goshen was surrounded by white settlers whose very presence interfered with village life. The converts may have been welcome at the Moravian village of Gnadenhutten, but at New Philadelphia, three miles north of the mission, it was another story. As the years passed, New Philadelphia became an increasingly hostile environment, constantly on the verge of erupting with threats against the Goshen mission, especially during the War of 1812. Had it not been for Benjamin Mortimer, Zeisberger's talented assistant, and William Henry and his family, who were educated natives, Goshen would not have survived Zeisberger's death. While Mortimer was initially a novice, he tutored under the great teacher for ten years and became as skilled as his mentor. Fortunately, his replacement, Abraham Luckenbach, who had gone through the horrible White River mission experience, was equally talented.

It is through Mortimer and his diaries that we get a small glimpse of Goshen mission life. While he recorded literally hundreds of different incidents, most of them fell within seven general categories: planting, growing, and gathering food; religious activities; building, trading, and industry; sickness and health; relations with white and native neighbors; schools and education; and miscellaneous events. Using some of Mortimer's own words, we will explore each of these activities.

PLANTING, GROWING, AND GATHERING OF FOOD

The basic Indian economy—native or Christian mission—rested on the success or failure of the corn crop. Corn was the staple ingredient of the Indian diet. From the ground cornmeal came the many appetizing and tasty meals that graced the Indian table. A successful harvest meant plenty; failure could mean starvation. The native Indian population grew thousands of bushels of corn each year, and this skill was carried over into the mission villages. In 1798 at the Fairfield mission in Canada, they had over 300 acres under cultivation. Initially, all planting was done without the use of plows. In a Mortimer entry under June 16, he explained the supposed advantages of the method: "16th. We heard that the Indian corn in all the settlements down the river was nearly destroyed by worms. Ours, on the contrary never appeared more promising at this season, which difference may arise from the circumstance of the white settlers plowing their corn fields, while our people only have theirs in small spots, which leave sufficient grass between for the worms to feed on."[3]

It was four years after the founding of Goshen before the villagers received their first plow, sent as a gift from Bethlehem to William Henry. The following year, 1803, they received the second. Each spring the local white neighbors plowed the Goshen plantations. Most of these fields were on the east side of the river, directly opposite the village. While extremely fertile, the land was subject to frequent flooding, and on some occasions the crop was destroyed, requiring replanting.

While corn was the main crop, other vegetables were planted also, either on the plantations or in the small individual gardens behind each convert's home. Pumpkins, turnips, beans, cabbage, and squash were grown each year.

Mortimer gives us a vivid picture of the torturous work required to prepare the ground for planting, and at the same time he describes an interesting anecdote about the village dogs. This incident occurred in May 1803, less than a month after they received the first plow.

> *7th.*
>
> Br. Urich finished plowing for us. We white brn. have about 4-1/2 acres of arable land in a state of cultivation, the greater part of which is under the management of Br. Mortimer. Besides this, we have some small pieces of meadow ground. This is the first year that we have been able to get any of it ploughed. After being cleared, and by means of the grubbing hoe, freed from innumerable roots, brushwood ivy, (which in this place is a work of more than ordinary labor and difficulty) all the grass & weeds have been pared off, and the earth repeatedly overturned by means of the hoe. In this way, by unremitting industry, and the greatest bodily exertions, made at times almost beyond our strength, are improvements effected at our settlement. . . .
>
> It may be noticed here, as a peculiarity of Indian settlements, that on account of the great number of dogs kept & the hunger that frequently prevails among them, it is necesssary to have the corn fields at a considerable distance from our town, to render them less subject to their depredations. The dog of an Indian eats corn like a horse, a cow, or a swine. These happily can be prevented from destroying a field by means of good fences, which are no defense against dogs.[4]

The destruction was not confined to the cornfields. Four years earlier, Mortimer had cautioned the residents of the village to protect themselves against an entirely different problem with the village dogs.

> *July 31st [1799]*
>
> The windows in our houses, which consist of paper rendered more transparent by being rubbed over with bear fat were much torn and injured by this tempestuous weather. It may easily be conceived that these kinds of windows are subject to speedy decay and destruction. Insects eat small holes through them and the changes of the weather render them rotten. Besides here the Indian dogs, when hungry, are apt to devour them, on which account it is proper to defend the outside approach to them with a high fence.[5]

Once again, Mortimer complained about dogs and fences.

13th. (May 1802)

It had been the standing rule wherever we had lived not to keep any bitches in our town, as among so many dogs as they were obliged to have to hunt with, they occasioned an insufferable noise. Those therefore of our town who had any would do well to make away with them immediately.

Ever since we had been here, there had been a great scarcity of corn among us in the spring. The chief reason of which was that they had not planted enough. They should therefore enlarge their fields & at the same time enclose them with good fences. Whoever has a field that was not well-fenced could not reasonably complain if his plantation was injured by breaking in of cattle, much less had he a right to demand payment for the same.[6]

Depending on the weather, the corn planting season usually took place the first two weeks in May, and the other vegetables usually planted two weeks later. Seldom would a killing frost occur after the end of May.

Other grain crops were also planted at Goshen. In 1800 Zeisberger had experimented with oats. Although successful, it never became a major crop at the village. With the advent of the plow, they sowed the first wheat crop in 1803 and continued each year thereafter to produce numerous acres of grain.

In 1804 they harvested the first peaches, a bumper crop of more than 150 bushels. The story of the thriving peach and apple orchards had its inception in the fall of 1798, shortly after their arrival at Goshen. During one of the frequent trips to Georgetown, four of the Brethren (not identified) were given peach seeds by the storekeeper, a Mr. Griffin. The seeds were planted immediately, and in the spring of 1801 the young saplings were transplanted to an orchard near the village and secured by a stout fence. The next fall they ate their first peaches. Mortimer noted, "these were the first mission-grown peaches since they lived at old Schoenbrunn (1772–77)."

The first substantial crop was harvested on September 16, 1804, all due to the foresight of four Brethren. Peaches, and later apples, became a cash crop. In September, during the harvest, some were dried and others were sold to many of their white neighbors. By 1809 the fruit harvest was an annual ritual, with their neighbors gathering at festivals held at Goshen to celebrate the occasion.[7]

The fall corn harvest usually began after the first heavy frost, which dried the milk in the grain and prevented spoilage. This normally occurred in the first two weeks of October. Once the harvest began, it was not uncommon for the Indians to remain in the fields overnight cutting and stacking the corn for transport to the village during the day. There was always a shortage of horses, and they had no wagons. The shocks were carried on their backs or in wheelbarrows. Since some of the plantations were several miles from the village, it was backbreaking labor, especially for the missionaries who usually harvested their own crops. In the later years it was not unusual for the village Indians to assist in the harvest of their white neighbors' crops, thus providing additional income for the Indian family.

Cattle, swine, and chickens were the sources of meat, milk, and eggs. Although the herds and flocks were not as abundant as those at the old Schoenbrunn, they were essential to the food supply, especially for providing milk for the children. Most of the families had at least one cow. The hogs, however, occasionally became an irritant. Never confined to pens, they were allowed to roam the forest to find their own food. In February 1804 Mortimer exhorted the Brethren to correct a problem plaguing the village: "19th. It was found necessary today to remind our brn. to remove to a distance from the town, the many hogs which have died here lately. These animals are at present so numerous here that since the late heavy fall of snow & severe weather, our brn. have found it impossible to support them properly without running the risk of feeding away all corn which was destined for their own sustenance."[8]

Eight years later hogs again were the subject of his diary, in a different but interesting context: "31st. (May 1812) Locusts now made their appearance here in greater numbers than ever have been known in these parts since the recommencement of the settlements on this river. For some weeks past, as they were coming out of the earth, the hogs fed and thrived on them. They now served as food for the fowl, and the Indian children also fried & ate them."[9]

Supplementing the income from grain crops was the annual winter sugarboiling. The combination of favorable weather and proliferation of the sugar maple trees made the production of sugar one of the most profitable endeavors at Goshen. Depending on the weather, the production usually began in late January or in the early weeks of February. The sap began to flow with the first warm days and stopped when the buds broke on the maples. Surveying the diary entries of thirteen years, from 1800 to 1812, we find the earliest beginning date for sugar production to be January 23 and the latest completion date April 11.[10] Mortimer gives us an excellent description of the process, explaining the history and impact of the product on the Indian economy. Note that this entry was written on Sunday and that the Brethren had returned to attend the day's services.

16th. (Sunday March 1800)
   Many of our people returned home to the public preaching which was held by Br. Mortimer from Luke 11:14. In the afternoon they went back to their

sugar camps where they dwell at the present, having with them all their household & furniture, and their cattle. Old and young now regale themselves on the decocted juice of the sugar maple tree. At this time last year, when our people were in want of bread, sugar formed a principal article of their food. It is accounted extremely wholesome for those especially who have eaten much meat during the winter, answering all the purposes of the common garden vegetables, and conveying at the same time far more nourishment to the human system. The Indians, who at this season especially eat sugar like bread, have generally good teeth.

The manufacturing of sugar from the sugar maple tree, has been carried on from time immemorial by the Indians, though not anciently to the extent that it is at present, for the want of those utensils with which European art has now furnished them. When hatchets were unknown among them, it must have been very difficult to make troughs to collect the sap of the trees. Without iron or brass kettles, they had to labor under much inconvenience in boiling it. . . .

The present Indians never make sugar from the red or white maple, as the white people often do, but always from the sugar maple tree, which is seldom to be met with in abundance, except on the richest of land in the inland parts of this continent.

The Chippewas carry on the manufacture to the greatest extent, which may arise from their occupying a tract of country where, in the winter, the hunting season is seldom so considerable as to take up their whole attention, and where the spring frost continues for the greatest length of time, which it is known produces plentiful running sap. They bring great quantities of sugar for sale to Michilimackenau & Detroit.

The best region for the manufacture of maple sugar probably lie[s] to the northwest of the 42 latitude. Where we dwell at present, the sugar season has been commonly but short, though this defect is in some measure made up by the sap's possessing a richness which is unknown in northern climates. Here is also a better stock of excellent sugar trees growing on our settlements. In Pettquotting, some of our brn. and sis. had to go 20 miles to their camps. Here they are all at present within two miles around us.[11]

Little can be added to Mortimer's description of sugarmaking at Goshen. In this incident the converts returned to the village for the Sunday service, but usually, they remained at the sugar camps as long as the sap flowed. Separated for weeks at a time from the controlling influences of the missionaries, on occasion they reverted to some of their old practices. Several entries in 1806 explain the problems of these extended absences. This incident occurred one year after the tragic suicide of Ignatius's son Henry, and the village animosity continued to linger on, as did the problem with Pfautz and Shane, the liquor dealers.

12th. (March 1806)
The behaviour of the Pfautzes & Shane on this occasion was as mean and pitiful as can be conceived. . . . Our people are at this season at their sugar

camps and consequently no longer under our eye. This opportunity, the Pfautzes and Shane made use of to entice them to purchase whiskey, and took in payment their sugar and clothing at a very low valuation.

Palm Sunday 30th.

At length, after an almost continual state of intoxication, some of our people returned into town. Br. Zeisberger discoursed to them shortly, concerning the day we celebrate, and then in strong and affecting terms represented to them the dreadful consequences that would ensue if they continued in that sinful course of life which they had led lately.[12]

Within the native Indian villages, the planting and harvesting of vegetables and the boiling of sugar were almost exclusively done by the women. While at the missions, the women organized and directed the activity but received considerable help from the men. Learning the skill of husbandry was an important part of the training in mission villages, and the missionaries encouraged the men to participate in this activity. The diaries indicate that they met with considerable success.

It is not surprising that hunting was the most popular activity among the men at Goshen. From boyhood, the native Indian was an expert hunter, and seldom a month passed before one or more of the families would go on the chase. Most of this activity, however, was confined to the winter and spring hunts, with the former being the most organized and productive. These two hunts were normally activities in which the entire family—father, mother, and children—participated. There were two basic purposes for the hunt: the gathering of food and the collection of furs to be sold later at David Peter's store at Gnadenhutten, or to some white trader.

The fall hunt usually began in the first or second week in November and continued until just before the Christmas celebration, which next to Easter was the highlight of the religious year at the mission. The spring hunt began after the sugar making, usually the latter part of March or the first week in April, and seldom lasted more than one month. The Indians usually returned by Easter to participate in the Holy Week ceremonies. During the fall hunt, they would remain in the woods for the entire season, building regular hunting camps of small bark huts usually many miles from the mission village. It was customary for one of the Native Helpers to accompany each of the hunting parties "who occasionally discoursed to and admonished them about their Christian responsibilities."

Mortimer filled his diary with interesting hunting anecdotes, and over the course of the years provided a vivid picture of this activity. In November 1799 he entered the following comment: "12th. Many of the brn. went on the so called fall hunt. This is the principal hunting season of the whole year, and is compared by our Indians to the harvest of the white people. It lasts here from the second week in November till about Christmas during which time the deer are taken in greatest numbers, and their skins are the most valuable for every kind of use and fetch the highest prices."[13]

One month later, he again discussed the subject of hunting and noted that the native Indian hunters would "travel yearly to the extent of hundreds and perhaps thousands of miles on their excursions, and meet with others who have come equally far from other regions."[14]

The men did the hunting, returning with their catch to the camps, where the women and children would skin the animals, scrape and prepare the pelts, and dry the meat. Hundreds of deer and bear were felled in any given season. On May 28 during the hunting season of 1800, Mortimer recorded a total kill of 196 bears. No exact annual count for deer was ever recorded, but the catch always numbered in the hundreds. The following year, early in the season, they returned with seventeen bears and, several weeks later, with fifty deer. Certain members of the congregation were more proficient hunters than others. Thomas White Eyes, the son of the famous White Eyes, seemed to be the best hunter in the village. In 1803 he killed four bears on one day and three the next. Within the same month he had killed fifty-six deer. During the same year, Mortimer noted, "he sent back to the village over 100 skins, and James returned with 40 skins." In 1806 Christian Gottlieb returned from one trip with twenty deer pelts, and one month later Joachim and James returned with 120. The following year, on December 20, Mortimer noted that "the hunters returned with seven horse loads of skins." Transporting their kill became the most difficult part of the hunting process. In the course of the season they would make numerous trips back to the village with skins and meat, then return to the woods to continue the hunt.

Other useful products were also found in the woods and meadows. In the fall the women gathered walnuts and hickory nuts. On October 24, 1799, Mortimer noted: "The women gathered hickory nuts to make soup of which are this year very numerous. The juice of them is also used instead of milk added to their mush, by those who have no cows." Blueberries, which they called whortleberries, were considered a delicacy and baked into the corn bread.

RELIGIOUS ACTIVITIES

No other aspect of mission life was pursued with more vigor and demanded more attention than religious education. The scheduling of religious activities was rigorous and called for at least two daily meetings of the congregation. The first, in the morning following breakfast, was entirely religious and consisted of Scripture reading followed by preaching, instruction, and prayerful advice. Another meeting in the evening dealt with the more secular and civil aspects of mission life. Plans for the daily operation of the village were discussed, and assignments for the following day's chores were made. Views were exchanged on personal and family disagreements, and those accused of violating village rules or those who were the objects of wayward behavior were admonished. Behind these formal meetings was the constant work of the native assistants who were members of the Helpers' Conference. Most of the personal disagreements were resolved by these men and women. This service was followed by many prayers and their favorite activity, hymn singing. The Indians were accomplished singers. Quite often their white neighbors came to the services just to hear the congregation sing.

Despite this rigorous schedule, these meetings were interrupted during the hunting and sugar-making seasons, as most of the converts were absent. Cancellations were especially more frequent as the membership declined following the drunken frolics associated with Henry's suicide in 1805.[15]

Zeisberger firmly believed that the key to solving the transition from native culture to "civilization" could only be found through religious education. Like other European missionaries, he never questioned the singularity of his religion, ignoring the fact that native culture had long survived quite well without Christianity.

The essence of Zeisberger's Christian philosophy was contained in the first statute of village regulations, "All converts must worship one God, but the one and only true God who made all creatures, and came into this world in order to save all sinners." Only through Christianity could the ultimate salvation and the brotherhood of man be accomplished. Religious pluralism was a concept unthinkable in Zeisberger's mind.

Thirty years before the Goshen experience, he once had a spirited and argumentative conversation with a Seneca chief while on the road to the Allegheny region. At the end of the discussion he summed up his Christian-Indian philosophy in one paragraph. "Behold, these are the words which I come to tell the Indians. You say they are created in order to roam through the forest and run after bears and deer. Oh, no, my friend! They [the Indians] are made for higher purposes. Believe me, it is God's will that they, too, should be saved."[16]

The Indian congregations were structured similarly to the white Moravian congregation back in Bethlehem. The choir system, however, which divided the members into groups of single men, single women, small girls, and small boys, large girls, large boys, married couples, etc., was never adopted. The Indians would not have permitted their children to be separated from the family as they were in Bethlehem. The single men's and women's choirs were also not formed. Zeisberger contended that younger, unattached singles created problems, principally sexual, and they were discouraged from living at the village. This rule did not apply to widows or widowers. Presumably the older folks were not troubled with this problem.

The single exception was the married couples' choir. This group met frequently, especially on the anniversary of their baptismal day. The Indians did not celebrate birthdays—most did not know their birth date, but they never forgot the day of their baptism. Lovefeasts were held on these days and were accompanied by fervent singing of hymns followed by much animated conversation. On the evening of June 1, 1800, William Henry played host at a typical lovefeast and baptismal party. Mortimer described the proceedings.

> In the evening those who had their baptisimal day kept a solemn meeting & lovefeast together. . . . It was held in the house of our brother William Henry who also presided. He first discoursed for about ten minutes to the company, about twenty in number, speaking of the grace conferred in holy baptism, and the happiness of living to our Saviour. After the singing of a few verses, the company were invited to partake of what was set on the table, which consisted of meat, vegetables, tea, and cakes of wheat flour. He afterwards discoursed a second time; verses were sung again, each one of the guests beginning one alternately. Another exaltation was held by Br. Will. Henry. The company then broke up. At their respective homes many continued singing with their families till a late hour.[17]

Communion was held on a regular schedule, but administered only to communicants. The congregational lovefeast was a community affair with all the population of the village invited, including the natives. Such events were anticipated with great enthusiasm. The origin of the lovefeast came from the early Christians and was celebrated by the breaking of bread following the Resurrection and the day of Pentecost. Later it became customary to gather the church families together to partake of a simple meal before receiving the Holy Communion. These gatherings were called "feasts of love," from the Greek word *agape*, referring to the highest type of spiritual love, and were occasions for worship and for celebration of the risen Christ.

The lovefeast was adopted by the Moravians in Herrnhut as early as 1727. Usually coffee or hot chocolate with a sugar cake are served, while the congregation sings appropriate hymns. The tradition is still carried on among the Moravians and is a symbol of the love and brotherhood of the Christian faith.

The highlights of the religious calendar were Christmas and Easter. All the villagers looked forward to these holy days, especially during the first few years of the mission. The Christmas season was a happy time, particularly for the children. The service began on Christmas Eve with a joyful lovefeast. Everyone was invited. At the end of the service lighted tapers were given to the children, which always prompted squeals of delight and much babbling conversation. Christmas Day, was a day-long celebration with preaching and hymn singing. Their cares were forgotten and goodwill prevailed. Mortimer explains the Christmas season of 1804.

[Sunday] 23d
A few strange Indians were present. One of them, a half Mohawk, who had frequently celebrated Christmas at Brant's town on Grand river in Upper Canada, said that he was come to see how we kept Christmas here. [This was Moses Mohawk, see part 3, burial 8.]

Christmas Eve the 24th in the evening,
All inhabitants here, at a lovefeast, which was held by Br. Mortimer, called to mind with joyful hearts, the manifestation of God in the flesh. The history of this great event was read, & in a prayer on our knees, fervent thanks & praise were brought to the triune God for the great plan of our redemption, through the incarnation and death of Jesus Christ. At the conclusion, lighted tapers were as usual presented to the children and others, and Br. Hagen distributed written verses in Delaware treating of the blessing accruing from the birth of Jesus.

25th
Br. Zeisberger preached from Luke 2:10, 11. In an especial meeting for the children, he recommended to them to unite after the example of the angles in singing praises to God for the great love that he has displayed to us poor men.[18]

In sharp contrast to the Christmas service was the Easter observance, which was a most solemn occasion. It began on Wednesday with all communicants participating in the symbolic and humble gesture of washing of the feet. On the following day, Maundy Thursday, the missionaries began with the reading of the passion story to the entire congregation. The readings continued on Good Friday evening. The following day was called Great Sabbath and another meeting was held with a lovefeast. On Easter morning the services began at sunrise, and Mortimer usually wrote "it was held partly in the cemetery and partly in the Church." During the graveyard service, special prayers were said for those converts who departed in the past year. Mortimer records the Easter season ceremonies of 1803.

[Wednesday April] 6th
   The communicant brn. & sis, after hearing the history of our Lord's washing his disciple's feet, and a discourse & prayer by Br. Zeisberger, had the same administrated to them by us.

Maundy Thursday 7th
   They partook of the Holy comm. together, in a sweet sense of the divine presence. Previous thereto, the history of the institution of the Lord's supper was read to them by Br. Mortimer. . . .

Good Friday 8th
   Yesterday and today all our people were attentive hearers of the history of our Lord's passion; we trust to an abiding blessing for their hearts.
   In the evening was the burial of the child Ketura, daughter of Anna Sophia who departed to our Savior on the 6th, age 7 years [see part 3, burial 20]. . . .

Easter 10th
   We assembled at the break of day and the morning being fine, prayed part of the litany for the day around the graves of our departed brn. & sis., which were as usual at this festival neatly cleaned from weeds, and handsomely rounded. This meeting, & another at which the history of the resurrection of our Lord was read, was held by Br. Zeisberger. Br. Mortimer preached from John 11:25.26. Br. Haven kept the cong. meeting.[19]

Today it takes little imagination to stand in that quiet, tree-lined Goshen cemetery and see the ghostly apparitions of Indian men and women, with weatherworn heads bowed, standing among the graves of those they loved, celebrating the resurrection of their Savior.

BUILDING, TRADING, AND INDUSTRY
Building

   The first communal activity at all of Zeisberger's many missions was the building of a temporary meetinghouse or church which housed the missionaries. Constructed from small saplings and peeled bark, the structures were based on saplings bent in the shape of a U with their ends buried in the ground. Other saplings were woven horizontally between the uprights and the whole structure was covered with bark, except for doors usually at each end. This served as the temporary building for several months until permanent log cabins could be built. This same pattern held true at Goshen, and the temporary meetinghouse was started on October 19, 1798, twelve days after the missionaries arrived at the Goshen site. Ten days later, Zeisberger complained that the work was progressing "not as fast as in former times." By December 12, the building was completed. Normally these temporary structures could be constructed in two to four days. The diaries give no clues explaining the delay. However, the delay was a portent of the future of public buildings at Goshen. While Zeisberger's permanent home was finished by the Nazareth builders on November 3, 1798, the new permanent log church was not begun until five years later, in 1803. In the meantime, they met in the windowless temporary building. On September 22 Mortimer recorded the modest ground-breaking ceremony.

> *22d*
>
> We had at length the joy to see the beginning made of the building of our new church, *which through various hindrances, could not conveniently be attempted till now.* As soon as the four first logs of which it is to be composed were placed in a square, but before they were fitted into each other the brn. & sis. were called to the spot by the ringing of the church bell.[20] Br. Zeisberger then addressed them in a few words, stating that as we lived here as a congn. that had received the word of God, and were determined to keep it, it was proper that we should have a church where we could meet to hear it; and that we were all well when all of our neighbors were sickly, it might be that this good health was given us by God, on purpose that we might now be able to erect this building . . . .[21] [Emphasis added]

The "various hindrances" noted by Mortimer must have continued for the next seven years, since the building was not completed until 1810, more than a year after Zeisberger's death. By then the temporary meetinghouse, built in 1798, had decayed to the point of collapse and was unsafe for congregational meetings. During the interim period they met in one of the larger homes.

Construction of the schoolhouse, which was normally the second public building constructed in mission villages, followed the same pattern except it never progressed beyond the temporary structure. Following Zeisberger's death and Susan Zeisberger's departure in 1809, the Zeisberger house served as the school building. Goshen is the only Zeisberger mission that survived more than four years which did not have a permanent church and schoolhouse. Mortimer's "various hindrances" is the only reference in eight hundred pages of his mission diaries to vaguely offer any explanation. The delay in building these structures was certainly not for the lack of know-how. A diary entry in August 1799 describes the creative skill found among the Goshen converts:

Aug. 16th

Yesterday the young brn. went hunting together and today they all helped each other in raising the timbers of their houses, in the construction and workmanship of which they shew great superiority over all other Indians that we are acquainted with. They even excel the white people on the frontier, professed carpenters and masons excepted. We have no where in the settlements seen chimneys so well built, except by those who follow the trade as their profession. In the setting of timbers with the hatchet, in the smoothing of it with the broad-axe and plane, and in the splitting of clapboards, they have acquired much expertness. They can also supply the most necessary articles of house furniture that are made of wood or wicker-work.[22]

The only explanation (albeit a weak one) that would account for the lack of permanent construction might be found in the small number of converts living at the village after the 1805 incident of Henry's suicide, but this does not explain why these buildings were not constructed prior to this date.

Trading

Indians developed skills of negotiating and trading goods with the white man that would rival the talents of today's chief executive officers of multinational corporations. Clever and shrewd, artful and cunning, they drove hard bargains, not only with their own people, but also with the many English and French traders who visited the mission. They knew the market, even to the extent of knowing the prices of bear and deer skins all the way to Philadelphia. A Mortimer entry in April 1804 reveals their shrewdness: "17th most of our brn. went again in the bear hunt. A French trader from Detroit now offers them six dollars [cash] for each skin; for they keep it a profound secret from him that they have been informed that their price is now only three dollars in Philadelphia."[23]

On October 26, 1799, just one year after the converts arrived on the Muskingum, David Peter established his trading post and store at the new Gnadenhutten white settlement. Josua was his first customer, purchasing a blanket for $1.26. Four days later, David Zeisberger, the second customer, purchased several pounds of lath nails for sixteen cents. In less than a year Brother Ludwig Knauss began his blacksmith shop near Peter's store, saving the Indians a long trip to Georgetown. Convenient though these new facilities were, problems soon developed. Those shrewd Indian traders quickly discovered Mr. Peter was not competitive with the going market. After all, business was business, so they took their trade elsewhere. The whole situation created some embarrassment for the missionaries. Mortimer explains in an entry on June 3, 1800:

It is a circumstance that occasions us some concern, that though the Directors of the Heathen Society in Bethlehem have established a store in Gnadenhutten, chiefly with the view of serving the Indian congn. here and being generally useful to the mission, yet at present there is but little prospect that these desirable objects can be effected agreeable to wish. From Br. Peter who has the management of the store our brn. & sis. always experience kindness & friendship; but the traders from the northward, who stroll about the country and live in the Indian manner, can generally afford their goods at a much lower price than he [Peter] can, while they give a higher price for most kinds of skins.[24]

Certainly "kindness and friendship" were desirable, but not at the expense of the Indian pocketbook. David Peter, however, proved to be a resilient and clever trader. Within a few months he successfully responded to the marketplace and captured most of the fur trade in the area, thus redeeming the missionaries and causing a sigh of relief back in Bethlehem.

Industry

Furs and meat, the harvest of the hunt, were not the only products produced at the mission villages. Several converts were expert carpenters, especially Ignatius.[25] Many of the men were skilled at canoe making, each canoe selling for twenty to twenty-five dollars; and both men and women were experts at basketweaving, brooms, and chair making. Later in the mission history, wagon loads of over one hundred baskets and brooms were frequently taken to Pittsburgh, Washington, Pennsylvania, and Wheeling. As mentioned above, the products of their orchards and the sugar from boiling sap were sold to their white neighbors. The skins of the deer were made into moccasins, clothing, and other leather goods. Bear skins made ideal blankets for their white neighbors for those cold nights along the Muskingum. Despite this prodigious display of craftmanship, cash was always in short supply. Husbandry, with their crude methods of production, never produced quantities sufficient for a cash crop.

SICKNESS AND HEALTH

Smallpox, the scourge of Indians since their first contact with white people, was never a problem among the Goshen converts. Not one case was ever reported. There were several scares, but they turned out to be only cowpox. Unknown to Mortimer, the frequency of cowpox was a blessing. Halfway around the world, Edward Jenner, in London, was just beginning his experiments inoculating an eight-year-old boy with the cowpox vaccine, on May 14, 1776. Within a few years this procedure began to eradicate the dreaded smallpox. On July 23, 1817, Edward Jenner's vaccine finally caught up with the Goshen converts; all twenty-six were vaccinated for smallpox. But it came far to late for the Indian converts' ancestors who had paid the horrible price. In many instances, smallpox epidemics killed over 90 percent of a village population.

The Goshen Indians were not, however, less susceptible to other diseases of the white people. During the Easter weekend mentioned above, Mortimer recorded the death of seven-year-old Ketura, daughter of Anna and Johann Adam. At the same time he speculated in some detail on the cause of the many deaths at Goshen, especially among the younger folks.

Good Friday, 8th [1803] . . .

She [Ketura] is the twentieth corpse which has been committed to our burying grounds during the short time of our abode here. Eighteen of them were persons not above 30 years of age, while in the Gnadenhutten congn., which is considerably larger than ours and consisting chiefly of young people, not a person under that age has during the same period of time departed this life! The consideration of the great mortality that has taken place among us here induced Br. Zeisberger lately in a prayer in the church, to beseech our Saviour, if not inconsistent with his holy will, for his own name's sake & for the propagation of his gospel, to maintain & increase the number of his congn. here.

We have observed that all the deaths here except two have taken place in houses, ten in number, where the Muskingum water is with few exceptions made use of throughout the year for drink. During the dry sickly season, which commonly lasts from July till Novr., no other water is easily to be obtained, as a small creek near our town is then dry, & spring water is not to be had, but going for it *nearly half a mile*, and ascending a steep hill. The houses where the Muskingum water is not in common use, are 7.[a] One of the two deaths therein was the late Br. Edwards, and the other a young man who hurt his health by overexertion on a journey hither. Almost all our brn. & sis. in Gnadenhutten drink spring water.[b] In Fairfield no water is drunk out of the river, as the bank on which the town is built abounds in springs.[c]

a. Not all the above mentioned dwellings are at present inhabited. The greatest number of houses that have at one time stood in Goshen was 21.

b. The communication which the Muskingum has with stagnant waters between Old Schoenbrunn and this place, and the slow current which the river has before the town, may render its waters more unwholesome here than in other places.

c. Fairfield, during the last four years has upon the average, had at least three times as many inhabitants as Goshen; yet the number of deaths there has not been so great. The majority of them were aged & infirm persons, who could not have undertaken the journey hither. The mortality here, as above observed, has been chiefly among the *young people*.[26]

Mortimer had probably never heard of diphtheria or typhoid fever, which may have caused some of these deaths, but he did come close to the probable cause—contaminated water. His diaries frequently referred to "remittent or intermitting fevers and severe colds, attended in most instances with coughing, pains in the limbs & particularly in the head, and at length with a temporary deafness which lasted one or more weeks."[27] While some of these symptoms could have been the result of the common cold, others suggest malaria. The low swampy area around Old Schoenbrunn and even Goshen was heavily infested with mosquitoes and, at the time of the missions, probably the notorious genus *Anopheles*, the carrier of this disease. This contention is supported by the fact that most of the sickness occurred from July through October, at the height of the mosquito season in this area.[28]

Consumption, "the white plague," also took its toll among the Indians; however, it never reached epidemic proportions. During the seventeen years of their wilderness wandering, the mission recorded six deaths from tuberculosis, four women and two men. During the twenty-three years of the Goshen mission there were only two deaths, both men. Interestingly, all of these deaths were converts under forty.

Other ailments appear occasionally in the diaries: gangrene, fever and ague, measles, ulcers, and worms. These seldom proved fatal. Zeisberger recorded an interesting diary entry in July 1793 during his stay at Fairfield. "Friday, 5. Salome, David's wife, become suddenly so ill that her death was expected. She had inward convulsions, and all remedies failed. Among other things was given her a vermifuge, whereupon she passed an extraordinary strange sort of worm, such as is found in horses, wherefrom so many die in this country, and then she grew better."[29]

Treatment of the various sicknesses contracted by the Indians was an ever present problem to Zeisberger. Some of the converts insisted on resorting to their native Indian doctors, who were forbidden to live in the villages. Most of this treatment was based on witchcraft. In the section of part 3 on burial 2, Francis James, is a quote reflecting on Zeisberger's opinion of such cures. While at New Schoenbrunn in 1779, he recorded the following statement regarding the normal nursing care given the sick:

> Care and attention for the sick amounted to but little, the Indians being poor nurses. So long as they can go out they lie on the hard bed of boards; no longer able to do this they are laid on the ground near the fire, possibly on grass or hay, a small hole in the ground under the patient serving as a bedpan. In time of sickness their diet consists of thin soup of pounded corn, without either butter, fat, or salt. Not until a patient is convalescent is he allowed any meat. There are Indians who have considerable knowledge of the virtue of roots and herbs, learned from the fathers, and who bring about relief.[30]

Bleeding was the first remedy administered to ward off an expected spell of sickness. Mortimer gives us an example: "Sunday 15th [May, 1803] . . . Nearly all of our sis. here chose to get bled today—probably because the weather was warm. Such whims are frequent among them. It is not unusual that half the town thinks proper to vomit, or have other evacuations, for which strong potions are given often at the evident risk of health."[31]

RELATIONS WITH NEIGHBORS

In August 1805 Mortimer gives us a glimpse at the typical day's schedule at Goshen. He wrote, "there was a constant traveling through this place the whole day." Seldom was there a diary page that did not record some party coming or going from the mission. The frontier wilderness was a lonely place and those who traversed it longed to see the face of a human, be it Indian or white. Positioned as it was on the edge of the settlements, Goshen received a flood of visitors. The missionaries, ever watchful for another opportunity to save a soul for Christ, encouraged such visitations. Mortimer, on October 8, 1799, described the benefits of this Christian brotherhood.

> We remarked with particular pleasure in this place, that the very same characteristic spirit of brotherly love, which discovers itself so frequently and amiably among our white brn. & sis., when those who live in distant places visit or become acquainted with each other, and which is derived from consciousness of the like experience of divine grace, and the assurance of our close union in Christ as the head and Saviour of his Church is also equally perceptible in the connection between our Indian brn. & sis. When heathen Indians arrive here, they are treated with kindness and hospitality. They are lodged and fed gratuitously, the friendly pipe is handed to them, and they are conversed with in the most social manner. All this is however mere customary civility. It is acting according to the rules of Indian politeness and good breeding in the observance of which our brn. & sis. might by no means be deficient.[32]

Goshen Neighbors: Native Indians

For the first twelve years (1798–1810), most of the mission's native Delaware neighbors were clustered far to the west in ten villages along the White River in Indiana. The exceptions were a small village of Captain Pipe's Delaware Wolf clan at Sandusky, and Armstrong's Town (Greentown) near present Mansfield, Ohio. Natives from all of these villages came to visit Goshen.

From the beginning of the mission in 1798, and for the next fourteen years until the War of 1812, numerous messages arrived at Goshen encouraging the converts to move to the native villages along the White River area. The Delaware chiefs were particularly active during the initial part of this period between 1801 and 1807.[33] But the converts were always wary of these solicitations, especially following the debacle that occurred at the White River mission in 1806. William Henry, having served a brief period as the Delaware head chief, was the focal point of most of these proffers. An incident developed in 1807 that clearly shows how cleverly Indian diplomacy functioned. Henry, now almost seventy, had lost none of his skill as an Indian negotiator and statesman. The dispatch received from the new Delaware chief was quite similar to those received in 1801 before the beginning of the White River mission. The message was delivered by James, a convert and the husband of Sophia.[34] James had also taken the dispatch to Fairfield, but they passed it on to Goshen. It is singular because it expresses the devotions of a stalwart convert totally dedicated to mission life. Mortimer, on February 27, 1807, described William Henry's answer.

> He proposed in the most friendly terms, to thank his friends the chiefs for their message, to express his joy that they had now land of their own, and to wish them much happiness there; to tell them that when he heard that all other Delawares moved thither he would perhaps follow their example; that he had received the word of God, which had comforted his heart, and made it feel well, on which account he would never part with it; that he did not seek outward advantages as land or riches, but above all things, his soul's welfare; that he should be very glad to hear that they also were so disposed; that he could not promise that he would ever move to them; but if he heard that they had a desire to receive the word of God, he would think about it; & if he came bring his teachers with him.[35]

During most of this period (1798–1810), Goshen continued to enjoy friendly relations with the inhabitants' cousins in Indiana, but there were ominous rumblings among the centers of the native population. Late in the first decade of the nineteenth century, the two Shawnee brothers Tecumseh and Tenskwatawa began to develop their plan to organize a resistance movement among the western Indians. Conceived by Tecumseh, the plan was designed to form a confederacy of the western Indians to check further encroachment by the American government.

One nasty event, reported by Mortimer in 1810, came directly from the Shawnee brothers' activity and had its origin in the earlier incident of Ignatius's son Henry's suicide, which continued to plague the mission.

> *August 2,*
> The heathens here made a clapboard fence around the grave of the Indian Henry, who died and was buried here as a heathen, at some distance outside of

our burying ground, in March 1805. They performed then the heathenish ceremonies said to be customary among the Monsies on such occasions, which
consist chiefly, as we were told, in their filling their mouths with whiskey &
then blowing it out with violence all over the grave & surrounding fence. This
contemptible usage—quite in character for poor heathens who are fond of
spirituous liquors—we did not endeavor to prevent here. It is rather quite
agreeable to us, that this grave should ever be considered as containing the
corpse of a person who though he lived & died in the congn., was no believer,
but a mere heathen and an enemy of the gospel.[36] [Emphasis added]

The disappointment deep within the recesses of Mortimer's mind was re-
vealed in the pages of his diary.

Goshen Neighbors: White

The Goshen Indians' relations with their white neighbors followed
almost the same pattern as those of their western Indian relatives. For the
first few years they enjoyed a friendly and cordial association. But by 1806
the activities of the Shawnee brothers, particularly Tenskwatawa's action among the Delaware along the White River, gave cause for concern
among the white settlers along the Muskingum.

As noted earlier, there were two white settlements near Goshen. Gnadenhutten, whose residents consisted of friendly white Moravians, was
founded by Heckewelder in 1798. The second community, three miles
north of the mission at New Philadelphia, was founded in 1803 by John
Knisely and thirty white settlers from Bedford, Pennsylvania. They were
two very different groups of white immigrants.

Gnadenhutten was located eight miles south of Goshen on the east side
of the Muskingum. Organized initially by the Society of the United Brethren for the Propagating of the Gospel Among the Heathen, Heckewelder,
its founder, dreamed of another Bethlehem, this time on the Muskingum.[37] It was to serve as the supply base for the proposed far-flung
Moravian missionary effort, with the terminal and training grounds at
Goshen. Three years after it was founded, the Goshen Indians had available to them at Gnadenhutten a gristmill, sawmill, blacksmith shop, and
trading store, all operated by congenial and hospitable neighbors who
were dedicated to the expansion of the Moravian missionary program. No
longer did they need to travel the fifty-five miles to Charleston and
Georgetown. There was a veritable flood of communications between the
two settlements with people coming and going almost daily. During
1798, just three months after the Zeisberger converts arrived on the Muskingum, there were twenty-two references to Gnadenhutten in the Goshen diaries. In 1799, there were eighty-three.

Much of this close relationship between Goshen and Gnadenhutten can be attributed to Heckewelder's personal admiration of Zeisberger. Together they had suffered the horrors of the Great Dispersement, the trial at Detroit, and the refounding of the mission program at New Gnadenhutten and Pilgerruh. Heckewelder knew full well that Zeisberger was nearing the end of his life and that Goshen would be his final effort. Now an octogenarian, Zeisberger's health would no longer permit the agony of wilderness travel, and he wanted to make those last years as comfortable as possible.

Heckewelder visited the mission frequently and was most welcomed by the mission personnel. But as the agent of the Society for the Propagating of the Gospel (SPG) he had his own agenda. With an incredible burst of energy, Heckewelder's last twelve years on the frontier, from 1798 to 1810, saw him travel seven times from Gnadenhutten to Bethlehem, a round-trip distance of 820 miles. He brought his family to the village in 1801, where they remained during all of his traveling for the SPG. In the fall of 1810, two years after Zeisberger died, Heckewelder returned with his family to Bethlehem. By then the officials at Bethlehem had abandoned any further plans for mission expansion using Goshen and Gnadenhutten as bases of operation. Heckewelder made one final trip to Gnadenhutten after the end of the War of 1812, then returned to Bethlehem to retire. He died on January 23, 1823, and is buried there among so many of his fellow missionaries.

The missionaries, during the first decade of the nineteenth century, were not without problems with some of the white village residents in both Gnadenhutten and New Philadelphia. Again, the following incident is the direct result of Henry's suicide. Recorded by Mortimer in May 1806, this event occurred more than a year after the young man's death and represents at least one incident which prompted Mortimer to pour out his heart in bitter resentment against his fellow Moravians. It is one entry in which he seems to have been oblivious to the effect it might have had when the diary reached the Bethlehem elders.

3rd.

Br. Hagen visited in Gnadenhutten. In the evening, Indians came here drunk from that place. This is not the first time that this has happened. To be thus wounded, even in the house of our friends, is painful to us in the extreme, and would quite discourage us in the service of the gospel among the poor Indians. . . . Whether any person at Gnadenhutten gives whiskey to the Indians for their own use, or that of others, or at times lets white people alone have it and refuses it to Indians, are to us trivial circumstance. But that our Indians actually obtain it there, and to excess; that they see it there disposed without moderation or reserve to numbers of people who in their hearing blaspheme our holy redeemer, and before their eyes refrain from no wickedness; these are sources of the most pungent grief to us; because they seem to announce the utter ruin of our mission. How can we request any person whatever not to intoxicate the Indians when the answer has been given: Why may we not do so, as well as Mr. _____ of Gnadenhutten? And must we not, both before Indians and white people to whom we belong, when we reflect how inconsistent such conduct is with the professions and promises that have been heretofore so liberally made before the world?[38]

Despite the one incident noted above, and perhaps several other minor differences over trading of goods at Peter's store, Goshen's relationships with Gnadenhutten were always cordial and friendly.

For nine years following its founding in 1803, a similar observation could be made for the settlers at New Philadelphia, despite Mortimer's initial misgivings on their arrival in the valley.[39] With the exception of the problems with the liquor merchants Pfautz and Shane, Goshen enjoyed quite friendly relations with most of the inhabitants, especially the Knisely family, the founders of the village. On many occasions New Philadelphians visited the church services at the mission village and the missionaries were repeatedly complimented on their work among the Indians. For an eight-year period between 1804 and including 1811, there were fifty-three references to New Philadelphia in Mortimer's diary. With the beginning of active hostility during the War of 1812, the situation dramatically changed. During the two years 1812 and 1813, there were sixty-two references to New Philadelphia in the diaries. With Indians living on their doorsteps, these former Pennsylvania residents conjured up visions of the old days of bloody Indian incursions against their isolated farms and homesteads. While the Goshen Indians might seem outwardly friendly, the settlers believed the village attracted visits from hostile native friends from Indiana.

The stereotype of American Indians in the nineteenth century pictures them inveterate liars, thieves and at worst, cowards. Even Zeisberger once wrote, "They are masters in the art of deceit and at the same time very credulous; they are given over to cheating and stealing, and are not put to shame when caught."[40] Today the Indian is pictured as the noble savage; a large tear slowly drops from his eye as he watches white people contaminate his unsullied wilderness. The truth probably lies some place between these two extremes. Mortimer, however, tells us in October 1800 of at least one incident of a white man's culpability.

[Sunday] 19th
    Josua returned home from hunting. . . . He found that during his absence his house had been robbed of sundry articles of value to him among them a fleam, and lancet, which he had procured last year from Bethlehem in order

to be able to serve the brn. and sis. with bleeding. Suspicion immediately fell upon a white man whom he had lodged a few nights before, and who was seen on that evening following, when none of the family was at home, hovering about his premises as if in search of something. Our Indian brn. are kind to all strangers who come here, affording them gratis both lodging and provision. The white people whom they have entertained, have not always well requited this generosity. In several instances in the course of this year, they have robbed the houses or camps of their benefactors. This makes us very cautious about harboring people who are unknown to us, and shews the propriety of having our doors furnished with good locks. Far in the Indian country, where the white people do not travel, this precaution is not necessary. It deserves to be mentioned, to the credit of our people, that in no instance since we have been here have they, to our knowledge, been charged or even suspected with theft by any white people. On the contrary, many who had lost their horses or cattle have expressed a wish that they might be brought here as to a place of safety.[41]

SCHOOLS AND EDUCATION

While the missionaries placed great emphasis on education, they were forced to compromise the Goshen school schedules for three reasons. The first was the interference of the annual hunting, harvesting, and sugar-gathering activities. The children were an integral part of all of these food-gathering operations. Second, because of Zeisberger's advanced age, Mortimer assumed most of the responsibilities as the head missionary and could not always shoulder the role of schoolmaster. During the first few years, unless he had assistance, the schooling was neglected. Third, the rapid decline of the mission population, especially following the incident of Henry's suicide in 1805, left few children to attend the school. Despite these handicaps, the program appears to have had some success.

On August 6, 1799, ten months after their arrival, Mortimer began the first Goshen school with eleven children. He also noted: "A few up-grown persons also occasionally attended." This assembly began in the temporary building constructed for this purpose. The first session ended on November 1, with the beginning of the cold weather and the fall hunt. On January 8, 1800, he recorded: "The brn. began to hew timbers for the school house. A hindrance was, that several of them have of late had the misfortune to break their hatchets & cannot get others nearer than Charlestown, which is 60 miles from here." This permanent building was never completed and no satisfactory explanation is given in the diaries. As previously noted, school was continued in the temporary building, or the missionary's home, until Zeisberger's death and Susan's departure in 1809. The sessions were then held in the Zeisberger home.

During the first semester, Stephen, the Vorsteher (leading helper), arrived with letters and dispatches from the Indian brethren at Fairfield. His arrival gave Mortimer an opportunity to reflect on the advantages of Indian literacy.

Oct. 8th [1799]

Stephen had brought with him many letters for our Indian brn. & sis., as well as for us, from their friends and former acquaintances. It deserves notice, that our people are fully sensible of the many advantages of being able to express themselves by the help of written letters, in preference to the sending of verbal messages, as is the practice among the heathen Indians. The young people therefore excercise themselves diligently in this art, and some who have never had the opportunity of receiving regular instruction are become considerable proficients therein.[42]

The school semester began on May 27, 1800, following the sugar boiling and the spring hunt. Mortimer gives us an excellent explanation of the educational objectives of the mission program.

We regard it as a matter of great importance to the future welfare of the congn., and the progress of the gospel among the Indians, that the youth in our congn. be diligently instructed both in Indian & in English languages. The cleanly and decent appearances of the children, and the joy which they manifest on beginning to attend school again were highly pleasing to us.

The Indians with whom we are connected are known to be no way inferior to Europeans in the capacity for acquisition of useful knowledge. We have no where observed a more eager and steady desire to improve in what is useful, than is discovered by our younger brethren. They all wish to learn to read and write, and in spite of numerous disadvantages, and mostly untaught, several have made progress therein.[43] It is much to be lamented, that for many years past, the brn. who have been in the service of the missions, have not had it in their power to improve this happy turn and propensity, to the furtherance of the work of God, in the manner that they wished to do.[44]

This first annual school year continued well into the summer and ended on August 31, 1800, giving the children several months of vacation before the beginning of the fall hunt. The school sessions, following no regular pattern, changed depending on other events in the village schedule. During most of the years, however, winter sessions began in the later part of November or early December and lasted until early February, when the sugar-boiling season began. Classes would start again in early April and last until midsummer. With the exception of 1801, there are diary references each year to school activity. However, the enrollment never exceeded fourteen students in any given year. Mortimer, Haven, Hagen, Luckenbach, and Proske were listed as the various instructors.

SOME MISCELLANEOUS EVENTS IN VILLAGE LIFE

Tecumseh, in one of his far-ranging visits to the south in 1811, is reported to have met the Creek at their town of Tuckhabatchee, on the Tallapoosa River near present Montgomery, Alabama. He was soliciting military support for his planned uprising against the Americans. Fearing his words were falling on deaf ears, he made a prediction. "Your blood is white. You have taken my talk, and the stick, and the wampum, and the hatchet, but you do not mean to fight. I know the reason. You do not believe the Great Spirit has sent me. You shall know. I leave Tuckhabatchee directly, and shall go straight to Detroit. When I arrive there, I will stamp on the ground with my foot and shake down every house in Tuckhabatchee."[45]

Taking no chances, the Creek counted the days following his departure. At the appointed day he was to arrive, a mighty rumbling was heard —the Indians ran from their houses—every house in Tuckhabatchee was shaken down. It was not Tecumseh, however, but the famous earthquake at New Madrid on the Mississippi River. At Goshen, on December 16, 1811, they clearly felt the shock and also the aftershocks of January 23 and February 7, 1812.

The New Madrid earthquake is considered the second largest earthquake known to modern history. The shock waves were felt as far away as Canada in the north and the Gulf Coast to the south. The area of the greatest shaking was about forty thousand square miles, and the principal shock produced waves of sufficient amplitude to shake down chimneys in Cincinnati, Ohio, four hundred miles away. At Goshen, Mortimer describes this great "Act of God."

Dec. 16th [1811]
    Several shocks of earthquakes were experienced & as we learnt afterwards through the greater part of United States.[46]

Jan. 23rd [1812]
    There were several shocks of an earthquake felt here, and in particular one at 1/2 past 8 o'clock in the morning, more severe than any of those on the 16th Ultimo. None of our brn. & sis. could recollect that they had ever till lately witnessed anything of the kind before, and in common with the rest of the inhabitants of the country were much alarmed at these unusual phenomena. We ex-

plained to them the supposed cause of earthquakes, and exhorted them to put their trust in our Lord, & not to be afraid, but at the same time to pray for the grace to be ready for whatever might be his will with them. An Indian chief who hunts at the present not far from here, gives out, that the late earthquakes took place because the great spirit was not pleased that the white people had taken possession of so much of the Indian country, and had lately killed so many Indians on the Wabash [at the Battle of Tippecanoe].[47]

Feb. 7th [1812]

At about 1/2 past 3 o'clock in the morning, there was a very severe shock of an earthquake here. The concussions lasted nearly half an hour. The morning was perfectly calm & the moon shone dimly. In the evening at about 8 & 1/2 past 10 o'clock, there were two other pretty severe shocks, though not nearly equal to that in the morning. In general about this time slight earthquakes were very frequent, and sometimes lasted for hours successively. In many persons they produced headaches, & disordered state of the stomach resembling sea-sickness. We were told of instances in the neighborhood of children who after an earthquake were obliged to vomit. These concussions of the earth, the dreadful apprehensions that were at this time very generally entertained of an Indian war, the prognostications of a so-called prophet among the whites in Virginia, & a variety of other occurrences, made many people in these parts suppose that the end of the world was near at hand.[48]

Ten years before the earth rumblings at Goshen, an astronomical visitor produced similar reactions among the populace of the village. On January 7, 1801, at 8:30 P.M. a "fiery meteor" passed from the west to the east over the village. From Mortimer's description, it was a spectacular sight. "Illuminating the whole atmosphere to a greater degree than the full moon," he further said, "it exceeded the sun in its apparent size."[49] These natural phenomena were mysterious and wondrous to the Indians, and this incident was no exception among the Goshen residents.

~~~~~

NINE

Without Their Beloved David

The suicide of Henry on March 30, 1805, and the resulting rupture of the very fabric of the Goshen mission cast a deep shadow over the last four years of David Zeisberger's life. Normally of robust constitution, he began to have recurring periods of sickness and took to his bed frequently. Twice, in June and July of 1805, at the height of the insurgency, he was bedfast for lengthy periods. In 1806 his health improved somewhat, but beginning in February 1807 there was a definite change, and throughout the first six months of the year, he suffered almost continuously. By November of 1808 he was again confined to his bed, and it became obvious that David Zeisberger was dying.

Reaction to Henry's suicide is shown graphically in the population figures of the mission.[1] The census for 1803 closed with forty-six converts, and the following year there were thirty-seven. Most of the nine members lost during that year had moved to the new Pettquotting mission.[2] In 1805 there was a net loss of fifteen, and at year's end only twenty-two members remained. The loss of the fifteen—Ignatius's family and his friends—can be directly attributed to the suicide incident. It was not until Zeisberger's death in November of 1808 that the population again began to grow. Two years later under Mortimer's adroit leadership the membership reached thirty-five.

The most shocking development of this whole incident is the animosity that seemed to be directed against Zeisberger personally. Mortimer gives us an entry in May 1806 that demonstrates the depth of the Indians' resentment: "[Sunday] 4th., there was no meeting here as hardly any of our people were at home. A drunken Indian, a young man who had spent much time here, with *horrid imprecations and threats against Zeisberger*, struck his tomahawk with violence close behind him into the ground. There seems to be now among the Indians in general, a furious wild and ungovernable spirit, such as has not been usual in former peaceful times."[3] [Emphasis added]

Thus David Zeisberger became the object of the unpredictable and capricious nature of the Indian personality. Forbidding the burial of a suicide's body on sacred religious ground was beyond the converts' comprehension. Denied the privilege, the Indians retaliated with the one thing that wounded their teacher and protector the most — they turned to the bottle. Zeisberger and Mortimer fought back using the tool that had always solved the problem in the past. They mounted their pulpit. Day after day the diaries detailed sermons on drunkenness. The frequency of drunken behavior reached its height in October 1806. Mortimer recorded Zeisberger's poignant reaction to their detestable binges.

[Sunday October] 26th.

   In the afternoon Br. Zeisberger delivered an earnest exhortation to all the adult inhabitants here, upon the subject of drunkenness, of which several instances have of late occurred among us. He warned them against this sin . . . if [they] persisted it, would prove the ruin of their souls & bodies, and infallibly also destroy our town & settlement. . . . In former times, when strangers came to see us, the brn. always preached the gospel to them, and that no drunken Indian was then suffered as now, to enter into any of our own congn. settlements. He desired the brn. & sis. to consider these things, and to make up their minds as to their conduct in the future, remembering that if our own town and settlement was ruined, *they alone would be to blame for it.*[4] [Emphasis in original]

The day following this sermon William Henry came to Mortimer's cabin with some of the converts to speak privately about the Zeisberger sermon. After promising to refrain from further drinking and to vigilantly prevent drunken natives from coming to the village, he made the following objections to the Zeisberger charges.

[Monday October] 27th.

   1. Though in the large Indian congn. that formerly resided at Old Schoenbrunn, there might not have been a single instance of drunkenness, yet divers inhabitants of that place, when at a distance from home, were frequently guilty of it.
   2. The great murders of our Indians that took place at Gnadenhutten [1782], and the invitations [from the native chiefs] that have been given to the congn. at Pettquotting, are the cause why our congn. has had no permanent access from among the heathen, and our numbers have of late years decreased.
   3. Last of all our brn. objected as follows: "We have seen" said they, "with our own eyes, drunkenness among our brn. in Gnadenhutten, for some years past, whenever we have been there; and believe that it is not taken so much amiss of them, as it is of us." On being answered by us, that it was not the brn. but other people who got drunk there, they replied: "that the brn. there allowed the drunkenness, as they sold out liquor for it."[5]

Mortimer agreed and noted that Henry's observations "were also consistent with the truth." He had no other choice. He had heard the old converts tell stories of the clandestine trysts with the bottle beyond the village limits of old Schoenbrunn. He also knew the constant concern of the native Indians for the safety of their brothers at Goshen. The Gnadenhutten massacre was frequently on their minds despite the twenty-four years that separated them from the event. And he was fully aware of the inconsistent behavior of the Moravians in Gnadenhutten regarding liquor sales to both Indians and white people.

Disregarding his audience back in Bethlehem, Mortimer then took the next eight diary pages to pour out his frustrations. All too frequently the Indians had viewed scenes of drunkenness among the white men at Gnadenhutten who had purchased liquor at Peter's store. "Was not this," Mortimer cried, "the very wickedness of which they were being accused? How shall we answer and reconcile such inconsistencies, and how shall we conduct ourselves so as to prevent their baneful effects?" Although seldom underlining passages in his diary, he continued, with emphasis *"We feel that our admonitions to the Indians against drunkenness are, in consequence, deprived of their former weight; & that they lose thereby their respect for the Brethren congn. in general."*

"Without apology" he continued to explain the eight-year battle against the use of liquor at the village. From the beginning of the settlement they had been "zealously attentive" to guard against the introduction of liquor among the converts. As early as 1798 they petitioned the territorial governor, Arthur St. Clair, and the assembly to prohibit the sale of liquor at the three tracts owned by the society. After a spirited session of the assembly, they succeeded and a prohibition bill was passed, Mortimer wrote, "in terms as full & handsome as could be expected." Only because a majority of the legislators had the "highest confidence" in the Moravians to act with "probity and laudable enterprise for the benefit of the Indians" were they successful. But there had been opposition to the legislation.[6] The opponents had accused the Moravians of attempting to set up a monopoly for the trade of spirituous liquor on their own three tracts. Unwittingly, that is precisely what occurred. Mortimer explained:

As since then [the passage of the act], the Society's storekeeper at Gnadenhutten—the only person on the three tracts in whose sale of spirituous liquor the Society has interest—has, and for years successively, dealt publickly in the same, *While all other persons on the three tracts considered themselves as prohibited so to do. . . .* therefore, in the eyes of the quick-sighted world around us the opposers of the act were right in their vile insinuations concerning us, and we are an artful, designing, hypocritical people, whose professions are not to be believed nor secret views trusted. In addition to all this, it is a known fact, that the Indians in whose welfare we pretended to be much interested, have also occasionally obtained liquor there [at Gnadenhutten] to excess.[7] [Emphasis added]

Several years after the act was passed, it was repealed by the assembly.

Mortimer's act of self-recrimination was futile. Living among the on-rushing tide of white migration, there was little he could have done to change the situation. Time and again Zeisberger had fled with his converts from the influence of the white immigrants only to be forced deeper into the wilderness. Noble as their experiment was, it appears to have been beyond any person's solution. Zeisberger must have known, as he lay dying on his cot that November in 1808, that his battle with life was nearing the end. He longed to join his beloved Savior. At 3:30 P.M. on November 17, he passed away. (See part 3, burial 29 for the details of the last month of his life.) The fight was over, the torch now passed to another.

AFTER ZEISBERGER AND THE COMING OF THE WAR OF 1812

When Zeisberger died on that cold November afternoon, Mortimer was alone at Goshen. Dispatches had been sent to Bethlehem warning against a one-man stewardship, and on January 1, 1809, Abraham Luckenbach arrived in the valley to be Mortimer's new assistant. Since the aborted attempt and his near death at the White River mission in 1806, Luckenbach had returned to Bethlehem. During the two-year period between the close of the White River mission in 1806 and the Mortimer call for assistance in 1808, Luckenbach had been a busy man.[8] He first spent seven months in the eastern settlements. Then in August 1807 he was back at Goshen gaining proficiency in the Delaware dialect. He carried with him in 1807 a Bethlehem commission to explore the possibilities of expanding the mission work among the Delaware along the Miami, St. Mary's, and Sandusky rivers. During the spring and summer of 1808, accompanied by Johann Haven, the assistant at Pettquotting, he traveled among the natives, visiting the tribes in these areas and the Delaware village at Gigeyunk (now Fort Wayne, Indiana). By November 1808 he returned to Bethlehem to report on the results of his extensive travels. Two months later he was back on the Muskingum in response to Mortimer's call.

The thirty-two-year-old Luckenbach spent the next thirty-four years among the Christian Delaware. However, he remained at Goshen in 1809 for only three months. With the close of the Pettquotting on April 25, 1809, Johann Haven was now free to return to Goshen. Luckenbach was then assigned to assist Denke at the Fairfield mission. Just short of one month after Luckenbach's departure, Johann Haven arrived at Goshen to act as Mortimer's new assistant.

1809

After Zeisberger's death on November 17, 1808, Benjamin Mortimer's skill as an organizer and administrator quickly became evident. He began a series of moves to enhance the flagging morale and to upgrade conditions among the converts. Building on the pledges made at Zeisberger's deathbed, he rallied the remaining converts to a renaissance at Goshen. Charles Henry was granted a license to begin a ferry across the Muskingum, which facilitated access to New Philadelphia. Some 269 white persons now lived at the little village just three miles north of Goshen. The previous year the town had become the seat of recently organized Tuscarawas County. No longer would the local citizens be compelled to travel the seventy-five miles to Zanesville to conduct their county business. In April 1809 the converts tore down and rebuilt the old frame structure that housed the church bell. On the same day Mortimer noted, "There is more activity here than there has been for the last seven years, in making repairs & improvements about their houses."[9]

After spending most of her time at Gnadenhutten following her husband's death, Susan Zeisberger decided to return to Bethlehem. A tearful lovefeast was held on August 4, and she left the village six days later.[10] Since the Zeisberger home had just recently been remodeled, it now became the new church and schoolhouse. Nine days later the converts tore down the old church structure and on September 9 completed a new fence around the cemetery.

Near the end of September 1809, Mortimer dispatched Haven and two of the Henry brothers, John and Christian Gottlieb, to the Indian village of Sambosink (Armstrong's Town near present Mansfield, Ohio). The brothers were sent to proselytize among the natives in an effort to expand the Goshen population and bring additional converts to the Savior. They returned on October 2 with a cheerful report but no prospective converts. In November Haven again left the village, this time alone, traveling north to Cleveland and along the southern shores of Lake Erie to the Indian villages along the Pettquotting and Sandusky rivers. Perhaps some of the apostates from these areas could be induced to return to the fold. The winter had already set in, but despite the difficulties, Haven traveled over three hundred miles before returning on December 28, 1809, with a discouraging report. By the end of the year Mortimer noted that there were twenty-nine members of the Goshen mission, an increase of six converts since the previous year. It was a modest beginning.

1810

Shortly after the beginning of the new year, Heckewelder returned from the state capital with heartening news. At Chillicothe he successfully petitioned the state officials to issue incorporation papers to the Society of the United Brethren for the Propagating of the Gospel Among the Heathen. The Indian lands were now recognized and protected by the state of Ohio. It would be Heckewelder's last major contribution to the mission program on the Muskingum. Eight months later, on October 1, he left the valley and returned with his family to Bethlehem.

Heckewelder's replacement, Gottfried Sebastian Oppelt, had arrived from Bethlehem earlier in the spring. Oppelt had surprised everyone when he drove into the Goshen mission on May 16 with his long-suffering wife and three children. The contentious and quarrelsome head missionary at Pettquotting was to be the new agent of the SPG. By now the church fathers had forgotten the self-serving and carping letters that he wrote from Pettquotting and were willing to give him another chance.[11] Oppelt stayed at Gnadenhutten for the next eight years. Surprisingly, he did a creditable job as the society's agent on the Muskingum, working tirelessly to protect the Goshen converts from the wiles of a few unscrupulous white neighbors at New Philadelphia. This was especially evident during the turbulent years of the War of 1812.

Additional changes were also made in the spring of 1810. Johann Haven, who had served as Mortimer's assistant for only one year, returned to Bethlehem on May 25 and disappeared from the mission diaries. His replacement, John Hagen, arrived the following November. Hagen, after an earlier apprenticeship at Goshen, served five years at Fairfield.[12] He assisted Mortimer at Goshen for the next two years.

Other changes were taking place around the struggling Indian mission. In the first decade of the nineteenth century, the white population in Ohio increased dramatically. The Ohio census takers in 1810 counted 230,760 residents in the new state, an increase of over 245 percent since 1800.[13] In the next decade it increased another 150 percent. At Goshen Mortimer was also experiencing a renewed interest among the native Indians. Frequently, forty to sixty Indians would visit the church services, taxing the little building's capacity to hold the crowds. He closed the year with thirty-five converts—the highest figure in the last five years. It would never again reach this level.

Indications of the growing white population were evident by the variety of different religious leaders that visited the mission. On July 12, 1810, the physician and clergyman Dr. Christian Espich visited Goshen, telling Mortimer that he planned to establish a Lutheran congregation at New Philadelphia. Four days before Dr. Espich's visit, the Methodist ministers in the area conducted the first of a number of large camp meetings held near Goshen. Just twelve days before Dr. Espich's visit, the Methodist circuit rider Rev. Francis Travis visited the mission. All of these visitations indicated a demand for religious instruction among the growing white population.

Activities of a more secular nature were also occurring to meet the needs of the growing community. The common pleas court sat at New Philadelphia twice during the year, and the Supreme Court of Ohio met there on August 6. During the same month, the Tuscarawas County commissioners passed through the village with the state surveyors, laying out a new level road just above the river bank to New Philadelphia, thus eliminating the large hill on the old road immediately in back of the mission.

At the same time there were ominous and depressing signs coming out of the West of events that could interrupt this tranquil environment along the Muskingum. Mortimer's entries on March 31, April 22, and June 4, 1810, explain:

31st.

   The account was brought hither, that the Wyandots at Sandusky had lately murdered several of their own people in the same summary manner which was practiced on the Woapikamikunk (White River) during the time Br. Kluge and Br. Luckenbach lived there.[14]

22nd.

   David and Silas arrived here from Pettquotting. They confirmed the reports we had heard, of the murders which the Wyandots of Sandusky had lately committed among themselves; & added that the Delawares on the Woapikamikunk had also some time since killed twelve of their people.[15]

4th.

   An Indian of the name of Tobias came here. He was baptized as a child in Old Schoenbrunn & resided on the west side of the Mississippi. This Indian related that within the last year the Delawares there had killed 20 of their own people, charged with witchcraft.[16]

The Prophet's new Master of Life religion, espoused principally by the young men of the tribe, had spread like wild prairie fire among the western Indians. The horrors of witchcraft killings were continuing. What began so abruptly in June of 1806, as witnessed by Kluge and Luckenbach at the White River mission, was now occurring among the neighboring native Indians: Shawnee, Delaware, Wyandot, and many other western tribes, especially those living in Indiana and Illinois, were rapidly becoming rabid disciples of Tenskwatawa. The movement had already destroyed the Moravian mission on the White River and would shortly cause dramatic repercussions at Goshen.

1811

The new year at Goshen, however, began on a favorable note. Over sixty Indians attended the New Year's lovefeast. But the euphoric atmosphere lasted for only six weeks. On February 17, after a lingering illness, William Henry died.[17]

With the exception of Henry's suicide, none of the forty Indian deaths in Goshen affected the village and the future mission life so much as the loss of this great and lovable man. He was the patriarch of the principal family living at Goshen. It was his wise counsel and intricate knowledge of the native Indian life that repeatedly kept the mission program from destruction.

Two months following Henry's death, Nicodemus was stabbed at New Philadelphia by his son-in-law, Montgomery Montour, in an altercation concerning Nicodemus's daughter. He died several weeks later of his wounds. The incidents connected with this murder kept the mission occupied for the next two months.

By September Abraham Luckenbach had returned from his residency at Fairfield. He had been commissioned by the church elders at Bethlehem to try one more proselytizing effort among the tribes along the Sandusky. This time Hagen accompanied him. In light of the witchcraft killings on the frontier, it was an impossible assignment. Remarkably, they stayed for almost a year but accomplished nothing. The native Indians were in no mood to listen to the white missionaries about God. The threat of war seethed across the western Ohio and Indiana frontier.

On September 20 Mortimer noted in his diary: "The post brought us the account that the Militia of the Indiana territory, under orders of Gov. Harrison, were about to march against the so-called Shawnee prophet & his adherents. We communicated this intelligence to our Indn. brn., to guard against their being unnecessarily alarmed by the exaggerated reports that circulated among the whites and their own people."[18]

THE SHAWNEE MESSIAH

Among the Indians, prophets were neither unique nor surprising. As with most societies, during stressful times they sought refuge in strong leaders. While Tecumseh, the Prophet's brother, fits this stereotype, Tenskwatawa, originally called Lalawethika, is an anomaly. Their father was the famous Shawnee Puckeshinwa and their mother, Methoataske, was a Creek. From childhood, the handsome and dynamic young Tecumseh, "Panther passing across," displayed unusual Indian talents and rapidly became a leader among his people.

When Tecumseh was six, his father was killed at the Battle of Point Pleasant in October 1774, during the Lord Dunmore's War. Shortly after his father's death, Tecumseh's mother gave birth to triplets. However, only two survived, Lalawethika and Kumskaukau. Unlike Tecumseh, whose training during his youth exemplified Shawnee standards, Lalawethika's early childhood was fraught with difficulty. When he was five, and following the Bowman raids on the Shawnee villages in 1779, Methoataske abandoned the boys. She fled across the Mississippi with several members of the Shawnee tribes. The young boys were taken into the home of their older brother Chiksika and their sister Tecumpease. The two older children raised the three younger boys. Unlike Tecumseh, Lalawethika was not a handsome child and tended toward corpulence, which prevented him from excelling in childhood games with other children. He became frustrated and began to compensate for his failures by developing a bullying and bragging personality that earned him his nickname, Lalawethika (The Rattle, or Noisemaker). While still a child, an accident caused the loss of his right eye, adding to his disfigurement. As a young man he became addicted to alcohol, which further alienated him from the warriors of the tribe. Despite his undesirable personality, his brother Tecumseh permitted him to travel with the tribe as they moved farther westward. In his midtwenties, Lalawethika married and began to raise a family. Miserably inept at hunting, he preferred to remain in the village, so other members of the tribe were required to provide meat and provisions for his family. Relying more and more on relatives and friends to feed his wife and children, Lalawethika sank deeper into alcoholism and became the laughing stock of the village. Shortly after the turn of the century, he came to know Penagashea (Changing Feathers), an old medicine man of Tecumseh's village who taught him about herbs, healings, and incantations. In 1804 the old medicine man died and Lalawethika attempted to take his place. But because he was so universally distrusted, he met with little success. After an epidemic in 1805, which he had promised to prevent, Lalawethika's stature as a medicine man plummeted.

Late one cold April evening he fell into a deep trance. His wife and neighbors believed him to be dead and began to make preparations for his burial. After several hours he began to stir and finally regained consciousness. The shaken Indians crowded around his bedside as he began to tell tales of death and resurrection.

Lalawethika, according to his tale, had indeed died and his soul had been carried to a mountaintop by two young warriors. Here resided the Master of Life, who permitted him to look out over the mountain to a celestial paradise with fertile cornfields and lush forests populated with abundant game. This could all be available to the Shawnee people if only they changed their ways, gave up the pleasures, especially liquor, and the other favors they received from the white settlers, particularly the Americans. He assured his audience that he was a changed man. No longer would he drink the white man's liquor. The Master of Life had shown him the way to salvation, and henceforth he would be known as Tenskwatawa (The Open Door), the self-appointed religious leader of the Shawnee and all other Indian tribes. Several months later he had more visions. In August 1805 he led his growing band of young followers to a new village at Greenville, Ohio.[19] Little is known of Tecumseh's role during the initial phases of his brother's rise to religious prominence. He did accompany Tenskwatawa and his disciples to Greenville and seems to have assumed a secular role in running the village. It was shortly after this move that Tenskwatawa traveled to the White River and participated in the killing of the Delaware at the White River mission. There is some evidence that Tecumseh opposed these killings.[20] Governor Harrison, at Vincennes, became increasingly alarmed at the rapid spread of the new Indian religion and particularly at the large congregation of Indians at Greenville who lived within the land assigned to the Americans following the Treaty of Greenville. Reacting to the witchhunts along the White River, he challenged all the Indian tribes to test the Prophet's credentials. In a cicular letter to all the tribes he advised the Indians, "Demand of him some proof at least of his messenger of the Deity? If God has employed him, he has doubtless authorized him to perform some miracles, that he may be known and received as a prophet."[21]

Apparently Harrison was unaware that several astronomers had visited the Ohio Valley in the spring of 1806 to observe the total eclipse of the sun, scheduled to appear in June. Somehow, through unknown sources, Tenskwatawa learned the precise date of this astronomical event. On June 16 he gathered all of the faithful around his village, and at the appropriate time he demanded "the sun to stand still." The results of the eclipse ended the doubts among all of the skeptics.[22]

By the spring of 1808 the Greenville village had outlived its usefulness for the Shawnee brothers. The center of Indian action was now in the Indiana territory. In April they moved to the junction of the Tippecanoe and Wabash rivers. Within the next two months they built the village of Prophetstown.

In the meantime, Governor Harrison had been quietly negotiating treaties with the tribes favorable to the American cause. Between 1803 and 1809 he signed thirteen treaties with the Delaware, Shawnee, Wyandot, Miami, Eel River Miami, Chippewa, Wea, Kickapoo, Piankashaw, and Kaskaskia. Two other treaties were also negotiated during this period by William Hull, the new American commander at Detroit, with several of the same tribes. In these treaties the Indians effectively surrendered most of their remaining land in the new state of Ohio and large portions of their Indiana and Illinois territory.[23]

Throughout the latter part of the decade, Tecumseh desperately tried to remain on good terms with Harrison while he quietly built his support among the more recalcitrant members of the native Indian tribes. During the first part of the summer of 1809, Tecumseh traveled among the tribes along the Mississippi River only to return in August to find that the chiefs had planned to sign the final treaties. It was too late for Tecumseh to stop the meeting, and obviously Harrison had not invited him to the council to be held at Fort Wayne. On September 30, 1809, at the conclusion of the treaty conference, Harrison, with a perfectly straight face, stated, "This is the first request that your Father [Pres. James Madison] has ever made of you and it will be the last, he wants no more of your land." Both sides knew the spurious nature of his remarks. But regardless, the Indians signed, transferring over three million acres of Indian lands to the United States. Harrison had gone too far. An embittered Tecumseh vowed to kill the chiefs who signed the document and warned Harrison that he would kill any surveyors or settlers who tried to enter the newly acquired land.[24] He spent the next two years enlisting support for his confederacy, which ranged far north into Canada and west across the Mississippi. He was a whirlwind of activity, but met with only limited success.

By the summer of 1811, great congregations of Indians had visited the Prophet's village on the Tippecanoe, and Governor Harrison became increasingly concerned for the safety of the white settlers at Vincennes. During this period he had several altercations with the Prophet, which served only to heighten the tension. In August Harrison again met with Tecumseh, who assured him peace may yet be possible. In the meantime Tecumseh planned to visit the southern tribes and told Harrison, "he wished everything to remain in its present condition."

Harrison was now convinced that his only chance of defusing Tecumseh's efforts was to launch a military expedition against Prophetstown. On September 26, 1811, he marched out of Vincennes toward the village. En route he stopped to build several forts to protect his provisions and an orderly retreat, if necessary. The army of almost one thousand soldiers emerged from the forest just one mile east of Prophetstown on November 6.

During Harrison's approach, Tenskwatawa vacillated. Tecumseh had warned his brother before leaving on his southern trip not to participate in any hostile actions. Shaking himself from his lethargy, the Prophet sent a delegation to meet the governor, suggesting that they confer the next day. Harrison, against the advice of his subordinates, pulled back several miles to a camp along Burnett's Creek. Here he formed the army into a hollow rectangle to await the morning. That evening the men slept on their arms.

With another vision from the Master of Life, Tenskwatawa's indecision dissolved. He would remain in the camp and continue his incantations while his men were instructed to infiltrate the American army that evening, and kill Harrison, which would cause the army of white men to fly into the woods like frightened birds. His warriors had little to fear from the hated white man's bullets. The Master of Life had promised him they could brush them aside like the mosquitoes on a warm summer night. Shortly after 4:00 A.M. on November 7, his warriors began to creep toward the American lines. Almost immediately they were discovered, and the battle began. While the initial volley from the Indians surrounding the camp took a heavy toll, Harrison, who had already risen, rallied his troops and at dawn ordered a bayonet charge. The Indians had no stomach for the cold steel, and the bullets killed with a deadly thud. It was too much for the Prophet's men. They gave way and retreated to the village in great disorder. The battle of Tippecanoe brought an abrupt end to the Prophet's ministration. When his hostile warriors fled the battle, back into the village, his life was threatened, despite his assurance that he had new medicine to reclaim the defeat. Only the interference of his friends saved him. On the day following the battle, Harrison entered the now abandoned village and burned it to the ground, destroying over five-thousand bushels of corn secretly buried in the woods. When Tecumseh returned in January 1812 and viewed the destruction, his wrath was beyond control. He seized his brother by the hair and threatened to kill him if he ever interfered with his Indian movement again. Tenskwatawa's days as a prophet were at an end.[25]

Despite all the turmoil that raged across the countryside, Mortimer closed the year 1811 generally optimistic. While a glimmer of hope remained within his heart, his frustration and despair is clearly evident in the following diary entry written on December 31, 1811. It is perhaps one of the most sagacious and perceptive of all his entries. He had lived at Goshen for eleven years. At the end of the year 1811 he recorded seven fewer members than the previous year. But there was sadness in his heart as he wrote.

(December) 31st.
Nearly the same individuals who spent Christmas with us were here again. At 11 o'clock at night we had an agreeable lovefeast with them. . . . We hope, trust and pray that, according to the scripture promise, the word spoken is not in vain, though we do not, & have not ever since the white people have been so much our near neighbors, seen the same encouraging fruit of our labor, that we did during the first years of our abode here. . . . We should be thankful, if circumstances would permit us to pay more attention than we do, to the instruction of their children, who ought if possible to receive their Christian education. True as is this gloomy picture of the state of things in this place, we were, however, very thankful that we could close the year with a sense of the peace of God still continuing among us. Our few brn. & sis. seemed to wish to begin anew to live for our Saviour. . . . For a long time they had been much cast down, from being in a manner overpowered in principle by the presence here of many confused, discontented or evil-minded Indians who had formerly belonged to our congn. These, during the last months of the year, seemed to be gradually leaving us. Perhaps when things had come to the worst, a new period of grace is about to commence among them. Living together here by themselves they have at least this advantage, compared with residing again among the heathen, that when they fall into sin, their hearts are not anew so blinded and hardened by the temptations to follow heathenish practices, and they are not led, against their better knowledge, to seek therein an imaginary satisfaction, and a comfort against the stings of conscience. What they hear over and over again, that if any man sins we have an advocate with the Father, Jesus Christ the righteous; and he is the propitiation for our sins, and not for ours only, but also for the sins of the whole world. . . . We have, however, much cause to wish that their hearts were more established in grace, & that with full purpose of heart they would cleave unto the Lord.[26]

1812

While the principal shocks of the New Madrid earthquake occurred two weeks before the end of the year, the aftershocks on January 23 and February 7 were more severe at Goshen than were the first tremors. To the Indian psyche they were "dreadful apprehensions" and "prognostications" of the end of the world.[27] Two months later the post from Bethlehem brought additional unwelcome news. President Madison had called on Governor Meigs for 1,200 militia "to march immediately for Detroit."

Mortimer explained the reaction of the Goshen converts to this news: "[April]16th. This will occasion much uneasiness among the Indians in general, who are alarmed at nothing so much as at the marching of the militia. It was the militia of this country and not regular troops that murdered so many, in cold blood, in the year 1782 at Gnadenhutten."[28]

To add to Mortimer's problems, he received word from Bethlehem on May 7 that he would shortly be transferred to a Moravian pastorate in New York. Unfortunately, the church elders did not simultaneously appoint his replacement. When the announcement was made to the congregation, he noted their immediate reaction: "The communication caused some agitation among them and they seemed to be generally afraid they would now be left without a teacher, and, as they said, for want of hearing the gospel fall more into sin, thus perish eternally." Regardless of his instructions from Bethlehem, he solemnly promised not to leave before another teacher was assigned to the village. This seemed to calm their fears.

THE WAR OF 1812

The War of 1812 was primarily a frontier war.[29] It is not the purpose of this narrative to discuss causes and campaigns, but it is to show how one of the major disasters of the war greatly affected the small Moravian settlement of Christian Indians at Goshen.

Perhaps the most hapless and pathetic character of the war was Gen. William Hull. After a close vote by the Twelfth Congress, President Madison declared war on June 18, 1812. Three weeks later, Hull, the commander of Detroit, received orders from Secretary of War William Eustis to invade Canada. Hull replied that he would cross the Detroit River in a few days. Good to his promise, he moved across the river and into Canada on July 12, occupying the small community of Sandwich, now Windsor, Ontario. Quivering at the thought of bloodshed, he remained there, inactive, for three weeks. After receiving word that a combined British and Indian force had captured Fort Michilimackinac at the Mackinac Straits, Hull envisioned hordes of hostile Indians coming south to attack him, so he abandoned his position and returned to Detroit on August 8.

Hull's British counterpart, Maj. Gen. Sir Isaac Brock, was in charge of the small British army and Tecumseh's Indians. He was the exact opposite of his adversary. Brave and daring, he stood six-feet-three-inches tall —every inch a soldier. Tecumseh, when they first met, remarked, "This is a man." At dusk on August 14, Tecumseh led his 600 warriors across the Detroit and surrounded the fort. The next day Brock demanded Hull's surrender. Buoyed by the fear of criticism from his officers, he summoned up his courage and refused Brock's offer. At four o'clock in the afternoon of August 15, the British cannons opened fire. While some damage was done, the fort was not threatened. With lighted fuses in hand, Hull's men waited for his command to retaliate. The order never came. The next morning Brock crossed the river with 730 of his own men. Round after round poured into the fort as Hull sat in a stupor in his tent, cannon balls rolling around him. Finally, after hearing Tecumseh had surrounded the fort, he ordered his son, a captain, to raise the white flag in ignominious surrender. One hour later Brock occupied the fort.

Hull was subsequently court-martialed, convicted on all charges of cowardice and on most charges of neglect of duty and conduct unbecoming an officer. A senator from New York, Martin Van Buren, led the prosecution. Most of the incriminating testimony came from Duncan McArthur and Lewis Cass, both Ohio men. McArthur, from Chillicothe, Ohio, became governor in 1830, and Cass is better known as the territorial governor of Michigan (1813–31). The court sentenced Hull to hang, but Madison pardoned him in consideration of his distinguished revolutionary war service.[30]

Most of Hull's men came from the Ohio militia—just part of over 26,000 Ohio enlisted men and officers to serve in the War of 1812.[31] Many of those men came from areas near the Goshen mission. Following their parole by Brock, they returned to their homes passing through Goshen, creating horrendous problems for Benjamin Mortimer and John Hagen.

By July 1 the news from Washington, D.C., reached the Goshen village. It had an electrifying effect throughout the area, especially in the white communities, where the people had already lived through the horrors of many Indian wars. Visions of attacks in the night and rumors of hostile Indian activity flooded the countryside. The Christian Indians at Goshen immediately came under suspicion. The militia had been called to muster at New Philadelphia on August 1. Mortimer provided a clear picture of the white apprehension in a prophetic diary entry five days before that muster:

[Sunday,] 26th.
   A draft of militia was made this week throughout our county, and the men received orders to hold themselves in readiness for the defense of their country. This requisition fell hard upon many heads of families, and others, to whom it was very inconvenient to leave their homes; and numbers were under much anxiety, that if during their absence, an Indian war should break out on the frontier nearest us, their families would be unprotected, and in great danger of their lives. It was also believed, that the circumstance that the Indians reside at

this place, render the situation of the neighboring white inhabitants more critical than it otherwise would be; as here, it was apprehended, hostile Indians might secrete themselves; and from knowledge that they could obtain here of persons and places, devise plans for future mischief among the white people.

The report was circulated, too, that such inimical Indians were already arrived here; that by day they were not seen, but that they assembled here during the night. It was in consequence said without reserve, that before the militia marched, the settlement here must be destroyed. Many declared that if they saw a strange Indian here they would shoot him, and shoot any Indian who would take their part; which was in fact nothing less than uttering a threat of murder against all the inhabitants here; and some said plainly, that every Indian here must be killed. The different militia companies were mustered, and the drafts made on Thursday; and on Friday in particular these alarming expressions were communicated to us.[32]

Mortimer correctly predicted the events that occurred over the next six months. He sat down and fired off a letter to the governor in which he explained his situation. Another was sent to Mr. Varumn, the Indian agent at Sandusky. It was a pleading appeal warning all native Indians not to appear at Goshen. Three days following the mustering of the militia, he went to New Philadelphia to discuss the situation with Colonel Bay, the area commander.

Within a week after he wrote the prophetic entry, they had the first scare at the small village of Canton twenty-five miles north of Goshen. Reports of an Indian incursion forced three hundred people in that neighborhood to flee to the village. While the report proved false, tension continued to mount throughout the area. Three days later, in the dead of night, a party of twenty men from New Philadelphia appeared at the Goshen village and aroused Mortimer from a deep sleep. Reports of strange Indians headed for the mission had been spread in New Philadelphia. After a thorough and futile search of the mission, the disappointed posse members grumbled back to their homes.

On August 17 Goshen received the first vague reports of Brock's attack on Detroit. Six days later the extent of the humiliating defeat became known in the Muskingum valley. Between August 27 and September 7 Hull's defeated troops straggled through the mission on the road south toward their homes. Mortimer did his best to feed the hungry and dispirited men who frequently threatened the villagers.

In the meantime Colonel Bay gathered the militia at New Philadelphia. On September 2 they left the village, marching to join Harrison in northwestern Ohio. The next day Abraham Luckenbach arrived back at Goshen from his unsuccessful proselytizing trip to the Sandusky with

John Hagen. Forced to leave the area, he prudently abandoned his quest for additional converts. Unfortunately, on the return trip, he was compelled to leave his sick companion at Wooster, Ohio, under the care of a friendly white family. Three weeks passed before the ailing Hagen arrived back at Goshen.

In New Philadelphia resentment against the Goshen Indians had now risen to a fever pitch. "The state of things about us," Mortimer wrote, "were now truly awful." Their friend James Clark, the county clerk, had written a letter to Mortimer strongly suggesting that the Indians be moved further east, as he could no longer guarantee their safety. "Humanity cries aloud for the hand of protection to be extended to the innocent Indians who have submitted their all to the protection of the U. States, but yet I am sorry to state that I have no difficulty in saying that in my opinion they will not remain undisturbed in their present place of residence."[33]

Clark was also referring to the destruction of Chief Pamaxit's village at Greentown, near present Mansfield, Ohio. The village was the home of a few native non-Christian Indians who were ordered to leave the town by the area militia commander. He assured the village inhabitants that their property would be protected by his troops. Shortly after they left, neighboring whites plundered and destroyed all the Indian property and burned the village to the ground. This was precisely what Mortimer feared would happen at Goshen if the converts were forced to move.

Mortimer initially agreed to Clark's suggestion and wrote on the same day that he would comply. Several hours after he dispatched his letter, he began to receive strong reactions against the removal from his immediate white neighbors. They insisted he resist the frantic reactions of the New Philadelphians and remain at Goshen. "The difficulty," he noted in his diary, "was to get the whole neighborhood to think so."

On September 17, two days after they received Clark's letter, Mortimer, Luckenbach, and several of their friendly white neighbors visited New Philadelphia. They offered Clark a compromise. "Our proposal," wrote Mortimer, "was that Clark and his friends should, at our expense, hire any number of credible persons that they might think proper, to answer the double purpose of being guards over, and spies upon the conduct of our Indians. They should watch and guard them by day and night, report daily every occurrence among them to some civil or military officer, and cause every Indian who might offend against the law, or act suspiciously, be treated accordingly." He further suggested they should assist in scouting and follow every track of a strange Indian that might be discovered. He would furnish horses for their use in this service. Mortimer assured Clark that "they considered all the enemies of the U. States as their own," and he would personally board the guards in his own home at the village. After a lengthy and thorough discussion, Clark and his friends agreed to the proposal.

Two days after accepting Mortimer's plan, the Goshen residents had another scare. News arrived of four more white militiamen killed near Greentown by hostile Indian natives in retaliation for the burning of the Indian village. This was exactly what was feared would occur at Goshen if they were forced to abandon the area. When the news reached New Philadelphia, fights broke out in the village between those who wanted the Indians to leave and those who opposed their departure. Several of the protestors were confined to the county jail. These events notwithstanding, Mortimer's plans for the guards proceeded, and two men, Peter Edmonds and Daniel Warner, were appointed and began their watch. Several days later two additional men were added to the spy team.

Mortimer was slowly beginning to gather support for the Goshen Indians. On the morning of September 20 he drafted a broadside to be posted throughout the county. It called for their white neighbors to remain calm, appealing to their better judgment in solving the problem.

TO THE CITIZENS OF NEW PHILADELPHIA,
AND OF THE COUNTY OF TUSCARAWAS GENERALLY.
GENTLEMEN! The following remarks are respectfully submitted to your candor and good sense. Would it be for your advantage if the Goshen Indians were removed from their present abode? We have examples before us of the Greentown Inds. So soon as they were taken away from their towns, Indians who were out in the woods began to commit murders in that neighborhood. The tracks of Indians are also frequently discovered in this country; but as yet they have done no mischief any where among us. And they will, many people believe, do none in this country, for fear that vengeance should be taken upon the inhabitants of Goshen. But if the Goshen Indians be moved away, and their town burned, they will, it is feared by many, like the people near Greentown, be in great danger of suffering from other Indians; for all other Indians would be irritated by such treatment.

The Goshen Indians, Gentlemen, it is said, are desirous to give you every demonstration in their power, that they are faithful to you, and their country. They offer to accompany you on scouting parties, to consider your enemies as theirs, and if necessary, to fight by your side in time of danger. They wish spies to be placed by you in the town, to watch their whole conduct, report every occurrence among them, and cause every Indian who offends against the laws, or acts suspiciously, to be treated accordingly; and a generous reward has been offered to such spies for their service.

Dismiss, therefore Gentlemen, your distrust of the Goshen Indians! Consider them as your friends, and neighbors and believe them assuredly, that from the circumstance of these Indians residing among you, you are more safe from danger than any other frontier inhabitants of Ohio. 21 Sept. 1812.[34]

In the afternoon he traveled to New Philadelphia and secured approval from the county officials to post the bulletin throughout the county. Two days later Judge Roth and a party of his friends from Sugarcreek, a small community west of New Philadelphia, visited the mission in response to Mortimer's broadside. Mortimer had traveled throughout his neighborhood among the Methodists, Lutherans, and Tunkers, distributing copies of the bulletin and had stopped at the principal tavern in New Philadelphia to make known to all the object of the visit to Goshen. "They entreated us," Mortimer wrote, "to give up every idea of leaving this part of the country; for if we did so, they said, they saw plainly that the whole settlement, in every direction around us, must be broken up and ruined, as was the case in Greentown, when the Indians were moved away." Roth further promised to provide the Indians with food. Four days later the judge and his party returned with a wagonload of bread, wheat, flour, potatoes, and pumpkins for the village. The following day another wagon arrived with eighty pounds of flour.

Mortimer had won the battle. While there were other small incidents during the next four weeks, they were all minor and were solved promptly. On September 29 the guards were reduced to two, and by October 2 only one remained. For five months the patient Mortimer had delicately and adroitly diverted the forces of fear and prejudice. He had quietly guided the white population in this small section of the Ohio frontier to recognize that it was in their best interests to find an accommodation with his brown brethren.[35]

When the post arrived at the village on October 29, it included Mortimer's call to transfer to the New York parish. The recovering Hagen was to accompany him to the eastern settlements. The post also included the appointment of Abraham Luckenbach to the superintendency of the Goshen mission.

After "a short discourse and prayer," on November 17, 1812, Benjamin Mortimer, his wife and family, and John Hagen climbed aboard their wagons, leaving forever the Goshen mission. For fourteen years Mortimer had ministered to this little flock of Christian Indians.[36] For ten of those years, he lived under the aging shadow of David Zeisberger, the greatest of all the Moravian missionaries. But it was Mortimer who held the flock together in its greatest trials. Only Mortimer understood and anguished over the agony of Ignatius and Christiana caused by the suicide of their son Henry. Only Mortimer understood the double standards of the liquor sellers at Gnadenhutten. Only Mortimer's adroitness brought the mission through the trials of the War of 1812. Never again would the missionary program rise to the halcyon days of old Schoenbrunn and Gnadenhutten. Time had passed them by.

His replacement, Abraham Luckenbach, held on at Goshen for another eight years. Only the families of William Henry, the great Gelelemend, remained with a few of the women and older men and a handful of children. But year by year they fell deeper under the misery of their addiction to alcohol. Luckenbach stayed until May 20, 1820, and then was transferred to New Fairfield. During this period the mission population remained in the twenties. He was replaced by John Proske, who continued on at Goshen for another seventeen months.[37] On November 5, 1821, the last of the Leni Lenape left the Muskingum valley and moved to New Fairfield. The Christian missions on the Muskingum and Zeisberger's noble experiment came to an end.

≋

Part 3
*Record of Burials,
the Goshen Mission Cemetery*

Origins of the
Goshen Biographical Sketches

Indian cemeteries dating from the eighteenth and early nineteenth centuries are seldom found in North America, and in those that have been found, we rarely know the names of the deceased, dates of death, and certainly none of the biographical information. The Goshen cemetery is therefore an interesting exception. There were forty-four burials spanning a period of twenty-four years at Goshen—forty Indians and four whites. Of the Indian burials, nineteen were adults and twenty-one were children.

The eight hundred pages of Benjamin Mortimer's diaries provide intimate glimpses and many fascinating details of each of the Indians buried at Goshen. He gave special attention to every death among the Christian Indian congregation. Where possible, he wrote detailed obituaries and in many instances included long biographical sketches of the subject's life. References to the children's burials, however, were seldom longer than one line or one paragraph. I have included, under the children's burials, some relevant details concerning their parents. Adult entries, however, especially the key figures at the mission, ran to several pages.

The biographical information required for writing this section has been greatly enhanced by the work of Rev. Carl John Fliegel, a research assistant at the Archives of the Moravian Church at Bethlehem. From 1953 until his death in 1961, Reverend Fliegel read every word of twenty-five thousand pages of diary manuscripts in search of the elusive Walam Olum, or Red Score, the ancient and legendary pictorial history of creation supposedly conceived by the Leni Lenape. Today the prevailing opinion is the belief that the Walam Olum is a fanciful creation of a nineteenth-century native exhorter or prophet. Its author appears to have been acquainted with the biblical history of creation and may have learned to read and write in a Christian mission school. Most of the Moravian records are confined to the eighteenth century. This could account

175

for the fact that Fliegel found no record in the diaries on the Red Score, and why no Moravian diarist mentioned the Walam Olum.

While doing his research, Fliegel prepared a massive index consisting of an estimated 30,000 cards containing 135,000 entries. The index was subsequently printed in four volumes. Each baptized Indian convert was assigned a number, beginning chronologically with Abraham, the first Moravian Indian baptized on February 11, 1742. Each time Fliegel found a diary reference to Abraham (1) he entered a note in his index, recording the box number, folder number, and date. There are over 400 separate entries regarding Abraham. Benjamin Henry, the first burial in the Goshen cemetery, became convert 987. However, some of the later baptisms, especially a few young children born at Goshen, were not given a Fliegel number. These are marked in appendix G as NFN, or No Fliegel Number. A map of the cemetery can be found in appendix D.

Fliegel's work is an invaluable aid to modern scholars, especially those writing on the eighteenth century, the Moravian missions, and the life of David Zeisberger.

The notation following each entry (example, MCA B171/F4: 12–13) describes the location in the Moravian Church Archives where the information can be found under the date cited (in the example, it would be box 171, folder 4, pages 12 through 13). Subsequent references to the Moravian Church Archives are identified "MCA." Other sources are cited by author, title, and page reference.

≈≈≈

Burials 1–44, 1799–1823

1799

Burial 1
Benjamin, son of William and Rachel Henry
Goshen diary, August 11 and 12, 1799:

> *11th,*
> Early in the morning Benjamin departed this life. Bro. Zeisberger preached from 1 Tim. 1:15. . . .

> *12th,*
> The brn. [Brethren] cleared a pleasant & elevated spot of land for a burying-ground and opened a road to it. At 3 O'clock, after a funeral discourse in the church to about 50 persons, which was held upon the W.W. [watchword] of yesterday, concerning the happy lot of those who are called home to our Saviour; the congregation went there in procession; when Zeisberger in a fervent prayer solemnly dedicated this newly laid out place of interment to be a depository for the bodies of our departed brn. & sis., till the last trumpet shall call them forth at the general resurrection. Afterwards, the remains of our br. [brother] Benjamin, as the first fruits of the Goshen congn. [congregation] which has been transplanted into the church triumphant, were interred, during the prayer of the usual litany. (MCA B171/F4: 12–13)

The eighteen-year-old Benjamin was born on top of a hill just east of the Gnadenhutten mission in 1781. His family was fleeing from the colonial militia led by Colonel Brodhead, who had just raided and burned their village at Goschachgunk. A concern for the safety of his mother, Rachel, induced his father, Gelelemend, to secure a sheltered place for her to give birth to their child. They camped overnight near the Gnadenhutten mission, where they were safe from the militia.

In 1789, when Benjamin was eight, his parents moved to the Moravian mission at New Salem (Pettquotting) near present Milan, Ohio, on the Huron River. Here his father was baptized William Henry on

177

April 12, and his mother as Rachel on July 5. The family followed David Zeisberger and his Moravian congregations as they continued to move, fleeing the interference of the white settlers and hostile Indians. Benjamin was baptized at the Fairfield mission on the Thames River in Canada on December 25, 1793.

The entire family was among the thirty-three Indian converts who moved from Fairfield to Goshen in 1798. Benjamin, racked with the "white plague," died with tuberculosis within ten months after their arrival. Mortimer, referring to the young man, wrote: "He was of a mild, tractable, and good-natured disposition. His behaviour was quiet and inoffensive, and he was beloved by all his acquaintances."

Burial 2
Francis James, son of James and Sophia, the Younger
Fairfield, Canada, diary, June 12, 1798 (birth of James):

> *12th.*
>
> James and Sophia's son, born on the 10th was baptized by Br. Zeisberger in the evening meeting and received the name Francis. As the Delaware cannot pronounce the letters f, u, & v, they will call him Plancis. (MCA B161/F5: 9)

Goshen diary, September 13, 1799 (death of James):

> *13th.*
>
> Was the funeral of the child Francis, aged 14 months who departed this life yesterday morning, after a lingering illness. A poor family of heathen Indians had proffered their services to doctor him in a mysterious & superstitious manner,* and avowedly for the purpose of gain. The parents were, however, wisely deaf to this solicitation. (MCA B171/F4: 21)
>
> *[Mortimer placed this note on the margin of the diary:] "See Loskiel's Missions History, Part I, page 109."

Sometime during the 1770s, Rev. George Henry Loskiel asked Zeisberger to furnish him with a brief history of his experiences with the Indians. Loskiel planned to write a history of the Moravian missions in North America. In 1779 and 1780 Zeisberger wrote some eighty thousand words on the subject, subsequently sent to Loskiel and used in his *History of the Missions*, published in 1788. It was later translated by Christian Latrobe into English and republished in 1794. One-third of the book was the Zeisberger manuscript; Loskiel rather ungenerously gave him a one-line credit. Mortimer, in this entry on September 13, 1799, is subtly advising those readers back in Bethlehem that these were Zeisberger's observations, not Loskiel's. The following quotation is Zeisberger's original comment given to Loskiel on the subject of Indian doctors.

The doctors among the Indians are nothing but charlatans. Fancied skill and imagined ability to heal the sick are traced to dreams which these individuals may have had in their youth. . . . Older Indians, no longer fit for the chase, are particularly anxious to become medicine men, being able as such to not only maintain themselves but even to acquire wealth. Should one wish to be treated, payment must be ready, in value from £20 to £30, as soon as the doctor enters the home. If the payment is insufficient, it may be expected that there will be but little circumstance and ceremony, in which case, treatment will hardly avail. The doctor has the patient laid before him on the ground in the house or in the open, breathes upon him; or, taking a potion prepared from herbs and roots, blows it into the face and over the body of the sick—for they fancy themselves capable of curing the sick by breathing upon them and persuade the Indians that they have this power; or he makes horrible grimaces, tries to appear hideous and terrible and make such a noise with his howling that he can be heard in the whole town. (Zeisberger, "History of the Indians," 25)

Two years later, Francis's mother Sophia, the Younger, joined her young son in the tree-lined Goshen cemetery (see Burial 9).

1800

Burial 3
Lisetta, daughter of Israel and Salome
Goshen diary, November 24, 1799 (birth of Lisetta):

> *Sunday 24th,*
>   All the men among them went a-hunting, but some of the women remained here; Br. Mortimer preached from Luke 8:5 & upon the parable of the sower and the seed. Afterwards he baptized the daughter of Israel and Salome, born on the 21st., by the name of Lisetta. . . . There was no cong. meeting on account of the unfavorableness of the weather. (MCA B171/F5: 14)

Goshen diary, March 3, 1800 (death of Lisetta):

> *3rd.*
>   Was the funeral of Lisetta, the infant child of Israel & Salome, who departed this life yesterday morning, aged 14 weeks. (MCA B171/F6: 20)

Lisetta's mother, Salome, followed her in death exactly two years to the day, on March 2, 1802 (see burial 14).

Burial 4
Abraham James, son of James and Sophia, the Younger
Goshen diary, June 17, 1800 (birth of Abraham):

17th,

In the evening meeting, the son of James and Sophia, born on the 10th, was baptized by Br. Zeisberger by the name of Abraham. Br. Zeisberger took the opportunity of the father's coming to request the baptism of his child, to speak to him concerning his course in the cong., telling him that he should not rest satisfied with having obtained the forgiveness of his past transgressions, but should seek to enjoy all the happiness which our Saviour had in reserve for him. (MCA B171/F7: 15)

Goshen diary, October 6, 1800 (death of Abraham):

6th,

Early in the morning was the funeral of Abraham, the infant child of James and Sophia, who departed this life on the 4th, aged 4 months. (MCA B171/F7: 36)

James and Sophia lost another child. It had been just a year since the little boy Francis James died (see burial 2).

Burial 5
Gertraud, daughter of Johannes Thomas and Catharina Marie
Goshen diary, October 31, 1800:

31st,

Was the funeral of Gertraud, daughter of John Thomas and Catharine [Mortimer's English spelling of these names], who departed this life on the 29th, aged 7 years. She delighted in singing verses, which was her common employ, both at home and out of doors. Her heavenly-minded disposition seemed long to point her out as a candidate for a better world, to which she was unexpectedly called after a short sickness. At the discourse which was held previous to her burial, the children were exhorted to imitate her example. (MCA B171/F7: 41)

Burial 6
Beata, daughter of John and Anna Maria Henry
Goshen diary, November, 30, 1800:

Br. and Sis. Kluge went to Gnadenhutten, from whence brn. also visited here. There being no interpreter at home, Br. Zeisberger discoursed in the Delaware language from the text of the day 1 Tim. 2:5, concerning the advent of our own Lord in the flesh. Afterward was the funeral of the still-born child of John and Anna Maria Henry. As there had been no meeting here for about two weeks, on account of the absence of the brn., all our own people who were at home today, including the sick & decrepit, attended [the funeral] to the number of 30. (MCA B171/F8: 4)

A stillborn female child was referred to as *Beata*, the Latin word for "blessed infant daughter." *Beatus* is the Latin word for "blessed infant son."

1801

Burial 7
Sophia, the Elder, wife of Josua, Jr., and daughter of John Papunhank
Goshen diary, Monday February 2, 1801:

> 2d,
>
> In the afternoon, after a short discourse by Br. Zeisberger, was the funeral of Sophia, the wife of Joshua [Josua in German], who departed to our Saviour yesterday morning, after a lingering illness. She was the daughter of the celebrated Indian moralist and preacher John Papunhank, who was the first Indian that was baptized by Br. Zeisberger on the Susquehanna. In the year 1764 she was with the Indian congn. in the barracks in Philadelphia, where she was baptized by the late Br. Schmick 11 June the same year, and soon after [June 26] married the present widower by whom she had 10 children. Two of her upgrown daughters were killed in Gnadenhutten, at the well known massacre, one son and two daughters are still alive and are residents here [at Goshen]. After the dispersion of the Indian congn. at Sandusky, she was one of the first who came to live with the missionaries at new Gnadenhutten. She was a useful assistant in the work of the Lord and had a peculiar talent in speaking with new people from among the heathens, who were concerned for their salvation. (MCA B171/F8: 19–20)

Sophia and her husband Josua represented two distinguished families involved from the very beginning with the Moravian missionary movement in America. Her father, John Papunhank, first appears in the Bethlehem records in 1759 when he visited Philadelphia and Bethlehem. The Papunhank family was a small clan of Munsee Indians living, in 1752, at the village of Machiwihilusing on the Susquehanna River (now Wyalusing, Bradford County, Pennsylvania). The Munsee, originally called the Minisink, lived along the Delaware River north of the Delaware Water Gap, but they had subsequently moved over to the Susquehanna because of pressure from the growing white migration. John Papunhank had a reputation among the Indians as a preacher and a conjurer. The Indian psyche was particularly vulnerable to sorcery and legerdemain. There was, however, considerable sincerity in the machinations of Papunhank —he genuinely wanted to help his people.

Following a 1759 visit to the Nain mission when he received an intense indoctrination in Christian teaching, Papunhank returned to his village full of zeal to spread the word of Jesus—the "new found" son of

man. Through the teaching of Papunhank, the Munsee in the village
were intrigued by religion and applied to Bethlehem for a teacher. On
May 16, 1763, the mission board sent Zeisberger to the Papunhank village. The visit was so successful that he returned in June to attempt to
establish a mission. His first convert was John Papunhank, baptized on
June 26. But the mission work was quickly interrupted by the violence of
the Pontiac Uprising, and within a few weeks Zeisberger was compelled
to return to Bethlehem.

The Christian converts living at the existing missions of Wechquetank and Nain, located near Bethlehem, were now in jeopardy. White
mobs seeking to redress the depredations of the native Indian bands resulting from the Pontiac Uprising were threatening to kill all of the Indian converts around Bethlehem. In November 1763 Zeisberger was
instructed to take the 125 converts to Philadelphia, where they remained
under the protective custody of the Pennsylvania colonial officials.

Impressed with his new Christian state, Papunhank was granted
permission by the Pennsylvania governor to join the other converts at the
Philadelphia barracks. A contingent of more than twenty of the villagers
spent the next fifteen months in Philadelphia with the other Christian
Indians from Nain and Wechquetank. In 1765 all of the Philadelphia
converts, some ninety Indians, led by David Zeisberger, founded the new
mission on the Susquehanna at Friedenshutten near Papunhank's old
village. It was these converts who formed part of the nucleus of the
Schoenbrunn and Gnadenhutten missions on the Muskingum River in
1772. Papunhank remained a close associate and mission helper to
Zeisberger until his death at Schoenbrunn on May 15, 1775. His grave
may be seen today in "God's Acre" at the Schoenbrunn Village in New
Philadelphia, Ohio.

Josua, Sr., the father of Sophia's husband and a Mahican Indian, also
had a distinguished career with the Moravian missionary movement. He
was the tenth Christian convert of several thousand over the next one
hundred years. Baptized on September 4, 1742, at the first mission of
Shekomeko in Dutchess County, New York, he remained with the Moravian missions until his death thirty-three years later. In 1745, with the
close of the Shekomeko mission by the New York colonial assembly, he
moved his family to Bethlehem on August 12 and the next year to the
Gnadenhutten mission on Mahoning Creek near present Lehighton,
Pennsylvania. Here he became a Native Helper and a member of the
Helpers' Conference. Following the massacre at Gnadenhutten on the
Mahoning in November 1755, he assisted in founding the Nain mission
near Bethlehem and became one of the trustees. He and his family were
among the Indian converts taken under custody to Philadelphia in 1763.

While at Philadelphia, his son, Josua, Jr., married Sophia Papunhank on June 26, 1764. Fourteen days earlier the bride had been baptized by the missionary Johann Schmick.

Josua, Sr., continued to have a close association with Zeisberger and in 1768 acted as Zeisberger's guide over the Forbidden Path to Indian villages along the Allegheny River. Here they founded the mission of Goschgoschunk.

In 1772 father, son, and their families moved with Zeisberger to the Ohio country. Josua, Sr., and his wife Salome resided with the other Mahicans at the Gnadenhutten mission on the Muskingum, where he died on August 1, 1775. Today visitors to the site of the Gnadenhutten mission in Gnadenhutten, Ohio, can see his grave marker.

Following their fifteen-month custody in Philadelphia, Sophia and her husband Josua, Jr., followed their respective families to Friedenshutten in 1765. The old map of the village shows their well-built, square log house next to the Widow's House and near the church and schoolhouse. Across the street was her father's home. Here at the new mission of Friedenshutten they began their family. Anna, the first of ten children, was born on August 2, 1765. The second child, Bathseba, was born on May 10, 1767. Both of these children, Anna (at age seventeen) and Bathseba (at age fifteen), were victims of the Gnadenhutten massacre on the Muskingum on March 8, 1782. In Sophia's final obituary Benjamin Mortimer wrote: "It was a life of much trouble and hardship." For the next twenty years, with remarkable regularity—every fifteen months to two years—Josua and Sophia had another child, which was not unusual for either white or Indian families living on the frontier. Only half of these children reached adulthood.

There were few amenities in the wilderness of eighteenth-century America. Life was difficult and involved the ever-present search for the very basic necessities: food, clothing, and shelter. Zeisberger and his Moravian Christian missions always occupied that dangerous position between the two cultures: the native American Indian civilization on the one hand and the encroaching white pioneer migration on the other. Trying to maintain that delicate position between the two cultures, Zeisberger continued to move westward, and Sophia, Josua, and their families moved with him. From their first home at Friedenshutten, they moved sixteen times between 1765 and 1798 and suffered unspeakable adversity and turmoil. But it was a happy and captivating life despite the hardships.

Finally, in the snow-laden valley of the Muskingum and almost sixty years old, Sophia lay down on her cot, never to rise again, assured and happy that she would soon be in the arms of her Savior. Josua lived five more years before he was killed by his own Delaware kinsmen on March 17, 1806, in "a pillar of fire." He died at the White River mission (Indiana) as a Christian martyr. Although innocent, he had been accused of witchcraft by Tenskwatawa, "the Prophet," the treacherous brother of Tecumseh.

Burial 8
Moses Mohawk, husband of Rachel
Goshen diary, July 14 and 15, 1801:

> *14th*
> Moses departed happily to our Lord. So few of our Brethren were at home that we had to send to Gnadenhutten for four of them to return home in order to prepare his funeral.

> *15th*
> Early, after a short discourse by Br. Zeisberger upon the text of the day: "Behold now is the accepted time; behold, now is the day of salvation." 2 Cor. 6:2, the remains of our Brn. Moses were interred in our burying grounds. He was the second Indian of the Mohawk nation who has joined our congn. and the only one to remain with us. . . . The evening before he departed this life, he declared to Br. Mortimer as he visited him, that he was not at all afraid to die but desired to be with his Saviour, believing that the time would not be long. The words were delivered with an audible voice, eyes sparkling with joy, and a smile of exaltation. (MCA B171/F9: 8–9)

Only five years before his death, a lonely and puzzled young man—full of doubt and uncertainty—arrived at the Moravian Christian mission at Fairfield, Canada. He came from Brant's Town on the Grand River, the home of the famous Joseph Brant (Thay-en-dan-e-ge-a), brother to Molly Brant who married Sir William Johnson, the longtime Indian agent for the British colonies. Moses was born of Mohawk parentage sometime near the beginning of the American Revolution, about 1775. Following the Revolution his family became refugees, for they had been deprived of their land by the new United States government—the price the Mohawk paid for supporting the British during the war. The child, raised in an atmosphere of turmoil and confusion as a refugee, became a disturbed and perplexed young man seeking solace, like so many of his peers, in the bottom of the bottle. As his addiction grew, so did his concern for his future. He once told Zeisberger, "I might sometime be killed in a fit of intoxication, and my poor soul would be lost." Hearing about the Christian converts on the Retrenche River (now the Thames), he made his way westward to the Fairfield mission, arriving on January 22, 1797. According to his account, he had been baptized as a young man at the wish of his father, but "by whom, or for what purpose he did not know." He was willingly accepted at the mission, but his life as a Christian proved to be turbulent and indecisive.

For almost two years mission life satisfied him, and he presented no problems for the missionaries. On July 15, 1798, breaking his pledge to Zeisberger, he became involved with three friends in another drinking spree and resolved to leave the mission. Mortimer recorded: "On being encouraged by the Indian brethren, & assured to forgiveness, he seemed to take new courage. But his fresh transgression of today entirely broke his spirit." He left the mission.

Four days later Mortimer again refers to their problems with Moses:

> Today the unhappy Moses returned from the temporary exile into which he had been driven by the stings of a guilty and bewildered conscience. He soon came to Br. Zeisberger and expressed his sorrow for his late unseemly behavior, hoped that while intoxicated he had used no improper language to us and desired to know whether we would send him away from our town. If not, he would be glad to stay with us. Br. Zeisberger comforted him in all these respects and gave him the most fatherly and kind advice for his future conduct. (MCA B161/F5: 36)

Moses stayed at Fairfield for another year. In the meantime, Zeisberger left the Thames River location and founded the Goshen mission on the Muskingum River. On July 22, 1799, Moses arrived at Goshen with several other Indians who were allegedly on a hunting party. The hunting trip appears to have been an excuse to talk again with his beloved David, whom he loved as a father.

Shortly after his return to the Canadian mission, he married Rachel, a young Indian girl about his age. His new wife only added to his already mounting personal problems. In October, several months after the Goshen visit, he arrived back at the mission on the Muskingum angry and indignant. He was accompanied by his new bride and her brother, John Peter. Mortimer records his conversation with Zeisberger.

> He is much enraged because his wife Rachel had been taken away from him. He had seized her by force from her seducer but does not intend to live with her again, on account of her incontinent [unchaste] and base behavior to him. He declares that he was so angry with her on the journey, that he had thought of murdering her. From other sources we heard that her brother, John Peter, had also behaved very improperly. (MCA B171/F5: 6)

On October 21 Mortimer entered an interesting anecdote that took place at the same time relating to Moses' problems.

> Br. Zeisberger had a conversation with Abel, who with his wife Sulamith, & one of his children arrived with us on Saturday from Fairfield. Their wish to obtain leave to stay here was granted them. Abel is a young brother, and a somewhat

singular character. He is extremely fond of writing, and without having received any instruction is become a good proficient therein. His performance in this art would do credit to any school. He is a man of few words and can sometimes not at all be prevailed upon to speak. But he often expresses his thoughts in writing. He travelled from Fairfield with Moses, John Peter, & Rachel; and without their knowledge has committed to writing every sentiment delivered by them on the journey. (MCA B171/F5: 7)

Unfortunately, Abel's diary has not survived. Less than three months passed before Moses and Rachel were back at Goshen. On January 7, 1800, Mortimer recorded:

In the evening Br. Zeisberger sent for and had a long conversation with the unhappy Moses, who hunts in this neighborhood, with the view to see whether he could be helped in his present unfortunate circumstances. Apparently nothing could be done for him, as he said that he would never again be reconciled to his unfaithful wife. (MCA B171/F6: 13).

Rachel was with child and "the prospective father" planned to return to Fairfield, there to await the birth, at which time he would "claim her child as his own, give it to another person to nurse for him, and then dismiss her (Rachel) forever." The plan, as Zeisberger explained, was not very practical. Considering Rachel's transgressions, she would not be permitted to live at Fairfield. He burst into a flood of tears and said, "I came to the congn., because I wanted to be saved; but it seems that I shall be lost."

Three days after their conversation, Moses attended the evening church service. It was a particularly spirited session and ended with the singing of the hymn "Christ, Who Saves Us by His Cross." As they were singing the final verse, Rachel silently entered the back of the church, according to the diarist, "much distressed of mind." Following the service she spoke with Brother and Sister Zeisberger and "opened her heart to them." Before she left, Moses returned to the church and also joined them. He had now made up his mind not to return to Fairfield and believed that "he should, by and by, not be so angry and perhaps forgive her." The next day both were promised they could remain at Goshen. Mortimer closed the entry with, "There is now a pleasing prospect of their reconciliation."

According to Delaware custom, a prospective father absented himself from the village just before the birth of any of his children. Moses, following this precedent, was on a hunting trip at the time Rachel gave birth to the child on March 11, 1800. When he returned on March 23, he came to Zeisberger and "in the most humblest manner requested that his child might be baptized." To his great joy this was promised him (see burial 10).

Mortimer noted on Sunday March 30: "The baptism even of a child is a very weighty transaction, at which no one if possible fails being present." During the regular Sunday service, the church, crowded with villagers, witnessed the baptism of the new baby, Levi. Interestingly, Rachel's first husband was named Levi.

Rachel, like her husband Moses, had her share of life's problems. She was born and baptized at the Friedenshutten mission on the Susquehanna River (probably in 1771), then brought as an infant to the Ohio country. We first hear of her in 1789 at the Pettquotting mission (New Salem) where as a teenager she was accepted into the congregation. Several months later she married her first husband, Levi, on September 7, 1789. Three weeks prior to the marriage Levi had been baptized by Zeisberger as a new member of the congregation. For reasons known only to Rachel, shortly after their marriage he abandoned both the mission and his wife as the congregation was preparing to move north into Canada in 1791. The shock of her husband's departure scarred her emotionally. Mortimer once noted "that young women among the Indians who have no husbands are from various causes, in a particularly trying situation." Rachel was a prime example (see burial 15).

Following Moses' and Rachel's reconciliation and the birth of the child in the spring of 1800, a series of tragic events began that culminated in the death of all three of the family members. Moses died of tuberculosis on July 14, 1801. There was no craft, cunning, or duplicity in this young man. Mortimer later admitted, he was "very ignorant, and possessed no brightness of intellect, but his sociable & good-natured disposition, and quite inoffensive manners gained him the good-will of every one." Two months later, on September 12, their little son Levi joined his father. Exactly eight months later, on May 12, 1802, Rachel lay beneath the green oaks in the mission cemetery with her son and husband, and as Zeisberger said, "All were now safe in the arms of their Saviour."

Burial 9
Sophia, the Younger, wife of James
Goshen diary, August 15, 1801:

> 15th,
>   Was the burial of Sophia, daughter of Joshua [Josua and Sophia, the Elder], who departed happily to our Saviour yesterday. She was born & baptized at Gnadenhutten on the Muskingum in the year 1777. When 4 years of age, she went with her parents and the whole cong. to Sandusky. She was a hopeful child; was received into the cong. as a great girl, & admitted soon after to the comm. [Communion]. She was strict with herself and upright towards her

teachers. In Fairfield she married our Brn. James, with whom she lived in peace and harmony, and who on his side showed attention to, and care for her during her sickness, which could hardly have been expected of an Indian. Their marriage was blessed with three children, two of whom departed to our Saviour before her. From her childhood, she was of a weakly constitution. (MCA B171/F3: 14)

It had been just six months since Sophia's mother died. Mortimer erred by three years in stating the date of Sophia's birth. She was born on July 5, 1774, at old Gnadenhutten (MCA B144/F3: 59). She was therefore an impressionable child of seven at the time of the Great Dispersement in September 1781 when she and her family were forced to leave their peaceful valley. The little family remained by Zeisberger's side throughout the next twenty tempestuous years. Seven times they were forced to move before returning to the peaceful Muskingum valley they loved so dearly.

In the interim Sophia had married James, probably sometime in 1797. Their first child, Francis, was born June 10, 1798, at the Fairfield mission. The second child, Abraham, was born at Goshen on June 10, 1800. Both children died at Goshen (see burials 2 and 4). Mortimer mentions the death of a third child, Arnold, in 1806 (see burial 26).

The "peace and harmony" James enjoyed with Sophia during their stay at Goshen was short-lived. She developed, as Mortimer explains, "a painful swelling with which she was often troubled" and by which she was "rendered quite helpless." Only twenty-seven at the time, her affliction confined her to her home, and she became irritable and impatient with the sisters who assisted and nursed her. By the end of the year 1800, it became obvious the sickness would be fatal; however, she continued to insist throughout her confinement that she would accompany her father, Josua, to the new White River mission in the spring. Mortimer noted, "from which purpose she was with some difficulty dissuaded." The mission diary continues:

On the 10th Inst. [August 1801] she sent for Br. Zeisberger & told him that she was now very desirous to go to our Saviour & wished that he would soon call her to himself. She expressed the same ardent desire to him the next day; on which Br. Zeisberger answered: "That you are desirous to go to our Saviour is right & proper as you cannot become well again, & our Saviour will also take you to himself. One thing however I must tell you: You have for some time past grieved the Sisters who helped & nursed you, so that they were no longer willing to come to see you. Send for them (you know better than I do who they are) and beg them to forgive you. I know that they will do it cheerfully." She followed this good advice, and the Sisters assured her that they heartily forgave her everything with which she had grieved them. The same evening she partook of the holy comm., & was very happy. The day following she lost her speech & departed to our Saviour in the afternoon with the blessing of the congn. (MCA B171/F9: 15–16)

At the time of Sophia's death a group of "wild Indians" (Zeisberger's term for native or non-Christian Indians) was present in the village. Her death provided him with an opportunity to do some proselytizing. Contrary to the belief of most eighteenth-century Europeans, religion permeated day-to-day Indian life. They struggled daily to avoid alienating any of the sacred powers that governed their uncertain world. Because of the hostile environment in which they lived, they solicited the aid of the supernatural powers of good fortunes in this world, caring little for the promise of eternal happiness in the next. "Wild Indian" religious life revolved around the attempt to retain the goodwill of forces beyond their understanding or control through the belief in taboos, the observation of omens, and the search for strength in dreams and visions. Since they did not have a written liturgy, they did not appear to the white Christian missionaries—even Zeisberger—to worship God, at least not in the Christian sense. They did, however, pray for help to their *manito,* the mysterious power they believed was controlling the natural world that surrounded them, and they were generally content with the results of their efforts.

Mortimer, in his entry of August 15, 1801, gives us a direct quote from the Zeisberger sermon to the "wild Indians." There was no room for compromise in the mind of this true believer; his God had spoken clearly in the pages of his holy book. "If you wish to be happy, believe in him"—the reward was eternal life. It was a potent message for the mysterious and superstitious minds of those native Americans.

> I will also tell you of something of which you are ignorant. Behold, this person [Sophia] dies quite willingly & happily, because she believes in our Saviour! Whoever believes in him, is not afraid to die, because he knows that he goes to him, and will live with him forever. He leaves his body here, but God will raise it from the dead, & will give him a body that will live forever. If you wish to be happy, believe in him; he alone can save you, & no other. Perhaps you think now that what I tell you may not be true, but the time will come when you will see and be convinced of its truth. (MCA B171/F9: 16–17)

James, Sophia's husband, had a colorful life, full of startling contrasts and ambiguities. Shortly after his baptism at Pettquotting in 1790, he was dismissed from the congregation because of an unknown infraction of the rules; but after a long separation, he rejoined the mission in December 1792. Five years later he stabbed a fellow convert and was again dismissed from the village. Early in 1799 he was back with the congregation and, by the middle of the year, absolved of all his past sins. Mortimer wrote on July 28, 1799:

> 28th,
>   Soon after the cong. meeting, which was held by Br. Zeisberger, James came to him, and in a very contrite manner begged forgiveness for his transgressions, and the offences which he had from time to time given to the congn. This man is of such a character & disposition, and so circumstanced, that there seems to be no other alternative for him, if he would enjoy any true comfort of his life, but to repent of his sins, believe the gospel, and become thoroughly converted. Happily, by divine grace, he appears now to be convinced of this! (MCA B171/F4: 8)

He continued in this "thoroughly converted" state until after Sophia's death, displaying throughout her confinement unusual love and tenderness. But the loss of his first love unsettled the balance of his life. Shortly after her death he left Goshen. By the following July he was remarried and living at Fairfield. While associated with the missions for the next eleven years, he became a wanderer, living alternately at Goshen, Fairfield, and Pettquotting. By 1805 he was living at Pettquotting with his third wife, Rosina. For the next five years he made numerous trips between all three of the Moravian missions, delivering mail and escorting missionaries between the villages. A Fairfield diary entry on August 23, 1810, indicates that he no longer desired to "hear the word of God." Three years later, on June 21, 1813, he was killed in an altercation with a white man, who was subsequently acquitted of the murder. (For the genealogy of Sophia's and James's family, see appendix F.)

Burial 10
Levi, son of Moses and Rachel Mohawk
Goshen diary, September 13, 1801:

> Sunday 13th.,
>   After a discourse by Br. Zeisberger was the funeral of the child Levi, who departed to our Saviour yesterday, aged a year & a half. It is remarkable that his father Moses before his death, ardently and emphatically expressed the wish, that his son might follow him to our Saviour. The child was quite well at the time of his father's decease, but soon after fell into a rapid decline. (MCA B171/F9: 22)

Levi was born on March 11, 1800, and baptized by Zeisberger three weeks later on March 30. For additional information on his short life, consult burial 8 of his father, Moses, and burial 15 of his mother, Rachel.

Burial 11
Agnes, daughter of Ignatius and Christina
Goshen diary, September 26, 1801:

> *26th*
>   Was the burial of Agnes, the daughter of Ignatius & Christina, who departed this life on the 24th, aged 6 years. In the evening the commt. [communicants], who had previously been spoken with individually and found in pleasing course, had the grace to enjoy the holy sacraments of our Lord's body and blood. (MCA B171/F9: 23)

Agnes was born at Fairfield and baptized several days later, on May 13, 1795. For additional information on her parents, see burial 25 of her father, Ignatius, and burial 42 of her mother, Christina.

Burial 12
William Edwards, missionary
Goshen diary, October 8 and 9, 1801:

> *8th*
>   Early in the morning it pleased our Lord to take to himself the soul of our dear Br. Wm. Edwards.
>
> *9th*
>   Br. Heckewelder & Br. & Sis. Huebner came here from Gnadenhutten to attend the burial of Br. Edwards, which was at 2 o'clock in the afternoon. Br. Zeisberger observed in the discourse previous thereto, that Br. Edwards had lived 25 years among the Indians; & that in his old age had he chosen to go again to Bethlehem, whither he was invited, he might have lived much more comfortably there than he did here; but his attachment to the Indn. congn. was so great, that he resolved to die & be buried among them. (MCA B171/F9: 24)

William Edwards came late to the mission field. Born in England of Anglican parents, he joined the Moravians in 1749. He had just turned fifty-two before arriving at Schoenbrunn on November 4, 1776, to join Zeisberger. This was his first missionary assignment. Thus began an association that lasted for the next twenty-five years. Zeisberger and Edwards were kindred souls. Both were bachelors at the time they met, both were near the same age, and both shared the independence and loved the solitude they found living on the edge of the frontier. For those twenty-five years they shared the same life, fought the same battles, and reveled in their last years among the Indians spreading the seeds of their blessed Savior.

     Part 1 of our narrative explains the critical role William Edwards played in those years of wandering in the wilderness before returning to the Muskingum valley. He was especially active at the renewal of Zeisberger's mission work on the Clinton River at New Gnadenhutten. Edwards spent much of his time securing provisions and gathering the necessary food for the survival of the new mission. During the first three years (1782–85), the mission diary is filled with entries listing his numerous visits to Detroit. Leading small supply parties, Edwards secured food; purchased cattle, lumber, and building supplies; delivered mail; and escorted visitors to and from the mission.

Again, in the spring of 1791, with the beginning of the Indian Wars, Zeisberger assigned Edwards to negotiate with their British friends for a mission site at the mouth of the Detroit River. He finally secured the land for a temporary move and eventually received the grant for their permanent location at Fairfield.

With his arrival at Goshen in 1798, Edwards had the option to remain or to return to a life of ease back in Bethlehem. He refused to leave Zeisberger's side and chose to remain at Goshen. For three more years, the two inseparable old men ministered to their Indian brethren. Refusing to return to Bethlehem, William Edwards, on October 8, 1801, finally joined his beloved Savior and was buried among the Indians he loved so dearly.

1802

Burial 13
Rebecca, daughter of Abel and Sulamith
Goshen diary, November 2, 1800 (birth of Rebecca):

> *Sunday 2d.,*
> Br. Mortimer preached from Eph. 6:10–11, and baptized the infant daughter of Abel and Sulamith, born on the 24th Ult. [Ultimo], by the name of Rebecca. (MCA B171/F8: 1)

Goshen diary, January 2, 1802 (death of Rebecca):

> *2d.,*
> Was the funeral of Rebecca, the infant daughter of Abel & Sulamith, who departed to our Saviour on the 31st. Ult. Age 14 months. (MCA B171/F9: 35)

Rebecca's mother, Sulamith, was six months old when baptized by Johann Jungmann at Schoenbrunn on August 6, 1775. Surviving her daughter by only a few months, Sulamith died on June 25, 1803, in her twenty-eighth year at Fairfield, where she was buried.

Abel, Rebecca's father, was a remarkably gifted and naturally talented young man. While, like his wife, he also died young (on April 22, 1805), his short life is a fascinating story. It is told in detail under burial 24.

Burial 14
Salome, daughter of Josua, Jr., and Sophia, the Elder; wife of Israel
Goshen diary, March 4, 1802:

March 4th.
Was the funeral of Salome, who departed this life on the 2d. Inst. She was born at Friedenshutten in the year 1771, came with her parents, Josua & Sophia, to the Muskingum in the year 1772, where she lived at Gnadenhutten & New Schoenbrunn. At Pettquotting she was received into the cong., and admitted to the h. [holy] communion. From her youth up she was orderly in her behaviour, and there were traces of a work of the Holy Spirit upon her heart. She married Israel, the present widower, with whom she had three children, only one of whom is still living. For some years they lived very agreeably together, but at length through some unhappy occurrence, disharmony took place, and she fell into sin. She moved here with her husband in the year 1798, since which, though she was absolved, and readmitted to the h. communion we cannot on a whole give her the testimony, that her walk was an honor to the gospel. She had the unhappy propensity to make an improper use of her tongue, especially in conversation with new people who sought to become acquainted with the congn. Last fall she shamefully deprived herself of the h. commn. again. In the beginning of the present winter she fell into a lingering disease. About 4 weeks ago she sent for all the Sis. to request forgiveness of every thing wherewith she had grieved them, which was readily granted. She also desired to be absolved again in the name of our Saviour & the congn.; and hope was given her that her petition would not be denied, especially in case her dissolution appeared to be approaching. Probably from a sense of her unworthiness, or the belief that she would never recover again, this request was not repeated. Three days before her departure she lost her understanding, and shortly after, her speech. Her soul was commended in a fervent prayer to the merciful Friend of the backsliding sinners, who we believe received her to himself. Her age was 30 years. At her funeral, which the strangers who were here attended, Br. Zeisberger seriously exhorted all present, on no account whatever, to neglect or put off the concern of their everlasting souls till the last moment, as death might come sooner than they expected.
We found afterwards that Salome's unexpected death, and the circumstances with which it was attended, caused many serious reflections among our people. (MCA B171/F9: 41–43)

As noted above, Salome was born at the Friedenshutten mission on the Susquehanna in 1771. She was baptized on March 9, shortly after her birth. She married Israel on Feburary 21, 1789, at age eighteen. In the next ten years she had three children: Eleonora, in 1792; George, in 1798; and Lisetta, in 1799.

Salome is representative of the many converts who experienced difficulty living within the restrictive limits of mission villages. Zeisberger insisted the rules must be followed, and any infraction meant expulsion. Meekness, humility, and a desire to cooperate were essential characteristics. Living within these restrictions was a difficult task for the free-spirited, highly independent Indian natives. Salome, as noted by the diarist Mortimer, had her share of problems with mission life. But, like so many who preceded her, confession and forgiveness were always waiting at the village gates.

Burial 15
Rachel, wife of Moses Mohawk
Goshen diary, May 13, 1802:

> *13th*
> Was the funeral of Rachel, who departed to our Saviour yesterday. She was born and baptized at Freidenshutten on the Susquehanna, from whence she was brought as an infant here to the Muskingum. At Pettquotting, while still a girl, she was received into the congn. and admitted to the holy comm. Her first husband was Levi, who for some reason best known to herself, chose to forsake both her & the congn. at the time when we were under the necessity of leaving Pettquotting, to seek for the second time a place of refuge on the other side of the Lake [Erie]. This marred her whole future course among us, and was the occasion of her falling into many deviations. (MCA B171/F9: 61)

The last few tragic years of Rachel's life are recounted with Moses Mohawk, burial 8.

Burial 16
Anna Rosina, daughter of John and Anna Maria Henry
Goshen diary, October 24, 1802:

> *Sunday 24th.*
> In the afternoon was the funeral of Anna Rosina, the daughter of John & Anna Maria Henry, who departed to our Saviour yesterday, age 5 years and 3 months. We felt much compassion with the dear parents, who have buried seven of their children, and have now only one small infant remaining alive. Other children here were at this time dangerously ill. The present is always an unhealthy season among the children of our Indian brn. & sis. They eat large quantities of unripe fruits; particularly their own corn, (which when prepared and eaten sparingly by the white people is not always found to be a wholesome food), as [it] cannot but dispose the body to worms, and fill it with bad humors. Thus many a sound constitution is ruined in early youth. Add to this, most of the parents do at all times take but little care of the health of their

children. Accustomed themselves to a hardy life, they appear to be but little aware that dwelling now in warmer houses & enjoying other domestic comforts to which they were formerly strangers, their children require proportionably better nursing and attention. In conformity also to Indian maxims, they still continue the capital fault that they let their children have their will in everything. Thus for example; if a sick child, in the midst of a profuse sweat, expresses an inclination to be taken out of doors, be it even in the night and when it rains or is foggy, the desire according to their notion must forthwith be gratified. *Upon the whole, we have to lament that the cultivation of the minds of our Indian brn. & sis., has not kept pace with the small improvement that has been made in their outward condition.* (MCA B171/F11: 2; emphasis added)

Mortimer, like so many of his Christian missionary peers, had difficulty understanding the reluctance of native Indians to adjust to white cultural practices. In their rush to "reduce the Indian to Civility," they were confounded when the natives refused to comply. Native diet was essentially corn and meat while the missionaries' fare was primarily agricultural products. The cooking and preparation of these foods differed radically from native procedures. It is little wonder that the natives experienced dietary problems. Similarly, the raising of Indian children differed radically from white childrearing practices. Most native Indian tribes were quite permissive in raising their young, and the Delaware were no exception. Parents were indulgent with their children and rarely punished them for fear that mistreatment might result in the child being taken away from them by their creator. Also, mistreatment of their children might predestine rejection of the parents in old age, when it became essential for the aged parents to rely on their children for care. Zeisberger frequently registered complaints regarding this indulgence.

Burial 17
Anna Salome, daughter of Joseph and Beata
Goshen diary, November 8, 1802:

8th.

Was the funeral of Anna Salome, the infant daughter of Joseph and Beata, whose short race of but little more than one year ended on Saturday night last [November 6]. This child was naturally strong and healthy, and had no other disorder that we know of but the common ague & fever. While laboring under the sickness, instead of carefully guarded against dampness & cold, she was while in full perspiration taken but out of doors by her mother when it rained, and frequently made to lie on the wet ground while she gathered hickory nuts. Under treatment like this, what wonder is it that the Indians lose most of their offspring at an early age? It is much surprising that any of them actually arrive at years of maturity. (MCA B171/F11: 2)

1803

Burial 18
Jacob, son of John and Anna Maria Henry
Goshen diary, Janury 28, 1803:

> *28th.*
> Was the burial of Jacob, the last surviving child (from a total of eight) of John and Anna Maria Henry, who departed to our Savr. on the 26th, aged nearly 1 year and 2 months. He was of a healthy constitution; the immediate occasion of his last sickness was, that his mother about 10 days since went with him to see a female friend at some distance from here in the woods, with whom she passed a cold night. The next morning the child was taken ill of a disorder in his bowels, which baffled all the means made use of for its removal.
>
> When desired, and in cases where there appears to be no danger of our doing harm, we frequently administer medicine and offer our best advice to the sick. The misfortune is, we are sometimes not applied to till the last extremity, when a great variety of decoctions have been found to afford no relief, and the patient appears to be near his end. It was an excellent practice of the late Brs. Schmick & Jungmann when in the service of the mission, that they went from house to house *daily*. This is in fact the only way to become acquainted with the wants and situation of every family among us. Our dear people require being attended to, and taken care of, in many respects like children.
>
> Since the commencement of the settlement here, very nearly as many children have died as have been born. God must have wise reasons for permitting this. Perhaps he sees fit, that the present inhabitants of Goshen should be left without posterity: the children are too much beloved by him to be left exposed to the temptations of mature years. John Henry remarked on this occasion, that his only comfort was, the joyful hope of once seeing his children again with our dear Saviour. (MCA B171/F12: 17–18)

The poignant words of Mortimer fly across nearly two hundred years clearly revealing the love, sadness, and frustration he must have experienced on that cold January afternoon. Zeisberger and Mortimer (and their wives) were sacrificing their lives for a cause in which they believed, but it was not enough to protect their beloved flock.

Burial 19
Anna Maria Henry, wife of John Henry and daughter of Ignatius
   and Christina
Goshen diary, March 17, 1803:

17th.

Was the funeral of Anna Maria, the wife of John Henry, who departed to our own Saviour on the 15th. She was born to Ignatius & Christina at Old Schoenbrunn in the year 1773, was admitted to the holy communion at Pettquotting. In the latter place she also married. All her children, eight in number, departed this life before her. On the death of the last infant Jacob, in January last [see burial 18], she was inconsolable & expressed her ardent desire soon to follow him; declaring also, that her determination was, through grace, to remain faithful to our Saviour & the Congn. She was a truly converted person, her natural temper being extremely warm and resentful, in which of late years she altered much for the better. She was ever faithful to her husband and remarkably industrious and hard working. The great exertions which she made in cutting down trees, carrying heavy loads of firewood, and performing the other customary labors of the poor Indian women, were sometimes made at the expense of her health. Her constitution was naturally strong. She is now at rest with the redeemer of her soul, in whose atonement for her sins she gladly & sincerely believed. Her age was 30 years. (MCA B171/F12: 27–28)

Anna Maria lived among the Moravian Christians for her entire life. When she was seventeen, she married John Henry, on March 31, 1790, at Pettquotting. Her new husband was the son of William Henry (Chief Gelelemend). As Mortimer would say, "Her walk was in grace and a testimony to her Saviour."

John later married Anna Benigna, the thirteen-year-old sister of Anna Maria (see burial 36 for additional details on his life).

Burial 20
Ketura, daughter of Johann and Anna Sophia Adam
Goshen diary, April 8, 1803:

Good Friday, 8th.

In the evening, was the burial of the child Ketura, daughter of Anna Sophia, who departed to our Savior on the 6th. aged nearly 7 years. She was a healthy child till about a year ago, when she was seized with violent convulsive fits, which after some time subsided, though they appeared to have weakened her faculties. Her last sickness continued 9 days. (MCA B171/F12: 32)

Ketura's family lived at Fairfield, where she was born on April 9, 1796. Her father, Johann Adam was critically injured in a drunken altercation and died from his wounds on April 17, 1799, just two months short of his sixteenth birthday. Ketura and her mother subsequently came to Goshen. The mother, Anna Sophia, later remarried twice. Her second husband was Thomas White Eyes, the son of the late famous Chief White Eyes. For additional information on Anna Sophia and Thomas White Eyes, see burial 28. For further discussion of Ketura's death see "Sickness and Health," chapter 7.

Burial 21
Rachel, wife of William Henry (Chief Gelelemend)
Goshen diary, October 8, 1803:

   8th,
      Early was the funeral of Rachel the wife of Wilm. Henry, who entered into
   the joy of her Lord on the 6th. She was born somewhere near the banks of the
   Allegheny river, came to the congn. with her husband at Pettquotting, and
   was baptized & admitted with him to the holy communion. They have lived
   together in the married state, as nearly as we can compute, about 49 years, &
   have had 12 children, of whom three sons only are still alive, namely the brn.
   John, Charles, and Christian Gottlieb Henry, at the present residing here. She
   was a faithful and affectionate wife & mother, & was universally esteemed on
   account of her inoffensive, peaceable and obliging behaviour to every one.
   The most distinguishing features in her truly amiable character were meekness & lowliness of heart, and a poorness of spirit which has the promise of
   the kingdom of heaven. It was often remarkable to us, that though aged, when
   she came to the congn., & after appearing to have but a weak memory, she had
   learned by heart, and could join in singing, almost all the verses made use of
   in our church. From the time of her conversion, she remained faithful to the
   grace imparted to her. (MCA B171/F13: 34–35)

   Rachel and her husband were one of the most outstanding couples
in the history of Moravian mission work. Additional details of this
exceptional pair will be found in burial 33, William Henry.

1804

Burial 22
Joseph Warner, son of Benjamin and Bethiah (Warner) Mortimer
Goshen diary, January 3, 1804:

   3rd,
      Was the funeral of the child Joseph Warner Mortimer, who departed to our
   Saviour early yesterday morning, in a convulsive fit, aged 9 weeks & 4 days. Br.
   Mortimer took this opportunity to testify, from his own experience, that in
   hard trials, the word of God is through his Spirit the best & only sure support
   & comfort of those who have the grace to believe it. Among the Indians in
   general the idea is prevalent, & cannot as yet be eradicated among our brn. &
   sis., that most deaths are occasioned by the machinations of some person. The
   bro. & sis. & strangers present on this occasion were now told by a Br. in an
   affecting case in his own family that he received the painful stroke with resig-
   nation & humble submission, as from God alone, who has the sole power over
   life and death & does all things well; & that it is to us an unspeakable source of

consolation that we know that all believers and all children, when taken out of this world, will be happy forever with our Lord in heaven. (MCA B173/F1: 1)

Joseph's father, Benjamin Mortimer, an Englishman, joined Zeisberger and the mission field at Fairfield on May 25, 1798, just three months prior to their removal to Goshen. He remained by the venerable missionary's side until Zeisberger's death in 1808. Mortimer is the author of most of the mission diaries quoted in this narrative, and these are among the few Moravian diaries written in English. He and his wife remained at the Goshen mission until November 11, 1812, when they returned to Bethlehem. Subsequently, he became the pastor of the Moravian church in New York City, where he died November 10, 1834.

1805

Burial 23
Benjamin, son of Christian Gottlieb and Anna Susanna Henry
Goshen diary, April 4, 1805:

4th.
　　Br. Zeisberger kept the funeral of the child Benjamin Henry, born on the 26th Ult. [Ultimo], whom our Saviour pleased to take to himself yesterday. (MCA B173/F2: 10–11)

Burial 24
Abel, son of Thomas and Savina; great-grandson of Netawatwes;
　husband of Sulamith
Goshen diary, April 24, 1805:

24th.
　　Was the funeral of Abel, who departed happily to our Saviour on the 22d., aged as we suppose, about 35 years. He was the great-grandson of the well known Delaware chief Netawatwes, and came to the congn. at Old Schoenbrunn, with his father the late Brn. Thomas. When about 15 years of age, he had the grace, at his own earnest desire, to be washed from his sins by holy baptism, being at that time afflicted with a severe sickness, from which he however soon after recovered. As a boy he was remarkably reserved, seldom speaking to any one but his constant companions. When Br. Zeisberger began to keep school in Pettquotting, to the surprise of every one, he made far quicker progress in learning than anyone of the other young people there. He soon learned, both to read & write, & from that time forward these were his favorite employment, and he sought the like pleasures in such exercises. He wrote a neat, & legible hand, both English & German, and copied off every

translation into his native language that he could become possessed of. He had a reflecting mind, and much natural capacity for the acquisition of languages. During the time that he lived in Fairfield, he compiled a small Chippeway vocabulary, explained in Delaware; & he is supposed to have had pretty extensive acquaintance with that dialect. He had a fine voice for singing our tunes, & was after employed for many hours therein alone in his house.

A man of such natural & acquired talents seemed capable of becoming a shining ornament of our congn., had his unbroken temper been subsided by divine grace. But he was of a malicious, perverse, & obstinate disposition, and ever ready to fall into the sin of drunkenness. Availing himself of the superstitions prevalent among his nation, he knew how to make them afraid of him, by pretending that he had it in his power to cause whom he pleased to die. He knew well & to us was ever ready to acknowledge that this was a mere pretense of his; for when asked occasionally by Br. Zeisberger: How many devils he had?—he would frankly acknowledge that he had none, & no power to do any thing. Accordingly, when his late wife Sulamith, before her death about two years ago in Fairfield, desired him to use sorcery over her, he recommended to her rather to turn to our Saviour, & implore mercy & help from him only. From the time of our moving to this place, he & his late wife often travelled between here and Fairfield, commonly staying so long in each place, till they were sent away on account of bad behaviour. Last fall he came hither for the last time, & it was soon evident that he was in deep decline. He continued as heretofore frequently to attend meetings, but evinced for a long time not the least disposition to seek pardon of our Lord for his many sins. On the contrary, all the answers he gave to the kind admonitions of the brn., seemed to be those of an hardened infidel & scoffer. After the awful death of Henry on the 30 Utl. [see comments in burial 25], his sister Rosina gave him no rest, but continually teased him with the representation, that if he died in his present state, without forgiveness, he would also be buried like a dog outside of the burying-grounds & his soul would be lost. From her, however, he would accept of no advice; they quarrelled together, and she was obliged to discontinue her importunities. At length he turned penitent, and sent his brother Isaac to Br. Zeisberger on the 3d. Inst., soon after which his absolution followed, as above noticed. From that time forward he was no longer a child of darkness, but of the light; & his cheerful & serene countenance bespoke that happiness of his soul of which ever ready to testify. He became in truth an entire new man, and so complete a contrast to his former self, that those who had known him could not forbear expressing their great surprise thereat. He departed this life with joy, accounting it his highest bliss to be at home with the Lord. (MCA B173/F2: 15–18)

There are compelling characteristics about Abel that make him one of the most interesting subjects of this narrative. The blood of the great Netawatwes flowed in his veins, but he never quite reached the "state of grace" required for mission life and certainly did not become the "shining ornament" predicted by Mortimer. The sedate and serene life of the mission conflicted with his independent, wanderlust Indian nature. An entry on April 5, 1802, gives us a clue to this tendency in his character and the frustration he must have given the missionaries.

> *5th.*
>
> The Indian Abel, who for his disorderly behaviour had been ordered sometime since to leave the congn., in a letter to us very humbly confessed his faults, promised amendment, and desired that further patience might be had with him. He remarked that should he be obliged to go away from here, he would spend his time alone in the woods, among the wild beasts, without seeing the face of man. His letter would have been quite satisfactory, had it not been but too evident, both to us and the helper brn. that he had contrived to insert therein some sarcastic remarks, in a style of very keen satire. (MCA B171/F9: 45–46)

At least, on this occasion, his clever remarks and sly comments did not win the day, and even the veiled threat of a "heathen" life among the "wild beasts" did not convince his friends at the mission. His efforts to gain readmission failed. (Unfortunately the letter is no longer extant.) The next year, following the death of his "unrepentant" wife, Sulamith, at Fairfield, his attitude mellowed. By the fall of 1804 he was readmitted at Goshen. Had Abel been born white in the eighteenth century, his natural intelligence, quick wit, and sense of humor would possibly have made him a noteworthy man.

Another death occurred on March 30, 1805, which had a profound effect on village life and indirectly led to the death of Ignatius, one of the stalwart members of the congregation. The untimely death of his son Henry not only demoralized Ignatius and his family, but shocked all members of the mission and clearly demonstrates the limits of forgiveness and the strict interpretations the missionaries placed on their understanding of Christian doctrine. Some of the details of this incident have been previously discussed in chapter 7. What follows are liberal quotations from Mortimer's diary which clearly show the devastating effect that Henry's death had on the mission program and on all of the personnel involved, both the Indian converts and white missionaries.

Goshen diary, March 30, 1805:

> *30th.*
>
> The very affecting circumstance occurred, that Henry [Heinrich, in German], elder son of Ignatius & Christina, deliberately put an end to his life by poison. Nothing like this has ever before occurred in an Indian congn., though

among the heathens such deaths are common. His parents had for about a year past been apprehensive that his friends would bring him to an untimely end; but they little expected that he would choose to be his own executioner. When in his last agonies, they desired that he might receive absolution: a request that could not possibly be complied with as it was now too late, & he had to our or their knowledge never in his lifetime desired pardon of God or man for any of his numerous offenses. At this they were much offended with us, though they should have blamed themselves chiefly for having, in spite of all admonitions given their son a bad education.

To us it was painful that such a circumstance should occur in our place, though we believe that our Lord has been pleased to permit it for wise purposes. We must remark however, that this Henry has for some years past not been considered as any longer belonging to us, being in truth a perfect heathen. (MCA B173/F2: 8–9)

Goshen diary, March 31, 1805:

31st.

In the afternoon the relations buried the corpse of the deceased Henry, at the place permitted them at some distance from our own burying-grounds. Had it been desired, we white brn. would also have attended at the grave, and a short discourse would have been delivered. But they were too highly displeased on account of his not having received absolution, & at being refused leave to bury him near, & in the same line with our departed brn., to be able to ask such a favor. (MCA B173/F2: 9–10)

Reflecting back over these many years since young Henry's suicide, it is tempting to conclude that David Zeisberger made a monumental error. Perhaps so. But consider that as a young man Zeisberger studied in Bethlehem under the tutelage of Bishop Augustus Spangenberg, the leader of the Moravian Church in America. Spangenberg's many writings, especially his *Idea Fidei Fratrum,* clearly show the doctrinal position of the church regarding suicide. He called it "self murder" and deemed it a work of the flesh and inconsistent with the life of a believer. It therefore implies a separation of the victim from Christ and a yielding of one's life and action to the evil one. Hence, burial in the consecrated burial ground would have been inconsistent with the doctrinal position of the church. While on many occasions Zeisberger did forgive transgressions against his Christian message and willingly forgave and accepted the sinner back into the congregation, this one occasion he remained intransigent. Unyielding as he appears to be in this incident, think what must have gone on in the minds of both Zeisberger and Mortimer. These were dedicated and loving men devoted to their cause and their people. Between the lines of Mortimer's diary we can almost read the bitter disappointment and agony they personally felt in the lapses of this young man and, further, the feeling of responsibility in not having found a way to save this poor sinner.

The reader must remember the strict prohibition against suicide that prevailed in the eighteenth century, especially among church officials. While suicide may be more prevalent today, or at least accepted with more compassion, it remains difficult to accept for most professed Christians. It is still not an easy issue.

Henry was twenty-one at the time of his death. The following account of his father's death explains the impact the suicide had on village life.

1806

Burial 25
Ignatius, husband of Christina
Goshen diary, September 12, 1806:

> *12th.*
> Was the funeral of Ignatius, who departed to our Lord happily yesterday morning. He came as a youth to the congn. at Schechschiquanunk on the Susquehanna from whence he emigrated with the rest of the brn. & sis. there in the year 1772 to the Muskingum. In 1773 he was baptized at Old Schoenbrunn, & soon after admitted to the holy comm. During the trials that befell our Indian congn. in the following years, he was a brother who always remained faithful to his call and to the people of God, and the experience he had made of grace and mercy upon his own soul. . . . He always shewed much more inclination to follow husbandry, and the arts connected therewith, than hunting, which has, we believe more uniformly been the turn of the best characters that have been found among our Indians: *husbandry tending naturally to produce a regular orderly, industrious course of life; and hunting, if followed by alternate periods of idleness, dissipation, and excess.* The first years of his abode here were perhaps the most agreeable to him of any in his life, and it was then his full purpose to spend here the remainder of his days. As his family grew up, his troubles increased, especially from the female part of it, whose counsel to and control over him, was not always that of wisdom and goodness; and through his oldest son Henry, who in a fit of refractory disobedience, put an end to his existence in March last year. The kind, indulgent, tender heart of our late dear brother was now broken-down with sorrow; and he was for a short time, among other improprieties & sins, led to assume a harshness of demeanor toward his teachers, which we had never before witnessed in him. Thus disposed, he moved with his family to Pettquotting, where he soon became uneasy on account of the offense that he had given here, & in particular because he had grieved Br. Zeisberger. As he heard of the subsequent severe indispositions of

this his well-tried friend, he not only, with many tears, through Br. Oppelt [head missionary at Pettquotting] asked his forgiveness by letter; but hastened to receive the assurances of the same personally, as soon as his circumstances permitted; and the gospel, in which he gladly believed, remained, as heretofore his refuge, comfort and relief, amidst the numerous and very heavy afflictions to which he was now subjected. From the time that he left this place, his life was but a succession of trouble, and of wanderings from place to place; and his last sickness was short. . . . A week ago he returned from Charlestown with his family, and appeared quite emaciated & worn down. His last visits were to his teachers, whom he had learned to regard as his best earthly friends. On the 10th., agreeable to his request he received solemn absolution; & thence forward waited, with patient but earnest desire, to be home with the Lord. . . . White people attended his funeral, and helped to carry him to his grave. (MCA 173/F3: 2–6; emphasis added)

Ignatius's obituary is typical of most of the obituaries written by Mortimer; they deal primarily with the spiritual life of the deceased and relate only a few of the personal contributions made by the subject. Those of us living in the twentieth century may have trouble cutting through the verbiage of most nineteenth-century biographers to arrive at the facts. In biographies by some nineteenth-century writers like Mortimer, even the vilest scoundrel will be found an acceptable candidate for a seat in heaven at the right hand of Christ. This in no way is meant to be a reflection on Mortimer's sincerity, for he firmly believed in the program for Indian rehabilitation. But the clash of the two cultures is clearly evident in Mortimer's comments on hunting versus husbandry. In Mortimer's eyes hunting produced "idleness, dissipation, and excess," while husbandry contributed to "a regular orderly, industrious course of life." Hunting, to the native American Indian, was not a sport—as it was viewed by white settlers—but a matter of his very existence. For generations, the Indian economy had been supported by hunting and agriculture, and it was difficult to break this tradition. Hunting was not sport but serious work. For months at a time, in both the spring and winter, hunters traveled many miles to search for game, which they hauled on their backs to their villages. It was also an integral part of their culture, as the skins were traded to the whites for supplies which their economy desperately needed, and the meat was consumed by their own families.

Ignatius was a remarkable man. Except for one deviation at the time of the tragic death of his son, he remained a steady contributor to the mission program. Following his marriage on January 6, 1774, his growing family followed the trail of Zeisberger and the other converts from mission to mission for twenty-five years, until the family arrived at Goshen on May 26, 1799.

Ignatius followed Mortimer's advice and developed his skill as a husbandman and became an expert carpenter. In Mortimer's own words, several entries clearly show the extent of his skill.

Entry for September 9, 1799:

> 9th.
> William Henry and several other brn. went to Gnadenhutten. Ignatius is a good carpenter, generally spends the whole week there, as he has undertaken to build a dwelling house for Br. Heckewelder. (MCA B171/F4: 21)

Entry for September 26, 1799:

> 26th.
> Ignatius, who had long been at work in Gnadenhutten, and thereby been prevented from building a house for himself before winter set in as he intended, returned home again, in order to erect a temporary cabin for his family, to shelter them from the inclement weather of the approaching winter season. (MCA B171/F4: 23)

Entry for April 16, 1800:

> 16th.
> Ignatius went to Gnadenhutten to finish the house which he has contracted to build for Br. Heckewelder. (MCA B171/F6: 31)

Entry for May 4, 1800:

> Sunday 4th.
> Ignatius returned from Gnadenhutten, having finished all the work that he had engaged to perform there. We considered it as an honor to our congn., that he has been permitted to build the house which is designed for the habitation of the agent of the Heathen Society there [Society of the United Brethren for the Propagating of the Gospel Among the Heathen, of which Heckewelder was the agent], and is at first to be made use of for divine worship of the congn. We learned afterwards with pleasure, that he had discharged his contract to the entire satisfaction of Br. Heckewelder while his whole conduct had gained him the esteem & good-will of all the Gnadn. brn. and sis. *It is a remarkable circumstance, singular perhaps in the history of our times, that a converted heathen, formerly a savage, should build a religious meeting house for the use of a congn. of white Christians.* (MCA B171/F7: 1–2, emphasis added)

In September 1800, four months after finishing the Gnadenhutten structure, Ignatius was appointed the Master Builder and began to build a residence for Benjamin Mortimer at Goshen. He also continued to do carpenter work at Goshen, Gnadenhutten, and Warwick (probably near the present village of Tuscarawas, four miles south of Goshen). The death of Henry, however, and the treatment his family received from the missionaries immediately following the tragedy seem to have caused Ignatius to lose his confidence in the mission program and may have led to his death less than a year later.

Henry was born and baptized at the Clinton River mission of New Gnadenhutten in 1784. The first indication of Henry's problems occurred when he was seventeen and is recorded in the diary entry for May 19, 1801.

> *19th.*
> Ignatius returned with a heavy heart from a long and fruitless search for his son Henry among the camps of the wild Indians in the woods. He [Henry] left the congn. some time ago, since which the account was brought here, that another Indian had almost killed him. (MCA B171/F8: 50)

One month later Mortimer, on June 16, recorded this entry:

> *16th.*
> Henry, the son of Ignatius came here, owned his bad conduct, and begged leave to live here again. Br. Zeisberger desired him seriously to consider which was preferable, to live like a wild beast in the woods, or to be in the congn. (MCA B171/F9: 3)

Apparently the Zeisberger conversation had minimal effect on the young man's actions. Over the next three years he wandered in and out of Goshen. At the beginning of January 1802, he traveled to Fairfield with Christian Gottlieb Henry and returned four months later. In August of the same year he left the village again, returning three months later with a new wife, Anna Johanna, who had been baptized as a child at Pettquotting. The marriage lasted less than seven months. On June 24 of the following year, Henry again left Goshen, returning on November 28, 1803, with his second wife. That was too much for the exasperated Mortimer. He recorded, "Henry returned here after a long absence among the heathens, and he brought with him another wife. This young man has caused us much trouble." (Anna Johanna, the first wife, turns up in the Pettquotting diary on August 1, 1804, as the wife of a French trader.) Surprisingly, Henry was permitted to live at the village for the next year with his new, native Indian wife. On September 10, 1804, he left Goshen for Pettquotting. He returned alone for the final time on November 24, remaining in Goshen until he committed suicide on March 30, 1805.

Eight days after Henry's burial, Ignatius gave Zeisberger notice that he intended to move his family to Pettquotting. On April 16 Zeisberger made one final attempt to reconcile the distraught father:

16th.

Br. Zeisberger had an opportunity of conversing with Ignatius, concerning the mischief which occasions here. [Apparently, most of the village had engaged in a wild drinking party reflecting their disapproval of the missionaries' actions.] He [Ignatius] willingly took all of the blame upon himself. He got drunk, he said, in order to forget the death of his son. He and his party endeavor to get as many as they can to join them. Five only of our cong. have remained faithful, among whom are the two assistants Willm. Henry & Charles. . . . In these disturbing circumstances we looked to our Lord alone for help, who might easily have overruled the circumstances attending the death of Henry, so that it might have taken place elsewhere. (MCA B173/F2: 14)

The diary entries from both Pettquotting and Goshen during the eighteen months between Henry's and his father's deaths clearly show the demoralized condition of the parents. Subsequent to Henry's death, the family continued to live at Goshen for several months before transferring to Pettquotting. They remained at Pettquotting but made several visits to Goshen the following year. During one of these visits, Ignatius stopped at the village on his return home from Georgetown, where he purchased supplies for his family. He became seriously ill and died on September 11, 1806. Following her husband's death, Christina returned to Pettquotting, remaining until November 1807. She then came back to Goshen, where she spent the balance of her life. She died on October 23, 1821, and hers was the last adult burial officially recorded in the Goshen Indian mission diaries.

Burial 26
Arnold, son of James and Sophia, the Younger
Goshen diary, October 1, 1806:

Oct. 1st.,

Was the funeral of the boy Arnold, son of James, who departed happily to our Lord yesterday, aged about 10 years. He was a sensible child, over whom we could in general rejoice. The immediate cause of his death was, a hurt which he received sometime since, through his stepmother in Pettquotting. (MCA B173/F3: 6–7)

James, Arnold's father, was the final survivor of this small Indian family. His brother Francis died in 1799 (burial 2), his brother Abraham in 1800 (burial 4), and his mother Sophia, the Younger, in 1801 (burial 9).

1808

For some unexplainable reason, Mortimer's English diary for the entire year of 1808 is missing from the archives in Bethlehem. There is, however, a German extract supposedly written by Mortimer. It is from this shortened version that I have taken the following information. (The author is grateful to two Moravian scholars for the following translation of the 1808 diaries: C. Daniel Crews, Ph. D., and Albert H. Frank, D. Min.)

From the diary excerpts quoted in our narrative, the reader will begin to savor and appreciate the style and extent of detail covered by the Moravian diarist. Mortimer was typical of all Moravian missionaries: he did not write his diaries for his own enjoyment, but accepted the task as the responsibility of one missionary at each station. (Until his old age, Zeisberger always wrote his own diaries rather than turn this chore over to his assistant.) Periodically the scripts were sent back to Bethlehem and diligently read by the church leaders. Copies were then made and sent to the Moravian church headquarters in Herrnhut, Germany. Additional copies, usually extracts, were sent to the missions throughout North America and to other countries in which Moravian missions were functioning. Each missionary diarist was quite aware that he was "on stage" and wrote accordingly. It is important that the reader of these diaries keep this thought in mind. Seldom does one find the hidden subtleties and delicate nuances that may give the reader a glimpse of anything other than what was expected back in Bethlehem.

While Zeisberger, the senior member of the far-flung missionary staff, was probably given a free hand, Bethlehem prayerfully expected results, and that was not always measured in numbers of converts. Little objectivity can be gleaned from the mission diaries. These writers were certainly not without bias or prejudice. Neither were they impersonal or detached. Daily they faced the major problem that plagued the Europeans from the beginning of their contact with native Americans: how to reduce the Indian to civility? What was curious, however, was the terminology Europeans used. If their (the Europeans') culture was so superior, why was it necessary to "reduce" the native American to the level of European civilization?

Burial 27
Joseph, husband of Beata
Goshen diary, March 10, 1808:

> On the 10th of the body of Brn. Joseph who fell asleep blissfully on the 8th was buried. (MCA B173/F5: 3)

Joseph was eighteen at the time of his baptism at Pettquotting on Christmas Day 1789. His grandfather was John Papunhank, and he was a nephew of Sophia, the Elder (see burial 7). The diaries give us no details about his father and mother, but he was probably born at the Friedensstadt mission on the Beaver River in 1771. He married the sixteen-year-old Beata at Fairfield on January 28, 1792. Over the next thirteen years the couple had three children: Augustina in 1799; Anna Salome in 1801 (who died at age one, see burial 17); and Catherina in 1805. While not specifically mentioned by name, the young couple probably were among the thirty-three original converts who came with Zeisberger and Mortimer to Goshen on October 4, 1798. Less than three months later they returned to Fairfield. On May 26, 1799, just one month prior to the birth of their first child, they again moved to Goshen.

Later in the year Joseph had the opportunity to participate in a historic event. Mortimer described the incident in the August 10 diary entry:

10th.

William Buckingham [his correct name was Ebenezer], the surveyor arrived here with 6 men by water from Marietta, on their way to survey United States lands between the 7 Ranges and New Connecticut. At his desire he obtained leave to store some barrels of flour & other provisions here. (MCA B171/F4: 11)

The recently signed Treaty of Greenville (in 1795) granted to the United States all of the former Indian land east of the Muskingum (Tuscarawas) and Cuyahoga rivers. These men arrived to complete the first survey of this area. Today the surveyors' work is still known as the Buckingham Survey and is recorded on original Ohio survey maps. Joseph spent the next ten days assisting the Buckingham party with the survey.

In the spring of 1801, Joseph and his friend Israel traveled to Charlestown to purchase supplies, and on the return trip they discovered a stray horse and brought it back to the mission. This was a dangerous practice, and they could have been accused of stealing the horse. Mortimer explained in his diary entry of May 13:

13th.

By occasions that Israel and Joseph on their late return from Buffalo [also called Charlestown, now Wellsburg, Brooke County, West Virginia—a source for supplies], had brought a strange horse hither that had come to their camp. Our brn. were expressly told never to take charge of any horses or cattle that they might find in the woods and suppose to be lost, unless they & their owners were known to them. If strange horses & cattle came of themselves into our town, the case was otherwise. These brn. were afterwards told to take the horse that they had brought here to the very place where it had come to them in the woods, & there to leave it. These admonitions, it appears afterwards, were well received by our brn. (MCA B171/F8: 47)

Horse stealing, in many localities during the eighteenth and the early part of the nineteenth centuries, was a capital offense. The mere possession was enough to convince any white jury of guilt—especially if the suspect was an Indian—and quickly led the "thief" to the nearest tree, which served as a convenient gallows. The mission rule protected the flock against such charges.

On December 19, 1801, Mortimer noted that both Joseph and Beata became candidates for the Holy Communion. Normally the waiting period was only several months, but neither was accepted as a full communicant until almost one year later, on November 6, 1802. This lengthy delay in granting the couple full communicant status may explain a suspicion of subsequent problems the missionaries experienced with Beata.

Two days following their admittance as communicants, their little daughter Anna Salome died. The diary records the first criticism of Joseph's wife, Beata (see burial 17). Notwithstanding, both were appointed sacristans on December 21, 1802. (A sacristan was a lay helper doing certain church functions, such as preparing and serving the lovefeast and assisting with the preparation of Holy Communion.)

Joseph had developed a reputation for being an expert hunter. Mortimer's entry of June 13, 1803 records an example of his skill, but it also describes an episode relating to village life that later became the principal problem leading to the mission's destruction:

13th.

Early in the morning Joseph returned from hunting on the water, having had the rare luck, in one night to kill four deer. The next night he killed three. (They would watch the deer swim across the river and kill it as it emerged on the bank.)

A drunken Indian occasioned us some trouble. He had hid a small quantity of whiskey near the town, which he refused to deliver up to the assistants, unless he was paid for it. In the evening two persons belonging here went to drink with him, & fought together. Nothing of the kind would probably have happened, had it not been for the following unfortunate circumstances. A brother returned thirsty from hunting, & recollecting that his vinegar was beginning to turn sour (and in that state it is pleasant tasted), he drank so freely of it, as to be nearly intoxicated. Thus situated, he accepted the friendly invitation that was given to him to drink whisky, and took a companion with him. All the rest of our brn. staid home.

The above mentioned vinegar consists of the juice of the sugar maple tree, reduced by boiling to one fourth of its original quanity. When by standing in a warm place, it first begins to acquire taste, some Indians are so very fond of it, that they are often tempted to drink it to excess, before it becomes fit for its proper use. On this account vinegar is always scarce among them, which is the more to be lamented, as that made of sugar water is excellent in quality, & would be very wholesome for them to use with their food. Though our brn.

have occasionally got drunk with vinegar, yet the making of it has never been forbidden among them; but it has been found necessary some years since to prohibit them the use of molasses beer, which is made by boiling sugar or molasses with hops, which latter grew spontaneously here in the forest. (MCA B171/F13: 6–8)

In March of the following year, 1804, Mortimer not only extolled Joseph's skill at sugarmaking, but gives us additional information on the necessity for the Indians to hunt:

March 27th.
Our brn. & sis. began to return into town from the sugar-camps. They have been pretty successful in sugar-making this season. Joseph alone has boiled 400 gal. Some of the brn. staid home during the whole time, & assisted the sis. at the work, but most of them were frequently out hunting, & had good success in killing bears, whose skins bear now about double the price that they did formerly, & are mostly paid for by the traders in ready money. (MCA B173/F1: 9–10)

Catherina, Joseph and Beata's last child, was born on July 21, 1805. For the next three years Joseph's life is shrouded in the enigmatic and obscure words of Mortimer's diary. Only cryptic and murky references are made to Joseph's problems with his wife. During the last half of 1805 the marriage began to experience trouble. Shortly after Catherina's birth, Joseph was warned to "resist the influences of his wife," and the family was absent for more than a month from the village, finally returning on August 31. Two weeks later Joseph "paid his last visit to us" and set off with his family, moving to Pettquotting. Over the next two years they made several visits to Goshen, but they never again resided permanently at the village. Joseph apparently returned to Goshen without his wife late in the year 1807. The only clue we have is Mortimer's entry on December 31: "Joseph has been deserted by his wife." He died three months later, on March 8, 1808, of unknown causes.

Beata eventually returned to the village, married again, and became quite troublesome to the later missionaries. She lived at Goshen until July 27, 1821. Then, shortly before the mission was abandoned, she left the village and the church with her children.

Burial 28
Joseph, son of Thomas and Anna Sophia White Eyes
Goshen diary, November 24, 1805 (birth of Joseph):

24th.
Br. Mortimer preached from Gal. 3.27, and baptized into the death of Jesus, the son of Thomas and Anna Sophia, born on the 22d by the name of Joseph. (MCA B173/F2: 39)

Goshen diary, June 24, 1808 (death of Joseph):

> 24th
>> The body of the child Joseph was buried, having fallen asleep on the 22nd at the age of 2 years and nearly 7 months. He had been stricken with an illness since last autumn. (MCA B173/F5: 10)

Joseph's mother, Anna Sophia, has been mentioned previously in the burial diary as the mother of Ketura (see burial 20). Her first husband, Johann Adam, was killed in an altercation with a white man prior to Ketura's birth. We have no official record of her marriage to Thomas White Eyes. We do know they were considered man and wife at the mission by June 1801. A diary entry on May 17, 1805, indicates that Thomas abandoned her five months before the birth of Joseph. She was married a third time, to an Indian named Guley, and maintained her connections with the Goshen mission until its close in 1821.

Thomas White Eyes, the son of the famous Captain White Eyes, was Joseph's father. After the Delaware were forced to sign the Treaty of Greenville in 1795, the principal chiefs moved their capital to the White River region of Indiana. Thomas, originally called Joseph like his famous father, stayed behind. In December of 1798, shortly after the founding of Goshen, he turned up at the new mission applying for admittance. Wary initially, Zeisberger "patiently tolerated" the young man and finally baptized him as Thomas on January 6, 1802. For the next three years he struggled to make the transition from native Indian to Christian convert. Born into a prominent native family and torn between the two cultures, Thomas never quite made the passage. Popular with the Delaware, especially among the native Indians, he excelled in all of their skills, especially hunting. The diaries give us a glimpse into his mastery of this craft:

> *August 23, 1802:*
>> Our brn. Tho White Eyes returned from 9 weeks hunt during which he had killed 110 deer.

> *August 3, 1803:*
>> James returned from hunting having killed 40 deer & Thomas sent home by his wife the skins of 110.

> *February 25, 1804:*
>> Thomas had this week been so fortunate as to kill eight bears.

> *March 26, 1804:*
>> Thomas returned from hunting, having killed twelve bears & one elk.

In the diary entry for the Monday following Easter 1803, Mortimer gives us a rare glimpse into the Moravian attitude regarding the transition from native life to Christian mission life. Undoubtedly, the following

Zeisberger observation reflects the long, fifty-year experience he had with "wild Indians." It also attests to the compassion both missionaries felt regarding the plight of Thomas White Eyes.

April 11, 1803:

Br. Zeisberger today visited Thomas, who has of late appeared to shun our fellowship, and is reported to be on the eve of marrying another wife from among the heathens. We asked him if he was still among the believers, & on his answering in the affirmative, represented to him in affectionate but serious terms how inconsistent his conduct was with his profession and what would be the consequences if he persisted herein. He reminded him how happy he had been after his baptisim, so that we had all rejoiced over him, and that it was, through the fellowship which he maintained with the heathens, that he had become otherwise disposed. Thomas's behaviour for a few days afterwards, till he went hunting again, seemed to indicate that this conversation had had a salutary effect upon him.   Being the son of a famous man among the Indians (late Capt. White Eyes), & a good hunter, he is much courted among them. Allimi [his uncle and the brother of Captain White Eyes], has more than once tried to persuade him to go from here to the Woapikamikunk [the capital of the Delaware nation on the White River in Indiana] and was the cause of his making the journey last winter with the chiefs to the city of Washington. [Thomas had been invited to visit President Jefferson in Washington during January 1803.]

A heathen family who often visit here, want to persuade him to leave his present wife, and intermarry among them. To this end he was made drunk in February last, that an opportunity might be taken to exact such a promise from him. Thus his unsuspecting and ingenuous mind has to struggle with various temptation, from which it can alone be preserved by divine grace.

Experience fully proves, that when souls are once converted to our Saviour from among the wild Indians, it is absolutely *requisite* to their growth in grace and godliness, that they thenceforward renounce the world, with its afflictions and lusts, quit & separate themselves as much as possible from their former heathenish connections & friendships, hear the word of God frequently & seek pleasure in the company of their fellow Christians. Whoever cannot resolve to live thus, & at the same time pay more attention than is usual among the heathens to domestic duties, (with which the life of a hunter is at variance), is in great danger of making shipwreck of his faith, of which we fear that we have woeful example here, Gideon & Thomas, not to mention others. (MCA B171/F12: 35)

Caught between the two cultures, Thomas decided against mission life at Goshen by the spring of 1806 and moved to the Indiana territory, stopping at the White River mission. Luckenbach, the missionary at White River, described his reception on arrival.

23rd.

[May 1806] without thinking of first asking permission, Thomas White Eyes came here bag and baggage, to live with his sister, who is also a wicked person and one who came here without asking our leave. Sorry as we were to see it, we could do nothing to prevent it, for we have not so much as one Indian brother to fall back on. (Gipson, *Moravian Indian Missions*, 43)

The twenty-nine-year-old missionary had several reasons to be apprehensive regarding Thomas White Eyes. Just three days before Thomas came "bag and baggage" to the mission, he and a number of his drunken friends with "horridly painted faces came into our village." Completely naked, they broke down the gates and attempted to ride their horses into the open door of Luckenbach's house. Gathering up the missionary Kluge and his wife and children, the other missionaries retired quickly to the woods. It is easy to understand why the missionaries were not willing to write the incident off as a boyish prank. Over the next year, Luckenbach recorded numerous other hair-raising incidents involving Thomas and his young friends. But with the close of the White River mission in September 1806, Thomas White Eyes, the intractable son of the great chief, passed from the scene and beyond reach of the missionary diaries.

Burial 29
David Zeisberger, head missionary
Goshen diary, November 4–20, 1808:

> *November 4, 1808:*
> Our beloved brother David Zeisberger was very weak and testified that he was completely ready to go the Saviour, except that he was not confident of the effects of his departure on our Indian brethren. Br. Mortimer called them together and spoke with them because of this, advising them to turn again to the Saviour and seek forgiveness of their sins from Him, come to Brother Zeisberger and ask him for forgiveness.
>
> *November 7, 1808:*
> Our Indian brethren visited Brother Zeisberger and asked him with many tears for forgiveness for everything with which they had grieved him and showed their determination to give their hearts completely to the Saviour and live to Him alone. Br. Zeisberger received them all very warmly with solemnity and love which was always characteristic of his dealings with them, showing his affectionate participation in their welfare, and warned them very earnestly, as their friend especially of drunkenness in which they had easily fallen, from which not a few of their souls had been lost.
>
> *November 8, 1808:*
> On the 8th the weather was very warm for this time of the year. Br. Zeisberger's illness became serious so that he could seldom be up. He was very lively at times and conversed with us.

November 11, 1808:

On the 11th Br. Zeisberger was a little better, than he had been for several days and was pleased and talkative. In regards to the Indians he expressed that our work among them would not be wasted, and he trusted to the Saviour, to hold his hand over it and that all would be blessed.

November 12, 1808:

On the 12th he was weak so that we decided to watch him day and night. The attack of colic from which he had suffered came yet again. After midnight he could only now and again say a few words and would not stand or sit by himself anymore.

November 13, 1808:

Br. Zeisberger today took a tender farewell of his beloved wife, and thanked her for all of her devotion; likewise from the Mortimers and their children and imparted his fatherly blessing. He mentioned all that had gone before and sent word on his condition after the meeting. He expressed to all who visited him, as usual very cordially, and said: "I will soon go to the Saviour." Toward midnight we thought his release was at hand and he himself longed to be blessed. . . . The continuing suffering which our beloved brother endured this night seemed to cause a fever which in the following days came and went every twelve hours. Every new attack was a further step towards eternity. When he occasionally suffered much, nothing eased his pains as when verses were sung, and especially those in the Delaware tongue which he himself had made for use at death beds of the Indians. The Indian brethren supported him with these. His soul was often in silent prayer. Sometimes one heard a sigh, for example, "Lord Jesus, I pray thee, come and take my soul to thee." Once when his sufferings were very great, he said: "You have never forsaken me in any difficult circumstances; you will not forsake me now," and soon thereafter as if he had received an answer to his prayer: "The Saviour is near, perhaps He will soon come and take me to Himself." He wished strongly to be released, that he was totally surrendered to God's will. The powerful faith and confidence which had brought him so wonderfully throughout his entire life, through all trials and difficulties, proved its strength also at the approach of death. And the sensation of the peace of God, which is higher than any curse, filled his heart and mind in Christ Jesus, and likewise surrounded his death bed.

November 17, 1808:

On the 17th the brethren Mueller and Heckewelder visited him once more, whereat he obviously rejoiced, that he was able to speak with them one more time. Soon after they had left him, one noticed an apparent change. All of the local Indians assembled themselves and gathered in his room, and sang verses from time to time, whereas he made known almost to the last his delight through his sighs. About 3:30 P.M. he gave his last breath and heaved a sigh. Br. Mortimer fell on his knees with all present and thanked the Saviour in a short prayer during which many Indians shed tears, that He had released him from his misery, that he had blessed his witness for the conversion of many and especially Indians and implored the Saviour that He would give us grace to follow his words and example, through which we might all, according to His will, be with the Lord in eternity. His age was 87 years, 7 months, and 6 days.

November 20, 1808:
On the 20th at eleven O'clock in the forenoon we held the burial of the body of our beloved Br. Zeisberger, the oldest missionary of the Brethren's unity. An extensive number had gathered from the neighborhood. Br. Mortimer preached on Revelation 12:11. . . . The Indian brother John Henry translated the address in the Delaware language. . . . A brief report of the life, work, character and last hours of his falling asleep was read. . . . The body was carried by three white brethren and three Indians. The litany was read in English at the grave. In the evening we held a lovefeast with our local Indians in which we remembered all the white brethren who had lived among them and now have gone to be with the Lord, and also especially the last words of Br. Zeisberger. (All above November references in MCA B173/F5: 17–23)

What began in the spring of 1721 on the banks of the Oder River, deep within the heart of Europe, came to an end halfway across the world, on the Muskingum in the late fall of 1808. The struggle was over for David Zeisberger. He now lay quietly beside the soft stillness of the Muskingum River, his beloved home.

1809

Burial 30
Anna Maria, wife of Joachim
Goshen diary, June 6, 1809:

6th.
Was the funeral of Anna Maria, wife of Joachim, who departed happily to our Lord yesterday morning. She lived for some years as a child in the family of the second missionary of the name of Brainard [John Brainerd] at his mission settlement in New Jersey, where she learnt to speak the English language. In 1764, being then about 10 years of age, she was with our Indian cong. in the barracks at Philadelphia; from thence she went with them first to the Susquehanna, & then to the Ohio country. In Old Schoenbrunn she had the grace to be baptized, & was soon after married to the present widower Brn. Joachim, son of the well-known interpreter of that name, to whom she remained a faithful helpmate till death, namely about 30 years. At the time of the great dispersion of our Indian brn. & sis. during the war, she resided with her husband for some years in Kikeyunk [Gigeyuck, now Fort Wayne, Indiana] & on the Woapikamikunk [White River]. In Fairfield and Pettquotting she was in various ways a very useful assistant in the congn.

When the settlement at the latter place was to be broken up this spring, she, as well as her husband was firm in the determination to come hither. . . .

This excellent sister always distinguished herself in Pettquotting, by the faithful support that she afforded her teachers in every case where her assistance was called for, & especially in trying circumstances. On many occasions it was found very advantageous to make use of her talents as an interpreter; for she had not only the full command of a flow of words, to express with precision and energy what it was wished might be made known through her, but if intimated to her as agreeable, she was ready also to avail herself of such opportunities to add her own strong testimony to the truth. But it was not in word only, but in *deed* too, that she was ever ready to assist when called upon. In an endeavor of this kind, about two years ago, where her object was to help another sister, who was in the greatest distress, she received an inward hurt, which brought on a long sickness, from which she never perfectly recovered. At times she vomited blood, & appeared to get better again. This spring she was very infirm, but our Lord strengthened her to make the journey hither with her family and Br. Haven, & granted thereto the most favorable weather. . . . Every day she came to see Brn. Mortimer, & we considered her a valuable acquisition to our small community. . . . Though very poor, she was contented, & complained of nothing. We did not suspect that the remarkable disposition of heart which she manifested, was to be an indication to us that she was now ripe for eternity; & that her journey hither, was proper only in order that she might be laid to rest here, at the commencement of a new row in our burying-ground, & opposite a still more remarkable witness of the truth, our never to be forgotten Bro. Zeisberger [see the cemetery map, appendix D]. About nine days ago she was again seized with a vomiting of blood. She lay afterwards quite composed, & expressed herself perfectly ready to go to our Lord. . . . Her age was 55 years. (MCA B173/F6: 7)

The sharp mind and keen wit that Anna Maria displayed in her later life must have challenged John Brainerd as he took this bright little child into his home. Nothing is known of her parents, and we can presume she was an orphan or abandoned. John was the brother of David Brainerd (1718–47), a Presbyterian missionary who worked among the Delaware, Seneca, and Tuteloes, until his untimely death from tuberculosis at age twenty-nine. Well known for his missionary work, David's diaries and journals are still widely read among certain religious groups today. His brother John continued his missionary labors following David's death and established a mission the following year at Cranberry, New Jersey. By 1751 most of those converts had abandoned his mission and moved to Gnadenhutten, the Moravian mission on the Mahoning.

Anna Maria is next found as a ten-year-old experiencing the fifteen months of protective confinement in Philadelphia under David Zeisberger's leadership. Interestingly, it would be another eleven years before she was baptized, November 12, 1775, at Gnadenhutten, Ohio. At that time she was listed as a widow and the mother of one-year-old Anna Justina. The diaries are silent on her activities during this eleven-year period, which indicates that she lived among the "wild Indians." Four years later she married Joachim, and their first child, Martin, was born in 1780. Two other children followed, Henriette in 1789 and Johann Jacob in 1790. Henriette died in 1791. Anna Justina and Martin survived their mother.

Her husband, Joachim, came from a distinguished Delaware family connected with the missions almost from their inception. Joachim's uncle, Gottlieb, was "the first fruits of the Delaware nation" baptized by the Moravians in 1745. His father, also Joachim, was an expert German interpreter, and the son became equally talented and adept at this skill.

Following the Great Dispersement in 1781, when the British and hostile Indians removed the converts from the Muskingum valley, the family wandered among the native tribes in northern Ohio and Indiana. Most of this time they lived at the Miami Indian village of Gigeyunk. On November 11, 1788, they returned to the Pettquotting mission and remained with the Christian converts for the balance of their lives.

In the early spring of 1804 the family was living at the Fairfield mission and became part of the original group that founded the second mission on the Pettquotting. In June 1809 the second Pettquotting mission was abandoned. On this occasion the Munsee chief at Sandusky insisted that the converts at Pettquotting come and live with him, as Goshen was a place "where the white people will kill and burn you." The remark was an explicit reference to the massacre at Gnadenhutten in 1782. Most of the converts agreed, except for Joachim and his family. Anna Maria spoke for the family, as Mortimer noted, "in her plain, sensible, and cool manner":

> That she did not expect any such thing, as the present was a time of profound peace between the Indians and the white people. If however, there were grounds to apprehend such an event, that would not intimidate her, or cause her to alter her purpose. Should she be murdered here in cold blood, and be burnt, what was that but burning the body? It was a suffering that would be soon over. Whereas they, by forfeiting the congn. and going to live again among the heathen, put themselves into the danger that their souls as well as their bodies would be tormented forever with the devils in hell-fire. Her resolution, she said, was to live & die in the congn. (MCA B173/F6: 7)

Was it a premonition that she would live only two more months? Joachim, the faithful husband of thirty years, lived on until January 14, 1814. He died at Dundas, a small village near present Hamilton, Ontar-

io, Canada. In most of those intervening years he lived at the Fairfield
mission in Canada. For fifty years the Christian Moravian converts had
been fleeing white interference with their missions. It is ironic that the
last battle of the War of 1812 on the western frontier was fought one mile
from their village. After the battle, on October 5, 1813, William Henry
Harrison destroyed the Fairfield mission. Within two years Fairfield rose
again despite the misguided deeds of Harrison's troops.

1810

Burial 31
Rebecca, daughter of Christian Gottlieb and Anna Susanna Henry
Goshen diary, August 18, 1810:

> *18th.*
> Was the funeral of Rebecca, daughter of Christian Gottlieb and Anna
> Susanna, who departed to our Lord last evening, age 7 months. (MCA
> B173/F7: 14)

Rebecca was the sixth of ten children eventually delivered to the
Christian Gottlieb Henry family. She was born on January 3, 1810. After
many years of outstanding service to the mission, her father, the youngest
living son of William Henry, died tragically on February 9, 1823, racked
with alcoholism. The mother, Anna Susanna, disappeared from the
diary during the same year, fleeing from the violence of her husband. Details of both figures are covered in the report of the last burial of the
Goshen cemetery (see burial 44).

Burial 32
Nancy, daughter of John and Anna Benigna Henry
Goshen diary, November 4, 1810:

> *Sunday 4th.*
> The public meeting was from John 14:1–3 after which was the funeral of
> the child Nancy, daughter of John Henry & Anna Benigna, who departed to
> our Lord early yesterday morning, aged 1 year & 8 months. (MCA B173/F7: 22)

Nancy's mother, Anna Benigna, was thirteen when she married John
Henry and seventeen at the birth of Nancy, the second of her three
children. Within nineteen months she joined her infant daughter in the
Goshen cemetery (see burial 36).

1811

Burial 33
William Henry, the Delaware chief Gelelemend or John Killbuck, Jr.
Goshen diary, February 17 and 19, 1811:

17th.,
    Very early in the morning, Brn. Wm. Henry departed this life. There was no meeting, as almost every person here had been up during the night. Indians that were scattered out in the woods were sent for.

19th.,
    At 1 o'clock in the afternoon was the funeral of Brn. Wm. Henry, which Br. Miller from Beersheba, & other brn., out of particular response for the deceased, came here purposely to attend. The discourse was from John 11:25–26, after which some memories of his course of life were communicated. Much solemnity prevailed, & many tears were shed by the Indians.
    Our brn. Wm. Henry Killbuck was born in the year 1737 near the Lehigh Water gap in Northampton County, Pennsylvania. He well remembered the great snow that fell in the winter of 1740–41, when he was 4 years of age. In his youth he moved with his family and friends to this side of the Allegheny mountains, where he first had an opportunity of hearing the gospel, when he was about 35 years old. As he was by birth entitled to the chief office among his nation who were at that time very numerous, compared to what they are at present, he was even then active in all their public affairs. Meanwhile he embraced every opportunity to come & hear the gospel, and paid frequent visits to the missionaries, which were much blessed to him. He often in those days expressed a desire to come & live with the congn. but the missionaries advised him rather, on account of his political connections & the exigencies of the time, to continue among the heathen, & remain only their good friend. When the revolution commenced, many Delaware Indians, & especially their young people, were much inclined for war. Our late brother, in conjunction with the other chiefs, made use of all his influence to promote peace; for he was, from the time that he heard the gospel, an enemy to war & bloodshed and the friend of all men, whether Indians or whites. During the war that followed, in which at length, contrary to his advice, nearly all of his tribes engaged, he retired in the year 1781 to Pittsburgh, where he and other Indians remained for some years. Willm. Henry was considered there as an American officer, and as such he rendered important service to the country. After peace took place, he went with his family in the year 1787 [actually 1788], to live with the congn. which then resided at Pettquotting. It was on Friday when he obtained leave to live there, & that day of the week was ever afterwards, on that account, particularly weighty to him. The next year he had the grace to be baptized, & was soon after admitted to partake of the h. comm. As an Indian war soon broke out again, he went with the congn. to Canada, where he resided about 8 years till the

troubles were over & the settlements here could be commenced. He spent the last 12 years of his life in this place [Goshen] in peace & quietness, & was universally respected by all who knew him, both Indians & white people. . . .

It was his fervent wish & prayer also for his children & his children's children to the latest generations, that they might have the same blessed experience of our Saviour that he, through grace, enjoyed & that it might be communicated to many other Indians. . . .

About 7 years ago his wife Rachel, with whom he had lived agreeably for above 40 years, happily departed this life. . . . Within the last few years, his constitution which was naturally strong, began to break. It was his desire, & perhaps expectation too, that when he came near to depart this life, he might with a distinct voice, and the most perfect serenity of mind, be able to speak to others of the happiness of his heart, and give them a last powerful admonition to walk in his footsteps, in order that they also might depart this life happily. . . . About twelve days before his end, as we had heard that he was yet anxious concerning himself; & that some of the Indian brn. & sis. had expressed doubts, whether he was really in a happy state of heart, or not; Br. Mortimer examined him quite closely, to see if he had anything more on his mind that could prevent his blessed departure to our Lord. The answer that he gave, however, in presence of his sons was very satisfactory. At one time he said with a loud voice: "Don't think that old William Henry did not tell you the truth," and immediately stretched out his hand to Br. Mortimer & said very friendly: "I salute you, my brother!" From that time his weakness evidently encreased [*sic*] from day to day, until it pleased our Lord graciously to release him from all pain, by taking his soul to himself early Sunday morning last. His age was 74 years. He left behind him 3 sons [John, Charles, and Christian Gottlieb], who are living in this place, from whom he has many grandchildren. His eldest son, John, by particular favor of the Congress of the United States, spent some years in his youth as a student at Princeton College, New Jersey.

He left this charge to his sons: to cleave faithfully to our Lord and his word, never to forsake the Brethren, not to leave this place till a congn. of the Brn. is fixed somewhere in the Indian country, and never to aim to become chiefs or head men in the congn, which, he said he had always observed, shewed an improper spirit, and led the heart astray from simply following our Lord. This valuable and truly respectable brother will, we fear, be much missed among us. (MCA B173/F7: 2–7)

During the twelve years that John Killbuck, Jr. (Gelelemend), lived at the Goshen mission, Mortimer used his baptismal name William Henry, the name given to him by Zeisberger during his baptism on April 12, 1789. The name came from a legend following the defeat of the British colonial forces at the battle of the Monongahela in 1755, the first major battle of the French and Indian War. According to the legend, the eighteen-year-old warrior Killbuck, fighting with the French and Indians, was captured and condemned to death by the British. He was rescued by William Henry, a major in the British forces who later became a prominent judge from Lancaster. So grateful for his rescue, Killbuck promised Henry the highest compliment he could bestow—to assume his name. Truth or legend, when he was baptized thirty-four years later at Pettquotting, he asked Zeisberger to give him the name William Henry.

Little doubt remains, and most Moravian historians believe, that Henry (Gelelemend, or Killbuck, Jr.) was the most outstanding of all the Moravian converts. Certainly he was the highest ranked among all the Delaware who accepted Christianity. (The position of his grave beside Zeisberger in the cemetery does not indicate his status as a Delaware chief, but is simply coincidental as to the time of his death—the next male adult subsequent to Zeisberger.)

Young Killbuck, following the Delaware tradition, belonged to the Unami (Turtle) clan of his mother. Since the Delaware were matrilineal, they took their clan affiliations from their mother rather than from their father. His father, John Killbuck, Sr. (Bemineo), was the eldest son of Netawatwes. The Killbucks had long been prominent among the Delaware and originally lived near the Lehigh River, where John, Jr., was born in 1737. In 1755, during the French and Indian War, his father participated with Shingas and Captain Jacobs in bloody raids against the white frontier. Following the war Killbuck, Sr., moved his family to the Beaver River in western Pennsylvania, where he served as Netawatwes's Turkey lineage counselor. Later, in 1764, the family moved to the Muskingum River area. While never enamoured of the Moravian mission program, and at times quite hostile, he supported the Americans during the Revolution and visited Philadelphia in 1771, taking his son, John, Jr., with him. Although blind, he went as far as Pittsburgh in 1779 with another delegation on its ways to Philadelphia. He died not long afterwards.

His son, Killbuck, Jr., was designated the successor to Netawatwes in 1775. Upon the old chief's death in 1776, Killbuck, Jr., became the head chief of the Delaware. He was reluctant from the beginning to assume the office, wishing to join the Moravians and forgo the responsibilities of tribal government. Even before Netawatwes's death on October 31, 1776, Killbuck pleaded with both his grandfather and Zeisberger to let him join the Christian converts. Zeisberger discouraged the move, believing he could be of greater assistance to the Christian cause in his role as head chief.

Following the April 1776 founding of the Lichtenau mission, just several miles from the Delaware capital at Goschachgunk, Zeisberger was frequently invited to attend the meeting of the Delaware Council.

During Killbuck's short tenure as head chief (1776–1778), Zeisberger and Killbuck played an instrumental role in keeping the Delaware neutral.

These years were filled with confusion and turmoil; the tribe's chiefs were torn between the opposing British and American colonial forces. Following the death of the influential chief White Eyes, on November 10, 1778, Killbuck, Jr., lost his principal support. The Delaware Council broke their neutrality and joined the British. The commander at Detroit, Major Arent De Peyster, put a price on Killbuck's head—dead or alive. He resigned his post as head chief and became a fugitive. In January 1779 Col. John Gibson, then the commander at Fort Laurens, offered Killbuck and his family the protection of the fort. He did not accept the invitation but continued to remain close to the missions of New Schoenbrunn, Gnadenhutten, and Lichtenau. Following the birth of his last child, Benjamin, in the spring of 1781, he accepted Gen. Daniel Brodhead's invitation to move to the Pittsburgh area under the protection of the American colonial forces.

We know little of his activity between the years 1781 and 1787. However, among the papers of Judge William Henry of Lancaster, Killbuck's namesake, was found an original draft of a petition written by Mortimer on January 5, 1805, and cosigned by Zeisberger. The letter, a memorial to the then-governor of Pennsylvania, Thomas McKean, appealed to His Honor for a firm deed confirming the chief's ownership of an island on the west side of the Allegheny near Pittsburgh. Killbuck, Jr., related in the letter that he lived there, under the protective custody of the Americans, for six years following his flight from the Muskingum valley in 1781. There is conflicting evidence as to the length of his residency on Killbuck Island. He and his family next appear in the diary of June 30, 1788, arriving at the mission of Pettquotting, on the Pettquotting River (Milan, Ohio).

After the Great Dispersement in 1781, Zeisberger had gathered together the remnants of the Muskingum valley converts, and 123 were then living at Pettquotting. In a series of diary entries by Zeisberger, beginning on June 30, we have a partial explanation of the Killbuck family's sojourn on the Allegheny.

Pettquotting diary, Monday June 30, 1788:

> Today finally came Gelelemend [Killbuck, Jr.], *already in his third year of his journey from the Fort [Pitt] hither,* with his whole family, and encamped in sight of our town, where many of our Indian brethren visited him. [Emphasis added]

Pettquotting diary, Tuesday July 1, 1788:

> At the early service, which Br. Edwards held, Gelelemend, above mentioned
> was present, with three sons, one already grown.

Pettquotting diary, Thursday July 3, 1788:

> Brother Edwards held early service. David then spoke with Gelelemend, who
> expressed to him his desire and longing to be with the church again, for he
> had twice been expelled on the Muskingum, when we were there, for he was
> then very much involved in the affairs of chiefs, and at last became chief in
> Goschachgunk. Now, however, that he is free and has nothing more to do
> with affairs, although last year the Delaware chiefs visited him and proposed
> to him to come again and be chief, but he had declined, we could not refuse
> him for the third time, but received him, after the assistant had first spoken
> with him and his wife. . . . He said to Br. David, whom he had not seen for
> seven years, that he had countless times wished himself with us, for in Pitts-
> burgh, where he retired during the war, he was often no day sure of his life,
> on account of the militia; when then he thought of going to us over the
> lake, he knew not how to come because of the Indians, who likewise wished
> his life. He was quite revived and cheerful when he got permission to be one
> of our inhabitants, for he was much cast down and in fear he might be
> rejected. If the chiefs in such condition come to us, we will receive them
> heartily and cheerfully, show them love and kindness. (Bliss, Diary of David
> Zeisberger, 1:419, 420)

Gelelemend made one more trip on behalf of his native Delaware
brothers, and it almost cost him his life. At Fort Harmar, located at the
junction of the Muskingum and the Ohio [now Marietta], another treaty
conference was called by United States commissioners. Since the Treaty
of Paris in 1783, which concluded the Revolution, the British had ceded
to the new United States all of the Indian lands westward from the Ohio
to the Mississippi rivers. Indian reaction was immediate. King George
III may have agreed to this concession, but in the minds of the Indians he
had no rights of ownership. The British had no claim; thus they could
make no binding agreements, especially since the Indians had never
been consulted during the treaty negotiations. It took six years of
bloodshed to resolve the differences.

Sometime during the conference, Gelelemend was attacked and brut-
ually beaten by his native Indian enemies. He was unconscious for three
days and spent the next three weeks confined to his bed before recovering
sufficiently to return to the mission on February 12, 1789. Two months
later to the day, Zeisberger finally baptized him "into Jesus' death, with
the name William Henry." The missionary noted in the diary:

April 12, 1789:
    It was as if he alone should have grace and honor, for in his whole family there was movement and ferment, his wife, two grown sons, and yet others begging with many tears for baptism (but they all fell away.) He sat and kneeled at his baptism like an honorable old man. Already for many years he wished to be in the church, and although it was through many by-paths and crooked ways, the Saviour at last reached his end with him. May he help him further and let him thrive! (Bliss, *Diary of David Zeisberger,* 2: 24)

Thus the fifty-two-year-old William Henry realized his lifelong dream—he finally became a Christian convert. Zeisberger's faith in this quiet and gentle man was not misplaced. For the next twenty years, until Zeisberger's death, they remained inseparable. "Billy" became a tower of strength for the missionary movement and time and again interceded to solve the weighty problems that bore down on the beleaguered Christian Indians.

Within another year, William Henry's entire family was baptized at Pettquotting: the two oldest sons on May 31, 1789; his wife Rachel on July 5 of the same year; and the youngest son, Christian Gottlieb, on April 4, 1790.

The next eight years on the Thames River in Canada were quiet and successful, away from the turmoil of the Indian wars in the States. On August 15, 1798, a small party of thirty-three converts under Zeisberger's supervision and guided by William Henry left the Fairfield mission. They were returning to the Muskingum to begin once again in the peaceful valley they all called home. (Appendix F lists the burials of the Henry family at Goshen.)

Burial 34
Nicodemus, husband of Henrietta

A brisk April evening settled over the quiet Indian mission. Only low, muffled voices could be heard above the forest sounds. Suddenly the shrill shouts of a boy crying "Brother Mortimer, Brother Mortimer" disrupted the stillness. Goshen was about to encounter a chilling experience.

Goshen diary, April 10 to May 1, 1811:

April 10, 1811:
    Late in the evening a boy brought the melancholy intelligence hither, that the half-Indian Montgomery Montour, had, near New Philadelphia, given his father-in-law Nicodemus, a stab with a large knife, which was believed would prove mortal. The blood, it was said, gushed out of his mouth as well as from

the wound, & he was unable to move from the spot. It was further added, that Joachim had come immediately to Nicodemus's assistance, & Montour had badly wounded him in the arm. On hearing this, every man here armed himself and went up to New Philadelphia, and the women and children sought refuge in the house or on the premises of Br. & Sis. Mortimer. During the night we had but little sleep, as we often heard the cries of Indians on the other side of the river & did not know what might be going forward there.

April 19, 1811:
19th, early, Montour came into the town. As he crossed the street, by mere accident he espied Br. Mortimer, on which he drew his large knife out of the sheath and holding it up, declared with an audible voice, so that every person in town could hear him, that with that knife he would kill him too, because he spoke against the Indians getting drunk. Soon after he went again to New Philadelphia. Br. Mortimer wrote to the Justice there, who as well as others, was for committing him to jail: but after much deliberation, nothing was done as all there were afraid of him, or doubtful what steps it would be most proper to take in the matter. . . .

Soon after, we heard that Montour was returning here, with his face painted black, & to appearance very angry. Br. Hagen [Mortimer's assistant] immediately set off to get some of our neighbors out of their settlements to come hither, but before he could return with the three men who afterwards remained over two nights with us, Montour had come to the house of Br. & Sis. Mortimer. On his entrance quite unexpectedly, the children screamed for fear of him, and ran off. After cursing them, he asked in a fierce manner for Br. Mortimer. Sis. Mortimer, who at that moment was alone but able to answer him quite composedly, that she did not know where he was. Br. Mortimer however immediately appeared, shook hands with and addressed him with all friendship. He then also became friendly towards us, & tried to excuse his conduct on the preceding night as well as he could. We gave him victuals, as he said that he was hungry, and he left peaceably.

At the time that he came thus to Br. & Sis. Mortimer's house, the Indian men were still all about and near Nicodemus; we had just heard that he [Montour] had attempted to kill a white man in New Philadelphia, (only 4 miles from here). . . . In the course of this day, Nicodemus sent several times to Br. Mortimer to come and see him, but he could not leave the home.

April 20, 1811:
20th, Br. Mortimer went with two men to New Philadelphia to see Nicodemus and speak with the doctor. Nicodemus's wound, it appears, had been made with extreme violence through the lower part of his left shoulder bone, into the lungs. The Indians had very soon given up all hopes of his recovery. They applied however, to the surgeons in New Philadelphia, who examined and dressed the wound and pronounced, with some confidence, a cure to perhaps be possible. . . . Nicodemus was brought today by water into our town.

Sunday April 21, 1811:

21st. At noon, Montgomery Montour left here privately with a boy, as he said for Greentown & the White River [Armstrong's Town, or Pemaxit's Town, near present Mansfield, Ohio]. Yesterday, as he was quite sober, his courage had forsaken him. He heard in various ways, that Indians and white people were against him, & wished that he be punished, according to law. Two Indians declared publickly, that if Nicodemus should die of his wounds, they would with their own hands kill Montour. It was the universal opinion among them, that the stab with the knife was an act of premeditated malice; it was given without any just ground of provocation, & he was not drunk at the time. It was known that Nicodemus had for substantial reasons threatened to take his daughter away from him again; and that he had much ill-will against him on that account. Every occurrence, therefore, now alarmed him, and he was afraid to remain here any longer.

May 1, 1811:

1 May, was the funeral of Nicodemus, who yesterday happily departed this life. He was born on the East Branch of the Susquehanna in the year 1767. About 1789 he came to the congn. at Pettquotting, was baptized 6 Jan. 1789 [by Gottlob Senseman], and soon after admitted to the holy communion. His course since he joined the congn. was varied. Sometimes for a succession of years he walked worthy of his call as a believer in the gospel; at other times his natural corruption had powerful sway over him. He was, however, never without strong convictions as to what was right and wrong. For the last two years he would rather have lived in the Indian country than at this place. . . . He, as well as his wife, was often wavering in his mind, whether he should remain here or return to Sandusky to his relations and friends. . . . Yet still, from his discontent about the place of his abode, he was at times much given to drunkenness, and of course according to the common Indian habit, a promoter of this same [practice] in others. Every admonition however, that was given him about his behavior, he received in good part, and was after grieved about himself. . . . On the 23rd. he was, at his request, solemnly absolved in the presence of all the Indians, after he had publickly declared before them, that from the bottom of his heart he forgave the man who had given him the hurt of which he had to die. . . . Afterwards of his own accord, he particularly desired of & expected a promise from his eldest son, and from the other Indians who had declared that they would revenge his death by that of Montour, that they should not do so. The 24th, the surgeon visited him for the last time, and declared an inward mortification to be advanced. Many white people came to see him daily, among whom was Dr. Reppich of Canton. As long as he had senses, Br. Mortimer, at his desire, prayed aloud daily, for and with him beside his couch, he seemed to regard him as his best earthly friend, speaking and smiling to him as long as he could. His bodily sufferings were great, and lasted 12 days; but throughout, there was a feeling of the peace of God around him. . . . His age was 43 years. He has left a wife and 8 children. (MCA B173/F7: 11–15)

Seldom did a single incident so monopolize the life of the little mission. While the culprit, Montgomery Montour, was not one of the regular baptized inhabitants, he was not unknown to the thirty villagers. He first appeared at Goshen on May 5, 1803, eight years prior to the incident. The diary entry for that day noted his arrival and explained that he was the son of Thomas Montour who had been killed in the revolutionary war. It further related that Thomas was the son of Andrew Montour and the grandson of Madame Montour. Both were friends of Zeisberger and the Moravians. Andrew, in 1745, acted as their guide on the first trip made into the Iroquois country. It was during this journey that Augustus Spangenberg, Zeisberger, and Schebosh were adopted into the Iroquois nations (see burial 29). Andrew and his mother, Madame Montour, were well known throughout the American colonies and served as interpreters and confidential agents for the British, especially during the French and Indian War. The Madame came from French nobility and Indian extraction. She was captured as a young girl and raised by either the Seneca or the Oneida (the record is not clear), and is first mentioned in colonial history in 1711 as an interpreter.

Montgomery Montour, her great-grandson, again visited Goshen in June of 1803 and spent two months in the village. During this time he lived with Charles Henry, the second son of William Henry. Montour had no serious objections to Charles, except a reluctance to listen to his irritating proselytizing efforts. On June 30, the day of his departure, Charles complained: "When he spoke to his visitor of our Saviour, Montour often interrupted & contradicted him, pretending, merely because he can read, to a better knowledge of the word of God & divine things. 'Do you not think,' Montour once said to Charles' wife, 'that I am better & know more than you & Charles? I can read & you cannot' " (MCA B171/F13: 11). Mortimer's entry for the day drips with sarcasm. The arrogance shown by Montour was not appreciated at the Moravian mission and was the antithesis of what was expected from a Christian convert.

Two months later, Montour was back in the village. Mortimer wrote:

August 14, 1803:
    Br. Haven preached from Numb. 14:21, and Zeisberger held the congregation meeting. Montgomery Montour signified to the latter his intentions of laying out a farm on our land at some distance from our town, which he was informed could not be permitted him. Being educated among the white people, he has some knowledge of farming & carpenters' work. Everything pleased him here except the strictness of our rules, which, as may be supposed arises from his attachment to a vice-ridden life. (MCA B171/F13: 16)

In the next few years nothing further came from his attempt to begin the farm near Goshen. Montour visited the village in 1804, again in 1805, and then disappeared from the diary for two years. In the spring of 1807 he spent one week at the village after returning from a trip to Washington, D.C. He had been called to Washington by a congressional committee to testify as to the validity of Delaware signatures on a recent treaty. The diary entry gives us some appreciation of the importance federal authorities placed on his opinion.

30th.

[April 30, 1807] The Indian, Montgomery Montour, proceeded further into the Indian country. He related to us that a main object of his journey to the federal city was to represent, in behalf of the Delaware Indians, that the signatures of their chiefs to the treaty that was held on the Miami of the Lake, nearly two years ago [July 5, 1805, at Fort Industry, on the left bank of the Maumee River in present Toledo, Ohio]. The land [Montour claimed], commonly called the New Purchase, and ceded to the United States was a forgery; as those chiefs did not attend that treaty, and were at the time some hundreds of miles distant from the place the treaty was held; and that the Delawares did not wish to give up their rights to that part of the country. In consequence, he said, a bill had just passed congress, whereby some sections of land were to be reserved for the Delawares, so long as they continued to reside therein, and cultivate them. A printed law of the United States which we received at this time, seemed to confirm this narration. Montour assured us, that the Indians would now be under no necessity of leaving Pettquotting, unless they chose to do so. (MCA B173/F2: 5) [This was the treaty that eventually resulted in the closing of the second mission on the Pettquotting.]

Montour appeared twice at Goshen before that fateful day in April 1811 when he stabbed Nicodemus. On October 31, 1809, the diarist recorded that "Montgomery Montour, an Indian of some note, came on a visit here." His departure two weeks later was just as uneventful: "17th. Montgomery Montour set off on his way home." Again on November 11, 1810, Mortimer tersely recorded that "Montgomery Montour arrived here from the White River." For eight years, off and on, they had hosted this unusual Indian. While he may have disagreed with the missionaries' Christian philosophy, not a shred of evidence during that time indicated any vicious characteristic in his personality. We will have to look elsewhere to account for his violent act of the following April. He remained in Goshen for five months, from November 11, 1810, to April 21, 1811, ten days after the stabbing.

Montour's victim and father-in-law, Nicodemus, had a multifarious life as a Christian convert. He lived for twenty years among the Moravians, but those were years frequently interrupted by periods of banishment for infraction of mission rules. His principal relapses were caused by liquor, in-laws, and his own ambivalence—an explosive combination for a mission convert. He was never quite sure if he preferred the closely regulated, secure, and peaceful life of the mission or the independent, precarious, and assailable life of a "wild Indian." Frequently he was dismissed for drunkenness, only to be readmitted after "seeking forgiveness for his transgressions."

While rather unique among Moravian converts, virtually nothing is known of the early life of Nicodemus and of his wife, Henrietta. When baptized at Pettquotting, on January 6, 1791, he was twenty-three and probably married. Eight months later, their first child, Mattheus, was born.

Following the boy's baptism, Nicodemus and the growing family followed Zeisberger until they arrived at Fairfield in May 1792. Henrietta was baptized on September 11, 1791, at Warte on the Detroit River. The couple remained at Fairfield for ten years, except when the father was dismissed for being "drunk and quarrelsome." Their time at the mission was the most contented period of their marriage. The next eleven years were filled with wanderings and dissatisfaction.

In May 1803 Nicodemus and his young son first appeared at Goshen during one of his frequent periods of banishment. Mortimer wrote:

31st.

[May 31, 1803] Nicodemus arrived yesterday from Fairfield with his son Mattheus [now twelve years old]. He had a long conversation with Br. Zeisberger respecting the bad life he had led for some time past, which it is his desire to amend. The next morning he set off to fetch the remainder of his family. (MCA B171/F13: 4)

Eight days later we have a confirmation of his plans to move the family to Goshen. Mortimer's entry not only involved Nicodemus, but reveals an interesting observation regarding the relations between the Delaware and their neighbors at Fairfield, the Chippeways (Chippewa-Ojibwa tribes).

8th.

[June 8, 1803] Chippeways, on their way through our town, paid a visit to Br. Mortimer. The shyness observable between the Delawares and Chippeways is very remarkable. They seem never to be sociable with each other. Every white man as well as Delaware who comes here is saluted and treated friendly. A Chippeway, on the contrary, is hardly looked at & no Indian asks them into his house, speaks to, or offers him anything to eat. He is regarded as an intruder in this part of the country who has no right to hunt here. Our brn. & sis. planted today for Nicodemus, who will arrive here with his family too late to do the work himself. (MCA B171/F13: 4–5)

Unfortunately, Nicodemus's wife and in-laws did not share his enthusiasm for the Goshen move. Three weeks after he left Goshen, the Indian grapevine brought word of their disapproval. Mortimer noted on

June 24: "We heard that the relations of Nicodemus' wife had dissuaded her from coming here. He [Nicodemus] was described as much dejected on this account." By the following October we find a more hopeful Mortimer entry:

22d.

[October 22, 1803] Nicodemus and Bartholomaus [Nicodemus' brother], came here with their families from Pettquotting, and expressed a strong desire to be reunited to the congn. Our brn. & Sis. received them with joy & furnished them with dwellings. (MCA B171/F13: 47)

For the next two months they were provisional members of the village, and finally, on January 1, 1804, they were accepted officially. Unfortunately, their wanderings were not over. Within four months, he and his brother, Bartholomaus, were in violation of the house rules—Nicodemus for drunkenness, and his brother on a far more serious infraction. On several occasions, and without notice, Bartholomaus had entered the home of several white neighbors looking for liquor. On at least two of these visits he surprised and frightened a young mother and her children. Zeisberger, who was extremely conscious of relations with the whites, immediately ordered the brother and his family to leave the village.

Both families left Goshen on April 1 and moved to Pettquotting. They lived at the Huron River mission for the next five years, except for several short visits to Goshen. Early in November 1809, they again applied for permission to return to the Muskingum valley. Mortimer gave his consent and the families returned on January 11, 1810. They remained there for the next fifteen months, until Nicodemus's death.

Torn between the two cultures, Nicodemus, like his biblical counterpart, was full of questions and frustrated by his own human dilemma. As Mortimer wrote, "He was never without strong conviction as to what was right or wrong," but "often wavering in his mind, whether he should remain here or return to Sandusky" and join his native friends. To the missionaries the answer was elementary, the choice was God or the devil. To Nicodemus it was a far more complex problem.

The mission diaries seldom recorded family disagreements, and no entries can be found indicating any controversy between Nicodemus and Montour. However, sometime between November 1810 and the following April, during Montour's residency at the mission, there must have been a heated discussion over the daughter. Given Nicodemus's proclivity for in-law problems and Montgomery Montour's arrogant and self-serving attitude, it is little wonder the situation exploded into violence on April 10, 1811, ending in the tragedy on May 1.

Henrietta remained at Goshen for two and one-half months after her husband's death and then moved the family to Sandusky.

Burial 35
Charles, son of John and Anna Benigna Henry
Goshen diary, August 3, 1811:

> Aug. 2d
> Was the funeral of the son of John Henry & Anna Benigna, who was born yesterday, baptized immediately afterwards by the name of Charles, & then shortly after was taken home to our Lord. (MCA B173/F8: 7–8)

Charles was the last person interred in 1811. Why he was buried among the girls rather than the boys, as was traditional, we are at a loss to explain (see burial map, appendix D). Additional details of Charles's mother and father, John and Anna Benigna Henry, are found in the commentary for burial 36.

1812

Burial 36
Anna Benigna, wife of John Henry; daughter of Ignatius and Christina
Goshen diary, May 22, 1812:

> 22d.
> Was the funeral of Anna Benigna, the [second] wife of John Henry, who departed to our Lord early yesterday morning. She was born & baptized at the winter abode of the Indn. congn., on Capt. Elliot's farm [near Malden Centre in Upper Canada] on their way from Pettquotting to Fairfield, in the year 1791. At an early age she married, & being brought to bed of her first child on the way between here and Pettquotting, the company with which she travelled so hastened with her on the journey, that when she arrived at the latter place, she was very ill, & apparently at the point of death. In her distress she sought & found the grace of our Saviour, & was soon after received into the congn. . . . She was of a still quiet & meek disposition, lived in uninterrupted peace and every one, was dutiful towards her aged mother and in the different relations of wife and mother walked worthy of the gospel. . . . So exemplary & valuable a young sister we would very gladly have kept her among us. Our Lord thought otherwise, & for a considerable time past has been preparing her for a happy exit out of time. When her departure drew near, nothing troubled her but the thoughts of leaving her only surviving child, her husband & mother. But she became of length easy on their account too, & being assured of the forgiveness of her sins, she declared that she was now ready to depart. (MCA B173/F9: 2–3)

The reality of the early nineteenth century comes vividly alive in the short life span of Anna Benigna Henry. Born on September 8, 1791, at the small mission of Warte (near present Malden Centre, Ontario, Canada), she married John Henry on April 26, 1804, in the thirteenth year of her life. Within thirteen months she was the mother of Rachel, who was born under severe conditions that almost cost her life. She bore two more children, who both preceded her in death: Nancy died on November 3, 1810 and Charles on August 1, 1811 (burials 32 and 35). Her father Ignatius (burial 25) and her mother Christina (burial 42) are also buried at Goshen. Between the lines of the Mortimer obituary we can read the sadness and pathos he felt for this child. She was only twenty at the time of her death.

Her husband, John Henry, the oldest son of William Henry, had previously married Anna Benigna's sister, Anna Maria, who died in 1803 (see burial 19). At the time of Anna Benigna's death, the couple had one surviving child, Rachel—the first daughter of Anna Benigna. Both wives of John Henry had ten children who died in infancy.

After Anna Benigna's death, John lived on at Goshen until it closed in 1821. The last diary entry referring to him was on September 19 and indicated that he was sick with a fever. Like so many of the converts still at Goshen, he was frequently charged with drunkenness. Just two weeks before his sickness, he was dismissed as the official interpreter of the village because of his drunken behavior. Sometime during the latter part of 1821 and the first few months of 1822, he moved with his small family to New Fairfield. He remained there until 1837, when he became part of sixty-one disgruntled members of the mission who broke away and emigrated to the Nebraska territory. They left New Fairfield on July 17, 1837. John, now seventy-four, survived for five months of the slow and tedious trek, but he died in December near the banks of the Kansas River before they reached their destination.

Anna Benigna Henry was the only person to die at Goshen in 1812. (Consult appendix F for a complete list of deaths and burials within the Henry family while living at Goshen.)

1813

Burial 37
Anna Caritas, second wife of Charles Henry
Died January 27, 1813

The early life of Anna Caritas is shrouded in mystery. She first appears among the Brethren records at the Detroit River mission, where she was baptized on September 11, 1791. Zeisberger gives us a clue to her ancestry in the entry for that date:

> In the afternoon we had the first baptism here of an adult, among them a white girl who, when a child had been taken in the last war by the Indians, and given to our Theodora [a widow] in place of a child before she came to us. Since she asked for baptism and we could not find out whether, when a child, she had been baptized, having reason to doubt about such a baptism, as she was from a neighborhood on the frontier where there are few inhabitants, and where there were only a couple of houses far away from the settlements, we concluded and thought: It is better at all events that she should be twice baptized than that she should live in doubt about her baptism all her life. Thus at her request, with the approval of the Saviour, she was baptized by David Zeisberger into Jesus' death, receiving the name of Anna Charity [English translation for the German *Caritas*]. (Bliss, *Diary of David Zeisberger*, 2: 214; MCA B173/F10: 10)

Throughout the many Indian wars of the eighteenth century, literally thousands of white people were taken captive by the Indians, adopted, and raised among the tribes. This was one alternative to replace their dwindling population, which was being depleted by war and disease. A striking number of these captives preferred to remain among the Indians rather than return to white civilization. In his recent book, *The Invasion Within*, James Axtel gives us a vivid insight into this practice. After extensive research Axtel concluded: "They stayed because they found Indian life to possess a strong sense of community, abundant love, and uncommon integrity—values that European colonists also honored, if less successfully." He also noted other attractive values of Indian life: "social equality, mobility, adventure and the absence of those cares and corroding solicitudes which often prevail with us" (pp. 302–27).

In a diary entry of March 6, 1791, Zeisberger explained how Indians captured these prisoners.

> Some Tawas [Ottawas] from over the lake arrived on their way to get prisoners. This is the Indian custom; if the son or daughter of a man or woman dies naturally, or in any other way, they give to a captain a black belt of wampum, with the desire that he will go out and bring back a prisoner in the place of the dead. He gets together a company, goes out, and if he obtains a prisoner he shaves and paints his head so that he looks like no white man and he hangs this same belt about his neck which is a token that he is to remain alive and when he comes to the proper place he is delivered to the one who gave the belt and taken into the family in place of the [lost] child. Such was the business of these warriors, who had with them such a belt. (Bliss, *Diary of David Zeisberger*, 2: 160)

Anna Caritas appears to have been the victim of one of these raids. The journals do not list the precise date of her marriage to Charles Henry, but the first indication of such a marriage is found in a diary entry on September 2, 1803. In a brief trip to Pettquotting, "Charles and Anna returned to Goshen after retrieving their horse lent to Bartholomaus." Bartholomaus was the natural son of Theodora, or the adopted Anna's brother.

Anna Caritas lived an exemplary life among the Christian Indians, becoming a sacristan in 1796 and a valuable Native Helper in 1803. She also appears to be the second wife of Charles Henry. While Fliegel does not list the marriage of the first wife, Benigna (902), there is an entry under November 15, 1789, listing the marriage: "In the evening William Henry's son Charles was married to Benigna Nanticoke [Samuel Nanticoke's daughter], both were unmarried" (Bliss, *Diary of David Zeisberger*, 2: 65). Benigna and Charles later separated, and she subsequently married Moses.

It was not unusual for Indian couples to dissolve their marriages, which continued only at the pleasure of each party. Zeisberger provides a quick glimpse of Indian mores on this subject in his "History of the North American Indians," written for George Henry Loskiel in 1779–80 during the Zeisbergers' stay at New Schoenbrunn:

In studying the Indians, their mode of life and deportment toward each other, particularly the relations between the sexes, it is safe to say that one does not learn to know them well until they become concerned about the well-being of their souls and confess the evils that weigh on their consciences. One may be among them for several years and, not knowing them intimately as stated, but regard them as virtuous people. Far from it. Impurity and immorality, even gross sensuality and unnatural vice flourish among them, according to the testimony of the Indians themselves. . . . As they marry early in life, the men in the eighteenth or nineteenth year, the women in the fifteenth or sixteenth, or earlier, one would imagine that the Indians should increase rapidly and would have many children. Yet an Indian may become old and have but few children, for the family ties are only too frequently and easily broken on slight provocation, even when there are children. Only as the parties advanced in age and cannot readily form other connections, are the matrimonial relations apt to be permanent. Owing to the instability of family relations, children are often neglected. This does not argue that the Indians do not love their children, As every creature loves its young, so the Indians do love their children, are indeed, very fond of them, especially as they mature and return the affection. *But sin and lust bring about unnatural conditions.* It seems as if a curse rested upon them and that they were destined to become extinct. There is another clan of Indians who live with their wives because they love their children, and at the same time have concubines, who do not live in the house, because the rightful wife will not suffer this. The latter will generally be content to remain with her husband. I have known cases where the Indian would have two wives in his house, but this is rare.

Yet there are Indians, even among the savages, who maintain peaceable and orderly family lives. Among them larger families are the rule, there being often eight to ten children. (Pp. 20–21; emphasis added)

With due respect to Zeisberger "sin and lust" did not bring about the rapid decline in Indian population, but, rather, the decline was brought on by the white settlers' disease, liquor, and the on-rushing and insatiable demand for Indian land by the white settlers. It was natural for these zealous missionaries, a product of their time and age, to look askance at any moral or sexual criterion that deviated from those accepted by Christian standards. Tribal law already outlawed adultery but placed no particular prohibition on premarital sexual activity. The young people began sexual exploration early in their teens and found no particular shame in their behavior. But to the missionary their scanty dresses and bare breasts only intensified the problem. David McClure, a missionary who visited the Schoenbrunn area in 1772, leaves a description of several days spent with the Delaware at Gekelemunkpechunk (Newcomerstown, Ohio). His host was Gelelemend (William Henry), who provided a house and assigned his son John to protect him:

> Several of the aged Councillors had lived with one wife from their youth; but a great part of husbands & wives at Kekalemahpehoong [his spelling of the Indian village name] had separated and taken others. I was astonished at the profligate description which young [John] Killbuck (whose father had directed him to lodge in my house and to wait on me), gave me himself. He slept in a loft which was ascended by a ladder at the further end of the house. He conducted a squaw up the ladder every night. I asked him, one day, if it was his wife? He said no. I admonished him for his conduct. He said, he was 19 years old, and had had several wives, and that he wanted one more, and he should be happy. It is natural to expect that but few children, can be the fruits of such unbounded licentiousness. On an average they are about 2 or 3 to a family. (McClure, *Diary of David McClure*, 91)

"Unbounded licentiousness," indeed. The author can only observe that we have made the full circle from John (Killbuck) Henry's indiscretions of the eighteenth century to the trial marriages of the late twentieth century. For millennia prior to white contact, the Indian had lived in relative peace and contentment. While many of his cultural practices differed radically from white Christian missionary mores, any attempt to radically alter his life-style only added to the burden of transition and acculturation.

Burial 38
Nancy, daughter of Christian Gottlieb and Anna Susanna Henry
Died August 2, 1813

Amid all the turmoil of troops marching past the Goshen mission during the War of 1812, the diary entry for June 27 announced the birth of: "a healthy and happy new daughter to Christian Gottlieb and Anna Susanna Henry." One month and six days later she was dead, another statistic to the high rate of child mortality among the Indian population. Nancy was the eighth of eleven children born to Christian and Anna Henry (Fliegel, *Index* 1:82–84; MCA B173/F10: 41).

1814

Burial 39
Carolina Louisa, daughter of Abraham and Rosina
    (Heckedorn) Luckenbach
Died October 12, 1814

Carolina Louisa, the first child of the Luckenbachs, died two months and ten days after her birth. By that date, Luckenbach was the head missionary of the village, having replaced Benjamin Mortimer on November 17, 1812. He married Rosina Heckedorn, from Lititz, on September 8, 1813. Luckenbach remained at Goshen until May 29, 1820, then accepted a call to serve at New Fairfield. After a long twenty-three-year stay at New Fairfield, in failing health, he returned to Bethlehem in June of 1843. He died there in 1854 at seventy-three (MCA B173/F11: 35).

1815

Burial 40
Thomas (Amaniechge)
Died April 3, 1815

Thomas, with the Indian name Amaniechge, meaning "Young Turkey Cock," is the mystery burial in the Goshen cemetery. Little is known of him. He arrived at Goshen on December 2, 1813, as a homeless native Indian. Twenty-seven days later he was seriously burned during an epileptic seizure. He continued to live at Goshen for the next year. In October he disappeared, apparently lost in the woods while suffering another seizure. Days later he struggled back into the village. After repeated appeal, Luckenbach consented and baptized him on March 31, 1815. Three days later he died. The secret of his identity lies buried with him in the Goshen cemetery (MCA B175/F1: 13).

1818–1823

Burial 41
Beatus, the infant son of Charles and Deborah Henry
Died July 2, 1818

After Anna Caritas's death (burial 37) in 1813, Charles Henry was married a third time, to the young Indian girl, Deborah. She was born at Fairfield on February 5, 1797, and was eighteen at the time of her son's death. Despondent over losing her child and disgruntled with Charles and mission life at Goshen, Deborah left the village on July 27, 1821. She returned to New Fairfield and died five months later, on December 23, 1821. Charles remained until September 8, when Brother Proske, the last missionary at Goshen, reported, "He is on his way to New Fairfield to cause more trouble." Charles spent the rest of his life at New Fairfield, dying there on May 24, 1837 (MCA B175/F4: 6–7; B3191/F4, Charles Henry 954; B3191/F6, Deborah 1556; see also Fliegel, *Index* 1:99).

Burial 42
Christina, wife of Ignatius
Died October 23, 1821

Christina's life prior to her husband Ignatius's death on September 11, 1806, is covered in the burial sketch 25. She left Goshen for a brief period following his death, then returned to the village in November 1807, just one year before Zeisberger's death. If her age, as reported at her death, is correct, she would have been seventy. Several entries in 1813 record serious concern for her son, Philippus, who was twenty-six. The diary entries do not explain the reason for her despair. Confronted with extreme poverty, as was common with aged widows, she received numerous gifts from the Society for the Propagating of the Gospel. She remained at Goshen for the balance of her life and died, at age eighty-four, on October 23, 1821, just seven days before the congregation was notified of the closing of the mission. She and her husband, Ignatius, represent one of the most poignant narratives of the Goshen mission (Fliegel, *Index* 1:88; MCA B175/F8: 20).

Burial 43
John, son of Christian Gottlieb and Anna Susanna Henry
Died September 22, 1822

John, the last of the eleven children of Christian Gottlieb and Anna Susanna Henry, was born on January 17, 1822, after the mission closed. He lived for nine months. Three more children from this marriage are buried in the Goshen cemetery: Benjamin, burial 23; Rebecca, burial 31; and Nancy, burial 38. At the time of John's death, the mission had been closed, but a handful of the Indians resided at the village. Life for the remaining few became one drinking orgy after another. Nine months later, when Brother de Schweinitz visited the village on July 14, 1823, he found it deserted (Fliegel, *Index* 1:197; also "Gnadenhutten Diary of the White Moravian Settlement" [First Moravian Church, Gnadenhutten, Ohio], 96).

Burial 44
Christian Gottlieb, son of William Henry and husband of
  Anna Susanna Henry
Died February 9, 1823

While drinking was a constant annoyance among Zeisberger's converts as long as he lived, the disruption of village life was kept to a minimum. Shortly before his death in 1808 it became an ever-increasing problem, especially after Mortimer's departure in 1812. The diaries are filled with entries on this topic. Normal village life, including regular church services and school, was totally disrupted. Christian Gottlieb was one of the worst offenders. In the final years of his life he became totally debauched.

We have scanty information as to his precise age. At his baptism in 1790 he is described as an "older boy," probably about fourteen. If that is correct, he would have been forty-eight at his death. He married Anna Susanna on December 6, 1796, at Fairfield. She was his only wife. Three years later their first child, Jeremias, was born on October 22, 1799. Between Jeremias and the last child, John, born January 19, 1821, the couple had, with great regularity, eleven children.

Christian Gottlieb accompanied Heckewelder and the Edwards party to Gnadenhutten in June 1798, making him among the first converts to return to the Muskingum valley in seventeen years. Zeisberger and the balance of the Brethren followed in August. In June of the following year, Christian moved the pregnant Susanna from Fairfield to Goshen, and in

October, Jeremias was born. Thus began an exemplary life of service to his family, the mission, and the federal government. He made frequent trips to Charlestown, Buffalo, Fairfield, and Pettquotting, delivering correspondence, carrying supplies, acting as a translator, bringing the mail, and gaining a reputation as a successful hunter. During the War of 1812, he worked as a spy for the United States government.

For twelve years Christian Gottlieb lived a blameless life. But on October 30, 1810, we have the first entry discussing an incident that would later portend disaster. "Christian Gottlieb was sorry for having been drunk." With haunting and increasing regularity it would appear again and again among the diary entries, until the close of the mission in 1821. By then, he had lost all respect, all honor, and had become known as the mission's troublemaker and town drunk. The final entry is found in the diaries of the Gnadenhutten, Ohio, First Moravian Church on February 11, 1823:

> Brother Rauschenberger conducted the funeral in Goshen of the Indian, Christian Henry Killbuck, who died on the ninth. He had been in New Philadelphia on the eighth where he drank too much whiskey, and as he was on his way to Stonecreek, where his family was camping this winter, and he could not go on, it being very cold, and when he was brought into the house of a white man, he was almost frozen. He lay there until the following morning when he breathed his last. Before the body was buried, Brother Rauschenberger spoke to the Indians and white people who were present with great vigor on the meaning of the daily text: "No one who puts his hand to the plow and looks back is fit for the kingdom of God." Luke 9:62. (99; see also Fliegel, *Index* 1:82–84)

Appendix A

Number	Name of Mission	Location	Founded	Abandoned
1	Shekomeko	Dutchess Co. N.Y.	Aug. 1740	Dec. 1744
2	Pachgatgoch	Kent Co. Conn.	Oct. 1742	Dec. 1762
3	Wechquanach	Dutchess Co. N.Y.	Oct. 1742	June 1753
4	Friedenshutten I	Bethlehem, Pa.	Sept. 1745	May 1747
5	Gnadenhutten I	Leighton, Pa.	June 1746	Nov. 1755
6	Shamokin	Sunbury, Pa.	June 1747	Dec. 1755
7	Meniologameka	Monroe Co. Pa.	June 1749	May 1754
8	Nain	Lehigh Co. Pa.	June 1758	April 1765
9	Wechquetank	Monroe Co. Pa.	April 1760	Oct. 1763
10	Tuscarawas (Post-Heck.)	Bolivar, Ohio	April 1762	Nov. 1762
11	The Philadelphia Incident	Philadelphia, Pa.	Oct. 1763	Mar. 1765
12	Friedenshutten II	Bradford Co. Pa.	May 1765	June 1772
13	Goschgoschunk	Forest Co. Pa.	June 1768	April 1769
14	Lawunakhannek	Forest Co. Pa.	April 1769	April 1770
15	Schechschiquanunk	Bradford Co. Pa.	June 1769	June 1772
16	Friedensstadt (Lagundo Utenunk)	Lawrence Co. Pa.	April 1770	April 1773
17	Schoenbrunn (Welhik Thuppeek)	New Philadelphia, Ohio	May 1772	April 1777
18	Gnadenhutten II	Gnadenhutten, Ohio	Oct. 1772	Sept. 1781
19	Lichtenau	Coshocton, Ohio	April 1776	April 1780
20	New Schoenbrunn	New Philadelphia, Ohio	April 1779	Sept. 1781
21	Salem	Port Washington, Ohio	April 1780	Sept. 1781

22	Captive Town	Wyandot Co. Ohio	Oct. 1781 March 1782
23	New Gnadenhutten	Clinton River, Mich.	July 1782 April 1786
24	Pilgerruh	Cuyahoga Co. Ohio	June 1786 April 1787
25	New Salem (Pettquotting)	Erie Co. Milan, Ohio	June 1787 April 1791
26	Warte (Detroit River)	Amhersburg, Ontario	May 1791 April 1792
27	Fairfield	Thames River, Ont.	May 1792 Oct. 1813 (Burned)
28	Goshen	Goshen, Ohio	Oct. 1798 Nov. 1821
29	White River	Near Anderson, Ind.	May 1801 Sept. 1806
30	Chippewa	East Sydenham Ontario	April 1802 Dec. 1806
31	Pettquotting 2d. Experience	Milan, Ohio	June 1804 April 1809
32	New Fairfield	Thames River, Ontario	Aug. 1815 April 1903

Compiled by Earl P. Olmstead, January 2, 1988.

Appendix B

THE GOSHEN MISSION: ANNUAL POPULATION STATISTICS

Year	Moravian Church Archives (Box/Folder: Page Number)	Married Persons	Single Men, Women, Widows, & Widowers	Children	Communicants	Baptized not incl. Communicants	Unbaptized Natives	Total
1798	(The mission began October 4, 1798)				Not Recorded			37
1799	171/6:11	28	5	17	21	25	4	50
1800	171/8:11	40	8	23	28	32	11	71
1801	171/9:34	28	6	20	14	31	9	54[a]
1802	171/11:6	30	4	14	16	21	11	48
1803	171/13:66	24	4	18	10	29	7	46
1804	173/1:36	21	5	11	11	20	6	37[b]
1805	173/2:44	13	3	6	7	11	4	22[c]
1806	173/3:33	13	1	9	7	13	3	23
1807	173/4:11	10	2	10	7	12	3	22
1808	173/5:26	9	3	12	6	15	3	24
1809	173/6:16	11	4	14	10	16	3	29[d]
1810	173/7:26	11	6	18	9	24	2	35
1811	173/8:15	10	3	15	7	18	3	28
1812	173/10:3	6	5	16	8	16	3	27
1813	173/10:7	8	6	12	7	18	1	26
1814	173/11:46	6	6	13	Not Recorded			25
1815	175/1:34	6	6	15	3	20	4	27
1816	175/2:40	6	9	14	4	16	9	29
1817	175/3:17	Not Recorded			5	14	7	26
1818	175/4:25	Not Recorded			4	16	7	27
1819	175/6:6	Not Recorded			4	16	7	27
1820	175/7:9	Not Recorded			5	21	4	30
1821	Mission closed November 5, 1821							

Source: Compiled from Moravian Church Archives.
[a]Founding of the White River mission.
[b]Founding of the Pettquotting second mission.
[c]Suicide of Ignatius's son, Henry.
[d]Abandonment of the Pettquotting mission.

Appendix C

POPULATION GRAPH OF THE GOSHEN MISSION, 1798–1821

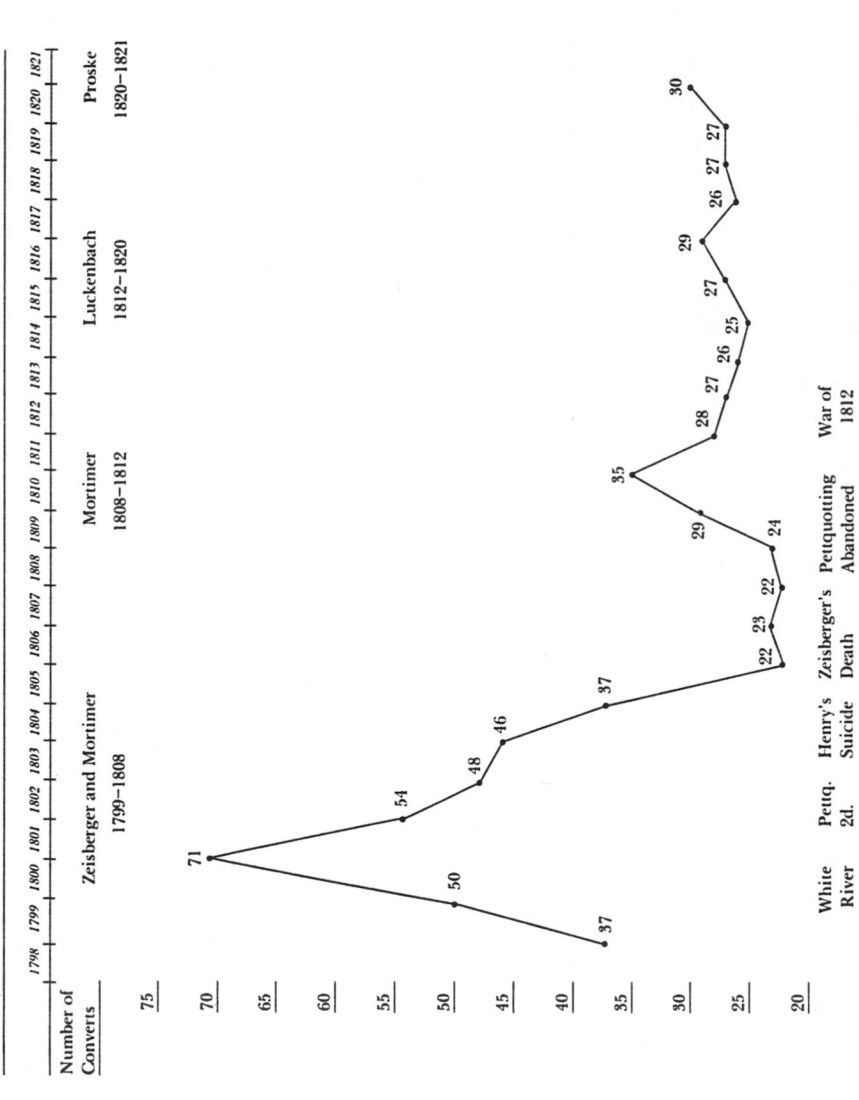

Source: Moravian Church Archives.

Appendix D

MAP OF THE INTERMENTS, GOSHEN MISSION CEMETERY, 1799–1823

↑ N

Adult Women

No.	Name	Date	Year
42	Christina Sophia	10/23	1821
37	Anna Caritas	1/27	1813
36	Anna Benigna	5/21	1812
30	Anna Maria	6/5	1809
21	Rachel	10/6	1803
19	Anna Maria	3/15	1803
15	Rachel	5/12	1802
14	Salome	3/2	1802
9	Sophia Younger	8/14	1801
7	Sophia Elder	2/1	1801
11	Agnes	9/24	1801
13	Rebecca	12/31	1801
6	Beata Henry	11/30	1800
5	Getraud	10/29	1800
3	Liseta	3/2	1800
16	Anna Rosina	10/23	1802
17	Anna Salome	11/6	1802
20	Ketura	4/6	1803

Girls

No.	Name	Date	Year
39	Carolina Luckenbach	10/12	1814
38	Nancy	8/2	1813
35	Charles	8/1	1811
32	Nancy	11/3	1810
31	Rebecca	8/17	1809

Adult Men

No.	Name	Date	Year
40	Thomas	4/3	1815
44	Christian Gotlieb Henry	2/9	1823
27	Joseph	3/8	1808
24	Abel	4/22	1805
25	Ignatius	9/11	1806
29	David Zeisberger	11/17	1808
33	William Henry (Gelelemend)	2/17	1811
34	Nicodemus	4/30	1811
1	Benjamin Henry	8/11	1799
8	Moses	7/14	1801
12	William Edwards	10/8	1801

Boys

No.	Name	Date	Year
22	Joseph Mortimer	1/2	1804
23	Benjamin Henry	4/3	1805
26	Arnold	9/30	1806
28	Joseph Henry	6/22	1808
41	Son of Deborah Henry	7/2	1818
43	John Henry	9/22	1822
2	Francis	9/12	1799
4	Abraham James	10/4	1800
10	Levi	9/12	1801
18	Jacob Henry	1/26	1803

Source: Moravian Church Archives.

A careful study of the plot layout will reveal the familiar pattern consistently used in all mission burial grounds. There are four separate plots: adult males (upper right), adult females (upper left), male children (lower right), female children (lower left). The author is at a loss to explain why Charles (burial 35) is among the girls. Race provided no distinction—whites were buried along with Indians in the order of their deaths.

Location: The Goshen mission cemetery is located on State Route 416 three miles below New Philadelphia, in Goshen Township, Tuscarawas County, Ohio.

Note: The underlined numbers above each name represent the chronological dates of the deaths at the mission.

~~~

Appendix E

I. We will know no other God but the one only true God, who made us and all creatures, and came into this world in order to save sinners; to Him alone we will pray.

II. We will rest from work on the Lord's day, and attend public service.

III. We will honor father and mother, and when they grow old and needy we will do for them what we can.

IV. No person will get leave to dwell with us until our teachers have given their consent, and the helpers (native assistants) have examined him.

V. We will have nothing to do with thieves, murderers, whoremongers, adulterers, or drunkards.

VI. We will not take part in dances, sacrifices, heathenish festivals, or games.

VII. We will use no tshapiet, or witchcraft, when hunting.

VIII. We renounce and abhor all tricks, lies, and deceits of Satan.

IX. We will be obedient to our teachers and to the helpers who are appointed to preserve order in our meetings in the towns and fields.

X. We will not be idle, nor scold, nor beat one another, nor tell lies.

XI. Whoever injures the property of his neighbor shall make restitution.

XII. A man shall have but one wife—shall love her and provide for her and his children. A woman shall have but one husband, be obedient to him, care for her children, and be cleanly in all things.

XIII. We will not admit rum or any other intoxicating liquor into our town. If strangers or traders bring intoxicating liquor, the helpers shall take it from them and not restore it until the owners are ready to leave the place.

XIV. No one shall contract debts with traders, or receive goods to sell for traders, unless the helpers give their consent.

XV. Whoever goes hunting, or on a journey, shall inform the minister or stewards.

XVI.   Young persons shall not marry without the consent of their parents and the minister.

XVII.   Whenever the stewards or helpers appoint a time to make fences or to perform other work for the public good, we will assist and do as we are bid.

XVIII.   Whenever corn is needed to entertain strangers, or sugar for love-feast, we will contribute from our stores.

XIX.   We will not go to war, and will not buy anything of warriors taken in war. (This last statute was adopted at a later time during the revolutionary war.)

Source: De Schweinitz, *Zeisberger*, 378–79.

*Languntoutenunk (Lagundo Utenunk) is Friedensstadt, and Welhik Tuppek (Welhik Thuppeek) is Schoenbrunn; see appendix A, numbers 16 and 17.

Appendix F

A. GENEALOGY, WILLIAM HENRY AND IGNATIUS FAMILIES

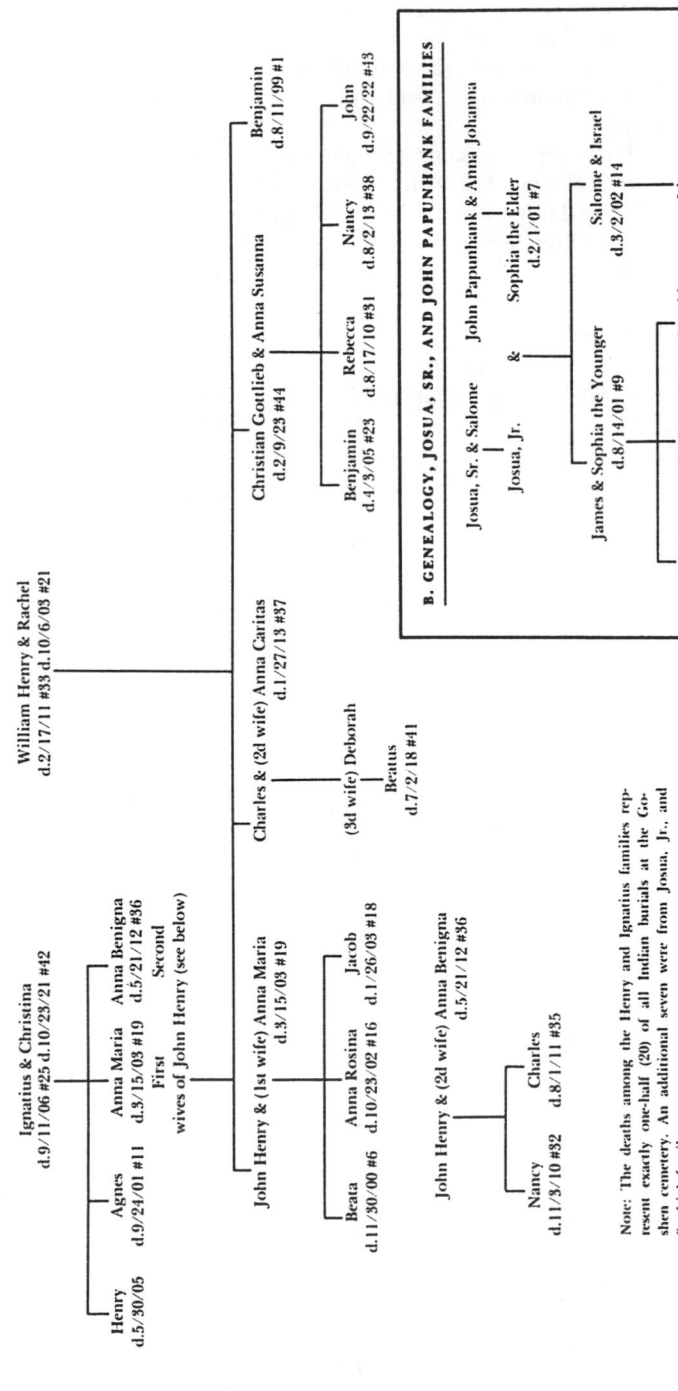

William Henry & Rachel
d.2/17/11 #33 d.10/6/03 #21

Ignatius & Christina
d.9/11/06 #25 d.10/23/21 #42

Henry
d.5/30/05

Agnes
d.9/24/01 #11

Anna Maria
d.3/15/03 #19
First

Anna Benigna
d.5/21/12 #36
Second

wives of John Henry (see below)

John Henry & (1st wife) Anna Maria
d.3/15/03 #19

Beata
d.11/30/00 #6

Anna Rosina
d.10/23/02 #16

Jacob
d.1/26/03 #18

John Henry & (2d wife) Anna Benigna
d.5/21/12 #36

Nancy
d.11/3/10 #82

Charles
d.8/1/11 #35

Charles & (2d wife) Anna Caritas
d.1/27/13 #37

(3d wife) Deborah

Beatus
d.7/2/18 #41

Christian Gotlieb & Anna Susanna
d.2/9/23 #44

Benjamin
d.4/3/05 #23

Rebecca
d.8/17/10 #31

Nancy
d.8/2/13 #38

John
d.9/22/22 #13

Benjamin
d.8/11/99 #1

B. GENEALOGY, JOSUA, SR., AND JOHN PAPUNHANK FAMILIES

Josua, Sr. & Salome

Josua, Jr.

&

John Papunhank & Anna Johanna

Sophia the Elder
d.2/1/01 #7

James & Sophia the Younger
d.8/14/01 #9

Francis
d.9/12/99 #2

Abraham
d.10/4/00 #4

Arnold
d.9/30/06 #26

Salome & Israel
d.3/2/02 #14

Lisetta
d.3/2/00 #3

Note: The deaths among the Henry and Ignatius families represent exactly one-half (20) of all Indian burials at the Goshen cemetery. An additional seven were from Josua, Jr., and Sophia's family.

Source: Moravian Church Archives.

~~~~

Appendix G

Burial Number	Died	Name	Relationship
		1799	
1	August 11	Benjamin Henry (987)	Son of William and Rachel Henry. Died of Consumption. Age: 18 years.
2	September 12	Francis James (1569)	Son of James and Sophia, the Younger. Age: 14 months.
		1800	
3	March 2	Lisetta (NFN)	Daughter of Israel and Salome. Age: 14 weeks
4	October 4	Abraham James (NFN)	Son of James and Sophia, the Younger. Age: 4 months.
5	October 29	Gertraud (1538)	Daughter of Johannes Thomas and Catharina Marie. Age: 7 years.
6	November 30	Beata (NFN)	Stillborn daughter of John and Anna Maria Henry.
		1801	
7	February 1	Sophia, the Elder (530)	Daughter of John Papunhank, wife of Josua, Jr. Age: 60 Years.
8	July 14	Moses Mohawk (NFN)	Husband of Rachel. Age: 25 years.

9	August 14	Sophia, the Younger (1329)	Wife of James. Age: 27 years.
10	September 12	Levi (NFN)	Son of Moses and Rachel Mohawk. Age: 18 months.
11	September 24	Agnes (1542)	Daughter of Ignatius and Christina. Age: 6 years.
12	October 8	William Edwards	Assistant missionary to David Zeisberger. Age: 77 years.

1802

13	December 31, 1801	Rebecca (NFN)	Daughter of Abel and Sulamith. Age: 14 months. Buried Jan. 2, 1802.
14	March 2	Salome (673)	Daughter of Josua, Jr., and Sophia, the Elder; wife of Israel. Age: 30 years.
15	May 12	Rachel (946)	Wife of Moses Mohawk. Age: 31 years.
16	October 23	Anna Rosina (1560)	Daughter of John and Anna Maria Henry. Age: 5 years.
17	November 6	Anna Salome (NFN)	Daughter of Joseph and Beata. Age: 1 year.

1803

18	January 26	Jacob (NFN)	Son of John and Anna Maria Henry. Age: 1 year, 2 months.
19	March 15	Anna Maria (936)	Wife of John Henry, daughter of Ignatius and Christina. Age: 30 years.
20	April 6	Ketura (1548)	Daughter of Johann and Anna Sophia Adams. Age: 7 years.
21	October 6	Rachel (957)	Wife of William Henry. Age: 65 years.

1804

22	January 2	Joseph Warner	Son of Benjamin and Bethiah (Warner) Mortimer. Age: 9 weeks, 4 days.

		1805	
23	April 3	Benjamin (NFN)	Son of Christian Gottlieb and Anna Susanna Henry. Age: 9 days.
24	April 22	Abel (959)	Son of Thomas and Sabina; great-grandson of Netawatwes; husband of Sulamith. Age: 35 years.

		1806	
25	September 11	Ignatius (726)	Husband of Christina. Age: unknown.
26	September 30	Arnold (1550)	Son of James and Sophia, the Younger. Age: 10 years.

		1808	
27	March 8	Joseph (961)	Husband of Beata. Age: 37 years.
28	June 22	Joseph (NFN)	Son of Thomas and Anna Sophia White Eyes. Age: 2-1/2 years.
29	November 17	David Zeisberger	Head missionary. Age: 87 years.

		1809	
30	June 5	Anna Maria (799)	Wife of Joachim. Age: 55 years.

		1810	
31	August 17	Rebecca (NFN)	Daughter of Christian Gottlieb and Anna Susanna Henry. Age: 7 months.
32	November 3	Nancy (NFN)	Daughter of John and Anna Benigna Henry. Age: 1 year, 8 months.

		1811	
33	February 17	William Henry (951)	a.k.a. Gelelemend and John Killbuck, Jr. Age: 74 years.
34	April 30	Nicodemus (977)	Husband of Henrietta. Age: 43 years.
35	August 1	Charles (NFN)	Son of John and Anna Benigna Henry. Age: 1 day.

1812

| 36 | May 21 | Anna Benigna (1515) | Wife of John Henry; daughter of Ignatius and Christina. Age: 21 years. |

1813

| 37 | January 27 | Anna Caritas (979) | Wife of Charles Henry. Age: unknown. Captured white girl, daughter of Theodora. |
| 38 | August 2 | Nancy (NFN) | Daughter of Christian Gottlieb and Anna Susanna Henry. Age: 1 month, 6 days. |

1814

| 39 | October 12 | Carolina Louisa | Daughter of Abraham and Rosina (Heckedorn) Luckenbach. Age: 2 months, 10 days. |

1815

| 40 | April 3 | Thomas (Amaniechge) (NFN) | Homeless young man. Age: unknown. |

1818

| 41 | July 2 | Beatus (NFN) | Son of Charles and Deborah Henry. Age: 1 day. |

1821

| 42 | October 23 | Christina (744) | Wife of Ignatius. Age: 84 years. |

1822

| 43 | September 22 | John (NFN) | Son of Christian Gottlieb and Anna Susanna Henry. Age: 9 months. |

1823

| 44 | February 9 | Christian Gottlieb (970) | Son of William Henry; husband of Anna Susanna Henry. On February 14, at the time of this burial, the mission was deserted. Age: 50 years. |

Indian converts

Adult male converts	9
Adult female converts	10
Female children	11
Male children	10
Total Indians	40

Missionaries

Zeisberger and Edwards	2
Missionary children	2
Total whites	4
Grand total	44

~~~~

Notes

1. The Muskingum River of Zeisberger's day is now known as the Tuscarawas River.

2. George Henry Loskiel, *History of the Missions of the United Brethren among the Indians of North America*, trans. Christian Latrobe (London: Burlinghouse, 1794), 2:7.

3. Both missions were located in present Tuscarawas County, Ohio—Schoenbrunn at New Philadelphia, and Gnadenhutten in Clay Township, at the present village of Gnadenhutten.

4. Paul A. W. Wallace, *Indians in Pennsylvania* (Harrisburg: Pennsylvania Historical and Museum Commission, 1961), 183.

5. David Jones, *A Journey of Two Visits Made to Some Nations of the Indians on the West Side of the River Ohio in the Years 1772, 1773, 1774* (reprint, Fairfield, Wash.: Ye Galleon Press, 1973), 89.

6. August C. Mahr, "Translations of the Schoenbrunn Diary, 1772–1777" (Columbus, Ohio Historical Society), 102b–103.

7. Ibid., 123a.

8. Ibid., 132a–132b.

9. Ibid., 136b.

10. See Goshen burial 12, part 3.

11. Mahr, "Translations of the Schoenbrunn Diary," 147a–147b.

12. Newellike first appeared in the mission diaries in 1765 during a visit to the Friedenshutten mission on the Susquehanna. At that time he was serving as the Munsee chief at Tunhannock Creek. The first message sent by Netawatwes to the Iroquois came to the Christian mission, then was passed through Newellike's village and forwarded to the Iroquois at Onondaga. Newellike was a regular visitor to Friedenshutten but was generally antagonistic toward the Christians and frequently refused to cooperate with requests to assist the mission. He and his people later moved to Grand Haven on the West Branch of the Susquehanna and in March 1774 he moved his family to Schoenbrunn. On May 12, 1774, he was baptized Augustinus by Zeisberger (Rev. Carl John Fliegel, *Index to the Moravian Records of the Moravian Missions among the Indians of North America* [New Haven: Research Publication, 1970], 1:51, 309).

13. Mahr, "Translations of the Schoenbrunn Diary," 148b.

14. Ibid., 153b.

15. Ibid., 154b.

16. Mahr, "Translations of the Schoenbrunn Diary," 155a. Schebosh (Running Water) was a white lay missionary, John Joseph Bull. He was a close personal friend of David Zeisberger. The two had been inseparable from the beginning of Zeisberger's ministry. Schebosh will be a familar character later in our narrative, see chapter 5.

17. Mahr, "Translations of the Schoenbrunn Diary," 155a.

18. Ibid., 155b.

19. Ibid., 159b–160.

20. J. E. Hutton, *A History of the Moravian Church* (London: Fetters Lane, 1909), 406–7.

21. I am indebted to Vernon Nelson, the chief archivist at the Moravian Church Archives in Bethlehem, Pennsylvania for arranging for the translation of the letter from the archives' holdings, and also to the assistant archivist Lothar Madeheim, who did the actual translation.

22. Edmund De Schweinitz, *The Life and Times of David Zeisberger* (Philadelphia: J. B. Lippincott, 1870), 456.

23. We have irrefutable evidence that this rumor was true. Nineteenth-century Moravian historians relied almost entirely on the Bethlehem archives for their Zeisberger research and maintained that he scrupulously kept a neutral stance between the two antagonists. However, during the first half of the twentieth century the Draper Manuscripts became available to scholars. Among the Fort Pitt records, especially the correspondence of General Brodhead, Zeisberger's letters were discovered. While there seem to be logical reasons for Zeisberger's correspondence, it does shed additional light on Colonel De Peyster's later hostility in 1781.

24. Reuben Gold Thwaites and Louise Phelps Kellogg, *Frontier Defense on the Upper Ohio Frontier 1777–1778*, Draper Series, vol. 3 (Madison: Wisconsin Historical Society, 1912; Millwood, N.Y.: Kraus Reprint Company, 1977), 93–95.

25. Ibid., 101–3.

26. The only account of this melodramatic and tension-laden ride is supplied by Heckewelder, writing some forty-two years after the event. The mission diaries, written on the day he arrived at Lichtenau, are quite casual and do not give the histrionic flare to the event supplied by Heckewelder. The account can be found in his *Narrative of the Missions of the United Brethren among the Delaware and Mohegan Indians* (Philadelphia: McCarty and Davis, 1820; reprint, New York: Arno Press, 1971), 176–82.

27. The primary source of the murder of White Eyes came six years after the event. The information was contained in a letter written on May 12, 1784, by George Morgan, the Indian agent, to Thomas Mifflin, the president of Congress. A second letter, confirming the first, was written four years later on September 25, 1788, to the Board of Treasury (George Morgan Papers, 1776–1789, National Archives, microfilm 247, roll 180, item 163. Copies of the manuscripts are in the author's files).

28. George Rogers Clark, *Sketches of His Campaigns in Illinois in 1778–1779* (Cincinnati: Robert Clarke and Company, 1869; reprint, New York: Arno Press and the New York Times, 1971).

29. New Schoenbrunn was located on State Route 416, just one-quarter mile south of present New Philadelphia, Ohio. Part of the old village site was destroyed by the construction of the Ohio Canal in 1825.

30. The Salem village was located on the western banks of the Tuscarawas River approximately one mile below present Port Washington, Ohio.

31. N. N. Hill, Jr., comp., *The History of Coshocton County, Ohio: Its Past and Present 1740–1881* (Newark: A. A. Graham, 1881), 213.

2. THE GREAT DISPERSEMENT

1. James Axtel, *The Invasion Within: The Contest of Cultures in America* (New York: Oxford Univ. Press, 1985), 329.

2. Ibid., 217.

3. Ibid., 218.

4. Ibid., 330.

5. R. Peirce Beaver, "American Missionary Motivation Before the Revolution," *American Society of Church History* 31, no. 2 (June 1912): 225.

6. Sometimes called Lagundo Utenunk, Friedensstadt (City of Peace), was located on the west bank of the Beaver River in Lawrence County, Pennsylvania, just a few miles below present New Castle. It was founded in April 1770 (see chapter 1).

7. David McClure, *Diary of David McClure, Doctor of Divinity, 1748–1820*, with notes by Franklin B. Dexter, M.A. (New York: Knickerbocker Press, 1899), 51.

8. Over the past two hundred years there has been considerable speculation regarding the fate of Fort Laurens. When was it destroyed? Zeisberger wrote in his diary that a party of converts visited the fort on July 24, 1780, and found it burned to the ground, supposedly by the Indians. This would have been ten months after it was abandoned on August 2, 1779 (Moravian Church Archives, Bethlehem, Pennsylvania, box 141, folder 10, July 24, 1780).

9. Randolph C. Downes, *Council Fires on the Upper Ohio* (Pittsburgh: Univ. of Pittsburgh Press, 1968), 204, and chap. 1, note 23.

10. Eugene F. Bliss, trans. and ed., *Diary of David Zeisberger: A Moravian Missionary among the Indians of Ohio* (Cincinnati: Robert Clarke and Company, 1885; reprint, St. Clair Shores, Mich.: Scholarly Press, 1972), 1:3.

11. Ibid.

12. Ibid., 9

13. Zeisberger, Heckewelder, and George Henry Loskiel, all writers of this period, referred to the location as the "camp on the Sandusky." Only De Schweinitz, the author of the nineteenth-century Zeisberger biography, called it "Captive Town." Because of its descriptive nature, I will follow the name used by De Schweinitz. Later references to Sandusky will indicate the native Indian villages in the area.

14. Consul Willshire Butterfield, *An Historical Account of the Expedition Against Sandusky under Col. William Crawford in 1782* (Cincinnati: Robert Clarke and Company, 1873), 180.

15. Bliss, *Diary of David Zeisberger* 1:24–25.

16. The converted men and women of the Helpers' Conference were the most trusted and loyal Indian converts of the village and assisted the missionaries in the operation of the mission.

17. Bliss, *Diary of David Zeisberger* 1:33–34.

18. Ibid., 37–38.

19. Ibid., 38–39.

20. Ibid., 42.

21. Ironically, just twenty-six days before this conversation, Commander Charles Cornwallis had surrendered the British army to General Washington at Yorktown (on October 19, 1781). The war was near conclusion, but neither De Peyster or Zeisberger were aware of this fact.

22. Bliss, *Diary of David Zeisberger* 1:37–43. All references to the Detroit trial are found within these pages of the Bliss book.

23. Zeisberger was describing the Great Swamp that ran southwest from Lake Erie in the

northwestern part of Ohio. The north boundary was bordered by the Maumee River. The south border ran from Sandusky southwest near the present cities of Fremont, Findley, and Delphos (see Carolyn Platt, "The Great Black Swamp," *Timeline* 4, no. 1 [February–March 1987]: 26–39).

24. De Schweinitz, *Zeisberger*, 531.

25. Bliss, *Diary of David Zeisberger* 1:54.

26. Ibid., 56.

27. Ibid., 56–57.

28. Ibid., 64.

29. The twenty-four-year-old Joseph died one month later. He was the first casualty of the Gnadenhutten Massacre, killed by Williamson's men on March 6, 1762.

30. In the summer of 1779, Simon Girty led a party of eight warriors from Detroit with specific instructions to kill Zeisberger. On July 4 they met the missionary and several converts in the woods traveling between New Schoenbrunn and Lichtenau. Only the intercession of several friendly native Indian warriors saved Zeisberger's life (Moravian Church Archives, box 147, folder 9, July 4, 1779).

31. Girty's biographer, Consul Willshire Butterfield, has called his life "tragically romantic." Published in 1890 (Cincinnati: Robert Clarke and Company), *The History of the Girtys*, still remains a most exciting work. Unfortunately, today we are interested in heroes rather than "scoundrels."

32. Bliss, *Diary of David Zeisberger* 1:68.

33. Ibid., 69. The request was immediately granted. That evening, the broken-hearted Zeisberger party slowly made the ten-mile trip back to the village.

34. Ibid., 74.

35. Ibid.

3. FROM DISASTER TO A NEW BEGINNING

1. The John Lieth family also received Zeisberger's permission to live at the Salem mission village for a short period in 1780, just prior to its abandonment. These were the only exceptions to the strict rule of "Indians only" at Moravian villages.

2. Charles N. Thompson, *Sons of the Wilderness: John and William Conner* (Indianapolis: Indiana Historical Society, 1937), 9–35.

3. Native Helpers were Indian converts who assisted the missionaries.

4. A reasonable facsimile of their cabin can be seen at the reconstructed Schoenbrunn village in present New Philadelphia, Ohio.

5. Consult the list of missions in appendix A.

6. Bliss, *Diary of David Zeisberger* 1:76.

7. Ibid.

8. Isa. 10:22 and 66:19. These verses were selected more than a year in advance. The books were printed in Herrnhut, Germany, the world headquarters of the Moravian church, then sent to all the Moravian outpost missions and churches.

9. Bliss, *Diary of David Zeisberger* 1:78–79.

10. Joseph Doddridge, *Notes of the Settlement and Indian Wars* (Wellsburg: By the author at the office of the *Wellsburg (Virginia) Gazette*, 1824; republished with additional material, Pittsburgh: John S. Ritenour and Wm. T. Lindsey, 1912), 268.

11. This was the same expedition that captured the Schebosh party as they were gathering corn to take back to the starving members of the mission at Captive Town.

12. Doddridge, *Notes*, 68. The Mingo Bottoms were on the west side of the Ohio River, several miles south of Mingo Junction, Ohio. There were several sites in this area called Mingo Bottoms or Mingo Springs.

13. Bliss, *Diary of David Zeisberger* 1:79–80.

14. By stealth two teenage boys, Jacob and Thomas, escaped the massacre. Jacob arrived at the Sandusky mission on or shortly before March 23, 1782. He later married Christina, the daughter of Schebosh and Christina, and remained with the congregation, becoming a faithful convert. The last diary reference to him appeared on January 14, 1814, at the Fairfield mission. Thomas disappeared from the diaries briefly after the massacre and did not reappear until July 6, 1785. His death the following year will be reported in our narrative during the converts' stay at Pilgerruh.

15. All the above references to the massacre are found in Bliss, *Diary of David Zeisberger* 1:39–81.

16. Butterfield, *Account of the Expedition Against Sandusky*, 39.

17. Consul Willshire Butterfield, *Washington-Irvine Correspondence: The Official Letters* (Madison, Wis.: David Atwood, 1882), March 8, 1782, p. 94. Ironically and unknown to Washington he wrote this letter on the same day as the Gnadenhutten massacre. Immediately after Irvine arrived at Fort Pitt he became aware of the tragic events on the Muskingum. On April 12, 1782, he wrote to his wife, cautioning her to be circumspect on discussing the incident: "Whatever your private opinion of these matters may be, I conjure you by all ties of affection and as you value my reputation, that you will keep your mind to yourself, and that you will not express any sentiment for or against these deeds;—as it may be alleged, the sentiments you express may come from me or be mine. No man knows whether I approve or disapprove of the killing the Moravians" (Butterfield, *Washington-Irvine Correspondence*, 345.

18. Butterfield, *Account of the Expedition Against Sandusky*, 63. The site was the same rendezvous used by the Williamson expedition, see note 12 above.

19. At that time, considerable acrimony revolved around the objective of the expedition and the quality of the men accompanying Crawford. Most of it came from early Moravian historians like Heckewelder who, in his *History, Manners, and Customs of the Indian Nations Who Once Inhabited Pennsylvania and the Neighboring States* (1876; reprint, New York: Arno Press, 1971, p. 283), called Crawford's men "a gang of banditte" and Loskiel who, in his *History of the Missions* (part 3, p. 188), refers to them as "a gang of murderers." Most of this malevolence was based on the mistaken impression that their objective was to destroy Zeisberger and the remaining converts, now located on the Sandusky River. Later accounts, especially those furnished by Butterfield in *Account of the Expedition Against Sandusky* (p. 70), have completely disproved this contention. Crawford's men, especially the officers, were pioneer farmers and were considered respectable citizens by their peers. Their objective was to destroy the native villages and punish the Indians who were responsible for the many depredations against their frontier settlements.

20. Butterfield, *Account of the Expedition Against Sandusky*, 259.

21. Bliss, *Diary of David Zeisberger* 1:88.

22. Ibid., 99.

23. Ibid., 100.

24. Ibid., 102. This use of the third person in the Zeisberger diary is typical of most of the Moravian diaries.

25. Ibid., 101.

26. Ibid., 104–5.

27. Ibid., 107–8.

28. Ibid., 108.

29. "Diary of David Zeisberger and Gottlob Senseman, Journey to Goschgoschunk on the Ohio and Their Arrival There, 1768," trans. Archer Hulbert and William Schwarze, The Moravian Records, *Ohio Archaeological and Historical Society Publications* 21(1912): 67.

30. Ibid.

31. De Schweinitz, *Zeisberger*, 580.

4. RETURN TO THE OHIO COUNTRY

1. Downes, *Council Fires*, 278.

2. De Schweinitz, *Zeisberger*, 584.

3. Downes, *Council Fires*, 277–309.

4. Moravian Church Archives, box 151, folder 6, item 3. Letter from Schebosh to Nathanael Siedel, November 4, 1782. Schebosh had left the starving converts on the Sandusky at Captive Town to secure the unharvested corn at New Schoenbrunn. His party was discovered there on October 25 by a group of one hundred militiamen and taken as prisoners to Fort Pitt.

5. De Schweinitz lists a total of fifty-three converts at New Gnadenhutten in 1784 (*Zeisberger*, 579); however, the Zeisberger diary does not show this figure, but records twenty-six Brethren absolved and readmitted to holy communion, five children born and baptized, three died, and two adult deaths.

6. Bliss, *Diary of David Zeisberger* 1:193–206.

7. Ibid., 236.

8. C. E. Sherman, *Original Ohio Land Subdivisions*, vol. 3 (Columbus: Ohio Cooperative Topographic Survey, 1976), 177.

9. It was this survey in 1797 that prompted Zeisberger to return to the Muskingum and found the Goshen mission in 1798 (Bliss, *Diary of David Zeisberger* 1:215; Sherman, *Ohio Land Subdivisions*, 97).

10. Bliss, *Diary of David Zeisberger* 1:243–47.

11. Ibid., 261.

12. Ibid., 265. See also Thompson, *Sons of the Wilderness*, 36.

13. Bliss, *Diary of David Zeisberger* 1:267.

14. Ibid., 278.

15. Ibid., 279, 280. There is some doubt as to the precise location of Pilgerruh. It probably was near the mouth of Tinker's Creek and the Cuyahoga River in Cuyahoga County, Ohio, near the village of Valley View.

16. Neither the missionaries nor the Indians gave this village the name of Pilgerruh. The name was assigned to the mission by the Moravian historian George Henry Loskiel. I will continue this tradition.

17. Bliss, *Diary of David Zeisberger* 1:281. Thomas was one of the two survivors of the Gnadenhutten massacre. He was probably nineteen at the time of his death.

18. Ibid., 298.

19. Downes, *Council Fires*, 298.

20. The Pettquotting is now the Huron River, Erie County, Ohio.

5. PETTQUOTTING: THE NEW SALEM

1. Both Loskiel and De Schweinitz referred to this mission on the Pettquotting River as New Salem. There were actually two missionary settlements at this location, the first be-

tween June 1787 and April 1791, and the second from April 1804 to September 1809. The diarist, in both instances, referred to these missions as the first and second experiences on the Pettquotting.

2. Bliss, *Diary of David Zeisberger* 1:442.

3. Ibid.

4. See burial 33, part 3.

5. Bliss, *Diary of David Zeisberger* 1:360; see also Butterfield, *Account of the Expedition Against Sandusky*, 178.

6. Fliegel, in his *Index*, devotes six pages to the activities of Schebosh, far exceeding most of the ordained missionaries. The references span a period of fifty years, from 1747 to 1807, and include 506 separate entries.

7. Bliss, *Diary of David Zeisberger* 1:431.

8. Eugene H. Roseboom and Francis P. Weisenburger, *A History of Ohio* (Columbus: Ohio Historical Society, 1956), 43.

9. Ibid., 56–57; see also Downes, *Council Fires*, 301.

10. Francis Jennings, *The History and Culture of Iroquois Diplomacy* (Syracuse: Syracuse Univ. Press, 1985), 157–201.

11. William H. Guthman, *March to Massacre* (New York: McGraw-Hill, 1970), 186.

12. Ibid., 194.

13. Bliss, *Diary of David Zeisberger* 1:385.

14. See chapter 4, note 8; Sherman, *Ohio Land Subdivisions*, 97; see also Kenneth G. Hamilton, "John Ettwein and the Moravian Church During the Revolutionary Period," *Moravian Historical Society Transaction* 12, nos. 3–4 (1940): 198.

15. De Schweinitz, *Zeisberger*, 608–11.

16. Bliss, *Diary of David Zeisberger* 2:4.

17. Ibid., 1:457.

18. Ibid., 2:158. The acceptance of the messenger's string would have indicated compliance with the instructions. Returning the string meant a subtle rejection.

19. Ibid., 166.

6. FROM THE DETROIT RIVER TO THE RETRENCHE

1. De Schweinitz, in his *Zeisberger* biography, appears to be the first Moravian historian to call the Detroit River mission "die Warte."

2. De Schweinitz, *Zeisberger*, 622. Zeisberger even suggested that McKee, Elliot, and Pipe's names be omitted altogether. The German edition was published in 1788 and the English translation, by Christian Ignatius Latrobe, in 1794. The Loskiel *History* carries the Zeisberger narrative up to 1787 and closes just at the beginning of the Pettquotting mission. Although the book is informative, it is fraught with numerous errors and gives a distorted picture of the native Indians. Loskiel did not come to America until 1802, when he finally met Zeisberger at the Goshen mission. He wrote his book while on assignment to a church in Livonia, Russia.

3. This conversation took place on June 8, 1791, slightly over a month after their arrival at the Detroit River (Bliss, *Diary of David Zeisberger* 2:189).

4. Ibid., 192.

5. Ibid., 186.

6. Downes, *Council Fires*, 317.

7. Guthman, *March to Massacre*, 203–5.

8. Bliss, *Diary of David Zeisberger* 2:193.

9. Ibid., 205.

10. Ibid., 228–29.

11. Ibid., 239–40.

12. For an explanation of the Fliegel *Index,* see Part 3.

13. Bliss, *Diary of David Zeisberger* 2:249.

14. "The Greenville Treaty," Address of Hon. Samuel F. Hunt, Delivered on the Occasion of the Centennial of the Treaty of Greenville, Aug. 3, 1895, at Greenville, Ohio, *Ohio Archaeological and Historical Society Publications* 7(1899): 238.

15. See chapter 4.

16. See Putnam's original Schoenbrunn survey map, page 96. These three tracts still appear on the current Tuscarawas County map.

17. Paul A. W. Wallace, *Thirty Thousand Miles with John Heckewelder* (Pittsburgh: Univ. of Pittsburgh Press, 1958), 340–72. Mortimer wrote a brilliant description in his forty-seven page journal describing the trip.

18. Bliss, *Diary of David Zeisberger* 1:526–27.

19. Moravian Church Archives, box 161, folder 5, page 1.

20. Ibid., 48.

21. Ibid., 46.

22. Zeisberger in all of his diaries never wrote in laudatory phrases of either his wife or himself. This perhaps accounts for the few references to Susan in the mission diaries.

23. Moravian Church Archives, box 161, folder 5, page 54.

24. Ibid., box 171, folder 14, page 22.

25. Ibid., 38.

26. This is presently the site of Bolivar, Ohio.

27. See Surveyor General John F. Mansfield's 1806 map of Ohio.

28. Moravian Church Archives, box 161, folder 5, pages 42–44.

7. THE GOSHEN MISSION

1. Moravian Church Archives, box 171, folder 2, page 1.

2. Ibid., 2.

3. Ibid.

4. Godfrey Haga, the wealthy Philadelphia merchant, had accumulated large land holdings in the Muskingum valley following the signing of the Greenville treaty. Heckewelder became his on-site agent, which probably made him one of the first real estate agents in Ohio. In the following narrative we will witness several of his sales on behalf of Mr. Haga. On Haga's death in 1825, he bequeathed over $250,000 to the Moravian church, an immense sum in those days.

5. Moravian Church Archives, box 172, folder 2, pages 4–5.

6. Georgetown was located in Beaver County, Pennsylvania, a few miles east of Chester, West Virginia, on the banks of the Ohio. Founded in 1793, it remains a small community still found on Pennsylvania maps.

7. Moravian Church Archives, box 171, folder 13, pages 19–20.

8. Ibid., 49.

9. Ibid., 55.

10. Ibid., box 173, folder 1, page 17.

11. Ibid., box 172, folder 2, page 29.

12. Ibid., box 171, folder 4, page 19.

13. This was the Moravian name given to the chief. The Delaware called him Teta Bokshke/Grand Glaise (One who has been split). He became head chief of the Turtle clan

in 1778 after White Eyes's death (Delaware Tribe of Western Oklahoma, *Turtle Children* [Anadarko, Ok.: Bureau of Indian Affairs, 1985], 32).

14. Moravian Church Archives, box 171, folder 6, page 27.

15. Ibid., 31.

16. For further details on Josua, Jr., and the White River mission, see part 3, burial 7, and appendix F for the genealogy of his family.

17. Lawrence Henry Gipson, *The Moravian Mission on the White River* (Indianapolis: Indiana Historical Bureau, 1938), 418–19. The shock of the indiscriminate killing taking place in and around their mission village was particularly difficult on Anna Marie Kluge, John Peter Kluge's wife. On March 27, 1806, nine days following the reported death of Josua, Luckenbach wrote this entry in his diary: "She [Anna Marie] passed the days and nights in constant fear and anguish. Her mind suffered from shock of the terrible experience and her heart was filled with terror. Our dear brethren can easily imagine how we must have felt under the circumstances, especially so when they remember that at the time we were quite alone in the midst of a wholly unrestrained wild people, who burned and murdered their own people, and who no longer listened to anybody, and we are quite worn out in body and soul, so that we hardly know what to do."

18. R. David Edmunds, *The Shawnee Prophet* (Lincoln: Univ. of Nebraska Press, 1983), 42–66.

19. See chapter 5.

20. Moravian Church Archives, box 173, folder 2, page 32.

21. Sherman, *Ohio Land Subdivisions*, 127.

22. Although Mortimer does not supply us with the method of Henry's suicide, it was probably done with the highly poisonous root of the May Apple (*Podophullum peltatum*), which would have been available at this time of year (Herbert C. Kraft, *The Lenape* [Newark: New Jersey Historical Society, 1986], 184; Heckewelder, *History, Manners, and Customs*, 258, 259).

23. Much of the personal details of this event are covered in part 3, burial 25. However, we will explore here the effects that the incident had on Goshen village life.

24. Moravian Church Archives, box 173, folder 2, page 12.

25. Kaschates, sometimes called Thomas Lyons, was an unbaptized native Indian. He and his family came to the village in 1800, and continued to live at Goshen for short periods of time until 1817. He was well liked by the missionaries (Fliegel, *Index* 1:240).

26. See part 3, burial 24.

27. Moravian Church Archives, box 173, folder 2, page 19.

28. See part 3, burial 25.

29. Moravian Church Archives, box 173, folder 2, page 20.

30. Ibid., 21–22.

31. Ibid., 29.

32. Moravian Church Archives, box 1571, folder 8, item 10.

33. Mortimer, in his obituary of Anna Marie, gives us several interesting details of the final days at the Pettquotting mission (see part 3, burial 30).

34. Moravian Church Archives, box 173, folder 6, page 10.

8. GOSHEN MISSION LIFE: AN OVERVIEW

1. See appendix A, mission 6 and mission 28.

2. The original construction and sequential order of the regulations are found in appendix E; De Schweinitz, *Zeisberger*, 378–79.

3. Moravian Church Archives, box 161, folder 5, page 10.

4. Ibid., box 171, folder 12, pages 39–40.

5. Ibid., folder 4, pages 9–10.

6. Ibid., folder 8, page 47.

7. References for this paragraph are found in Moravian Church Archives, box 171, folder 8, page 43; box 171, folder 11, page 1; and box 173, folder 6, page 14.

8. Ibid., box 173, folder 1, page 6.

9. Ibid., folder 9, page 5.

10. Ibid., box 171, folder 1, page 13; box 173, folder 1, page 11.

11. Ibid., box 171, folder 6, pages 21–22.

12. Ibid., box 173, folder 2, pages 6–7.

13. Ibid., box 171, folder 5, page 10.

14. Ibid., folder 6, page 8.

15. See chapter 7.

16. De Schweinitz, *Zeisberger*, 327.

17. Moravian Church Archives, box 171, folder 8, pages 11–12.

18. Ibid., box 173, folder 1, pages 33–34.

19. Ibid., box 171, folder 12, pages 32, 35.

20. In October 1799 the Brethren built a tower in front of the temporary church to accommodate a bell sent from Bethlehem.

21. Moravian Church Archives, box 171, folder 13, pages 28–29.

22. Ibid., folder 4, page 15.

23. Ibid., box 173, folder 2, page 13.

24. Ibid., box 171, folder 7, pages 13–14.

25. A detailed account of Ignatius's skill as a carpenter is shown in his burial account, part 3, burial 25.

26. Moravian Church Archives, box 171, folder 12, pages 32–34.

27. Ibid., box 173, folder 1, page 27.

28. August C. Mahr, "Health Conditions in the Moravian Indian Missions of Schoenbrunn in the 1770's," *Ohio Journal of Science* 50 (1949): 122.

29. Bliss, *Diary of David Zeisberger* 2:317–18.

30. David Zeisberger, "The History of the North American Indians," *Ohio Archaeological and Historical Society Publications* 19(1910): 24.

31. Moravian Church Archives, box 171, folder 12, page 42.

32. Ibid., folder 5, page 3.

33. See chapter 7.

34. See part 3, burial 9.

35. Moravian Church Archives, box 173, folder 4, page 3.

36. Ibid., folder 7, pages 13–14.

37. In 1798, during his trip with Edwards from Fairfield to the Muskingum, Heckewelder met an old Indian who previously lived near Bethlehem. Heckewelder informed him, "The Brethren still loved the Indians . . . and intended soon to build a new Bethlehem on the River Muskingum" (ibid., folder 5, page 12).

38. Ibid., folder 2, pages 12–13.

39. See chapter 7.

40. Zeisberger, "History of the Indians," 19:19.

41. Moravian Church Archives, box 171, folder 7, page 39.

42. Ibid., folder 5, page 3.

43. For example, consult the biographical sketch of Abel, part 3, burial 24, who proved to be one of the most exceptional students in the history of the Moravian missions.

44. Moravian Church Archives, box 171, folder 7, page 8.

45. James Penick, Jr., ". . . I will stamp on the ground with my foot," *American Heritage* 27, no. 1 (Dec. 1975): 82.

46. Moravian Church Archives, box 173, folder 8, page 12.

47. Ibid., 17.

48. Ibid., 18.

49. Ibid., box 171, folder 4, pages 9–10.

9. WITHOUT THEIR BELOVED DAVID

1. See appendixes B and C.

2. See chapter 7.

3. Moravian Church Archives, box 173, folder 2, pages 13–14.

4. Ibid., folder 3, page 9.

5. Ibid., 18.

6. In a footnote, Mortimer indicated this information came from their friend, Thomas Worthington, a member of Congress. He became governor of the new state of Ohio in 1814.

7. Moravian Church Archives, box 173, folder 3, pages 13–14.

8. Fliegel, *Index* 2:582–88.

9. Moravian Church Archives, box 173, folder 6, page 10 (April 27).

10. Susan Zeisberger lived in the Widows' House at Bethlehem for the rest of her life. She died on September 8, 1824, and is buried in the old cemetery at Bethlehem. The Zeisbergers had no children.

11. See chapter 7 for a description of Oppelt's experience at the Pettquotting mission and his complaints against the Zeisbergers and the Mortimers.

12. The similarity of these two names is confusing. Both men spent their apprenticeship at Goshen. Haven went on to Pettquotting in 1806 and Hagen went to Fairfield in the same year. Both returned to Goshen, Haven in 1809 and Hagen in 1810.

13. U.S. Bureau of the Census, *Historical Statistics of the United States, Colonial Times to 1957* (Washington, D.C., 1960), 13. The Ohio census takers counted 45,365 Ohioians in 1800.

14. Moravian Church Archives, box 173, folder 7, page 5.

15. Ibid., 7.

16. Ibid., 10.

17. See part 3, burial 33, for a biographical sketch of William Henry's life.

18. Moravian Church Archives, box 173, folder 8, pages 9–10.

19. R. David Edmunds, *Tecumseh and the Quest for Indian Leadership* (Boston: Little, Brown, 1984), 73–76.

20. Ibid., 85; and William H. Van Hoose, *Tecumseh: An Indian Moses* (Canton, Ohio: Daring Books, 1984), 108.

21. Edmunds, *Tecumseh*, 86.

22. During the spring of 1806 several teams of astronomers and other scientists traveled throughout Indiana, Kentucky, and Illinois establishing observation stations to study the eclipse scheduled to occur on June 16. Harrison must have been aware of such preparations, but if he was he evidently had forgotten about the coming eclipse when he wrote to the Delaware in April. Like Harrison, Tenskwatawa also was aware of the scientists' activities. He also knew that among the Shawnee such an eclipse was called Mukutaaweethee Keesohtoa, "the Black Sun," an event surrounded with dread, and supposely warning of future warfare (Edmunds, *The Shawnee Prophet*, 48).

23. Charles J. Kappler, *Indian Treaties, 1778–1883* (New York: Interland Publishing, 1972), 65–105.

24. Edmunds, *Tecumseh*, 122–23.

25. Ibid., 154–60.

26. Moravian Church Archives, box 173, folder 8, pages 13–14.

27. See chapter 8.

28. Moravian Church Archives, box 173, folder 8, page 21.

29. John Anthony Caruso, *The Great Lakes Frontier* (Indianapolis: Bobbs-Merrill, 1961) , 257.

30. Ibid., 268–73.

31. Roseboom and Weisenburger, *A History of Ohio*, 83.

32. Moravian Church Archives, box 173, folder 9, pages 7–8.

33. Ibid., 31.

34. Ibid., 44–46

35. Ibid., folder 7, pages 7, 8, and 9.

36. Ibid. To some extent, Mortimer's involvement in the partisan attacks against the missions can be found in the number of pages devoted to the Goshen diary for the three years of 1810, 1811, and 1812. In 1810 he required twenty-seven pages to relate the events of the year. In 1811, it took fifteen pages. Usually the diary was written on octavo sheets, which were approximately six inches by nine inches. For part of that year they used a sheet roughly double this size. In 1812 it took ninety-five octavo pages. During the months of August and September, at the height of his difficulty, he wrote fifty-seven pages. Benjamin Mortimer lived in New York for the balance of his life, dying on November 10, 1834.

37. "Gnadenhutten Diary of the White Moravian Settlement," 1821: 82.

Bibliography

Allen, Walser H. *Who Are the Moravians: The Story of the Moravian Church, a World-Wide Fellowship*. Bethlehem: Department of Publications—Moravian Church, 1966.

Axtel, James. *The Invasion Within: The Contest of Cultures in America*. New York: Oxford Univ. Press, 1985.

———. *The European and the Indian*. New York: Oxford Univ. Press, 1981.

Beauchamp, Rev. William M. *Aboriginal Place Names of New York*. Albany: New York Educational Department, Grand River Books, 1907.

———. *Moravian Journals Relating to Central New York 1745 to 1766*. Syracuse: Onondaga Historical Association, 1916.

Beaver, R. Peirce. "American Missionary Motivation Before the Revolution." *American Society of Church History* 31, no. 2 (June 1912): 216–26.

Bliss, Eugene F., trans. and ed. *Diary of David Zeisberger: A Moravian Missionary among the Indians of Ohio*. 2 vols. Cincinnati: Robert Clarke and Company, 1885. Reprint. St. Clair Shores, Mich.: Scholarly Press, 1972.

Brasser, T. J. "Mahican," In *Handbook of North American Indians*, ed. Bruce G. Trigger, 15:198–212. Washington, D.C.: Smithsonian Institution, 1978.

Brown, Parker B. "The Battle of Sandusky: June 4–6, 1782," *Western Pennsylvania Historical Society Magazine* 65(1982): 2, 116–51.

Butterfield, Consul Willshire. *An Historical Account of the Expedition Against Sandusky under Col. William Crawford in 1782*. Cincinnati: Robert Clarke and Company, 1873.

———. *History of the Girtys*. Cincinnati: Robert Clarke and Company, 1890. Reprint. Columbus: Long's Collage Book Company, 1950.

———. *Washington-Irvine Correspondence: The Official Letters*. Madison, Wis.: David Atwood, 1882.

Carter, John H. "The Moravians at Shamokin, Early Events in the Susquehanna Valley." In *Early Events in the Susquehanna Valley*. The Northumberland Historical Society. Millville: Precision Printing, 1981.

Caruso, John Anthony. *The Great Lakes Frontier*. Indianapolis: Bobbs-Merrill, 1961.

Clark, George Rogers. *Colonel George Rogers Clark's Sketches of His Campaigns in Illinois in 1778–1779.* Cincinnati: Robert Clarke and Company, 1869. Reprint. New York: Arno Press and the New York Times, 1971.

Darlington, Mary C. *History of Col. Henry Bouquet and the Western Frontier of Pennsylvania: 1744–1764.* New York: Arno Press, 1971. (Originally published in 1920.)

Delaware Tribe of Western Oklahoma. *Turtle Children.* Delaware Indian Child Welfare, title 2. Anadarko, Ok.: Bureau of Indian Affairs, 1985.

De Schweinitz, Edmund. *The Life and Times of David Zeisberger.* Philadelphia: J. B. Lippincott, 1870.

———. *The Moravian Manual, Containing an Account of the Moravian Church or Unitas Fratrum.* Bethlehem: Moravian Publication Office, 1869.

———. "Some Fathers of the American Moravian Church." *Moravian Historical Society Transaction* 2, nos. 4–5 (1886): 146–269.

Doddridge, Joseph. *Notes of the Settlement and Indian Wars.* Wellsburg: By the author at the office of the *Wellsburg (Virginia) Gazette,* 1824. Republished with additional material. Pittsburgh: John S. Ritenour and Wm. T. Lindsey, 1912.

Donehoo, Dr. George P. *Indian Villages and Place Names in Pennsylvania.* Harrisburg: Telegraph Press, 1928.

Downes, Randolph C. *Council Fires on the Upper Ohio.* Pittsburgh: Univ. of Pittsburgh Press, 1968.

Edmunds, R. David. *The Shawnee Prophet.* Lincoln: Univ. of Nebraska Press, 1983.

———. *Tecumseh and the Quest for Indian Leadership.* Boston: Little, Brown, 1984.

Fenton, William N., and Elisabeth Tooker, "Mohawk." In *Handbook of North American Indians,* ed. Bruce G. Trigger, 15:466–80. Washington, D.C.: Smithsonian Institution, 1978.

Ferguson, Roger James. "The White River Indiana Delawares: An Ethno-Historic Synthesis, 1795–1867." Ph.D. diss., Ball State University, Muncie, 1972.

Fliegel, Rev. Carl John. *Index to the Moravian Records of the Moravian Missions among the Indians of North America.* 4 vols. Moravian Archives, Bethlehem, Pennsylvania. New Haven: Research Publication, 1970.

Gipson, Lawrence Henry. *The Moravian Indian Mission of the White River.* Indianapolis: Indiana Historical Bureau, 1938.

Gist, Christopher. *Christopher Gist's Journal.* Edited by William M. Darlington. New York: Argonaut Press Ltd., 1966. (Originally published in 1893.)

Glatfelter, Charles H. *Pastors and People: German Lutheran and Reformed Churches in the Pennsylvania Field, 1717–1793.* Vol. 1, *Pastors and Congregations.* Breinigsville, Pa.: Pennsylvania German Society, 1981.

———. *Pastors and People: German Lutheran and Reformed Churches in the Pennsylvania Field, 1717–1793.* Vol. 2, *The History.* Breinigsville, Pa.: Pennsylvania German Society, 1981.

"Gnadenhutten Diary of the White Moravian Settlement, 1797–1824." First Moravian Church, Gnadenhutten, Ohio.

Goddard, Ives. "Delaware." In *Handbook of North American Indians,* ed. Bruce G. Trigger, 15:213–39. Washington, D.C.: Smithsonian Institution, 1978.

Gray, Elma E., and Leslia Robb. *Wilderness Christians: The Moravian Mission to the Delaware Indians.* New York: Russell and Russell, 1956.

Guthman, William H. *March to Massacre: A History of the First Seven Years of the United States Army 1784–1791.* New York: McGraw-Hill, 1970.

Hamilton, J., and K. Hamilton. *History of the Moravian Church.* Bethlehem: Interprovincial Board of Christian Education, Moravian Church in America, 1967.

Hamilton, Kenneth G. "John Ettwein and the Moravian Church During the Revolutionary Period." *Moravian Historical Society Transaction* 12, nos. 3–4 (1940): 85–429.

Hanna, Charles A. *The Wilderness Trail.* New York: G. P. Putnam's Sons, 1911.

Heckewelder, John. *History, Manners and Customs of the Indian Nations Who Once Inhabited Pennsylvania and the Neighboring States.* 1876. Reprint. New York: Arno Press, 1971.

———. *A Narrative of the Missions of the United Brethren among the Delaware and Mohegan Indians, from its Commencement, in the Year 1740 to the Close of the Year 1808.* Philadelphia: McCarty and Davis, 1820. Reprint. New York: Arno Press, 1971.

Hill, N. N. Jr., comp. *The History of Coshocton County, Ohio: Its Past and Present 1740–1881.* Newark: A. A. Graham, 1881.

Hunt, George T. *The Wars of the Iroquois.* Madison: Univ. of Wisconsin Press, 1940.

Hunt, Samuel F. "The Greenville Treaty." Address Delivered on the Occasion of the Centennial of the Treaty of Greenville, Aug. 3, 1895, at Greenville, Ohio. *Ohio Archaeological and Historical Society Publications* 7(1899): 218–40.

Hunter, William A. *Forts on the Pennsylvania Frontier 1753–1758.* Harrisburg: Pennsylvania Historical and Museum Commission, 1960.

———. "History of the Ohio Valley." In *Handbook of North American Indians,* ed. Bruce G. Trigger, 15:588–93. Washington, D.C.: Smithsonian Institution, 1978.

Hutton, J. E. *A History of the Moravian Church.* London: Fetters Lane, 1909.

Jacobs, Wilber R. *Diplomacy and Indian Gifts: The Northern Colonial Frontier, 1748–1763.* Lincoln: Univ. of Nebraska Press, 1950.

James, Alton. *John Papunhank: A Christian Indian of North America.* Dublin: C. Benton, 1820.

Jennings, Francis. *The Ambiguous Iroquois Empire.* New York: W. W. Norton, 1984.

———. "The Delaware Interregum." *Pennsylvania Magazine of History and Biography* 89(1985): 174–98.

———. *Empire of Fortune: Crowns, Colonies, and Tribes in the Seven Years War in America.* New York: W. W. Norton, 1988.

———. *The History and Culture of Iroquois Diplomacy.* Syracuse: Syracuse Univ. Press, 1985.

————. *The Invasion of America: Indians, Colonialism and Cant of Conquest.* New York: W. W. Norton, 1976.

Jones, David. *A Journey of Two Visits Made to Some Nations of the Indians on the West Side of the River Ohio in the Years 1772, 1773, 1774.* Reprint. Joseph Sabin, New York, 1865. Reprint. Fairfield, Wash.: Ye Galleon Press, 1973.

Kappler, Charles J. *Indian Treaties, 1778–1883.* New York: Interland Publishing, 1972.

Kopperman, Paul E. *Braddock at the Monongahela.* London: Feffer & Simons. Pittsburgh: Univ. of Pittsburgh Press, 1977.

Kraft, Herbert C. *The Lenape: Archaeology, History, and Ethnography.* Newark: New Jersey Historical Society, 1986.

Levering, Joseph M. *A History of Bethlehem, Pennsylvania 1741–1892.* Bethlehem: Bethlehem Times Publishing Company, 1903.

Loskiel, George Henry. *History of the Missions of the United Brethren among the Indians of North America.* Translated by Christian Latrobe. London: Burlinghouse, 1794. (Originally published in 1788.)

Madeheim, Lother. "Resettlement of the Moravian Indians in Nebraska Territory." Lecture delivered at the Moravian Archives, Bethlehem, Pennsylvania, February 6, 1983.

Mahr, August C. "Health Conditions in the Moravian Indian Missions of Schoenbrunn in the 1770's." *Ohio Journal of Science* 50(1950): 121-31.

————. "How to Locate Indian Place Names on Modern Maps." *Ohio Journal of Science* 53, no. 3 (May 1953): 129–137.

————. "Translations of the Schoenbrunn Diary, 1772–1777." Columbus, Ohio Historical Society.

McClure, David. *Diary of David McClure, Doctor of Divinity 1748–1820.* With notes by Franklin B. Dexter, M.A. New York: Knickerbocker Press, 1899.

Moravian Church Archives. *A History of the Beginning of the Moravian Church in America.* Edited by Rev. William N. Schwarze and Bishop S. H. Gapp. Vol. 1, *Translation of the George Neisser's Manuscripts.* Bethlehem, Pa.: The Archives of the Moravian Church, 1955.

O'Meara, Walter. *Guns at the Forks.* Englewood Cliffs, N.J.: Prentice-Hall, 1965.

Parkman, Francis. *The Conspiracy of Pontiac and the Indian War after the Conquest of Canada.* 2 vols. 10th ed. Boston: Little, Brown, 1893.

————. *Montcalm and Wolfe.* 2 vols. Boston: Little, Brown, 1902.

Peckham, Howard H. *Pontiac and the Indian Uprising.* New York: Russell and Russell, 1947.

Penick, James, Jr. ". . . I will stamp on the ground with my foot and shake down every house . . . ," *American Heritage* 27, no. 1 (Dec. 1975): 82–87.

Platt, Carolyn. "The Great Black Swamp," *Timeline* 4, no. 1 (February–March 1987): 26–39. Ohio Historical Society, Columbus.

Radloff, Ralph Mark. "Moravian Missions among the Indians of Ohio." Ph.D. diss., University of Iowa, 1973.

Reeves, J. C. "Henry Bouquet: His Indian Campaigns." *Ohio Archaeological and Historical Society Publications* 26(1918): 489–506. Columbus.

Reichel, Levin Theodore. *The Early History of the Church of the United Brethren, Commonly Called Moravians in North America. A.D. 1734–1748.* Nazareth: Moravian Historical Society, 1888.

Reichel, William C., ed. *Memorials of the Moravian Church.* Philadelphia: J. B. Lippincott, 1870.

———. "Wyalusing and the Moravian Mission at Friedenshutten." *The Moravian Historical Society, Transactions* 1, no. 5 (1871): 178–224.

Rishel, Dr. Jonas. *The Indian Physician.* New Berlin, Penn.: Joseph Miller, 1828. Reprint. Columbus: Ohio State Univ. Press, 1980.

Roseboom, Eugene H., and Francis P. Weisenburger. *A History of Ohio.* Columbus: Ohio Historical Society, 1956.

Roundthaler, Edward. *Life of John Heckewelder.* Edited by B. H. Coates. Philadelphia: T. Ward, 1847.

Sawyer, Edwin A. *The Religious Experience of the Colonial American Moravians.* Moravian Historical Society, vol. 18, pt. 1. Nazareth, 1961.

Sherman, C. E. *Original Ohio Land Subdivisions.* Vol. 3. Columbus: Ohio Cooperative Topographic Survey, 1976.

Sipe, C. Hale. *The Indian Chiefs of Pennsylvania.* Butler: Zigler Printing Company, 1927.

———. *The Indian Wars of Pennsylvania: An Account of the Indian Events in Pennsylvania of the French and Indian War.* Harrisburg: Telegraph Press, 1929.

Smith, Kenneth. *A Practical Guide to Dating Systems for Genealogists.* Printed privately, 1983.

Swanton, John R. *The Indian Tribes of North America.* Bureau of American Ethnology Bulletin no. 145. Washington, D.C., 1982.

Thompson, Charles N. *Sons of the Wilderness: John and William Conner.* Indianapolis: Indiana Historical Society, 1937.

Thwaites, Reuben Gold, ed. *Early Western Travels.* Cleveland: Arthur H. Clarke, 1904.

———. *France in America: 1497–1763.* American Nations Series, vol. 7. New York: Harpers, 1905.

———, and Kellogg, Louise Phelps, eds. *Frontier Defense on the Upper Ohio Frontier 1777–1778.* Draper Series, vol. 3. Madison: Wisconsin Historical Society, 1912; Millwood, N.Y.: Kraus Reprint Company, 1977.

U.S. Bureau of the Census. *Historical Statistics of the United States, Colonial Times to 1957.* Washington, D.C., 1960.

Van Hoose, William H. *Tecumseh: An Indian Moses.* Canton, Ohio: Daring Books, 1984.

Wainwright, Nicholas. *George Croghan: Wilderness Diplomat.* Chapel Hill: Univ. of North Carolina Press, 1959.

Wallace, Anthony F. C. "Women, Land and Society: Three Aspects of Aboriginal Delaware Life." *Pennsylvania Archaeologist* 17, nos. 1–4 (1947): 1–35.

Wallace, Paul A. W. *Conrad Weiser 1696–1760: Friend of Colonist and Mohawk.* New York: Russell and Russell, 1971. (Originally published in 1945.)

————. *Indians in Pennsylvania*. Harrisburg: Pennsylvania Historical and Museum Commission, 1961.

————. *Indian Paths in Pennsylvania*. Harrisburg: Pennsylvania Historical and Museum Commission, 1971.

————. *Thirty Thousand Miles with John Heckewelder*. Pittsburgh: Univ. of Pittsburgh Press, 1958.

Weinlick, John R. *Count Zinzendorf*. New York: Abingdon Press, 1956.

Weinland, Joseph E. *The Romantic Story of Schoenbrunn: The First Town in Ohio*. Dover, Ohio: Seibert Printing Company, 1930.

Weslager, C. A. *The Delaware Indian Westward Migration*. Wallingsford, Pa.: Middle Atlantic Press, 1978.

————. *The Delaware Indians: A History*. New Brunswick: Rutgers Univ. Press, 1972.

Wilcox, Frank N. *Ohio Indian Trails*. Cleveland: Gates Press, 1934.

Wright, Louis B. *The Atlantic Frontier*. New York: Alfred H. Knopf, 1951.

Zeisberger, David. "The History of the North American Indians," written 1779–1780, translated by Archer Butler Hulbert and William Nathaniel Schwarze. *Ohio Archaelogical and Historical Society Publications* 19(1910): 1–173. Columbus.

————. "Diary of David Zeisberger and Gottlob Senseman, Journey to Goshgoschunk on the Ohio and Their Arrival There, 1768." Translated by Archer Butler Hulbert and William Nathaniel Schwarze. The Moravian Records, *Ohio Archaeological and Historical Society Publications* 21(1912): 42–69.

Index

Abel, 120, 185–86, 192–93, 199–201,
  264n.43
Abraham (Sekima), 19, 47, 59, 60, 77, 92,
  126, 176
Adam, Anna Sophia. *See* White Eyes,
  Anna Sophia Adam
Adam, Johann, 141, 197, 212
Adam, Ketura, 137, 141, 197
Adams, John (U.S. president), 95, *109*
Agnes, 191
Alcohol use by Indians, 117, 119, 120,
  121, 125, 131–32, 134, 145, 146–47,
  152–55, 160, 161, 170, 184, 185, 197,
  200, 207, 210–11, 213, 214, 227, 229,
  230, 231, 233, 236, 239, 240, 246
Ancrum, Major, 69, 70
Anderson, Captain, 70, 71
Anna (daughter of Josua, Jr., and
  Sophia the Elder), 183
Anna Maria, 123, 216–18
Anna Salome, 195, 209, 210
Anton, 24, 126
Articles of Confederation, 79–80
Askin, John, 69, 70, 71, 86
Augustinus (Newellike), 17–18, 255n.12
Axtel, James, 35, 234

Basketry, 140
Battle of Fallen Timbers, 82, 91, 94
Battle of Tippecanoe, 151, 163
Bay, Colonel, 167
Beata (wife of Joseph), 195, 209, 210, 211
Beaver (Delaware chief). *See* Tamaqua
Beersheba, 111
Bemineo. *See* Killbuck, John, Sr.

Berries, 133
Bethlehem, Pennsylvania: Zeisberger's
  home in, 4; Moravian center at, x,
  4–5, 35; Moravian Church Archives
  at, xii, xiv, xvi
Big Cat, 17
Biggs, Capt. John, 55
Blackcoats, 5, 62
Blickensderfer, Matthias, 83
Blue Jacket (Shawnee chief), 82, 91
Boaz (Gegaschamind), 77, 123
Bouquet, Col. Henry, 101
Boyer, Margaret. *See* Conner, Margaret
  ("Polly") Boyer
Braddock, Gen. Edward, 91
Brainerd, David, 35, 217
Brainerd, John, 216, 217
Brant, Joseph, 88, 184
Brant, Molly, 184
Brock, Maj. Gen. Sir Isaac, 165–66, 167
Brodhead, Gen. Daniel, 32–33, 37, 38,
  52, 57, 177, 223
Broom making, 140
Buckingham, William (Ebenezer), 209
Buckongahelas (Delaware chief), 82
Buildings, by missionaries, 137–39
Bull, John Joseph. *See* Schebosh,
  Joseph
Burgoyne, Gen. John, 29
Butler, Gen. John, 58, 73, 74, 91

Captain Pipe. *See* Pipe, Captain
Captive Town, 39–40, 242, 257n.13
Carpentry, 140, 205
Cass, Lewis, 166

Catherina (daughter of Joseph and Beata), 209, 211
Chelloway, Billy. *See* William
Cherokee Indians, 73
Chiksika, 160
Chippewa Indians, 38, 59, 65, 66–67, 68, 77, 89, 92, 93, 118, 123, 131, 162, 230. *See also* Ojibwa Indians
Chippewa mission, 242
Christina, 118–21, 170, 191, 196, 201, 207, 232, 233, 238–39, 248, 259n.14
Clark, George Rogers, 30–31, 61, 80
Clark, James, 168–69
Colver, John, 108
Colver, Nathaniel, 108
Comenius, John Amos, ix
Conner, Henry, 52
Conner, James, 51, 52
Conner, John, 52
Conner, Margaret ("Polly") Boyer, 20, 51, 52, 59
Conner, Richard, 20, 51–52, 59, 65, 69
Conner, Susanna, 52
Conner, William, 52
Consumption, 142
Cook, John, 78, 84
Corn, 127–28, 129–30
Cornplanter (Seneca chief), 89
Cornwallis, Gen. Charles, 79, 257n.21
Cowpox, 140–41
Crawford, Col. William, 57–58, 59, 64, 79
Creek Indians, 150
Crews, C. Daniel, 208
Custaloga (Delaware chief). *See* Pankanke

David (Kutschias), 24, 90, 123, 142, 158
Delaware George, 17, 49
Delaware Indians, xi; conversion of, 14–15, 58, 72, 113–14, 155; Zeisberger's attempts to compromise with, xiv; hostility toward white settlers, 68, 82, 88, 101, 110, 159; land cessions by, 118, 162, 229; neutrality of and fighting by during American Revolution, 19, 29–30, 31, 33, 56, 57, 223; postrevolutionary conditions among, 65, 66,

113, 144; Unami (Turtle) clan, 10, 11, 17, 222; Wolf clan, 11, 40, 143
Demuth, Luther, xii
Denke, Christian Frederick, 123, 156
De Peyster, Maj. Arent Schuyler: actions against Zeisberger and converts, 37, 38, 223; assistance to Zeisberger and converts, 48, 53, 58, 59; Chippewa agreement with, 66; as governor of Detroit, 32, 33, 69; missionaries' treason trial conducted by, 41–45; summoning of missionaries to Detroit, 39–40, 49, 53, 65–66
Detroit: missionaries summoned to, 39–40, 40–50; missionaries' treason trial at, 41–45
Detroit River (die Warte) mission, 85–86, 87–93, 233, 242
Diphtheria, 142
Disease. *See* Health and disease
Doddridge, Rev. Joseph, 54
Dogs, 128–29
Duncan and Wilson (a Pittsburgh supplier), 71

Earthquakes, 150–51
Education of Indians, 79, 83–84, 133–34, 148–50, 199–200
Edwards, William: baptisms by, 119; birth of, 191; death of, 141, 191–92; at Detroit, 41, 50, 85, 86, 192; at Detroit River mission, 87, 192; at Gnadenhutten, 28–29, 31, 32, 36, 239; at Goshen, 97, 108, 192; grave of, xi, 117; at Lichtenau, 17, 25; at missionaries' treason trial, 41; move to Fairfield, 93, 192; move to Pilgerruh, 70; at New Gnadenhutten, 60, 63, 67, 68, 192; at Pettquotting, 85, 86, 224; at Pilgerruh, 71, 73; at Schoenbrunn, 191
Eel River Miami Indians, 90, 162
Elliot, Capt. Matthew: assistance to Zeisberger and converts, 85, 86, 87, 88, 90, 92, 232; as British spy, 29; expedition to remove Christian Indians from Muskingum valley, 37, 38; and missionaries' treason trial, 41; visit to Detroit River mission, 90

Espich, Dr. Christian, 158
Ettwein, Bishop John, xii, *11*, *12–13*, 36, 66, 67

Fairfield mission, xiv, 92, 93–94, 117, 123, 127, 141, 156, 184, 190, 209, 218, 219, 242
Fevers and ague, 142, 195, 233
Fire Lands, 118
Flemming, Mr. (a trader), 118
Fliegel, Rev. Carl John, 175–76
Forbidden Path, 7
Fort Finney, 65, 66, 69
Fort Hamilton, 82
Fort Harmar, 65, 80, 83, 224
Fort Henry (Wheeling), 26, 27, 28
Fort Industry, 118, 123, 229
Fort Jefferson, 82
Fort Laurens, 29, 32, 37, 38, 102, 223, 257n.8
Fort McIntosh, 64–65, 66, 67
Fort Recovery, 95
Fort Stanwix, 11, 64, 65, 81
Fort Washington, 80, 81–82, 88, 89, 90
Frank, Albert H., 208
French and Indian War, xiii, 6, 77, 79
Friedenshutten mission, 6–7, 8, *9*, 10, 92, 95, 182, 183, 187, 193, 241
Friedensstadt mission, 7, 36, 208, 241, 246–47, 257n.6
Fruit trees, 129, 140

Gangrene, 142
Gekelemukpechunk village, 10
Gelelemend. *See* Henry, William (Gelelemend)
George III (king of England), 81, 224
George Washington's Indian War, 81
Gibson, Col. John, 55, 66, 223
Gigeyunk, 90, 91
Girty, Simon, 29, 37, 48–49, 64, 258n.30
Gist, Christopher, 101
Glikhikan. *See* Isaac (Glikhikan)
Gnadenhutten mission, x, 6, 8, 16, 19, 25, 28–29, 31, 32, 36, 38, 54, 55, 66, 67, 68, 79, 95, *96*, 107, 116, 153, 154, 165, 182, 183, 217, 241, 258n.29; reoccupation of, 108, 111, *112*, 127, 139–40, 141, 145–47, 157
Goschachgunk village, 15, 18, 25, 27, 32–33, 37, 39, 102
Goschgoschunk mission, 7, *8*, 241
Goshen cemetery, xi–xii, xiv, 141, 156, 175–76, 217, 245, 249–53
Goshen mission, x; construction of, 137–39, 205; establishment of, xi, xiv, 3, 97–98, 242; land patent for, *109*; location of, 95, *96*, 109–10; move to, 98–103; problems within, 119, 152; settlement around, 110–12, 126, 143–48; visitors to, 143
Gottlieb, 218
Gray, Lord George, 69

Haga, Godfrey, 108, *109*, 262n.4
Hagastaes, 62
Hagen, John, 136, 146, 150, 157, 159, 166, 168, 170, 226, 265n.12
Haldimand, Sir Frederick, 64
Hamilton, Henry, 17, 28, 31, 32
Hand, Gen. Edward, 26, 27, 28, 29
Harmar, Gen. Josiah, 81–82, 84, 88–89
Harrison, William Henry, 159, 161–63, 167, 219
Hartline, Waldo, *12–13*
Haven, Johann Benjamin, 117, 118, 122, 123, 137, 150, 155–56, 157, 217, 228, 265n.12
Health and disease, 140–43, 194–95, 236. *See also* Medicine
Heckedorn, Rosina. *See* Luckenbach, Rosina Heckedorn
Heckewelder, Johanna Maria ("Polly"), 50, 60, 67
Heckewelder, Johann Gottlieb Ernest. *See* Heckewelder, John
Heckewelder, John (Johann Gottlieb Ernest): as assistant to Zeisberger, x; at Bethlehem, 24, 73, 83, 95, 108, 112, 146, 157; in charge at Lichtenau, 31; correspondence with Fort Pitt, 27; and death of Zeisberger, 215; departure from Pilgerruh, 73; at Detroit, 41, 50, 60; at Fairfield, 97, 108; at Gnadenhutten, 24, 29, 108, 145, 205, 239; at

Heckewelder, John (*cont.*)
  Goshen, 97, 98, 101, 107, 108, 191;
    map of Gnadenhutten by, *112;* map of
    Pilgerruh by, *72, 73;* marriage of, 32;
    meeting with Pomoacan, 48; at mis-
    sionaries' treason trial, 41; move to
    Lichtenau, 16, 19–20, 24, 29; move to
    Pilgerruh, 70; at New Gnadenhutten,
    67, 146; at Pettquotting, 83; recall to
    Detroit, 50; at Salem, 32, 36; at Schoen-
    brunn, 8, 18, 19, 21; as SPG resident
    agent, 83, 146, 157, 205; survey by, 83,
    95; on the Tuscawaras, 101, 102
Heckewelder, Sarah Ohneberg, 32, 50,
  67, 73
Hehl, Matthaeus, 21, 23–24
Hendricks (Mohawk chief), 5
Henrietta, 225, 230, 231
Henry (suicide victim; son of Ignatius
  and Christina), 118–22, 134, 144–45,
  146, 152, 159, 170, 200, 201–3, 206,
  207, 243, 244
Henry, Anna Benigna, 197, 219, 232–33
Henry, Anna Caritas, 233–34, 235, 238
Henry, Anna Charity. *See* Henry, Anna
  Caritas
Henry, Anna Maria, 180, 194, 196–97,
  233
Henry, Anna Rosina, 194–95
Henry, Anna Susanna, 219, 237, 239
Henry, Beata, 180–81
Henry, Beatus, 238
Henry, Benigna Nanticoke, 235
Henry, Benjamin (son of Christian Gott-
  lieb and Anna Susanna Henry), 199,
  239
Henry, Benjamin (son of William and
  Rachel Henry), 33, 98, 176, 177–78,
  223
Henry, Charles (son of John and Anna
  Benigna Henry), 232, 233, 245
Henry, Charles (son of William and Ra-
  chel Henry): baptism of, 77; death of,
  238; as ferryman, 156; at Goshen, 198,
  207, 228; marriages of, 233, 235, 238;
  at Pettquotting, 76
Henry, Christian Gottlieb: baptism of,
  77, 225, 239; children of, 219, 237, 239;
  death of, 219, 239–40; at Goshen, 97,
  98, 102, 156, 198; as hunter, 133; mar-

riage of, 239; at Pettquotting, 76; as
  spy during War of 1812, 240; travel to
  Fairfield, 206
Henry, Deborah, 238
Henry, Jacob, 196, 197
Henry, Jeremias, 239, 240
Henry, John (son of Christian Gottlieb
  and Anna Susanna Henry), 239
Henry, John (son of William and Ra-
  chel Henry): baptism of, 77; children
  of, 180, 194, 196, 219, 232; comments
  on son's death, 196; death of, 233; at
  Zeisberger's funeral, 216; at Goshen,
  156, 198; marriages of, 197, 219, 233,
  236; at Pettquotting, 76; at Princeton
  College, 221
Henry, Nancy (daughter of Christian
  Gottlieb and Anna Susanna Henry),
  237, 239
Henry, Nancy (daughter of John and
  Anna Benigna Henry), 219, 233
Henry, Rachel (daughter of John and
  Anna Benigna Henry), 233
Henry, Rachel (wife of William Henry):
  baptism of, 77, 178, 225; birth of, 198;
  children of, 76, 177–78, 198, 248;
  death of, 198, 221; funeral of, 198;
  marriage of, 198; move to Goshen, 98;
  at Pettquotting, 76
Henry, Rebecca, 219, 239
Henry, Maj. William, 77, 95, 222, 223
Henry, William (Gelelemend): as advisor to Netawatwes, 10; and alcohol
  use by Indians, 153–54; baptism of,
  14, 76, 77, 95, 177–78, 220–25;
  biographical notes on, 11, 14, 220–25;
  birth of, 11, 220, 222; children of, 33,
  76, 177–78, 197, 198, 221, 248; conversion to Christianity, 77, 144, 225; death
  of, 159, 220–21; as Delaware
  chief, 16–17, 29, 114, 144, 222–23; at
  Detroit River mission, 87; exile of, 33,
  223; at Fort Harmar treaty conference,
  224; at Goshen, 98, 121, 127, 171, 207;
  as host to missionary David McClure,
  236; lovefeast hosted by, 135; marriage
  of, 198; move to Goshen, 100; neutrality during Revolution, 17, 33; origin
  of baptismal name of, 77, 95, 221–22;
  as pacifist, 14, 222; at Pettquotting,

76; plow given to, 127; return to Muskingum valley, 3, 14, 225; as supporter of missions, 10, 11, 17; travel to Gnadenhutten, 205
Herrnhut, Saxony, ix, 4, 23
History of the Missions (Loskiel), 87, 178
Horse stealing, 209–10
Huebner, Rev. Louis, *112*, 191
Hull, Gen. William, 162, 165–66, 167
Hunting, 125, 126, 132–33, 134, 148, 149, 204, 210–11
Hus, John, ix
Hutchins, Thomas, 83

Ignatius, *112*, 118–21, 140, 152, 170, 191, 196, 201, 203–7, 232, 233, 238–39, 248
Indian Wars of 1790, 65
Invasion Within, The (Axtel), 35, 234
Iroquois Indians, 5, 6, 10, 65, 89
Irvine, Gen. William, 57
Isaac (Glikhikan), 25
Israel (husband of Salome), 179, 193, 209

Jacob, 20, 54, 55, 67, 72, 90, 259n.14
James, 98, 133, 144, 178, 179–80, 188, 189–90, 207, 212
James, Abraham, 179–80, 188, 207
James, Arnold, 188, 207
James, Francis, 98, 142, 178–79, 180, 188, 207
Jefferson, Thomas, 213
Jenner, Edward, 140–41
Joachim (friend of Nicodemus), 133, 218, 226
Joachim (son), 123, 216, 218–19
Johnson, Sir John, 63
Johnson, Sir William, 11, 184
Jones, David, 14
Joseph (husband of Beata), 195, 208–11
Joseph (son of Teedyuscung), 79
Josua, Jr.: arrival at Detroit River mission, 87; children of, 183, 187, 193; death of, 116, 183–84; as first customer of David Peter, 139; marriage of, 183; martyrdom of, 184; as messenger, 18, 54, 85; at missionaries'

treason trial, 41; move to Fairfield, 93; robbery of, 147–48; travel to White River mission, 188; at White River mission, 116
Josua, Sr., *9*, 126, 182–83, 248
Jung, Michael: at Captive Town, 40; at Detroit, 50; at Detroit River mission, 87, 91; move to Detroit River mission, 86; move to Fairfield, 93; at Pettquotting, 74; return to Bethlehem, 67; at Salem, 36; travel to New Gnadenhutten, 60
Jungmann, Anna Margaretha: at Bethlehem, 24, 67; endangered during American Revolution, 18, 20; at Goshen, 112; move to Lichtenau, 19, 20, 23; recall to Detroit, 50; at Schoenbrunn, 8; travel to New Gnadenhutten, 60
Jungmann, Johann Georg: as assistant to Zeisberger, x; at Bethlehem, 24, 67; at Captive Town, 40; endangered during American Revolution, 18, 20; at Goshen, 112, 196; and health of the Indians, 196; move to Lichtenau, 19, 20, 23; at New Schoenbrunn, 36; recall to Detroit, 50; reconstruction of house at Schoenbrunn, *13;* at Schoenbrunn, 8, 192; travel to New Gnadenhutten, 60

Kaschates (Thomas Lyons), 120, 263n.25
Killbuck, Christian Henry. *See* Henry, Christian Gottlieb
Killbuck, John, Jr. *See* Henry, William (Gelelemend)
Killbuck, John, Sr. (Bemineo), 10–11, 222
Killbuck, William Henry. *See* Henry, William (Gelelemend)
Killbuck Island, 223
King George's War, 5
Kluge, Anna Marie, 116, 118, 180, 214, 263n.17
Kluge, John Peter, 115, 116, 118, 158, 159, 180, 214
Knauss, Ludwig, 139
Knisely (Kneisley), John, 111, 145, 147

Lagundo Utenunk. *See* Friedensstadt mission

Latrobe, Christian Ignatius, 63, 178

Lawunakhannek mission, 10, 60, 77, 241

Lecrone, Susan. *See* Zeisberger, Susan Lecrone

Leni Lenape Indians. *See* Delaware Indians

Levallie, Francis, 50

Levi, 187, 194

Lichtenau mission, x; abandonment of, 32, 241; burning of, 33; establishment of, 16, 222, 241; Heckewelder in charge of, 31; movement of converts to, 19–21, 23–24, 29; search for site for, 15

Lieth (Leeth), Elizabeth ("Sally") Lowery, 78

Lieth (Leeth), John, 78, 258n. 1

Lisetta, 179, 193

Lititz, Pennsylvania, 25, 35

Little Turtle (Miami chief), 81, 82, 91

Livestock, 130

Logan, Col. Benjamin, 73, 80

Lord Dunmore's War, 52, 160

Loskiel, Rev. George Henry, 87, 122, 178, 235

Luckenbach, Abraham, 115, 116, 118, 127, 150, 155–56, 158, 159, 167, 170, 171, 213–14, 237, 238, 244

Luckenbach, Carolina Louisa, 237

Luckenbach, Rosina Heckedorn, 237

McArthur, Duncan, 166

McClure, Rev. David, 36, 236

McCormick, Alexander, 47

McIntosh, Gen. Lachlan, 29, 32, 37

Mack, Martin, 6, 124

McKee, Alexander: British Indian agent, 68, 69, 85, 86, 87, 88, 92, 93; as British spy, 29; expedition to remove Christian Indians from Muskingum valley, 37

Madison, James, 162, 164, 165

Malaria, 142

Marriages, Indian, 235–36, 247

Master of Life religion, 158–59, 161, 163

Mather, Cotton, 34, 35

Measles, 142

Medicine, 142–43, 179, 196, 226. *See also* Health and disease

Meigs, Gov. Return J., 164

Melanthy (Shawnee chief), 73

Meniologameka mission, 241

Miami Indians, xi, 28, 68, 81, 82, 84, 88, 110, 162

Mifflin, Thomas, 256n.27

Mingo Indians, xi, 17, 18, 20, 23, 28, 73, 89

Minisink Indians. *See* Munsee Indians

Mohawk, Levi, 186–87, 190

Mohawk, Moses, 136, 184–87, 190

Mohawk, Rachel, 184, 185, 186, 187, 194

Mohawk Indians, 5, 88, 184

Montour, Andrew, 228

Montour, Madame, 228

Montour, Montgomery, 159, 225–29, 231

Montour, Thomas, 228

Moravian Church in America, training of missionaries by, 5

Moravian Daily Text, 54

Moravians: choir system of, 134–35; Helpers' Conference of, 40, 119, 134, 257n.16; lovefeasts held by, 135–36; method of conversion used by, 35–36; missionary training for, 5; Mission Helpers' Conference, 84; New World missions of, ix–x, 35; Ohio settlements of, 111; origins of, ix, 4; Provincial Helpers' Conference, 110; religious calendar of, 136–37; religious education stressed by, 133–37; town plan used by, 61, 72, 73, 107; use of the lot for decision-making by, 21–23, 24

Morgan, Col. George, 24, 256n.27

Mortimer, Benjamin: as assistant to Zeisberger, x, 3, 56, 95, 97, 113; authorship of mission diaries, xv, xvi, 3, 97, 113, 124, 127, 199, 207–8; at Bethlehem, 112, 199; comments on lives of individual Indian converts, 183, 187, 188, 190, 201–3, 210–11, 218, 228, 230; death of, 199, 266n.36; Zeisberger's farewell to, 215; on Zeisberger's sermon to the "wild Indians," 189; on Zeisberger's work with Indian converts, 185, 186, 206; at Fairfield, 95, 97, 99, 199; at Goshen, 107, 108, 113, 123,

127, 156, 165, 166, 168–70, 199, 205, 209, 214, 226, 239; as head missionary, 123, 152; on Indian adaptation to white culture, 194, 195, 212; on Indian culture, 196, 204, 230; marriage of, 112; mission population during tenure of, 113, 152, 156–57, 164, 244; on Moravian history, 178; move to Goshen, 98–101, 102–3, 107; obituaries by, 121, 175, 178, 183, 204, 232–33; opinion of Indian converts, 178, 187, 197, 201; petition by, 223; prayers by, 215–16, 227; preaching by, 99, 111, 130, 136, 179, 192, 198–99, 216; recall from Goshen to New York, 165, 170, 199, 239; as schoolteacher, 148, 150; work with Indian converts, 184, 192, 205, 217, 220, 233

Mortimer, Bethiah (Warner), 112, 198, 226

Mortimer, Joseph Warner, 198–99

Moses, 184–86

Mosquitoes and disease, 142

Munsee Indians, xi, 17, 18, 19, 48, 57, 91, 110, 117, 145, 181–82

Nain mission, 6, 65, 181, 182, 241

Nanticoke, Samuel: arrival at Detroit, 59; inspection of Fairfield mission site, 92; as messenger, 61, 67, 72, 73, 85; move to Pilgerruh, 70; search for mission site on Black River, 74; travel to New Gnadenhutten, 60

Nanticoke Indians, 68

Netawatwes (Delaware chief): biographical notes on, 10; death of, 16, 222; Zeisberger's relationship with, 7, 10, 15; fame of, 199; at Goschachgunk, 15; impact on success of missions, 7, 10; at Lichtenau inauguration, 16; as pacifist, 14; proselytizing of, 14; visit to Friedenshutten, 7

Newcomer (Delaware chief). *See* Netawatwes

Newellike (Delaware chief). *See* Augustinus

New Fairfield mission, 171, 233, 237, 238, 242

New Gnadenhutten mission, 60–63, 65, 66, 67, 69, 71, 79, 242

New Madrid earthquake (1811–12), 150, 164

New Philadelphia, 111–12, 147, 156, 157, 158, 166, 167–68, 169–70

New Salem mission. *See* Pettquotting mission

New Schoenbrunn mission, x, 31–32, 36, 39, 56, 107, 142, 241, 256n. 29

Nicholas, 97, 98, 101

Nicodemus, 102, 123, 159, 225–27, 229–31

Oats, 129

Ohio Historical Society, xi, xii

Ohio, settlement of, 80–82, 108, 110–12, 156, 157–58

Ohneberg, Sarah. *See* Heckewelder, Sarah Ohneberg

Ojibwa Indians, xi, 110. *See also* Chippewa Indians

Oppelt, Gottfried Sebastian, 112, 117, 118, 122, 157, 204

Oppelt, Mrs. Gottfried, 112, 118, 122, 157

Orchards, 129, 140

Ordinance of 1787, 80

Ottawa Indians, xi, 38, 66, 70, 71, 110, 118, 234

Pachgatgoch mission, 241

Pamaxit (chief), 168

Pankanke (Delaware chief), 14

Papunhank, John, 9, 181–82, 208, 248

Papunhank, Sophia. *See* Sophia, the Elder

Peter, David, 132, 139–40, 147, 154

Peter, John, 185–86

Pettquotting mission, 74, 75–79, 82–86, 100, 108, 131, 187, 189, 218, 223, 242; reoccupation of, 117–18, 120, 122–23, 152, 206–7, 218, 229, 242, 260–61n. 1

Pfautz, David, 120, 121, 131–32, 147

Pilgerruh (Pilgrim's Rest) mission, 71–74, 146, 242, 260n. 15

Pipe, Captain (Delaware chief): advice and assistance to missionaries, 72–73,

Pipe, Captain (*cont.*)
74, 85, 87; alliance with British, 17, 18, 33, 37; complaints against missionaries, 37, 42–43; at missionaries' treason trial, 40, 41–45, 53; relations with Goshen mission, 143; and removal of missionaries from Muskingum valley, 38
Plowing, 127–28
Pomoacan: and abandonment of Gnadenhutten, 24; advice to missionaries, 74; attack on Fort Henry, 26; complaints about missionaries, 37, 47, 53; link with Seneca black belt message, 62; opposition to Moravians, 27; and removal of missionaries from Muskingum valley, 38, 48–49; support for missions from, 25, 28
Pontiac (chief), 101
Pontiac Uprising, 6, 11, 101, 182
Post, Christian Frederick, x, 4, 14, 78, 101, 102
Power of the Gospel, The (Schussele), 8
Proctor, Col. Thomas, 89
Proske, John, 150, 171, 238, 244
Putnam, Gen. Rufus, 80, 95
Putnam, William Rufus, 95, *96*

Rachel, 16, 50, 55
Rebecca, 192
Red Eagle (Delaware chief), 32–33
Renatus, 65, 97, 98, 100
Reppich, Dr., 227
Revolution, American: British allies among Indians during, 17; end of, 64; impact on Indian missions, xi, xiii, 10, 63; Indian neutrality during, 17; problems between settlers and Indians following, 80–82, 86, 88–91, 94–95
Rosch, Albert, *12–13*
Rose, John, 57, 58
Roth, John, x
Roth, Judge, 170

St. Clair, Gen. Arthur, 65, 80, 82, 88–89, 90, 154
Salem mission, x, 32–33, 36, 39, 55, 67, 68, 78, 95–*96*, 241, 257n.30

Salome (wife of Israel), 179, 193–94
Salome (wife of Josua, Sr.), 183
Schebosh, Christina, 78, 79
Schebosh, Joseph: adoption into Iroquois nations, 78, 228; at Bethlehem, 66; biographical notes on, 78; birth of, 78; captured by militia, 66; death of, 78, 79; marriage of, 78; move to Gnadenhutten, 19, 24; move to Lichtenau, 29; obituary of, 79; obtaining supplies for Pilgerruh, 70, 71; and search for Goschachgunk mission site, 15; trip to Bethlehem, 48; trip to new Gnadenhutten, 66, 74
Schebosh, Joseph, Jr., 48, 55, 56, 258n.29
Schechschiquanunk mission, 241
Schmick, Johann: death of, 25; endangered during American Revolution, 18; at Friedenshutten, 92; at Gnadenhutten, 8, 19, 118; at Goshen, 108, 196; and health of the Indians, 196; objection to abandonment of Schoenbrunn, 19, 21, 23–24; at Philadelphia, 181, 183; portrait of, *26*; relationship with Zeisberger, 25; return to Lititz, 24–25
Schmick, Johanna Heid, 8, 18, 24–25, *26*
Schoenbrunn cemetery, xii, 182
Schoenbrunn mission, x; abandonment of, xiii–xiv, 19–21, 23–24, 241; archaeological excavations at, xii, *12–13;* confirmed for Moravian Indians by Congress, 67, 68, 95; Conner family at, 51, 52; Zeisberger's desire to return to, 68; establishment of, xi, 7–8, 126, 241; maps of, xii, *11*, *12–13*, *96;* reconstruction of, xii, xviii, *13, 20;* reoccupation of, 107; rules governing life in, 124; rules imposed on Indians at, 246–47
Schussele, Charles, *8*
Scott, Brig. Gen. Charles, 89
Seidel, Bishop Nathanael, 23, 36, 66
Sekima (Munsee chief). *See* Abraham (Sekima)
Sem, 19–20
Seneca Indians, 7, 62, 78, 89
Senseman, Anna Maria, 50, 60, 67, 84, 86, 87

Senseman, Christian David, 50, 67
Senseman, Gottlob: at Bethlehem, 67; at
    Detroit, 41, 50, 60, 92; at Detroit River
    mission, 86, 87, 92; at Gnadenhutten,
    36; at missionaries' treason trial, 41;
    move to Fairfield, 92, 93; at Pettquot-
    ting, 84; recall to Detroit, 50
Shamokin mission, xvii, 6, 124, 241
Shane, Mr. (a trader), 120, 121, 131–32,
    147
Shawnee Indians, 17, 18, 29, 38, 47, 48,
    51, 52, 56, 58, 59, 61, 62, 65, 66, 68, 69,
    72, 73, 80, 82, 102, 110, 118, 159, 162
Shekomeko mission, 182, 241
Shingas (Delaware chief), 101, 222
Smallpox, 140–41
Smith, John, xiii
Snake, Richard (chief), 94
Society of the United Brethren for the
    Propagating of the Gospel Among the
    Heathen (SPG), 63, 83, 95, 96, 108,
    140, 145, 146, 157, 205, 238
Sophia, the Elder, 181, 183, 187, 188,
    193, 208
Sophia, the Younger, 98, 144, 178,
    179–80, 187–90, 207
Spangenberg, Bishop Augustus, 5, 25,
    78, 202, 228
Stephen, 85, 149
Subsistence, 127–33
Sugarmaking, 126, 130–32, 134, 140,
    148, 149, 211
Suicide, 118, 119, 201–3
Sulamith, 185, 192, 199, 200, 201
Syphilis, 79

Tamaqua (Delaware chief), 10, 68, 101
Tatamy (Delaware chief), 4
Tawa Indians. *See* Ottawa Indians
Tecumpease, 160
Tecumseh (Shawnee chief), 73, 116, 144,
    150, 160–63, 165–66, 184
Tedpachxit (Delaware chief), 114–15,
    116
Teedyuscung (chief), 79
Tenskwatawa ("the Prophet"), 73, 116,
    144, 145, 158–59, 160–63, 184, 265n.22
Theodora, 234, 235
Thomas (Gutkigamen): family of, 199;

travel to Detroit, 59; travel from Pil-
    gerruh to gain support for mission,
    65, 72, 73; visit to proposed village
    site near Sandusky, 74
Thomas (Amaniechge), 237–38
Thomas (scalped at Gnadenhutten mis-
    sion), 72, 259n.14, 260n.17
Thomas, Catherina Marie, 98, 100, 116,
    180
Thomas, Gertraud, 98, 180
Thomas, Johannes (John), 98, 100, 116,
    180
Tobias, 41, 158
Trade, between Indians and whites,
    139–40
Travis, Rev. Francis, 158
Treaty of Fort Stanwix, 11, 64, 65, 81
Treaty of Greenville, 82, 94–95, 102,
    110, 113, 118, 161, 209, 212
Treaty of Paris (1763), xiii
Tuberculosis, 142, 178, 187, 217
Tuscarawas County Historical Society,
    xii
Tuscarawas mission, 241
Typhoid fever, 142

Ulcers, 142
Unitas Fratrum, ix. *See also* Moravians;
    Unity of Brethren Church
Unity of Brethren Church, 4. *See also*
    Moravians; Unitas Fratrum
U.S. Constitution, 80

Van Buren, Martin, 166
Varumm, Mr. (an Indian agent), 167
Verrazano, Giovanni da, xiii

Walhonding River camp, 29
Wallace, Robert: family of, 55
Walum Olum, 175–76
War of 1812, 116, 147, 157, 165–71, 219,
    240
Warte mission. *See* Detroit River (die
    Warte) mission
Washington, Gen. George, 17, 31, 32,
    37, 57, 82, 89, 257n.21
Wayne, Gen. "Mad Anthony", 82, 91, 94

Wea Indians, 89, 162
Wechquanach mission, 6, 241
Wechquetank mission, 182, 241
Weigand, John, 66, 74–75
Weinland, J. E., xii
Wetzel, Lewis, 33
Wetzel, Martin, 33
Wheat, 98–99, 129
White Eyes, Anna Sophia Adam, 136, 141, 197, 211, 212
White Eyes, Captain Joseph (Delaware chief): as advisor to Netawatwes, 14; as advisor to William Henry (Gelelemend), 17; correspondence with Fort Pitt, 27; death of, 14, 17, 29, 256n. 27; in Muskingum valley, 14; namesake of, 212; neutrality during Revolution, 17, 27; at Schoenbrunn, 52; support of missions by, 10, 18–19
White Eyes, Joseph (son of Thomas and Anna Sophia White Eyes), 211–12
White Eyes, Thomas, 133, 197, 212–14
White River (Woapikamikunk) mission, 114–16, 144, 155, 158, 159, 161, 184, 188, 213–14, 242
Wilkinson, Lt. Col. James, 89, 90
William (Billy Chelloway), 41, 74, 88, 92
Williamson, Col. David, 55, 56, 57, 58
Wingenund (Delaware chief), 40, 41
Witchcraft, 142, 158
Women: education for, ix; tasks assigned to, 132, 133, 197
Worms, 142, 194
Worthington, Thomas, 265n. 6
Wyandot Indians, xi, 17, 24, 25–26, 28, 37, 38, 39, 40, 48, 50, 51, 53, 56, 57, 58, 61, 62, 65, 66, 68, 78, 87, 88, 118, 158, 159, 162

Zeisberger, Anna (sister of David), 4
Zeisberger, David: accounts of American attacks on Indians, 89–91; adoption into Iroquois nations, 228; approach to Indian conversion, 36, 189, 213; arrested as a spy, 5; association with William Edwards, 17, 192; attempts at neutrality during Revolution, 27–28, 37; baptisms by, 16, 77, 118, 187, 190, 212, 221, 222, 224; at Bethlehem, 4, 33; birth of, xii, 4; burial of, 216; at Captive Town, 39–40, 46, 47–48, 56; childhood and youth of, 4; congregational meetings held by, 190; consultation on Muskingum valley mission survey, 83; correspondence with Fort Pitt, 27–28, 37–38, 41, 43, 256n.23; death of, xi, xiii, 123, 138, 149, 152, 155, 214–16, 244; decision to decentralize missions in 1779, 31; decision to move to Pilgerruh, 67–68; at Detroit, 41–45, 49–50, 52–53, 58–59, 66, 70; at Detroit River mission, 86, 87, 88, 89, 91–92, 94; diaries of, xii–xiii, xiv, 208; education of, 4; and education of Indians, 79, 83–84; and effect of French and Indian War on Indian converts, 81; encouragement to William Henry to accept role as chief, 222; at Fairfield, xiv, 92, 94, 97, 98, 99, 230; at Friedenshutten, 6, 182; at Friedensstadt, 7, 36; friendship with Montour family, 228; funeral of, 216; at Gnadenhutten, 6, 8, 183, 239; at Goschgoschunk, 7, 15, 183; at Goshen, xi, xiv, 108, 112, 185, 209; grave of, xi, 217; on history of Moravian missions, 178; home at Schoenbrunn, xii, *13;* Ignatius's offense to, 120–21, 203–4, 206–7; on Indian adaptation to white culture, 134; on Indian marriage customs, 125, 235–36; Indians' anger at, 152–53; on Indians' capture of prisoners, 234; and Indians' relations with their children, 135, 195, 235; Indians' requests for forgiveness from, 202, 204, 214; insistence that Indians follow rules, 124–26, 134, 194, 228, 246–47; knowledge of Indian languages, 4, 5, 87, 180; at Lawunakhannek, 10, 60; letter from Christian Latrobe to, 63; at Lichtenau, 16, 19, 25, 222; life shaped by historical events, xii–xiii, 80; on Loskiel's *History of the Missions,* 87; marriage of, 33; meeting with Sir John Johnson, 63; meeting with Pomoacan, 48; message from Netawatwes to, 15; at missionaries' treason

trial, 41–46; as missionary to the Iroquois, 5, 6; missionary work by, xii, 4, 5, 6, 36, 51; mission population during tenure of, 32, 66, 73, 76, 83, 84, 91, 98, 111, 113, 114, 115, 117, 122, 148, 152, 223, 243–44, 260n. 5; at Moravian synod, 33; move to Fairfield, 93; move to Lichtenau, 19, 21, 29; move to New Gnadenhutten, 60; on Muskingum massacre, 54, 55, 56; at Nain, 6; at New Gnadenhutten, 59, 60–63, 65, 66, 192; at New Schoenbrunn, 31–32; obituaries by, 79; order to Nicodemus and Bartholomaus to leave, 231; paintings of, *frontis.*, *8;* at Papunhank Village, 182; personality of, 4; petition for confimation of William Henry's land ownership, 223; at Pettquotting, 74, 76–79, 81, 82–86, 199; in Philadelphia, 6, 182; at Pilgerruh, 70, 71–74; preaching at funerals by, 177, 180, 181, 184, 190, 191, 193, 199; preaching by, *8,* 122, 136, 137, 138, 153; problems with Indians during the Revolution, 18, 27–28; proselytizing by, 36, 189; refusal to allow burial of Henry in consecrated ground, 119, 153, 202–3; relationship with Conner family, 51, 52; relationship with Joseph Schebosh, 78–79; relationship with Netawatwes, 10, 15; relationship with Pomoacan, 53; relations with

Indians, 7, 24, 25, 33, 61, 222; removal from Muskingum valley, 38–39; return to Muskingum valley, 3, 14, 60, 67, 68, 74, 94, 95, 97, 98, 124; sacrifices for cause, 196; at Schoenbrunn, xi, 7, 19, 21, 23–24; sending of Weigand back to Bethlehem, 75; and Seneca black belt message, 62; at Shamokin mission, xvii, 6, 124; summoned by De Peyster, 40, 49; summons from Pomoacan, 48; travel along Allegheny River, 183; and use of the lot for decision making, 23, 24, 75, 86; at Wechquanach, 6; work with Abel, 200; work with Anna Maria at Philadelphia, 217; work with Henry, 206; work with Ignatius, 207; work with Joseph, son of Teedyuscung, 79; work with Lucas, 77; work with Moses Mohawk, 185–86; work with Sophia, the Younger, 188; work with Thomas (Gutkigamen), 72; work with Thomas White Eyes, 212, 213; work with William Henry, 76–77, 224, 225

Zeisberger, David (father of David), 4

Zeisberger, Rosina (mother of David), 4

Zeisberger, Susan Lecrone (wife of David), 33, 47, 50, 60, 73, 94, 99, 108, 112, 122, 138, 149, 156, 215, 262n. 22, 265n. 10

Zinzendorf, Count Nicholas Ludwig von, ix, 5

BLACKCOATS AMONG THE DELAWARE

was composed in 10/12 Baskerville on a Varityper system
by Professional Book Compositors, Inc.;
printed by sheet-fed offset on 50-pound, acid free,
Glatfelter B-16 paper stock,
with a four color frontis printed on 80-pound white enamel stock,
Smyth sewn and bound over .088″ binders' boards
in Holliston Roxite cloth, with 80-pound Rainbow Antique endleaves,
and wrapped with dust jackets printed in two colors
on 80-pound enamel stock and film laminated;
also adhesive bound with paper covers printed in two colors
on 10-point coated-one-side stock and film laminated
by BookCrafters, Inc.;
designed by Will Underwood;
and published by
THE KENT STATE UNIVERSITY PRESS
Kent, Ohio 44242